W9-DHO-024

SECOND EDITION

ESSENTIALS *of* YOUNG ADULT LITERATURE

Carl M. Tomlinson

Northern Illinois University

Carol Lynch-Brown

Florida State University

PEARSON

Boston   New York   San Francisco

Mexico City   Montreal   Toronto   London   Madrid   Munich   Paris

Hong Kong   Singapore   Tokyo   Cape Town   Sydney

Executive Editor: *Aurora Martínez Ramos*
Editorial Assistant: *Amy Foley*
Executive Marketing Manager: *Krista Clark*
Managing Editor: *Joe Sweeney*
Editorial Production Service: *Omegatype Typography, Inc.*
Manufacturing Manager: *Megan Cochran*
Electronic Composition: *Omegatype Typography, Inc.*
Cover Designer: *Linda Knowles*

For related titles and support materials, visit our online catalog at www.pearsonhighered.com.

Copyright © 2010 Pearson Education, Inc., publishing as Allyn & Bacon, 501 Boylston Street, Suite 900, Boston, MA 02116

All rights reserved. No part of the material protected by this copyright notice may be reproduced or utilized in any form or by any means, electronic or mechanical, including photocopying, recording, or by any information storage and retrieval system, without written permission from the copyright owner.

To obtain permission(s) to use material from this work, please submit a written request to Allyn and Bacon, Permissions Department, 501 Boylston Street, Suite 900, Boston, MA 02116 or fax your request to 617-671-2290.

Between the time website information is gathered and then published, it is not unusual for some sites to have closed. Also, the transcription of URLs can result in typographical errors. The publisher would appreciate notification where these errors occur so that they may be corrected in subsequent editions.

Library of Congress Cataloging-in-Publication Data

Tomlinson, Carl M.
    Essentials of young adult literature / Carl M. Tomlinson, Carol Lynch-Brown.—2nd ed.
        p.   cm.
    Includes bibliographical references and index.
    ISBN-13: 978-0-13-704314-9 (pbk.)
    ISBN-10: 0-13-704314-7 (pbk.)
   1. Young adult literature—History and criticism.   I. Lynch-Brown, Carol.   II. Title.
   PN1009.A1T55   2010
   809'.89283071—dc22

                                          2009027992

Credit: page 130: "A Weak Poem" by Roger McGough from *Bad, Bad Cats* (© Roger McGough (1997)) is reproduced by permission of PFD (www.pfd.co.uk) on behalf of Roger McGough.

Printed in the United States of America

10 9 8 7 6 5 4 3 2 1   RRD-VA   13 12 11 10 09

www.pearsonhighered.com

ISBN-10: 0-13-704314-7
ISBN-13: 978-0-13-704314-9

CONTENTS

CHAPTER FIVE

Historical Fiction

CHAPTER SIX

Nonfiction: Biography and Informational Books

CHAPTER SEVEN

Poetry

CHAPTER EIGHT

Literature for a Diverse Society

PART THREE   LITERATURE IN THE SCHOOLS   169

CHAPTER NINE

Teaching Strategies   171

CHAPTER TEN

Resistant Readers and Young Adult Literature

211

CHAPTER ELEVEN

Censorship, Classics, Accountability, Technology: Issues and Trends

232

FEATURES

Early Important Works

Notable Authors

Tables

Figures

Boxes

Essentials of Young Adult Literature is a brief, affordable, comprehensive textbook with rich resources—a compendium of information about young adult literature. It is tailored to a course in young adult literature but, by virtue of its brevity and affordability, is also suitable as a companion text for a course in teaching reading in middle and high school.

The primary focus of a course in young adult literature should be reading trade books, not reading an exhaustive textbook about young adult books. Students need direct experience with these trade books—reading them, reading them aloud to others, discussing them, writing about them, comparing them, evaluating them, applying them to their own lives, and thinking about sharing them with young people. We deliberately do not include book reviews and plot summaries within the narrative of the textbook. However, the recommended booklists at the end of each genre chapter contain briefly annotated titles.

One of our goals is to awaken or reawaken college-level students to the joy of reading. This reawakening can happen only if they experience the pleasure and excitement of reading excellent trade books. At the same time, the body of knowledge about literature and about teaching literature to young adults can be conveyed most efficiently through a textbook. *Essentials of Young Adult Literature* presents this body of knowledge in a clear, concise, direct narrative using brief lists, examples, figures, and tables in combination with prose, thus freeing class time for involvement with literature.

EATURES OF *ESSENTIALS OF YOUNG ADULT LITERATURE*

- Comprehensive coverage and content relating to young adult literature in an affordable paperback format
- A genre approach to literature
- A logical, well-organized structure
- Useful charts and tables on history, research, read-aloud recommendations, and examples of literature to use across the curriculum
- Notable author features for the genre chapters
- Definitions of terms that appear in bold italics
- Coverage of multicultural and international young adult literature, graphic novels, short stories, and picture books for older readers
- Clearly stated positions on current issues and trends affecting schools and literature: censorship, classics, accountability, and technology
- A chapter devoted to addressing the needs of resistant readers

- Recommended book lists that are logically organized and briefly annotated
- Awards recognizing young adult literature included in an appendix with listings of the winning titles

 FEATURES NEW TO THIS EDITION

- Hundreds of new young adult books in annotated lists and as examples throughout the book
- A new conceptual planning web on making moral choices
- A new section on poetry and technology
- Websites provided for Notable Authors in genre chapters
- A greater emphasis on young adult–classic literature pairings
- Informational Books section of the nonfiction chapter reorganized around topics of high interest to young adults
- Chapter 8, "Literature for a Diverse Society," redesigned to focus on culturally responsive teaching strategies and literature to support this concept
- Poetry featured in a chapter of its own, and plays moved to the chapter on teaching strategies
- A new section in the chapter on resistant readers about ways to collaborate with students' families
- A new section on trends in technology

 ACKNOWLEDGMENTS

Judy E. Hughes, Panama City, Florida, is a former middle school teacher whose love of literature has always inspired her students to read and respond creatively to literature and whose classroom practices with literature have inspired us.

We are grateful to our editor, Aurora Martínez, who made possible the publication of both editions of *Essentials of Young Adult Literature.*

For their generous help, good advice, and valued opinions concerning *Essentials of Young Adult Literature,* we wish to express our appreciation to the following reviewers: Dana Duffy Backs, School of Library and Information Science, Indiana University Bloomington; Lisa A. Hazlett, University of South Dakota; Katrina Hunter-Mintz, University of North Alabama; Goldie Johnson, Winona State University; Caroline S. McKinney, University of Colorado at Boulder; and Billie A. Unger, Blue Ridge Community & Technical College.

We are indebted to illustrator Pat Dypold for the cover of this edition of *Essentials of Young Adult Literature.* To us, the vibrant color and energetic lines of her cut-paper collage represent the energy, fervor, and directness of youth. The modern style speaks of young people's urge to live fully in the present.

YOUNG ADULTS *and* YOUNG ADULT LITERATURE

Part I provides introductory content for a course on young adult literature. This material will help teachers and librarians select, read, and evaluate young adult books to integrate into their classrooms and libraries.

Chapter 1 begins by defining young adulthood and young adult literature and presenting an overview of the history of young adult literature, including milestones in the evolution of the field and early important works. The value of this literature for young people is presented, augmented by extensive research evidence supporting its benefits for readers. The following section concerns evaluating and selecting books for young people and includes discussion on reliable selection sources. The chapter concludes with a discussion of approaches to studying young adult literature.

Chapter 2 presents important literature concepts—elements of fiction, fictional literary forms, and aspects of book format—and reviews these concepts for students. The major fictional literary forms—novel, short story, picture book, and graphic novel—are also discussed.

Although examples are given throughout this text of well-known modern classics as well as recent notable titles, we include no lengthy plot summaries or book reviews. We believe that more is gained from reading and discussing young adult books themselves than from reading *about* the books in a lengthy textbook.

chapter ONE

UNDERSTANDING YOUNG ADULTS *and* YOUNG ADULT LITERATURE

Change is always accompanied by anticipation, anxiety, excitement, or fear. In the years between childhood and adulthood, when people change rapidly and are old enough to be conscious of the process, finding reassurance, understanding, and the company of those who are sharing their experiences and feelings is comforting, if not vital. All these supports can be found in good stories for young adults.

DEFINITION OF YOUNG ADULTHOOD

The term "young adult" does not have a firm definition that suits everyone. It connotes other words, such as *puberty, adolescence,* and *teenager,* and these in turn suggest different things to different people. Even professionals in the fields of sociology, psychology, and education do not all agree on the meanings of these terms. In the United States and most other developed Western countries, young adulthood is associated with biological changes that all children go through and a growing sense of independence from adult caregivers. At some point and for varying reasons (economic, social, political, biological, or a combination), the transition to adulthood is complete, and young adulthood ends. These developments occur at different ages and at different rates for different people, yet the prevalent school configuration in the United States defines middle school as grades 6 through 8 (ages 11 through 14 for most students) and high school as grades 9 through 12 (ages 15 through 18 for most students). Therefore, we define *young adults* as 11- to 18-year-olds, recognizing that in some instances young adulthood may begin and end earlier or later.

DEFINITION OF YOUNG ADULT LITERATURE

Young adult literature, as defined in this text, is literature written for young people ages 11 to 18 and books marketed as "young adult" by a publisher. We will focus on what we consider to be the best of young adult literature while recognizing that a book does not have to be an award winner or receive rave reviews to have value for a reader.

Herz and Gallo in *From Hinton to Hamlet* (2005) established some criteria for young adult literature that may prove helpful.

- The main character is a teenager who is the center of the plot.
- The protagonist's actions and decisions are major factors in the plot's outcome.
- The events and problems in the plot are related to teenagers, and the dialogue reflects their speech.
- The point of view is that of an adolescent and reflects an adolescent's interpretation of events and people. (pp. 8–9)

In Chapter 2 the literary term *genre*—type or category of literature—will be discussed. Since young adult literature includes all traditional genres of literature from realistic fiction to poetry, we view it as a body of literature appropriate for individuals at a certain stage of development rather than a genre itself.

HISTORY OF YOUNG ADULT LITERATURE

The history of young adult literature parallels that of its psychological counterpart, adolescence, in that books for adolescents could not precede the concept of adolescence itself. Until the mid-eighteenth century, the United States was mostly a rural, agrarian society. Children were sent out to work as early as age 7, and by ages 15 or 16 were fully incorporated into the workforce of the nation. Independence from parents and families came to young people much earlier than it does today. Schools were scarce, and school attendance was seasonal, sporadic, and short-lived. Consequently, there was little need for books in the general population. In those days, adolescence did not exist.

The general acceptance of adolescence as a distinct stage of life emerged in the mid-twentieth century (Appleby, 1989; Wilder & Teasley, 2000; Cart in Beers & Lesesne, 2001), although its social, economic, and political roots developed earlier, as shown in Table 1.1. The efficiencies of industrialization and modern technology, as well as the passage of child labor laws, had removed most children from the workforce and placed them in schools by the early 1900s. Other factors—the Great Depression in the 1930s, a shift away from agriculture to industry, a resulting increase in educational requirements for employment, a demographic shift from rural to urban, and the growth of compulsory school attendance laws—extended this workplace-to-school transition to teenagers by the 1940s. Records from the National Center for Education Statistics show a 72 percent increase in the population of the United States from 1900 to 1940. In contrast, the number of high school graduates in the same period increased by more than 1,700 percent (Gopel, 2005). The emergence of the middle school movement in the 1980s in the United States resulted in the inclusion of middle-graders in the definition of young adult.

Of course, young people read and enjoyed books long before there was a body of literature labeled "young adult." Classics such as Emily Brontë's *Wuthering Heights* (1847), Charles Dickens' *Great Expectations* (1861), Jonathan Swift's *Gulliver's Travels* (1726), Jules Verne's *Journey to the Center of the Earth* (1864), and Mark Twain's *The Adventures of Tom Sawyer* (1876) and *The Adventures of Huckleberry Finn* (1884) may have been written for adults, but young people enjoyed them too. After the establishment of juvenile divisions in publishing houses in the 1920s and 1930s, a few noteworthy books such as *Seventeenth Summer* by Maureen Daly (1942) and *The Catcher in the Rye* by J. D. Salinger (1951) can be seen as precursors to today's young adult books, although librarians shelved them with books for adults.

Although the forerunners of the young adult book began to appear in the mid-nineteenth century, an emphasis on studying adult classic works of literature in high school held sway throughout the twentieth century, delaying the development of young adult literature. However, some of the early important works of young adult literature were published in the late 1960s and early 1970s, but this first flowering of young adult literature was diminished by the simultaneous publication of a plethora of books in which problems overpowered character development and plot. These gloomy novels did the field no good because they sustained for a time a widespread notion that young adult books were categorically of poor quality.

In the liberal political climate of the 1960s and 1970s many topics theretofore considered taboo for young adults (e.g., sex, drug abuse, war, the occult) were addressed head-on by pioneering young adult authors of contemporary fiction, as shown in Early Important Works of Young Adult Contemporary Fiction on page 7. In response, the number of censorship attempts on books rose steadily throughout the 1970s and 1980s. (See Chapter 11 for a discussion of young adult literature, banned books, and censorship.) Nevertheless, due in part to an increase in the number of teenagers in the 1990s, the field matured, blossomed, and came into its own with the better written, more serious, and more varied young adult books published during the last two decades.

TABLE 1.1   Milestones in the Concepts of Adolescence and Young Adult Literature

Date/ Era	Event	Significance
1892	Formation of the Committee of Ten (mainly presidents of well-known universities) (Aulbach, 1994)	Promotion of the study of English and literature throughout high school; establishment of foundations for a university-influenced canon of classic literature to be taught in high school by basing college entrance exams on knowledge of these books
Early 1900s	Growth of the middle class and educational institutions	Positive view by adults of obedience, self-restraint, dependency, conformity in young people
1904	Publication of *Adolescence* by G. Stanley Hall	First formal description of adolescence as a distinct psychological state
1911	Establishment of the National Council of Teachers of English	Signal of an early effort to broaden English curricula beyond the classics to meet the needs of a diverse, democratic society
1920s	Children's divisions established by many publishing houses	First indication of widespread acceptance of the importance of books for young people
1930s	The Great Depression (1929–early 1940s)	Encouragement of teenagers without work to go to high school
1957	Young Adult Services Division established by the American Library Association (name changed to Young Adult Library Services Association—YALSA—in 1992)	Recognition of the distinction between childhood and young adulthood and the books appropriate to each group
1960s–1970s	Civil rights and women's liberation movements; more permissive social and sexual climate	Encouragement of the publication of books by and about minorities and females; permission for publication of books for young people on topics heretofore considered taboo
1970s	Publication of many excellent works of young adult literature	Considered to be the first golden age of young adult literature
1973	Adolescent Literature Assembly of NCTE (ALAN) established	Forum for discussion of and advocacy for the reading of young adult literature in middle and high schools
1988	Margaret A. Edwards Award established	Acknowledgment of authors for their lifetime achievement in writing young adult books that have been popular over a period of time
2000	Establishment of the Michael L. Printz Award for Excellence in Young Adult literature	National recognition of young adult literature as a worthy body of literature

EARLY IMPORTANT WORKS *of* YOUNG ADULT CONTEMPORARY FICTION

Date	Literary Work	Significance
1967	*The Outsiders* by S. E. Hinton	Herald of the age of the realistic young adult novel; considered by many to be the prototypical young adult book
	The Contender by Robert Lipsyte	Early young adult book with an African-American protagonist
1968	*The Pigman* by Paul Zindel	Young adult book well received by critics; counters the argument that young adult literature is of poor quality
1969	*My Darling, My Hamburger* by Paul Zindel	One of the first young adult novels to address abortion
1970	*Are You There, God? It's Me, Margaret* by Judy Blume	One of the first young adult books to feature a frank treatment of female puberty
1971	*Go Ask Alice* by Anonymous (Beatrice Sparks)	One of the first problem novels; deals with the controversial topic of drug abuse
1972	*The Man Without a Face* by Isabel Holland	One of the first young adult books to address homosexuality
	Dinky Hocker Shoots Smack! by M. E. Kerr	One of the first young adult books to realistically portray family dynamics
1973	*A Hero Ain't Nothin' but a Sandwich* by Alice Childress	One of the first young adult books to address drug abuse
1974	*The Chocolate War* by Robert Cormier	A work that helped set a trend toward "dark" or "bleak" novels for young adults
1975	*Forever* by Judy Blume	A book dealing with the controversial topic of teenage sex; helps strike down taboos against frank discussion of such topics in books for young people
1988	*Fallen Angels* by Walter Dean Myers	A signal of the growing strength of multicultural writers and their writing
1989	*Weetzie Bat* by Francesca Lia Block	One of the first crossover novels; helps open writing for young adults to innovation and new forms

The postmodern movement, which emerged following World War II, has significantly influenced young adult literature. According to *Merriam-Webster's Encyclopedia of Literature*, **postmodern** refers to "any of several artistic movements that have challenged the philosophy and practices of modern arts or literature since about the 1940s. In literature this has amounted to a reaction against fixed ideas about the form and meaning of texts" (Kuiper, 1995, p. 899). Postmodernism has helped broaden the types of literature accepted into the mainstream, including graphic novels, novels in verse, docudramas, and novels of mixed genres.

Although it began as a trend in adult literature, postmodern works for young people are growing in number. Nikolajeva (1998) points out the defining characteristics of the postmodern literary work, the most recognized of which is genre eclecticism—writing that has aspects of more than one genre and ready acceptance of elements of popular culture such as film and television. Postmodern literature is also characterized by narrative structures that mirror life. That is, there are not necessarily distinct beginnings, middles, and endings; stories can be emotion-driven rather than event-driven; and stories may include multiple protagonists, perspectives, and narrators. Some postmodern stories include multiple plots or realities with parallel times and places. Authors of postmodern works sometimes encourage readers to take a more active role in the storytelling by using open endings or a choice of endings that invite readers to project subsequent events or by using less authoritative narration that leaves readers to draw their own conclusions. Another interesting feature of postmodern literature is *metafiction,* or having characters or the author talk about the act of creating the literary work and, by doing so, crossing the line between make-believe and real life.

The rising popularity of *crossover novels*—books read, and often marketed to, both young adult and adult audiences—is another manifestation of the trend toward broader definitions of what constitutes young adult literature. According to Cart (2004), crossover books are usually written by young authors, are often first novels or a collection of connected stories, have protagonists in their teens or twenties, are driven by right-of-passage issues, and are published as adult works. Conversely, many adults in their twenties and thirties are now reading young adult titles, effectively expanding the young adult market and significantly increasing sales. This trend is best exemplified by the *Harry Potter* publishing phenomenon that began in 1998 and attracted a huge adult readership.

BENEFITS AND VALUES OF YOUNG ADULT LITERATURE

Excellent works of young adult literature have a definite place in middle and high schools—as class study books in English classes, as reading material in other content-area courses, and as independent reading material. For those who are ready for them, classic works of literature also have value. In many instances these two bodies of literature can be used effectively in tandem. For example, analysis of young adult literature can set the stage for analysis of a particular classic work. Or students can be led to see thematic similarities between contemporary young adult literature and the classics. (See p. 185 for a discussion on pairing young adult literature with classics.)

The primary benefit derived from reading excellent works of young adult literature is enjoyment. Good young adult literature accurately portrays the developmental and emotional stages of adolescence. Its relevance to teenagers is the basis for its appeal to them. Closely related to the benefit of enjoyment is the escape that reading offers to teens—escape from the pressures of school and personal problems with family or friends. Works of fantasy and humorous stories are particularly helpful in providing escape and relaxation.

Another important benefit of reading good literature is that it rewards the reader academically. Many of the research findings summarized later in the chapter in Table 1.2 state that when young people have access to and can choose reading material that is interesting and relevant to them, they read more, become better readers, and consequently do better in all content areas.

There is also a social and emotional aspect. Many works of young adult literature have as their main theme or a secondary theme developing sexuality and awakening romantic interest in another person. The best of these books offer guidance, comfort, and answers to the many questions young people have as they enter puberty and begin to experience romantic feelings for others.

Also, when a story is so convincingly written that readers feel as though they have lived through an experience or have actually been in the place and time where the story is set, the book has given them a valuable personal experience. Experiences such as these are broadening because readers are taken to places and times that they could never actually visit—and might not want to! Personal experiences with literature can be good mental exercises for young people, since they are asked to view situations from perspectives other than their own. By seeing the world around them in new ways and by considering ways of living other than their own, young people increase their ability to think critically and to better understand the different ways people live. Stories about real people can inspire young people to overcome obstacles, accept different perspectives, and formulate personal goals. Entering a world different from the present one can help young people develop their imaginations.

By introducing young people to stories and characters from other cultures and other countries, teachers and librarians help instill in them a foundation for understanding and accepting those who are different from themselves: they learn that all humans are, to some degree, alike. Walking in someone else's shoes by "becoming" a book character, particularly those characters whose lives are restricted by disabilities, gender, politics, poverty, or race, is beneficial to young people because it helps develop their senses of empathy, compassion, and social justice.

Stories based on actual events in the past help young people gain a greater appreciation for what history is and for the people, both ordinary and extraordinary, who made history. By reading stories set in the past, young readers of today can relate on a more personal level with their predecessors and the events that affected their lives. History presented in this way, because it is more interesting, has been shown to be more memorable and its lessons more readily learned.

Often, characters are placed in situations that require them to make moral decisions. Young readers naturally consider what they themselves would do in such a situation. As the story unfolds and the character's decision and the consequences of that choice are disclosed, readers discover whether their own decisions would have had positive outcomes. Regular experiences with these types of stories can help young people formulate their own concepts of right and wrong.

Pleasure, escape, help with personal problems and questions about sexuality, improved reading and writing skills, inspiration, moral development, and developing senses of empathy, compassion, and social justice are some of the important benefits and values derived from reading good young adult literature. Whether it is humor, suspense, wonder, or finding themselves in the story that keeps young people reading, the ultimate benefit of positive experiences with young adult literature is that they often lead to a lifetime of learning and reading enjoyment.

VALUATING AND SELECTING YOUNG ADULT LITERATURE

Teachers and librarians should select the best available material for literature and reading instruction, reading in the content areas, and read-alouds. In making book selections for young people, consider the suggestions in the following subsections.

Know the Reader

The best teachers tend to know their students well, both as a group and, as far as possible, as individuals. For those who work with young adults this is no small challenge, since the operative word at this stage in life is *change,* as 11- to 18-year-olds make the transition between childhood and adulthood. The most apparent change in young adults is their physical growth, with its accompanying awkwardness, self-consciousness, mood swings, and awakening interest in sex. Also apparent are changes in socialization patterns, primarily the need to be with or communicate with peers and to establish independence from parents and other adults. Less apparent, but just as important, is the development of cognitive skills and higher-order thinking processes that make young adults capable of more complex reasoning and communication.

In light of their increased cognitive skills, young adults, if provided with an array of good reading materials, are capable of making their own book choices and should be given opportunities for doing so. Middle and secondary school teachers and librarians can benefit from the importance of peer influence and the increased desire of teens to communicate with one another by providing many opportunities for young people to select from a wide variety of literary choices and to share with one another their responses to the books they read. Teens who speak up in favor of reading exert a strong influence on their peers' decision to read and to select certain books.

A person's interests have been shown to be one of the most powerful forces to motivate reading. But teens' interests, both as a group and individually, are highly diverse and change rapidly, so assessment of student interests by teachers or librarians must be free of any preconceptions and must be done regularly to be effective. For students who need or ask for help in selecting books, the teacher's or librarian's first consideration will be what topics are of interest to them. This is particularly important in the case of resistant readers. (See Chapter 10 for a discussion of students who are resistant readers.) Anderson, Shirey, Wilson, and Fielding (1987, p. 288) reported the results of four experimental studies in which "rated interest accounted for an average of *thirty times* as much variance in sentence recall as readability." They also reviewed and analyzed various other studies on interestingness of reading materials and concluded that "interestingness of children's reading materials has strong and pervasive effects on learning" (p. 299). Knowledge of young people's friends, social activities, hobbies, skills (athletic, academic, artistic), and hopes or plans for the future is helpful in recommending books to them.

Book recommendation or selection must also be based on the students' reading abilities and the mode of delivery. Books selected for whole-class assigned reading should fit all students' needs, interests, and reading levels. Even the most able students who are forced to read uninteresting, irrelevant materials often stop reading voluntarily (McKenna, Ellsworth, & Kear, 1995). Students reading independently usually fare best with materials that are at or slightly below their assessed reading ability, but keen interest in a topic would enable them to read with good comprehension material that is slightly above their readability level.

Another consideration in making good book recommendations for readers is their maturity level. Individual rates of development and influences of home, culture, and school will result in greatly varying levels of maturity within any classroom. For this reason, selections of reading material for whole-class use could be based on the general maturity level of one's students, but selections for independent reading material should be determined by the individual's maturity level. For example, the treatment of war in Rosemary Wells' *Red Moon at Sharpsburg* (2007) and Margaret McMullan's *How I Found the Strong* (2004) would be appropriate for middle-grade classes, but Walter Dean Myers' much more graphic treatment of this topic in *Fallen Angels* (1988) and his *Sunrise Over Fallujah* (2008) would be more appropriate for eleventh- or twelfth-grade class reading or independent reading for a younger but more mature student.

Know the Books

Teachers and librarians who are well-read and current with young adult literature are more likely to be able to suggest books that will be of interest to their students. Sharing information about books with colleagues, being familiar with notable young adult authors, and reading book reviews are alternative ways to learn about good books. Teachers and librarians will, of course, want to have read any book they plan to use as reading or teaching material with a class.

Knowing the major authors writing for young adults and having a general idea of the kinds of books they write can help a teacher or librarian make good book suggestions. Knowing something interesting about the author—that she helps build libraries in developing countries (Ann Cameron) or that he has participated in the Iditarod dogsled race in Alaska (Gary Paulsen)—can motivate a person to read that author's books. (See the Notable Authors feature in each genre chapter.)

Reliable Selection Sources

Several book award programs have been established for the purposes of elevating and maintaining the standards of books for young people and for honoring the authors whose work is judged by experts in the field to have the greatest literary merit. Teachers and librarians can use these award lists as resources for selecting excellent works to share with young adults. Appendix A contains lists of winners of the following major national awards for books for young people.

- Michael L. Printz Award for Excellence in Young Adult Literature
- National Book Award for Young People's Literature
- Newbery Medal
- Carnegie Medal (annual British award)
- Boston Globe–Horn Book Award for text
- The Governor General's Literary Award for text (annual Canadian award)
- Book of the Year for Older Readers Award (annual Australian award)
- Coretta Scott King Award for writing
- Pura Belpré Award for writing

- Margaret A. Edwards Award
- Phoenix Award

Journals that review young adult trade books are an important source of current titles. In addition, these journals contain articles discussing effective strategies for incorporating literature into reading and content-area instruction and for bringing young adults and books together. Each of the publications in the following list offers evaluative annotations and suggested grade-level ranges for books reviewed. Review journals that cover the full spectrum of literature from baby books to adult books are not included here.

- *The ALAN Review,* published three times a year by the National Council of Teachers of English's Assembly on Literature for Adolescents
- *English Journal,* published bimonthly by the National Council of Teachers of English
- *The Horn Book Magazine,* published bimonthly by Horn Book, Inc.
- *Journal of Adolescent and Adult Literature,* published eight times a year by the International Reading Association
- *School Library Journal,* published monthly by Reed Elsevier, Inc.
- *Voices from the Middle,* published four times a year by the National Council of Teachers of English
- *VOYA–Voice of Youth Advocates,* published bimonthly by Scarecrow Press.

Bibliographies offer many carefully selected and annotated titles organized around themes or topics and indexed to assist teachers and librarians. NCTE publishes two bibliographies, each with over a thousand titles, for middle and high school students: *Your Reading: An Annotated Booklist for Junior High and Middle School Students* (Brown & Stephens, 2003) and *Books for You: An Annotated Booklist for Senior High* (Beers & Lesesne, 2001). These sources are updated regularly.

Annual book lists are developed by library and education organizations and are accessible online. Notable among these are

- "Best Books for Young Adults" developed by the American Library Association. www.ala.org/ala/yalsa/booklistsawards/bestbooksya/bestbooksyoung.htm
- "Teachers' Choices" developed by the International Reading Association. www.reading.org/resources/tools/choices_teachers.html

RESEARCH ON READING AND YOUNG ADULT LITERATURE

From its beginnings in the mid-twentieth century, the proponents of young adult literature have encountered resistance to its use in schools from administrators, high school teachers, and university professors who adhere to the notion that only the classics are of sufficient literary quality to be taught to young adults. A full discussion of this issue can be found in Chapter 11. The first part of this section will address research on teachers' attitudes toward the use of young adult literature in schools today.

The second section will deal with research on the effects of using young adult literature with young people in middle and high schools.

The resistance to using young adult literature in high schools is documented in Krickeberg's (1995/1996) national survey of 481 secondary English teachers. Her respondents stated that only ninth- and tenth-grade low- to average-ability students would benefit from using young adult literature. This finding is supported by Applebee (1994), who found that inclusion of young adult literature in high school is sparse, and Bushman (1996), who found that young adult literature was rarely used beyond seventh grade.

Krickeberg's respondents also stated that young adult books were often too controversial to consider using in class, but, oddly enough, two-thirds of these teachers had never taken a young adult literature course, and only one-fifth of them had read *one* of seventeen notable, recently published young adult titles (four-fifths had read none). Their responses also showed that the less knowledgeable they were about young adult literature, the less positive were their beliefs about it.

Another finding by Krickeberg deserves mention. Her respondents, most of whom did not believe that young adult literature was appropriate reading material for their students, indicated that their goal for teaching literature was to motivate students to become lifetime readers. This finding is perplexing, since young people are more likely to view reading as pleasurable and become lifelong readers if they are introduced to literature containing plots consistent with their experiences, themes of interest to them, main characters who are young adults, and language that corresponds to their own language. This statement is supported by reading-interest surveys of young people conducted in the last century (McBroom, 1981; Bushman & Bushman, 1997).

Research on the effects of using young adult literature in schools mainly concerns how it affects students' reading ability and attitudes toward reading. Often, because of the polarization of teachers into the "classics" or "young adult" camps, research studies compare students' learning and attitudes toward reading when using literature of one sort or the other. Important studies on young adult literature and motivation to read are summarized in Table 1.2. This body of research reveals important lessons for administrators and teachers in middle and high schools, as follows:

- Young people read more and more willingly if they are allowed to choose reading materials of interest to them.
- The more young people read, the more practice they get, and the better readers they become.
- Reading aloud to middle and high school students motivates them to read, to read a wider variety of books, and to love reading.
- Classical literature, mostly written for a well-educated adult audience, does not fully meet the needs, interests, and abilities of most young adults.

PPROACHES TO INTERPRETING YOUNG ADULT LITERATURE

The scholarly study of literature generally focuses on the meaning found in a work of literature and how readers construct that meaning. When readers subject a work to deep analysis through exact and careful reading, it is referred to as *new criticism* or *structural criticism*. In this approach, the analysis

TABLE 1.2   Important Studies on Motivation and Young Adult Literature

Researcher(s)	Subjects	Findings
Albright and Ariail (2005)	141 middle grade teachers in one Texas school district	Teachers in the survey • read aloud mainly to help students gain information from textbooks • read from a limited variety of types of texts • rarely read aloud nonfiction chapter books
Worthy, Patterson, Salas, Prater, and Turner (2002)	24 struggling, young resistant readers	Most effective factor in increasing a student's motivation to read was a reading instructor who tailored instruction to the student's unique needs, found materials that exactly fit the student's needs and interests, and took time to inspire the student to read.
Ivey and Broaddus (2001)	1,765 sixth-graders in 23 diverse schools in mid-Atlantic and northeastern United States	When asked what made them want to read in the classroom, students ranked as most important • free reading time and teacher read-alouds of literature as part of instructional time • quality and diversity of reading materials and a choice in selecting these materials Most favored free reading material • Magazines (77%) • Adventure books (69%) • Mysteries (68%) • Scary stories (59%) • Joke books (56%) • Nonfiction about animals (51%)
Follow-up study to Carlsen and Sherrill (below) by Cope (1997)	272 twelfth-graders from advanced, general, and remedial-level English classes, including resistant readers	Love of reading in students is promoted by • self-choice of books they find interesting • interesting books for assigned reading • being read to by a good reader Dislike of reading is promoted by • required reading of uninteresting books, mainly classics, before students are developmentally prepared for them • overanalysis of any single work • book reports • being forced to read aloud in class

Researcher(s)	Subjects	Findings
Stewart, Paradis, Ross, and Lewis (1996)	49 developmental reading students (scored below grade level on a standardized reading test) in grades 7, 8, and 9	After three years in a literature-based reading program, students overwhelmingly believed that, as a result of the program, they read better in terms of speed, fluency, comprehension and retention, and overall school performance. The attributes of the program that the students found most helpful were • choice over what they read • interest in what they read • being given time in school to read • reading practice
Carlsen and Sherrill (1988)	College students who were committed readers	Conditions that promoted a love of reading included • freedom of choice in reading material • availability of books and magazines • family members who read aloud • adults and peers who model reading • role models who value reading • sharing and discussing books • owning books • availability of libraries and librarians
Fielding, Wilson, and Anderson (1986)	Middle-graders	Students who read a lot at home showed larger gains on reading achievement tests
Livaudais (1985/1986)	1,020 students in grades 7–12	The reading activities students found truly motivational were • teacher read-alouds • freedom of choice in reading materials • owning books
Fader, Duggins, Finn, and McNeil (1976)	Boys, ages 12 to 17	Classrooms "saturated" with high-interest books and print for self-selected reading significantly improved low-achieving students' attitudes toward school, learning, and reading as well as their verbal proficiency and language comprehension.
Appleby (1967)	Three stratified (by ability level) groups of high school seniors: • 65 who took a one-semester individualized reading course • 65 who wanted to take the individualized course, but did not • 65 who took a required traditional literature course	Individualized reading group accomplished the objectives of a literature program as well as, if not better than, groups receiving other types of literature instruction.

of the words and structure of a work is the focus; the goal is to find the "correct" interpretation. Until the 1960s structural criticism held sway in most middle and high school literature classrooms. Many teachers continue to use this method today. Most teachers using this approach take the view that there is one correct interpretation of any work of literature. According to this view, reading is a process of taking from the text only what was put there by the author. Young readers' success with any work of literature is determined by how closely their interpretations match the "authorized" interpretation. Students' responses to literature are thus limited to naming (or guessing) the "right" answers to teachers' questions.

In 1938, Louise Rosenblatt introduced *reader response theory* or the *transactional view of reading.* She asserted that what the reader brings to the reading act—his or her world of experience, personality, and current frame of mind—is just as important in interpreting the text as what the author writes. According to this view, reading is a fusion of text and reader. Consequently, any text's meaning will vary from reader to reader and, indeed, from reading to reading of the same text by the same reader. Almost everyone has experienced reading a book only to discover that a friend has reacted to or interpreted the same book quite differently. Although Rosenblatt (1978) points out that the text of any book guides and constrains the interpretation that is made, an important corollary to her view of reading is that personal interpretations, within reason, are valid, permissible, and, in fact, desirable. Beach and Marshall (1990) point out that students' worlds of experience include (1) knowledge of various genres and literary forms gained from previous reading that can help them understand new, similar works; (2) social relationships that can help them understand and evaluate book characters' actions and motivations; (3) cultural knowledge that influences one's attitudes toward self and others (as in gender roles) and that can help readers understand their responses to story events; and (4) topic knowledge or knowledge of the world that can deepen readers' understanding of a text and enrich their response to it. Reader response theory, in accepting different interpretations of the same literary work, accommodates both traditional, genre-specific works and genre-eclectic, nonlinear, postmodern literature with its multiple perspectives and plots and demands on the reader to act as coauthor.

Another interesting aspect of Rosenblatt's theory is that reading is done for two distinct purposes: to take knowledge from the text (efferent reading) and to live through a literary experience, in the sense of assuming the identity of a book character (aesthetic reading). Whether we read efferently or aesthetically depends on what we are reading (e.g., a want ad versus a mystery novel) and why we are reading it (e.g., for information versus for pleasure). Rosenblatt's view of reading has important implications for the way teachers will encourage their students to respond to the literature they share with them. See Chapter 9 for a detailed discussion with suggestions and explanations of literature-related response activities.

REFERENCES

Albright, L. K., & Ariail, M. (2005). Tapping the potential of teacher read-alouds in middle schools. *Journal of Adolescent and Adult Literacy, 48*(7), 582–591.

Anderson, R. C., Shirey, L., Wilson, P., & Fielding, L. (1987). Interestingness of children's reading material. In R. E. Snow & M. J. Farr (Eds.), *Aptitude, learning, and instruction,* Vol. 3. *Conative and affective process analysis,* pp. 287–299. Hillsdale, NJ: Erlbaum.

Anonymous. (1971). *Go ask Alice.* New York: Harper.

Applebee, A. (1994). *Shaping conversations: A study of continuity and coherence on high school literacy curricula.* Albany, NY: National Research Center on Literature Teaching and Learning.

Appleby, B. C. (1967). The effects of individualized reading on certain aspects of literature study with high school seniors. (Doctoral dissertation, University of Iowa, 1967.) *Dissertation Abstracts International, 28*(7), 2592A.

———. (1989). Is adolescent literature in its adolescence? *ALAN Review, 17*(1), 40–45.

Aulbach, C. (1994). The Committee of Ten: Ghosts who still haunt us. *English Journal, 83*(3), 16–17.

Beach, R. W., & Marshall, J. D. (1990). *Teaching literature in the secondary school.* Belmont, CA: Wadsworth.

Beers, K., & Lesesne, T. S. (Eds.). (2001). *Books for you: An annotated booklist for senior high* (14th ed.). Urbana, IL: National Council of Teachers of English.

Block, F. L. (1989). *Weetzie Bat.* New York: HarperCollins.

Blume, J. (1970). *Are you there, God? It's me, Margaret.* New York: Bradbury.

———. (1975). *Forever.* New York: Bradbury.

Brontë, E. (2002/1847). *Wuthering Heights.* New York: Penguin.

Brown, J. E., & Stephens, E. C. (Eds.). (2003). *Your reading: An annotated booklist for middle school and junior high* (11th ed.). Urbana, IL: National Council of Teachers of English.

Bushman, J. H. (1996). Young adult literature in the classroom—or is it? *English Journal, 86*(3), 35–40.

Bushman, J., & Bushman, K. (1997). *Using young adult literature in the English classroom* (2nd ed.). Upper Saddle River, NJ: Prentice Hall.

Carlsen, G. R., & Sherrill, A. (1988). *Voices of readers: How we come to love books.* Urbana, IL: National Council of Teachers of English.

Cart, M. (2004). Carte blanche: What is young-adult literature? *Booklist, 101*(8), 734.

Childress, A. (1973). *A hero ain't nothin' but a sandwich.* New York: Putnam.

Cope, J. (1997). Beyond *Voices of Readers:* Students on school's effects on reading. *English Journal, 86*(3), 18–23.

Cormier, R. (1974). *The chocolate war.* New York: Knopf.

Daly, M. (1942). *Seventeenth summer.* New York: Dodd, Mead.

Dickens, C. (2002/1861). *Great expectations.* New York: Penguin.

Fader, D., Duggins, J., Finn, T., & McNeil, E. (1976). *The new hooked on books.* New York: Berkley.

Fielding, L. G., Wilson, P. T., & Anderson, R. C. (1986). A new focus on free reading: The role of trade books in reading instruction. In T. Raphael (Ed.), *The contexts of school-based literacy,* pp. 149–160. New York: Random House.

Gopel, E. C. (Ed.). (2005). *The world almanac and book of facts.* New York: World Almanac Books.

Hall, S. G. (1904). *Adolescence: Its psychology and its relations to physiology, anthropology, sociology, sex, crime, religion and education.* New York: Appleton.

Herz, S. K., & Gallo, D. R. (2005). *From Hinton to Hamlet: Building bridges between young adult literature and the classics* (2nd ed.). Westport, CT: Greenwood.

Hinton, S. E. (1967). *The outsiders.* New York: Viking.

Holland, I. (1972). *The man without a face.* New York: Lippincott.

Ivey, G., & Broaddus, K. (2001). "Just plain reading": A survey of what makes students want to read in middle school classrooms. *Reading Research Quarterly, 36*(4), 350–377.

Kerr, M. E. (1972). *Dinky Hocker shoots smack!* New York: Harper.

Krickeberg, S. K. (1996). A national teacher survey on young adult literature. (Doctoral dissertation, Northern Illinois University, 1995.) *Dissertation Abstracts International, 56*(10), 3895A.

Kuiper, K. (Ed.). (1995). *Merriam-Webster's encyclopedia of literature.* Springfield, MA: Merriam-Webster.

Lipsyte, R. (1967). *The contender.* New York: HarperCollins.

Livaudais, M. (1986). A survey of secondary students' attitudes toward reading motivational activities.

(Doctoral dissertation, University of Houston, 1985.) *Dissertation Abstracts International, 46*(8), 2217A.

McBroom, G. (1981). Research: Our defense begins here. *English Journal, 70*(6), 75–78.

McKenna, M., Ellsworth, R., & Kear, D. (1995). Children's attitudes toward reading: A national survey. *Reading Research Quarterly, 30,* 934–957.

McMullan, M. (2004). *How I found the strong.* Boston: Houghton.

Myers, W. D. (1988). *Fallen angels.* New York: Scholastic.

———. (2008). *Sunrise over Fallujah.* New York: Scholastic.

Nikolajeva, M. (1998). Exit children's literature? *The Lion and the Unicorn, 22*(2), 221–236.

Rosenblatt, L. (1978). *The reader, the text, the poem.* Carbondale: Southern Illinois University.

Salinger, J. D. (1951). *The catcher in the rye.* New York: Little, Brown.

Stewart, R. A., Paradis, E. E., Ross, B. D., & Lewis, M. J. (1996). Student voices: What works in literature-based developmental reading. *Journal of Adolescent and Adult Literacy, 39*(6), 468–478.

Swift, J. (2003/1726). *Gulliver's travels.* New York: Penguin.

Twain, M. [Samuel Clemens]. (2002/1876). *The adventures of Tom Sawyer.* Berkeley: University of California Press.

———. (2001/1884). *The adventures of Huckleberry Finn.* Berkeley: University of California Press.

Verne, J. (1995/1864). *Journey to the center of the earth.* New York: Random.

Wells, R. (2007). *Red moon at Sharpsburg.* New York: Viking.

Wilder, A., & Teasley, A. B. (2000). YA: FAQ (We're glad you asked!). *ALAN Review, 28*(1), 55–57.

Worthy, J., Patterson, E., Salas, R., Prater, S., & Turner, M. (2002). "More than just reading": The human factor in reaching resistant readers. *Reading Research and Instruction, 41*(2), 177–202.

Zindel, P. (1968). *The pigman.* New York: Harper.

———. (1969). *My darling, my hamburger.* New York: Harper.

chapter TWO

LEARNING
about BOOKS

In Chapter 1 we stated that reading is a fusion of text and reader and that each reading of a particular literary work results in a different transaction. Even a rereading by the same reader will result in a different experience. But if the transaction is different each time a book is read, how can general assessments of literary merit be made? Rosenblatt's answer is that, although the notion of a single correct reading of a literary work is rejected, *"given agreed-upon criteria,* it is possible to decide that some readings are more defensible than others" (1985, p. 36). Although each reading of a given literary work will be personal and distinct, there are certain generally-agreed-upon interpretations of that work by a community of educated readers. In this chapter, traditional literary elements are reviewed in order to heighten your awareness of literary criticism and to provide a more precise vocabulary for you to express your responses to books. Literary terms may also be considered as tools that your students can use to initiate and sustain conversations about literature. In using these terms in the classroom you can help students to acquire a literary vocabulary.

ELEMENTS OF FICTION

Learning to evaluate books can best be accomplished by reading as many excellent books as possible. Gradually, your judgment on the merits of individual books will improve. Discussing your responses to these books with students, teachers, and your classmates and listening to their responses will also assist you in becoming a more appreciative critic. Understanding the different parts, or elements, of a piece of fiction and how they work together can help you to become more analytical about literary works; this ability, too, can improve your judgment of literature. For a discussion of the elements of poetry, see Chapter 7, "Poetry"; for the elements of nonfiction, see Chapter 6, "Nonfiction: Biography and Informational Books." The various elements of fiction are discussed separately in the following sections, but it is the unity of all these elements that produces a story.

Plot

The events of a story and the sequence in which they are told constitute the *plot* of the story. In other words, the plot is what happens in the story. Plot is an important element of fiction to those who want to find excitement in the books they read. A good plot produces conflict to build excitement and suspense to keep the reader involved.

The nature of the *conflict* within the plot can arise from different sources. The basic conflict may be one that occurs within the main character, called *person-against-self.* In this type of story, the main character struggles against inner drives and personal tendencies to achieve some goal. Stories about adolescence will frequently have this conflict as the basis of the story problem. For example, in *Ghost Boy* (2000) by Iain Lawrence, 14-year-old Harold, an albino, struggles to know and accept himself and others.

A conflict usually found in survival stories is the struggle the main character has with forces of nature. This conflict is called *person-against-nature.* In *Wild Man Island* (2002) by Will Hobbs and *The Young Man and the Sea* (2004) by Rodman Philbrick, the main characters struggle to survive wolves, strong tides, a monster tuna, and ocean storms.

In other stories, the source of the conflict is found between two characters. Conflicts with peers, sibling rivalries, and rebellion against an adult are examples of *person-against-person* conflicts. For example, in *Bucking the Sarge* (2004) by Christopher Paul Curtis, 15-year-old Luther's conflict is with his mother, whose views on right and wrong collide with his own.

Occasionally, a story presents the main character in conflict with society. In young adult novels this conflict is most often about preventing environmental destruction by new technology or changing times, about surviving in an increasingly corporate culture, or about coping with political upheaval such as war. The conflict is then called *person-against-society.* In the environmental mystery *Hoot* (2002) by Carl Hiaasen, protagonist Roy attempts to preserve a habitat for burrowing owls against encroaching development. Another example is the thriller *So Yesterday* (2004) by Scott Westerfeld, in which the consumer culture is exposed. *Soldier Boys* (2001) by Dean Hughes and *Private Peaceful* (2004) by Michael Morpurgo, both war stories, also create this type of conflict.

In some stories the protagonist faces *multiple conflicts* in which, for example, a character may be in conflict with society as well as with other persons. In L. J. Adlington's science fiction novel *Cherry*

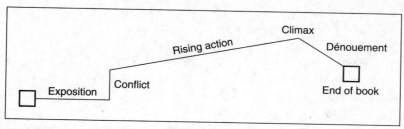

FIGURE 2.1   Diagram of a Progressive Plot

Heaven (2008), characters are in conflict with the dystopian society in which they find themselves and also in conflict with the former owners of that world.

Plots are constructed in many different ways. The most usual structures found in young adult novels are *chronological plots,* which cover a particular period of time and relate the events in order within the time period. For example, if a book relates the events of one week, then Monday's events will precede Tuesday's, and so on. *Lizzie Bright and the Buckminster Boy* (2004) by Gary D. Schmidt has a chronological plot. There are two distinct types of chronological plots, progressive and episodic. In books with *progressive plots,* the first few chapters are the exposition, in which the characters, setting, and basic conflict are established. Following the expository chapters, the story builds through rising action to a climax. The climax occurs, a satisfactory conclusion (or dénouement) is reached, and the story ends. Figure 2.1 suggests how a progressive chronological plot might be visualized.

An *episodic plot* ties together separate short stories or episodes, each an entity in itself with its own conflict and resolution. These episodes are typically unified by the same cast of characters and the same setting. Often, each episode comprises a chapter. Although the episodes are usually chronological, time relationships among the episodes may be nonexistent or loosely connected by "during that same year" or "later that month." An example of the episodic plot structure is found in Richard Peck's humorous novels *A Long Way from Chicago* (1998) and *A Year Down Yonder* (2000) about siblings' adventures with their grandmother in rural Illinois during the 1930s. Because episodic plots are less complex, they tend to be easier to read and often lend themselves to the recounting of humorous escapades. Readers who are new to reading full-length novels will find episodic plot novels especially appealing and fairly easy to comprehend. Figure 2.2 suggests how a chronological episodic plot might be visualized.

With greater frequency young adult novels are appearing with new plot formulations such as *complex multiple plots,* in which the traditional chronology is replaced by nonlinear plots that occur simultaneously. In Matt de la Peña's *Ball Don't Lie* (2005), a basketball story that involves race relations, a disjointed narrative with various viewpoints alternates between past and present and can be seen as a reflection of the internal life of the protagonist. Other stories are told through a multiplicity of protagonists, each of whom has a vantage point from which to unfold some portion of the story being told. Judith Clarke's *Wolf on the Fold* (2002) spans four generations of an Australian family through various adolescent and child characters who deal with harsh realities of poverty, war, and death. The loosely woven stories link members of the family and reveal shared family traits.

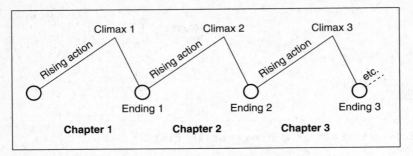

FIGURE 2.2   Diagram of an Episodic Plot

Authors use a *flashback* to convey information about earlier events in a chronological plot—for example, before the beginning of the first chapter. In this case, the chronology of events is disrupted, and the reader is taken back to an earlier time. Flashbacks can occur more than once and in different parts of a story. The use of a flashback permits authors to begin the story in the midst of the action but later fill in the background for full understanding of the present events. Such plots require a higher level of reading comprehension and can be challenging for less able readers. Teachers can help students understand this plot structure by assigning for reading good examples of stories using flashbacks, such as Virginia Euwer Wolff's *Probably Still Nick Swansen* (2002). Class discussion can then focus on the sequence of events and why the author may have chosen to relate the events in this manner. Figure 2.3 illustrates the structure of a book in which some events occurred before the beginning of the book.

A plot device that prepares readers for coming events in a story is *foreshadowing*. This device gives clues to a later event, possibly even the climax of the story. In Chapter 1 of Kenneth Oppel's *Airborn* (2004), the cabin boy's chance meeting with and rescue of a dying balloonist and hearing his tales of strange flying creatures foreshadow events to come a year later and prepare readers for the cabin boy's pivotal role in these events. You can alert students to one of the subtle ways authors prepare them for the outcomes of stories by discussing foreshadowing.

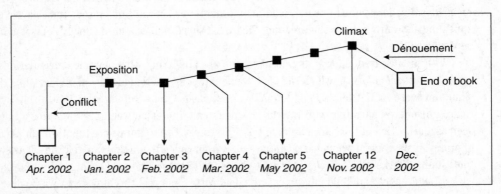

FIGURE 2.3   Diagram of a Flashback

Characters

Characters, the actors in a story, are another element of fiction vital to the enjoyment of a story. A well-portrayed character can become a friend, a role model, or a temporary parent to a young reader. Although young adults enjoy reading about exciting events, the characters must matter to the reader, or the events no longer seem important. How characters are depicted and how they develop in the course of the story are important to the reader. Two aspects to consider in studying a character are characterization and character development.

Characterization refers to the way an author helps the reader to know a character. The most obvious way an author can do so is to describe the character's physical appearance and personality. Portraying the character's emotional and moral traits or revealing her relationships with other characters are subtler and more effective techniques. In the most convincing characterizations, we come to know the character through a combination of her own actions and dialogue, the responses of other characters to her, and the narrator's descriptions.

Character development refers to the changes, good or bad, that the character undergoes during the course of events in the story. If a character experiences significant life-altering events, we, as readers, expect that the character will somehow be different as a result of those events. A character who changes in the course of the story is referred to as a *dynamic character.* For example, in Kevin Crossley-Holland's *At the Crossing Places* (2002), Arthur, a squire, lacks self-confidence at first, but during his preparation for becoming a crusader, he develops physically and morally.

In a work of fiction for young adults there are usually one or two main characters and some minor characters. Ideally, the main character, sometimes called the *protagonist,* will be a fully described, complex individual who possesses both good and bad traits, like a real person. Such an individual is called a *round character.* For example, in the realistic fiction novel *A Step from Heaven* (2001) by An Na, young Ju, the protagonist whose Korean family immigrates to America, is presented as a complex character dealing with the many challenges an immigrant must face. The character or force that is in direct opposition to the main character is called an *antagonist.* In Sara Zarr's *Story of a Girl* (2007), Tommy, the former boyfriend, a thoughtless and cruel antagonist, is shown to be vulnerable himself during the course of the story.

Minor or *secondary characters* are described less fully. The extent of description depends on what the reader needs to know about the character for a full understanding of the story. Some of the minor character's traits are described fully, whereas other facets of the character's personality may remain obscure. Because the purpose is to build the story and make it comprehensible, fragmentary knowledge of a minor character may suffice. In *Heat* (2006) by Mike Lupica, a sports novel portraying a positive image of Hispanic teens competing athletically, secondary character Manny is depicted as the catcher and a loyal mate to talented pitcher Michael Arroyo, the protagonist.

Occasionally, an author will insert a *flat character*—that is, a character described in a one-sided or underdeveloped manner. Although such one-dimensional people do not exist in real life, they may be justified within the story to propel the plot. Sometimes the character is shown as an all-evil or all-frivolous person; folktales, for instance, present flat characters as symbols of good and evil. In some stories, a flat character plays the role of *character foil,* a person who is in direct juxtaposition to another character (usually the protagonist) and who serves to highlight the characteristics of the other individual. A character foil may occur as a flat or a round character. For example, in Gordon Korman's *Born to Rock* (2006), Melinda, childhood friend of the protagonist, Young Republican Leo Caraway, is a flat character who makes Leo aware of who his biological father is. Melinda also serves as a character foil to Leo in her dislike of Republicans and distaste for Leo's interest in money.

The main characters in an excellent work of fiction for young adults are rounded, fully developed individuals who undergo change in response to life-altering events. Because young adults generally prefer protagonists of their age, or somewhat older, authors of books for young adults often face a dilemma: in real life, young adults usually have restricted freedom of action and decision making within the confines of a family, but a vivid and exciting story requires the main characters to be "on their own." Thus, in many young adult novels, authors arrange for parents to be absent, no longer living, or nonfunctioning.

Setting

The time and place(s) in which the story occurs constitute the *setting* of a story. The setting has a more or less important function depending on the story. For example, in historical fiction the authentic recreation of the period is essential to comprehension of the story's events. In this situation, the setting, fully described both in time and place, is called an *integral setting.* The story could not be the same if placed in another setting. For example, in the World War II historical novel *B for Buster* (2004) by Iain Lawrence, useful maps of the 1943 European war theatre are included.

By contrast, the setting in folktales is often vague and general. For example, "long ago in a cottage in the deep woods" is meant to convey a universal, timeless tale, one that could have happened anywhere and almost anytime except the present or very recent past. This type of setting is called a *backdrop setting.* It simply sets the stage and the mood.

Theme

The literary *theme* of a story is its underlying meaning or significance. The term *theme* should not be confused with *topic* or *theme* as used in the sense of a thematic unit of study. Although we sometimes think of the literary theme as the message or moral of the story, it can just as likely be an aesthetic understanding, such as an appreciation for nature, or a viewpoint on a current societal issue. To identify the theme, you may ask yourself what the author's purpose was in writing the story, or what the author is saying through this story.

A theme is better expressed by means of a complete sentence than by a single word. For example, students often suggest that a theme found in *Nothing but the Truth* (1991) by Avi is communication. A better statement of the theme is "Communicating clearly and honestly is important to good relationships in life." The single word *communication* may be a topic found in the story, but it is not an expression of the theme. It does not inform us of what the author wishes to declare about communication.

Readers with different life experiences may not identify the same theme. If we are to accept the notion of reader response, then we must accept that students may perceive the underlying meaning of a work in a number of different ways. Indeed most layered works of literature can be argued to have multiple themes. For example, in *Nothing but the Truth,* a reader may identify the theme as "Different people perceive truth differently, depending on their point of view or perspective." Other readers may identify the theme as "Communicating clearly and honestly is important to good relationships." A statement of a theme can be a beginning point for students to discuss why they have identified a particular theme, what parts of the novel convinced them of this, and whether they agree with the theme personally.

Themes in young adult literature should be worthy of readers' attention and should convey truth to them. Furthermore, themes should be based on high moral and ethical standards. A theme must not overpower the plot and characters of the story; young adults read fiction primarily for enjoyment, not for enlightenment. Heavy-handed, obvious, and didactic themes detract from a reader's enjoyment of a story. Certainly a well-written book may convey a moral message, but it should also tell a good story from which the message emerges. In this way the theme is subtly conveyed to the reader. For example, Kirby Larson's *Hattie Big Sky* (2006) demonstrates that family is not land nor a home but is instead a matter of heart.

Often adults write stories not for the pleasure of young people but to teach lessons in morality. We think of moralistic stories as existing only in the thinly disguised religious tracts for children and adolescents found in the 1800s, yet we must be alert to a tendency for some authors to use young adult literature as a platform to preach about drug abuse, animal rights, or other issues of contemporary interest. If the literary quality of these novels is weak, then the story and characters become secondary to the issue or problem. However, moral values embedded within the fabric of a powerful story may help readers increase their moral reasoning, develop a sense of right and wrong, and make choices for their own lives.

Style

Style is the way an author tells the story; it can be viewed as the writing itself, as opposed to the content of the book. However, the style must suit the content of the story; the two are intertwined.

Different aspects of style are considered in evaluating a work of fiction. Most obviously, you can look at the *words* chosen to tell the story. Are they long or short, common or uncommon, rhyming or melodic, boring and hackneyed or rich and challenging, impassive or emotional, standard dialect or regional minority dialect? The words should be appropriate to the story being told. As an evaluator of books for young adults, you will want to ask the following questions as you read: Why did the author choose these words? What effect was the author trying to achieve?

The *sentences* may also be considered. Do they read easily? Do they flow without the reader needing to reread to gain the meaning of the text? Sometimes an author chooses to limit the word choices to write a book that conveys the thought processes and voice of a young narrator. Such books may consequently fall within the lower range of difficulty. Yet in the hands of a gifted writer, the sentences will remain no less melodic, varied in length and structure, and enjoyable to read and hear than sentences in the best books at the highest range of difficulty. An example of a novel written in simple yet powerful language is *Out of the Dust* (1997) told in the form of free verse by Karen Hesse.

With greater frequency new or unusual forms are appearing in young adult literature, from novels told as a movie script, as in Walter Dean Myers' *Monster* (1999); novels in the form of a diary experimenting with poetic forms, as in Ron Koertge's *Shakespeare Bats Cleanup* (2003); novels in the form of letters, as in Iain Lawrence's *Lord of the Nutcracker Men* (2001); novels in the form of e-mails and phone calls, as in Catherine Stine's *Refugees* (2005); and novels drawing on letters, diary entries, lists, e-mails, and so on, as in Jaclyn Moriarity's *The Year of Secret Assignments* (2004). Styles acceptable in young adult literature have grown beyond traditional ways of telling a story.

The *organization* of the book may be considered by noting the paragraphs and transitions, length of chapters, headings and chapter titles, preface, endnotes, prologue, epilogue, and length of the book. For many readers chapter length is important. Shorter chapters appeal to students who read more slowly or whose attention spans are shorter. For example, Sharon Creech's *Ruby Holler* (2002) is a 310-page novel with many chapters, but each chapter is only a few pages long. The story's humorous and lighthearted mood, swift action, and quirky characters make it enjoyable for a wide range of readers.

Chapter titles can provoke interest, as well as provide the reader with clues to predict story events. Some books also provide the readers with a *prologue,* an introductory statement telling events that precede the start of the story. Adeline Yen Mah, author of *Chinese Cinderella: The True Story of an Unwanted Daughter* (1999), speaks directly to the reader in an informative prologue about the Chinese language. She invites the reader to become interested in a Chinese girl's language, history, and culture.

Some authors include an *epilogue,* a concluding statement telling events that occur after the story has ended. In *How I Live Now* (2004), Meg Rosoff describes an England during a third world war, but then in an epilogue adds a hopeful note of events taking place six years after the conclusion of the story. Occasionally, an author presents information on the sources or historical facts used in the story. In *Yellow Star* (2006), for example, Jennifer Roy places an author's note and a timeline of events in the epilogue.

Point of view is another aspect of an author's style. If the story is told through the eyes and voice of a *third-person narrator* (characterized by the use of *he, she, it*), then the reader can know whatever the narrator knows about the events of the story. In many stories, the narrator is *omniscient* and can see into the minds of all characters and be at many places at the same time. The reader of Jerry Spinelli's *Loser* (2002) can understand and interpret the story from many different perspectives because of Spinelli's use of the omniscient point of view. Other stories are narrated from the perspective of only one character in the story. In this case, the story is still told in the third person, but the reader knows only what that particular character can see and understand. This technique is called *limited omniscient* point of view. In Ron Koertge's novel, *Margaux with an X* (2004), the story is told from the viewpoint of Margaux, the cool protagonist who is attracted to uncool Danny.

Other times authors choose to tell the story through a *first-person narrator* (the use of *I*), usually the main character of the story. In such cases the reader gains a sense of closeness to the main character but is not privy to any information unavailable to this character. As you read, you will note that some authors have accomplished a first-person point of view by writing as though their main character were writing a diary or letters, as in *Flight to Freedom* (2002) by Ana Veciana-Suarez. Occasionally, a story is told in first person through the eyes of a minor character. In *The Captain's Dog: My Journey with the Lewis and Clark Tribe* (1999) by Roland Smith, a dog relates the historical events during the early-1800s Lewis and Clark expedition to search for the Northwest Passage.

A *shifting point of view* permits the reader to see events from different characters' points of view. This technique can be demanding on young readers' skill. When the point of view shifts, the author cues readers to the changing point of view, as Lynne Rae Perkins does in *Criss Cross* (2005). In this story teen friends offer their varying perspectives on life and on one another during the course of a summer in a small town. The use of several characters as protagonists is being seen more frequently in young adult literature and lends itself to displaying the various ways teenagers perceive one another in a school or social setting.

Symbolism is an artistic convention that authors use to suggest invisible or intangible meanings by analogy to something else through association, resemblance, or convention. Often a *symbol*—a person, object, or situation—represents an abstract or figurative meaning in the story in addition to its literal meaning. Some symbols are universal and can be found repeatedly in literary works; others may be particular to the story. For example, a farm often stands for love and security in works of literature. Some students may read only on a literal level, but they can be helped by teachers to note symbols in the books they are reading. If the symbolic feature recurs in the story, it is referred to as a *motif.* The number 3 is a common motif in folktales, for example.

A *circular plot structure,* often seen in adventure novels and quest fantasies, is a narrative device involving setting, character, and theme. Typically a protagonist ventures from home (or the starting place of the story), goes on a journey, often a dangerous one in which many challenges are overcome, and then returns home a changed person. The plot is usually chronological, with the events occurring in a setting that becomes a circle. By returning the character to the place where he started, the author can emphasize the character's growth or change while also highlighting the theme of the story. In Geraldine McCaughrean's *The Kite Rider* (2002), a son trying to save his widowed mother from a horrendous marriage departs on an adventure across China as a circus kite rider. While gaining strength from this experience, he also gains confidence and resolve from his inner journey in which he confronts his beliefs and prejudices before being reunited with his mother.

A story must be more than a plot and a character study, however; a story integrates all the elements of fiction into a pleasing whole. In drawing together these elements, authors create new worlds for their readers.

ICTIONAL LITERARY FORMS

In this book we address four fictional literary forms: the novel, the short story, the picture book, and the graphic novel. Titles of works in these literary forms are noted as such in the list of recommended books at the end of each genre chapter. Collections of short stories are indicated by **(COL)**, picture books are coded as **(PI)**, and graphic novels are noted by **(GR)**.

Novel

The *novel* is an extended fictional narrative, generally in prose, with full development of characters, settings, and plots dealing with human experience. Novels have been the mainstay of the literature program in most high schools since the nineteenth century. Middle schools have included novels in the curriculum but have also relied on anthologies of short stories and poems. Novels have the advantage of being able to develop fully the context in which the story is set, the feelings of the characters, and the attitudes of society, as well as the particular events of the story, in the course of the narrative. In novels many characters can be and often are developed. The writer may develop multiple though over-lapping plots and employ complex plot structures. Many young adults enjoy the greater depth, length, and complexity they find in novels, experiences most readers would not want to miss. Recommended novels can be found in the lists at the end of each genre chapter.

Short Story

The *short story* is a brief fictional narrative, generally in prose, designed to create a unified impression quickly and forcefully. British author of short stories and novels Jan Mark (1988) observed that a short story is "dealing with the moment at which change occurs: the seminal moment—after which nothing will ever be the same again. It is the challenge to the writer to choose the right moment and then to prove that he or she chose the right moment" (p. 44).

The short story has long predominated in literature anthologies used in middle schools, but until re-cently the stories included were written for an adult audience. Today many stories included in anthologies are written for young adults. Contemporary short stories can also be found in magazines for young people. See Appendix B for a list of magazines for young adults. The Paul A. Witty Short Story Award is given annu-ally to an author for an original short story published for the first time in the past year in a periodical for young people. *Cricket* magazine has been the most frequent publisher of the award-winning stories.

In the 1980s collections of short stories written for and about young adults began to be published. Don Gallo deserves much of the credit for this trend with his 1984 publication of *Sixteen: Short Stories by Outstanding Writers for Young Adults.* Gallo has continued to select and publish short stories for young adults, and collections by other anthologists and collections of short stories by individual writers have also been published since the mid-1980s. In an interview (Crowe, 1997), Gallo suggests that a short story that appeals to teenagers should

- be a good story
- grab the reader's attention with the opening lines of the story
- contain lively, readable, honest writing
- focus on teenage characters
- deal with issues and situations with which almost any teen can identify
- give readers something to think about while remaining entertaining

Short stories have many advantages for classroom use. Because of their brevity students will have time to explore a variety of topics in a short period of time. Short stories usually take 15 to 20 minutes to read aloud and are ideal for use as an introduction to a unit of study in content-area classes as well as English classes. Lesesne (1994) proposes using the short story in the classroom to introduce readers to different cultures and their customs, to explore new genres in the study of literature, and to serve as models for student writing. As noted, short story collections are coded **(COL)** in the Recommended Books lists at the ends of the genre chapters.

Picture Book

The *picture book* is a profusely illustrated book in which both words, generally in prose, and illustra-tions contribute to the story's meaning. In a true picture book the story would be diminished without the illustrations, and so we say that illustrations in picture books are integral or essential to the story. At one time picture books were considered appropriate only for young children, but in the 1970s picture books for older readers began to appear. These books are more sophisticated, abstract, or complex in themes and subjects and are written in response to increasingly visual modes of communication now prevalent in society. Consider some of the advantages in using picture books in middle and high schools.

- They can be used as teacher read-alouds for introductions and supplements to textbook-based units of instruction.
- They can be used in text sets (several books on the same subject) in class reading, analysis, and discussion by small groups of students.
- They can stimulate interest in a topic, and possibly provoke discussion, which would result in a deeper understanding of the content (Albright, 2000, 2002), as in Jacqueline Woodson's *Show Way* (2005), illustrated by Hudson Talbott, which discusses slavery through the history of quilts used as secret maps for freedom-seeking slaves in the 1800s.
- They can demonstrate applications of concepts (Alvermann & Phelps, 1998), as D. B. Johnson's *Henry Climbs a Mountain* (2003) does for the concept of civil disobedience.
- They often have factual content that reinforces or enhances that found in textbooks, as Karen Hesse's *The Cats in Krasinski Square* (2004), illustrated by Wendy Watson, does for a unit of instruction about the Holocaust by featuring two Jewish sisters, escapees of the Warsaw ghetto, and their courage.

Picture books are coded **(PI)** in the Recommended Books lists at the end of each genre chapter.

Graphic Novel

The *graphic novel* is an extensive book-length narrative form in which the text is written in speech bubbles or as captions to comic book–like illustrations. Graphic novels, sometimes referred to as long comic books, may be of any genre of literature and may be about any theme, topic, or subject. The term *graphic* refers to stories told through images and does not refer to the nature of the content, and *novel* refers primarily to length, not to whether it is fiction or nonfiction. Graphic novels may be hardcover or paperback, but they have enough pages to have a spine and to stand on a shelf.

Like comic books, graphic novels are usually written as sequential strips or panels that go across the page, within which are separate frames that are read from left to right and top to bottom. Each frame is read for the content of both text and picture in order to follow the action, after which the reader proceeds to the next frame to the right. As each row or panel is read, the reader moves to the next row or panel and begins again at the left. Dialogue is usually presented in a bubble pointing to the speaker; thought is presented in a wavy-line bubble with small circles leading back to the character whose thoughts are being conveyed.

Comics began in the United States, but have also thrived in Europe and Asia. *Anime,* animated Japanese television programs, such as Pokémon and Yu-Gi-Oh!, are often animations of *manga,* Japanese comic books. Anime artists typically draw characters with enormous eyes of different shapes and colors, and with large, distinctive heads of hair, often of unusual colors, such as lavender and green.

The television shows have been very popular in the United States among school-age students and have further primed young readers for graphic novels.

Graphic novels were rarely seen in the United States prior to the 1990s, but they have been growing in popularity over the last decade and represent a new trend in young adult literature. Early noteworthy graphic novels include

- *Maus: A Survivor's Tale* (1986) by Art Spiegelman. A Holocaust survivor's story.
- *Batman: The Dark Knight Returns* (1986) by Frank Miller. Batman is faced with the problems of a dystopian future.
- *Watchmen* (1987) by Alan Moore and illustrated by Dave Gibbons.
- *Sandman: Preludes and Nocturnes* (1991) by Neil Gaiman and illustrated by Sam Kieth, Mike Dringenberg, and Malcolm Jones III. The story of a man interested in capturing Death.
- *Bone* (1995) by Jeff Smith. An action-packed adventure of power and evil in which three cartoon cousins land in a mysterious valley full of monsters and magic.

Graphic novels, with their illustrations, spare text, and heavy use of dialogue, can serve as reading motivators because of their appeal for many students who are more visually oriented or who dislike reading.

Graphic novels evolved from comics but have taken on their own identity. The graphic novel is gaining in acceptance by young adults and by the professionals who study, review, and publish young adult literature, as evidenced by new graphic novel imprints from mainstream youth trade publishers. An example is the new imprint First Second, from Roaring Brook Press, launched in the spring of 2006. Charles McGrath (2004) in the *New York Times Magazine* points out that "comics are what novels used to be—an accessible, vernacular form with mass appeal" (p. 24). Michael Cart (2005) in a *Booklist* column titled "A Graphic-Novel Explosion" contends that graphic novels are "a literary art form that combines a tradition of excellent, carefully edited text with newly kinetic eye- and attention-grabbing visuals. [This art form] could be the salvation of young-adult reading. It could, in fact, offer a new kind of interactive engagement between reader and book" (p. 1302). If this statement is true, then it may be because "there is a . . . critical mass of artists uncovering new possibilities in this once-marginal form, and a new generation of readers, perhaps, who have grown up staring at cartoon images on their computer screens and in their video games, not to mention the savvy librarians and teachers who now cater to their interests and short attention spans" (McGrath, 2004, p. 26). More review journals including *School Library Journal* and *Booklist* are now reviewing graphic novels. Web resources to locate articles and reviews of graphic novels include http://my.voyager.net and www.graphicnovels.brodart.com. Graphic novels are coded **(GR)** in the Recommended Books lists at the end of each genre chapter.

BALANCE AND VARIETY IN BOOK SELECTIONS

In addition to the various literary elements that are central to the issue of quality, the age and development of the reader and the balance and variety among books are also important considerations. Which stories teachers choose to share with students is important, as Dressel (1990) found in studying the effects on fifth-grade students of listening to literature of higher and lower quality. The writing of students in this study was affected by the characteristics of the stories they heard and discussed. Varying choices will challenge students and enhance the resulting academic benefits for their language and cognitive development, as discussed in Chapter 1. Because young adults have a wide range of reading interests and abilities, you will need to provide your students with many different types of books, including novels, picture books for older readers, collections of short stories and poetry, graphic novels, books of plays, and works of nonfiction. Balance among *topics, literary forms,* and the *genres of literature* is essential.

The *mood* of the books must also be varied to include stories that are sad, humorous, silly, serious, reflective, dramatic, boisterous, suspenseful, or scary. A steady diet of light, humorous books might, at first, appeal to students, but eventually, the sameness will become boring. A teacher who selects works of literature with the same predominant mood over an entire year is ignoring the rapid change and growth in personal lives and choices that are the hallmark of young adults. Because their interests are changing as they grow and develop, you should introduce them to many different books that will help them as they meet new challenges.

A balance between male and female main characters is necessary to meet the needs of students of both sexes and to help them understand more fully the perspectives, problems, and feelings of members of the opposite sex. School library collections need to have a wide range of topics with a gender balance among the main characters. In addition, understanding and empathy for people with disabilities can be gained through portrayals in books of individuals, both young people and adults, with impairments. A positive image of people with disabilities needs to be conveyed in these books. Furthermore, young adults with disabilities need to see characters like themselves positively portrayed in books.

The representation of minorities as main characters is also essential if you are to present a realistic view of society and the world. Through well-written *multicultural literature,* readers can see that someone from a different race, ethnic group, or religion has many of the same basic needs and feelings that they themselves have. Literature by and about people different from oneself can help an individual develop an understanding and appreciation for all peoples. Young adults from minority groups will enjoy reading books in which others from backgrounds similar to their own play leading, and sometimes heroic, roles. Characters with whom one can identify permit a deeper involvement in literature and at the same time help readers to understand situations in their own lives.

International literature—that is, literature from other nations and regions of the world—needs to be included in classroom and library collections in order to guide students toward global understanding. Through reading books about young adults from other nations, your students will experience cultural literacy on a worldwide basis.

Classroom libraries are usually limited in scope; therefore, school and public libraries are necessary to provide the adequate balance and variety of books for students' research needs and independent reading. Frequent visits to the school library media center by the class and by individual students need to be arranged by the teacher and librarian.

 ## ATEGORIES OF LITERATURE

In Chapters 3 to 8, the main categories of books for young adults will be defined and explained, followed by book titles recommended for reading in each of the categories. Chapters 3 to 7 focus on the literary genres, as presented in Table 2.1. The number of the chapter in which each genre of litera-

TABLE 2.1   Genres and Topics of Young Adult Literature

Fiction				
Realistic fiction (3)	*Modern fantasy (4)*	*Historical fiction (5)*	Nonfiction (6)	Poetry (7)
Families	Modern folktales	Beginnings of civilization	Biographies	Lyric poems
Peers	Magical realism		Informational books	Narrative poems
Romance and sexuality	Stories of the supernatural	Civilizations of the ancient world		
Coming of age	Special fantasy situations	Civilizations of the medieval world		
Physical, emotional, mental, and behavioral challenges	Historical fantasy	Emergence of modern nations		
Communities	Quest adventures	Development of industrial society		
Adventure and survival	Science fiction	World wars in the twentieth century		
Sports		Post–World War II		
Mysteries				

ture is discussed is noted next to the genre. For the purposes of this textbook, a genre organization, a traditional, though admittedly imperfect, way of grouping literature, is the most practical, making it easy for teachers and librarians to organize learning and to demonstrate the wide spectrum of ideas and emotions that can be found in young adult literature. Because many students seek and select books for their independent reading by topics, such as mystery, adventure, romance, or friendships, we have also included subheadings of topics within each genre chapter and have arranged the recommended books by these genres and by the topical subheadings. In addition, brief annotations of recommended titles alert readers to some of the issues they address.

Understanding genre characteristics builds a frame of reference for readers of a particular genre and can ease the task of comprehension. Furthermore, as readers encounter postmodern works of literature that go beyond the traditional boundaries of a genre, knowledge of the traditional literary forms may help them understand what the authors are doing and help them gain new understandings from the shift in style.

Authors of young adult literature have been experimenting with works that blend characteristics of several genres, and as a result, genre boundaries are increasingly blurred (Laminack & Bell, 2004;

Kaplan, 2005). As discussed earlier in this chapter, novels for young adults written in the style of free verse and other verse forms are being seen with greater frequency. An example is Karen Hesse's *Out of the Dust* (1997), awarded the Newbery Medal and the Scott O'Dell Award for Historical Fiction in the same year. Novels in verse form are listed in this textbook under the particular narrative genre, such as historical fiction, rather than in the chapter about poetry. Works of magical realism, a literary mode that combines realism and fantasy, such as those of Virginia Hamilton (*Sweet Whispers, Brother Rush,* 1982), Francesca Lia Block (*Weetzie Bat,* 1989), and David Almond (*Skellig,* 1999), offer the reader new ways to perceive the world. Works of magical realism are discussed and placed in Chapter 4, "Modern Fantasy." Historical fantasy blends historical fiction and modern fantasy, as in Mary Hoffman's *Stravaganza: City of Masks* (2002). These works are also discussed and placed in Chapter 4. Other blended genres include works of fictionalized biography and informational books that contain elements of both fiction and nonfiction, as in Russell Freedman's *Confucius: The Golden Rule* (2002) and David Macauley's *Mosque* (2003); these works are placed in Chapter 6, "Nonfiction: Biography and Informational Books." These blended-genre works offer readers new perceptions and often provide heightened interest for readers.

Chapter 8, "Literature for a Diverse Society," diverges from the organization of genre and presents books organized by culture. Although multicultural and international books have been placed in a separate chapter for emphasis and ready access, many multicultural and international titles are also recommended in the genre chapters.

An overview of the genres, subtopics, and their relationships to one another is displayed in Table 2.1. These genres can be used in making balanced choices for library and classroom reading collections and for choosing books to read aloud.

REFERENCES

Adlington, L. J. (2008). *Cherry Heaven.* New York: Greenwillow.

Albright, L. K. (2000). "The effects on attitude and achievement of reading aloud picture books in seventh grade social studies classes." Unpublished dissertation, Ohio University, Athens.

————. (2002). Bringing the ice maiden to life: Engaging adolescents in learning through picture book read-alouds in content areas. *Journal of Adolescent and Adult Literacy, 45*(5), 418–428.

Almond, D. (1999). *Skellig.* New York: Delacorte.

Alvermann, D. E., & Phelps, S. F. (1998). *Content reading and literacy: Succeeding in today's diverse classrooms* (2nd ed.). Boston: Allyn and Bacon.

Avi. (1991). *Nothing but the truth.* New York: Orchard.

Block, F. L. (1989). *Weetzie Bat.* New York: Harper & Row.

Cart, M. (2005). A graphic-novel explosion. *Booklist, 101*(14), 1301.

Clarke, J. (2002). *Wolf on the fold.* Asheville, NC: Front Street.

Creech, S. (2002). *Ruby Holler.* New York: HarperCollins.

Crossley-Holland, K. (2002). *At the crossing places.* New York: Arthur A. Levine.

Crowe, C. (1997, March). Don Gallo: The godfather of YA short stories. *English Journal, 86,* 73–77.

Curtis, C. P. (2004). *Bucking the Sarge.* New York: Wendy Lamb.

de la Peña, M. (2005). *Ball don't lie.* New York: Delacorte.

Dressel, J. H. (1990). The effects of listening to and discussing different qualities of children's literature on the narrative writing of fifth graders. *Research in the Teaching of English, 24*(4), 397–414.

Freedman, R. (2002). *Confucius: The golden rule.* New York: Arthur A. Levine.

Gaiman, N. (1991). *Sandman: Preludes and nocturnes.* Illustrated by S. Kieth, M. Dringenberg, and M. Jones III. New York: DC Comics.

Gallo, D. (1984). *Sixteen: Short stories by outstanding writers for young adults.* New York: Delacorte.

Hamilton, V. (1982). *Sweet whispers, Brother Rush.* New York: Philomel.

Hesse, K. (1997). *Out of the dust.* New York: Scholastic.

———. (2004). *The cats in Krasinski Square.* Illustrated by W. Watson. New York: Scholastic.

Hiaasen, C. (2002). *Hoot.* New York: Knopf.

Hobbs, W. (2002). *Wild man island.* New York: HarperCollins.

Hoffman, M. (2002). *Stravaganza: City of masks.* New York: Bloomsbury.

Hughes, D. (2001). *Soldier boys.* New York: Atheneum.

Johnson, D. B. (2003). *Henry climbs a mountain.* Boston: Houghton Mifflin.

Kaplan, J. (2005). Young adult literature in the 21st century: Moving beyond traditional constraints and conventions. *ALAN Review, 32*(2), 11–18.

Koertge, R. (2003). *Shakespeare bats cleanup.* Cambridge, MA: Candlewick.

———. (2004). *Margaux with an x.* Cambridge, MA: Candlewick.

Korman, G. (2006). *Born to rock.* New York: Hyperion.

Laminack, L. L., & Bell, B. H. (2004). Stretching the boundaries and blurring the lines of genre. *Language Arts, 81*(3), 248–253.

Larson, K. (2006). *Hattie Big Sky.* New York: Delacorte.

Lawrence, I. (2000). *Ghost boy.* New York: Delacorte.

———. (2001). *Lord of the nutcracker men.* New York: Delacorte.

———. (2004). *B for Buster.* New York: Delacorte.

Lesesne, T. S. (1994). Forming connections and awakening visions: Using short story collections in the classroom. *ALAN Review, 21*(3), 1–8.

Lupica, M. (2006). *Heat.* New York: Philomel.

Macauley, D. (2003). *Mosque.* Boston: Houghton Mifflin.

Mah, A. Y. (1999). *Chinese Cinderella: The true story of an unwanted daughter.* New York: Delacorte.

Mark, J. (1988, January/February). The short story. *Horn Book Magazine, 64*(1), 42–45.

McCaughrean, G. (2002). *The kite rider.* New York: HarperCollins.

McGrath, C. (2004, July 11). Not funnies. *New York Times Magazine,* 24–33, 46, 55–56.

Miller, F. (1986). *Batman: The Dark Knight returns.* New York: DC Comics.

Moore, A. (1987). *Watchmen.* Illustrated by D. Gibbons. New York: DC Comics.

Moriarity, J. (2004). *The year of secret assignments.* New York: Arthur A. Levine.

Morpurgo, M. (2004). *Private Peaceful.* New York: Scholastic.

Myers, W. D. (1999). *Monster.* New York: Scholastic.

Na, A. (2001). *A step from heaven.* Asheville, NC: Front Street.

Oppel, K. (2004). *Airborn.* New York: HarperCollins.

Peck, R. (1998). *A long way from Chicago.* New York: Dial.

———. (2000). *A year down yonder.* New York: Dial.

Perkins, L. R. (2005). *Criss cross.* New York: Greenwillow.

Philbrick, R. (2004). *The young man and the sea.* New York: Blue Sky.

Rosenblatt, L. M. (1985). The transactional theory of the literary work: Implications for research. In R. Cooper (Ed.), *Researching response to literature and the teaching of literature: Points of departure* (pp. 33–53). Norwood, NJ: Ablex.

Rosoff, M. (2004). *How I live now.* New York: Wendy Lamb.

Roy, J. (2006). *Yellow star.* Tarrytown, NY: Cavendish.

Schmidt, G. D. (2004). *Lizzie Bright and the Buckminster boy.* New York: Clarion.

Smith, J. (1995). *Bone.* Columbus, OH: Cartoon Books.

Smith, R. (1999). *The captain's dog: My journey with the Lewis and Clark tribe.* San Diego: Harcourt.

Spiegelman, A. (1986). *Maus: A survivor's tale.* New York: Pantheon.

Spinelli, J. (2002). *Loser.* New York: Joanna Cotler.

Stine, C. (2005). *Refugees.* New York: Delacorte.

Veciana-Suarez, A. (2002). *Flight to freedom.* New York: Orchard.

Westerfeld, S. (2004). *So yesterday.* New York: Razorbill.

Wolff, V. E. (2002). *Probably still Nick Swansen.* New York: Simon Pulse.

Woodson, J. (2005). *Show way.* Illustrated by H. Talbott. New York: Putnam's.

Zarr, S. (2007). *Story of a girl.* New York: Little, Brown.

part TWO

GENRES of LITERATURE

In Part II we present the genres of literature as outlined in Table 2.1. We believe that the organization by genres, topics, and historical eras as found in Chapters 3 to 7 is the most convenient and helpful way for you and your students to locate books. We acknowledge from the outset that literary genres defy absolute definitions and that some people find them oversimplified. We acknowledge also that most books can be categorized within genres in more than one way because the stories address more than one topic. For example, stories about peers are often about families, too.

Please note that we have thoroughly integrated multicultural and international titles into Chapters 3 through 7. In addition, we devote Chapter 8 to literature for a diverse society in order to highlight the importance and current status of multicultural and international literature and to provide more extensive lists of recommended titles within these fields.

Special features in Part II deserve your attention. The Early Important Works features give you the history of the development of each genre at a glance. The lists of Notable Authors found in Chapters 3 to 8 will familiarize you with well-known creators of literature and help you make good choices for in-depth author studies. Our goal in the Recommended Books section at the end of each genre chapter has been to include the best recent books for young adults as well as a few older titles that continue to hold wide appeal for today's young adults. Please note that titles in the Recommended Books lists are organized by the same topic or historical era as in the body of the chapter, to facilitate locating specific types of books.

Other good titles for young adults may be found in the awards lists in Appendix A. These awards were selected specifically for their suitability for young adults. The history, criteria for selection, and lists of the winners by year are included for each award.

REALISTIC FICTION

Realistic stories for young adults openly address sad and harsh situations of life as well as happy and humorous ones. Readers of all ages enjoy stories about people who seem like themselves or who are involved in familiar activities.

chapter THREE

DEFINITION AND DESCRIPTION

Realistic fiction refers to stories that could happen to people; that is, it is within the realm of possibility that such events could occur. The protagonists of these stories are fictitious characters created by the author, but their actions and reactions are quite like those of real people. Sometimes events in these stories are exaggerated or outlandish—hardly probable but definitely possible and still fitting the definition of realistic fiction.

Realism in literature is a complex, multifaceted concept. Marshall (1988) considers various components of realism in literature, including factual, situational, emotional, and social. In good realistic stories, several of these components of realism occur, with varying degrees of emphasis. *Factual realism* is provided by descriptions of actual people, places, and events in a book, with facts that are recorded accurately. Usually in historical fiction and occasionally in realistic fiction, for example, the names and locations of actual places are included in the story, with accurate and complete descriptions. In Catherine Stine's *Refugees,* for example, communications occur between two teens, one in New York and one in Afghanistan, right after the actual September 11, 2001, attack in New York.

Situational realism is provided by occurrences that are not only possible but also quite likely, often in identifiable locations with characters of an identifiable age and social class, making the whole treatment believable. The survival story, which often hinges on a life-threatening situation, is an example of a story built on situational realism. Geraldine McCaughrean's *The White Darkness* relates the survival story of a troubled teenage girl who goes on a dangerous secret expedition to Antarctica with an obsessive and manipulative pseudo-uncle.

Emotional realism is provided by the appearance of believable feelings and relationships among characters. Rite-of-passage or coming-of-age stories often employ emotional realism. Beth Kephart's *Undercover* depicts loner Elisa, who writes love letters for boys to express their feelings to their girlfriends. She falls in love with one of the boys and discovers an ablity to express herself in this first person coming-of-age narrative.

Social realism provides an honest portrayal of society and its conditions of the moment, including both healthy and adverse conditions. Government, schools, courts, and economic systems as described in a story are examples. In Martine Leavitt's *Heck, Superhero,* Heck finds himself without a home when his mother's life spirals out of control and she abandons him. Heck tries to cope on his own and avoids authorities.

Contemporary realism is a term used to describe stories that take place in the present time and portray attitudes and mores of the present culture. Unlike early realistic books that depicted only happy families and were never controversial, today's contemporary realism often focuses on current societal issues, such as alcoholism, racism, poverty, and homelessness. These contemporary books still tell of the happy, funny times in young people's lives, but they also include the harsh, unpleasant times that are, sadly, a part of many lives. Abuse, neglect, violence, peer problems, the effects of divorce, drug abuse, physical and mental disabilities, disillusionment, and alienation from the mainstream of society are all topics that are included in the contemporary realistic novel.

Authors of contemporary realistic fiction set their stories in the present or recent past. But, in time, features of these stories, such as allusions to popular culture, customs, and dress, become dated, and the stories are therefore no longer contemporary, though they remain part of realistic fiction. In some cases the stories may continue to appeal to young readers because of the power of the storytelling. See the feature Early Important Works of Realistic Fiction for a brief glance at the history of this genre.

The ***problem novel*** is a contemporary realistic story that addresses a societal problem and, at times, is used as a synonym for the term *contemporary realism*. At other times *problem novel* is used as a derogatory term to refer to a story in which problems or conflicts overwhelm the plot and characterization. In these cases the novel is written to provide the author with a soapbox from which to lecture or as a vehicle for capitalizing on whatever societal problem is currently at the forefront of the news.

EARLY IMPORTANT WORKS *of* REALISTIC FICTION

Date	Literary Work	Significance
1719	*Robinson Crusoe* by Daniel Defoe (England)	One of the first desert island survival adventures; many imitators
1812	*Swiss Family Robinson* by Johann Wyss (Switzerland)	Most successful imitation of *Robinson Crusoe*
1868	*Little Women* by Louisa May Alcott (United States)	An early family story of great popularity
1876	*The Adventures of Tom Sawyer* by Mark Twain (United States)	Classic adventure story set along the Mississippi
1877	*Black Beauty* by Anna Sewell (England)	One of the first animal stories to deplore inhumane treatment of animals
1883	*Treasure Island* by Robert Louis Stevenson (England)	Classic adventure story with pirates
1934	*The Good Master* by Kate Seredy (United States)	Newbery winner set in Hungary; one of the first realistic stories featuring another culture and country
1938	*The Yearling* by Marjorie Kinnan Rawlings (United States)	Classic animal and coming-of-age story
1941	*In My Mother's House* by Ann Nolan Clark (United States)	One of the earliest stories to feature Native Americans
1951	*Catcher in the Rye* by J. D. Salinger (United States)	Novel of teenage rebellion, first published for adults, but later adopted by young adult readers
1964	*Harriet the Spy* by Louise Fitzhugh (United States)	Ushered in the New Realism movement in books for young people
1967	*The Outsiders* by S. E. Hinton (United States)	One of the first young adult books; focuses on gangs, social alienation, and adolescent rebellion
1967	*The Contender* by Robert Lipsyte (United States)	Early young adult book with African-American protagonist

(continued)

EARLY IMPORTANT WORKS *of* REALISTIC FICTION (CONTINUED)

Date	Literary Work	Significance
1968	*The Pigman* by Paul Zindel (United States)	Romance with alternating chapters by the male and female protagonist
1969	*My Darling, My Hamburger* by Paul Zindel (United States)	Realistic young adult story that addresses abortion
1970	*Are You There, God? It's Me, Margaret* by Judy Blume (United States)	One of the first young adult books with a female protagonist to feature a frank treatment of sex
1971	*Then Again, Maybe I Won't* by Judy Blume (United States)	One of the earliest young adult books with a male protagonist to feature a frank treatment of sex
1971	*The Planet of Junior Brown* by Virginia Hamilton (United States)	Realistic novel featuring minority main characters by an African-American author
1972	*The Man Without a Face* by Isabelle Holland (United States)	One of the first young adult books to feature homosexual protagonists
1972	*Dinky Hocker Shoots Smack!* by M. E. Kerr (United States)	Realistic portrayal of family dynamics
1973	*A Hero Ain't Nothin' but a Sandwich* by Alice Childress (United States)	Story addressing drug abuse, African-American protagonist, multiple points of view
1973	*A Day No Pigs Would Die* by Robert Newton Peck (United States)	Rural story about a father–son relationship, coming-of-age story
1974	*The Chocolate War* by Robert Cormier (United States)	Story featuring athletics, religion, gangs, and the pressures to conform

In problem novels the characters are often from dysfunctional families or ordinary families facing difficult problems. A protagonist usually feels isolated and is often alienated from adults. Parents are often missing, dead, or emotionally remote. The story is frequently told in the first person or from the point of view of the protagonist, sometimes in a diary form. Dialogue often predominates and represents a particular dialect or teen vernacular, much the way teens would talk, and may include profanity and informal usage. Sexuality, once taboo in books for teenage readers, is openly addressed. Other formerly taboo topics, such as death and physical abuse, are also addressed. Problem novels remind us that it is important to read literature carefully to find books worthy of teenage readers. Nonetheless, adolescents want and deserve to read books that honestly address issues and topics about which they are concerned or curious.

VALUATION AND SELECTION OF REALISTIC FICTION

The criteria for evaluating realistic fiction are the same as those for any work of fiction. Well-developed characters who manifest change as a result of significant life events, a well-structured plot with sufficient conflict and suspense to hold the reader's interest, a time and place suitable to the storyline, and a worthy theme are basic literary elements expected to be found in any work of fiction.

Some realistic novels portray adverse and discouraging social situations, such as homelessness and poverty; yet it remains important that the stories permit some cause for optimism. Adolescents need to trust that this world can be a good place in which to live and that it can be made a better place through the efforts of individuals. Adolescent readers also need to understand that problems can be overcome or ameliorated.

Themes in realistic stories often convey moral values, such as the rewards of kindness and generosity to others. However, these moral values must spring naturally from the story, as a by-product of the story itself, not as the main reason for the story. At times, adults write books for young people with the sole intent of teaching or preaching, and the story itself is nothing more than a thin disguise for a heavy-handed moral lesson. In fiction, the story is of paramount importance. The moral must not overwhelm the story but may be its logical outcome.

Realistic fiction must be believable, even though all aspects may not be probable. Some young adults and children have a tendency to criticize a story when the events are not probable. An example is *The Mysterious Benedict Society* by Trenton Lee Stewart, in which four gifted students are selected by responding to a newspaper ad for a secret mission to infiltrate the Learning Institute for the Very Enlightened. Other aspects of *The Mysterious Benedict Society* are more ordinarily realistic; for example, the characters are well developed and the relationships among the characters seem quite ordinary. Sometimes, an author approaches the edge of the believable range to produce a more exciting, suspense-filled story. The sacrifice of some probability for a good story can enhance readers' interest and pleasure.

Much of the controversy involving young adult literature centers on topics that are found in realistic fiction novels, such as premarital sex, pregnancy, homosexuality, and the use of profanity. Many of these controversial books fall within the types of realism labeled "Romance and Sexuality" and "Coming of Age" in the recommended reading list at the end of this chapter. Chapter 11 provides a discussion of issues surrounding controversial books and censorship.

An aspect of writing style that students greatly appreciate is humor. Although humor may be found in stories of any genre, it is more often found in realistic fiction. Humorous stories feature characters caught up in outrageous situations or involved in funny predicaments. Adolescents often are amused by the incongruities presented in these escapades, as in Polly Horvath's *The Canning Season*. Other humorous stories draw on wordplay for their humor. In the list of recommended books at the end of this chapter, books involving humor are frequently noted as such.

Many realistic works are presented as though written by one of the characters. A first person point of view can often successfully reflect the internal struggles and introspective stances taken by many teenagers as they grow toward adulthood. Some recent examples are *Sweethearts* and *Story of a Girl* by Sara Zarr, *Undercover* by Beth Kephart, and *Red Glass* by Laura Resau.

Selection of realistic fiction for classroom and library collections and for class assignments should be balanced among the different topics of realistic stories. A steady diet of serious problem novels does not offer the richness of experience to adolescents that they deserve, nor does it provide for the varied reading interests of a group of students. The mood of a book may be serious and deal with disturbing family situations, but not all books recommended to adolescent readers should be serious. Some lighthearted stories with humor or romance can help balance the literary diet. It is also important to introduce students to both female and male protagonists, as well as protagonists from different races and cultures.

Realistic fiction stories are easy for young adults to relate to and enjoy. They can often see their own lives, or lives much like their own, in these stories (Samuels, 1989). The theme of self-discovery is especially important to adolescent girls. Many middle school and high school students also report on reading interest surveys a keen interest in sports, adventure, mystery, and romance stories, making it plain that realistic fiction is an important genre for many young adults (McBroom, 1981; Carter & Harris, 1982; Higgenbotham, 1999; Hale & Crowe, 2001). Books of realistic fiction should be well represented in libraries and classrooms.

OPICS OF REALISTIC FICTION

The subject matter of realistic fiction includes the whole world of relationships with self and others: the joys, sorrows, challenges, adjustments, anxieties, and satisfactions of human life. Realistic books often treat more than one aspect of human life; thus, some realistic fiction books can be placed in more than one of the categories described in the following subsections.

Families

Stories about the *nuclear family*—young people and their relationships with parents and siblings— are a natural subject of books for adolescents. The period of time from middle school through high school is usually spent in close contact with family members. Stories often show the struggle between parents and adolescents who are seeking greater freedom and adolescents' evolving relationships with siblings. *Indigo's Star* by Hilary McKay and *The Big Nothing* by Adrian Fogelin are good examples of this type of book.

Extended families can also be found in adolescent literature. Aunts, uncles, grandparents, and cousins are important in the real lives of many teenagers and may also be enjoyed in stories written for teens. Sometimes a book will tell of an adolescent being raised by a member of the extended family, as in Polly Horvath's *The Canning Season;* other times a relative is portrayed as a supportive family member. See *Tending to Grace* by Kimberly Newton Fusco and *The Same Stuff as Stars* by Katherine Paterson.

The *alternative family* of today's world is also depicted in family stories. Not all family stories present the safe and secure world of healthy, intact families. Single-parent families, separation, divorce, and reconstructed families of stepparents and stepchildren are often the backdrop of stories today. For example, in *The Steps* by Rachel Cohn, the protagonist deals with the adjustment to a stepfamily. The difficulty adolescents encounter in adjusting to these new family situations becomes the primary conflict in some stories. Temporary family situations, such as foster care, are also described in books about family life. It is important for young readers to see families other than the typical mother, father, and two children portrayed positively in books.

In contemporary realistic stories the harshness of family life and relationships are often portrayed. While many young people are fortunate to have supportive families, many teens want to read about families with difficult and abusive situations, as in Nancy Werlin's *The Rules of Survival*. In reading about such harsh situations some students can better understand and deal with their own difficult lives; in other cases such stories help them understand the problems of some of their peers.

Peers

In addition to adapting to one's family situation, adolescents must also learn to cope with their peers. Many realistic stories show adolescents struggling for **acceptance by peers** in a group situation. School settings are common in these stories. Examples include *Amandine* by Adele Griffin; *Fame and Glory in Freedom, Georgia* by Barbara O'Connor; and *Donuthead* by Sue Stauffacher. Neighborhoods, community centers, and summer camps are other common settings. For instance, see *What They Found: Love on 145th Street* by Walter Dean Myers and *Breaking Rank* by Kristen D. Randle.

Developing **close friendships** is another focus of stories about peer relationships. Friends may be of the same sex or the opposite sex, of the same age or a very different age, or of the same culture or a different culture. A concern for friendship and how to be a good friend to someone are shared traits of these stories. *Big Mouth & Ugly Girl* by Joyce Carol Oates and *The Year of Secret Assignments* by Jaclyn Moriarty are good examples of this type of book.

Romance and Sexuality

Romance stories are popular with preteens and teens, especially girls. Some young teens are interested in romance but very shy and confused about relationships with a romantic partner. Literature showing romantic encounters becomes especially interesting to them at this stage of development. Some stories depict *boy–girl friendships,* as in *The Grooming of Alice* by Phyllis Reynolds Naylor and *Doing It* by Melvin Burgess. Other novels portray *physical attraction,* as in Iain Lawrence's *Ghost Boy*. Some stories portray abuse in a relationship, as in Chris Lynch's *Inexcusable,* in which a date rape occurs. Since the 1990s many stories of characters dealing with *pregnancy and teenage parenting* have appeared; some worthy examples are Margaret Wild's *One Night* and Angela Johnson's *The First Part Last.*

Young people become aware of their **growing sexuality** during preteen and teen years as they begin to mature. Some stories for older teens show *attraction between members of the opposite sex as well as members of the same sex,* with the beginning of sexual activity sometimes depicted in relationships. Stories that portray the struggle of young people coming to terms with a *homosexual* or *lesbian sexual orientation* are seen more frequently than they were in the past; other stories show the cruelty of society toward young homosexuals, lesbians, bisexuals, and transsexuals. See *Talk* by Kathie Koja, *Geography Club* by Brent Hartinger, and *Boy Meets Boy* by David Levithan.

Coming of Age

From birth to age 10, most children's lives revolve around family, friends, and classmates, but during the preteen and teen years a shift toward self-discovery and independence occurs. Rapid growth and change are seen in the physical, emotional, moral, and intellectual domains of life. These changes are reflected in books for adolescents and are referred to as **coming-of-age stories.** An adult novel, *Catcher in the Rye* by J. D. Salinger, which captured the attention of many young adults and thus became a well-known forerunner to young adult literature, falls under this coming-of-age topic. Sometimes books that deal with the trials and tribulations encountered during growth from childhood to adulthood are called *rite-of-passage* books. A rite of passage is an event in one's life that signals a change from child to adult. Examples of rite-of-passage books are *Olive's Ocean* by Kevin Henkes and *No Laughter Here* by Rita Williams-Garcia.

Physical, Emotional, Mental, and Behavioral Challenges

Many individuals must deal with difficult challenges in their lives. Some teenagers have disabilities; others have a family member or a friend with a disability. These disabilities may be *physical,* such as scoliosis; *emotional,* such as bipolar disorder, suicidal tendencies, anorexia, or substance abuse; *mental,* such as mental retardation or learning disabilities; *behavioral,* such as hyperactivity; or *multiple.* As obesity increases in frequency across society, more stories focus on the physical and emotional health challenges faced by young people dealing with this problem. Recent examples include *Fat Kid Rules the World* by K. L. Going, *Looks* by Madeleine George, and *Big Fat Manifesto* by Susan R. Vaught.

Appearing different or strange to others is especially difficult for adolescents who seek peer approval. Authors of young adult books are becoming increasingly sensitive to the need for positive portrayals of individuals with special challenges. Well-written, honest stories of such individuals in books can help adolescents gain an understanding of disabilities, can foster in them an ability to empathize with people who have challenges, and can help adolescents understand that they are not alone in their differences.

Some young adult books include a minor character with a disability, often a parent or a sibling of the protagonist; this type of story can be valuable in helping to develop among family members and classmates a greater sensitivity to individuals with disabilities. As inclusion of special education students into regular classrooms becomes a more common practice, this trend in young adult literature can be an important educational resource. As an example, Pete Hautman's *Invisible* deals with mental illness that is gradually increasing throughout the novel. Another example, Adam Rapp's *Under the Wolf, Under the Dog,* recounts 16-year-old Steve's struggles with drug abuse and suicide while dealing with family problems and peer rejection.

Communities

Part of growing up involves the discovery of one's membership in a *community,* a group extending beyond the family. In some young adult books we find school settings in which students, teachers, administrators, and at times parents comprise the community. Helen Frost's novel told through twenty-two poetic forms, *Spinning through the Universe: A Novel in Poems from Room 214,* shows students, the teacher, and the custodian writing their thoughts about the school and other topics. Walter Dean Myers' *Street Love* tackles social class lines in Harlem and their effect on young people. In James Howe's *The Misfits,* students closed out of all social groups form a new group to participate in school elections.

In other books the community setting is the neighborhood. An example is K. L. Going's *Saint Iggy,* in which urban life in housing projects is depicted, a community not often featured in young adult novels. Iggy wants to make something of his life against difficult odds and finds the parental care that he needs. Janet McDonald's novels *Chill Wind, Twists and Turns,* and *Spellbound* are also about a community of teens living in urban housing projects.

NOTABLE *Authors of Realistic Fiction*

Laurie Halse Anderson, author of novels that depict the raw emotions and turmoil of teenagers. *Speak; Fever 1793; Prom.* www.writerlady.com

Sharon Creech, author of novels about girls seeking their families to find themselves. *Walk Two Moons; Chasing Redbird; Granny Torrelli Makes Soup; The Wanderer; Ruby Holler.* www.sharoncreech.com

Chris Crutcher, author of realistic sports stories. *Ironman; Staying Fat for Sarah Byrnes;* and a collection of short stories, *Athletic Shorts.* www.chriscrutcher.com

Paul Fleischman, author noted for realistic and historical novels and poetry for young adults and for his use of unusual book formats. *Whirligig; Seedfolks; Seek; Breakout.* www.paulfleischman.net

Jack Gantos, author of Joey Pigza novels about a boy with attention deficit disorder, *Joey Pigza Swallowed the Key; Joey Pigza Loses Control; What Would Joey Do?* and semiautobiographical humorous works, *Heads or Tails: Stories from Sixth Grade; Jack's New Power: Stories from a Caribbean Year.* www.jackgantos.com

Will Hobbs, author of wilderness-based young adult novels: *Beardance; The Maze; Wild Man Island; Far North;* and *Ghost Canoe,* a mystery set along the Northwest coast. www.willhobbsauthor.com

Ron Koertge, author of many realistic young adult novels that depict universal adolescent concerns, including *Mariposa Blues; The Arizona Kid; Tiger, Tiger, Burning Bright; The Brimstone Journals; Stoner and Spaz.*

Chris Lynch, author of coming-of-age sports stories. *Iceman; Slot Machine; Shadow Boxer.* Also, *Gypsy Davey,* a story about parental neglect and poverty.

Walter Dean Myers, author of novels about African-American adolescents in city settings. *Scorpions; Monster.* www.walterdeanmyers.com

Gary Paulsen, author of nature survival adventures often set in northern United States or Canada. *Harris and Me: A Summer Remembered; Hatchet; Woodsong; Sisters/Hermanas.* www.randomhouse.com/features/garypaulsen

Suzanne Fisher Staples, author of stories that present conflicts within and between diverse cultures. *Shabanu* and its sequel *Haveli,* set in the Cholistan desert of Pakistan; *Shiva's Fire,* set in India. www.suzannefisherstaples.com

Nancy Werlin, author of suspenseful mysteries that present delicate subject matter while, at times, blending fantasy and realism. *The Rules of Survival; Double Helix; Impossible; Black Mirror; Killer's Cousin.* www.nancywerlin.com

Virginia Euwer Wolff, author of novels about unique teen characters. *True Believer; Probably Still Nick Swansen; Make Lemonade.*

Jacqueline Woodson, African-American author whose novels often treat sensitive issues of sexuality, abuse, and race. *I Hadn't Meant to Tell You This; From the Notebooks of Melanin Sun; If You Come Softly.* www.jacquelinewoodson.com

Community extends beyond country to communities around the world. With increasing interdependence among countries, young people will likely be more connected to an international community than ever before. Books set in foreign countries about life in another culture can help young adults develop an awareness of and sense of kinship toward people from other countries and an appreciation for people whose lives differ from their own. Examples include *Colibrí* by Ann Cameron, *Afrika* by Colleen Craig, and *Chanda's Secrets* by Allan Stratton.

Adventure and Survival

Facing physical danger, an external force, also contributes to the maturing process. Stories of *adventure and survival* feature young protagonists who must rely on will and ingenuity to survive life-threatening situations. Although most survival stories are set in isolated places, as in *Wild Man Island* by Will Hobbs, a growing number of stories are being set in cities where gangs, drug wars, and abandonment are indeed life threatening, as in *Tyrell* by Coe Booth. Adventure stories may be set in any environment where the protagonist faces the challenge of surviving alone or against great odds.

Sports

Sports stories often present a story in which an adolescent protagonist gains success in a sport but struggles with academics or with interpersonal relationships. John Coy's *Crackback* is a good example of a sports story in which the main character struggles to overcome the harsh criticisms of his coach and his father and to resist peer pressures to use steroids to enhance his playing. Matt de la Peña's *Ball Don't Lie* relates the story of a successful but frustrated 17-year-old basketball player who struggles to overcome poverty and his foster home background. Playing basketball at a recreation center offers him support he needs to overcome his many challenges. Some sports stories feature a protagonist who uses sports as an outlet for personal anger and frustration, as in Sis Deans' novel, *Racing the Past*. Traditionally written with males as the main characters, sports stories rarely feature females as protagonists. One example, however, is Kristi Roberts' *My Thirteenth Season*.

Mysteries

Mysteries range from simple "whodunits" to complex character stories. The element of suspense is a strong part of the appeal of these stories. In Nancy Werlin's *Black Mirror*, social isolation, mixed race, and suicide at a boarding school contribute to this complex and intriguing mystery. See also Cynthia DeFelice's *Death at Devil's Bridge*, a mystery in which 13-year-old Ben gets involved with illegal drugs and possible murder. Many mystery stories are realistic and could happen, but some mysteries have elements of the supernatural. These stories are placed in Chapter 4, "Modern Fantasy," under the category "Stories of the Supernatural."

The Edgar Allan Poe Award for Juvenile Mystery Novels can be helpful in selecting good mysteries—one of the most popular story types for intermediate-grade and middle-grade students. This award was established in 1961 by the Mystery Writers of America (www.mysterywriters.org) and is awarded annually in order to honor U.S. authors of mysteries for children and young adults.

Stories in the realistic fiction genre present familiar situations with which adolescents can readily identify, often reflect contemporary life, and portray settings not so different from the homes, schools, towns, and cities known to today's adolescents. The protagonists of these stories are frequently testing themselves as they grow toward adulthood. Young readers can therefore empathize and gain insight into their own predicaments. Your challenge will be to stay abreast of good realistic stories in order to provide a wide range of books that will entertain, encourage, and inspire your students.

REFERENCES

Carter, B., & Harris, K. (1982). What junior high students like in books. *Journal of Reading, 26*(1), 42–46.

Hale, L. A., & Crowe, C. (2001). "I hate reading if I don't have to": Results from a longitudinal study of high school students' reading interest. *ALAN Review, 28*(3), 49–57.

Higgenbotham, S. (1999). *Reading interests of middle school students and reading preferences by gender of middle school students in a southeastern state.* ED 429279. Dissertation.

Marshall, M. R. (1988). *An introduction to the world of children's books* (2nd ed.). Brookfield, VT: Gower.

McBroom, G. (1981). Research: Our defense begins here. *English Journal, 70*(6), 75–78.

Samuels, B. G. (1989). Young adults' choices: Why do students "really like" particular books? *Journal of Reading, 32*(8), 714–719.

RECOMMENDED REALISTIC FICTION BOOKS

Ages indicated refer to content appropriateness and conceptual and interest levels. Formats other than novels are coded as follows:

(GR)	*Graphic novel*
(PI)	*Picture book*
(COL)	*Short story collection*

FAMILIES

Abelove, Joan. *Saying It Out Loud.* Dorling Kindersley, 1999. Ages 13–18. Mother dying of cancer, dealing with family emotions.

Acampora, Paul. *Defining Dulcie.* Dial, 2006. Ages 12–15. A quirky road trip, a daughter grieving for her father.

Banks, Kate. *Dillon Dillon.* Farrar, 2002. Ages 10–14. Discovery of being adopted, identity, and adjustment.

————. *Walk Softly, Rachel.* Farrar, 2003. Ages 12–16. Diary, death of a sibling, family secrets.

Baskin, Nora Raleigh. *What Every Girl (Except Me) Knows.* Little, Brown, 2001. Ages 10–13. Seeking identity after death of mother.

Bauer, Joan. *Hope Was Here.* Putnam, 2000. Ages 13–18. Adjusting to life in small-town Wisconsin, local politics.

Bredsdorff, Bodil. *The Crow-Girl: The Children of Crow Cove.* Translated from the Danish by Faith Ingwersen. Farrar, 2004. Ages 9–12. Orphaned girl making a new family in Denmark.

Brooks, Bruce. *All that Remains.* Atheneum, 2001. (COL) Ages 12–18. Exploring the effects of death on young lives. Three thought-provoking novellas.

Brooks, Kevin. *Martyn Pig.* Scholastic, 2002. Ages 13–18. Dealing with an abusive alcoholic parent's death.

Budhos, Marina. *Ask Me No Questions.* Simon & Schuster, 2006. Ages 12–16. Immigrant Muslim family from Bangladesh after 9/11, secrets, immigration fears, and prejudice.

Choldenko, Gennifer. *Notes from a Liar and Her Dog.* Putnam, 2001. Ages 10–13. Telling lies, being the middle child in a family.

Cohn, Rachel. *Gingerbread.* Simon & Schuster, 2002. Ages 14–18. Adjustment to a stepfamily, abortion.

————. *The Steps.* Simon & Schuster, 2003. Ages 10–14. Adjusting to a new stepfamily in Australia.

Cole, Brock. *The Facts Speak for Themselves.* Front Street, 1997. Ages 15–18. Mother–daughter relationship, rape, murder.

Coman, Carolyn. *Many Stones.* Front Street, 2000. Ages 11–16. Adjusting to parents' divorce, dealing with a sister's death.

Conly, Jane Leslie. *While No One Was Watching.* Holt, 1998. Ages 10–13. Three siblings on a summer visit to their aunt in a small town.

Creech, Sharon. *Chasing Redbird.* HarperCollins, 1997. Ages 10–15. Family relationships, rebuilding an Appalachian trail.

————. *Heartbeat.* HarperCollins, 2004. Ages 10–14. Trying to understand her mother's pregnancy, her grandfather's memory lapses, and her best friend's changes. Free verse.

—————. *Ruby Holler.* HarperCollins, 2002. Ages 9–13. Finding a family, twins, country life.

—————. *Walk Two Moons.* HarperCollins, 1994. Ages 12–15. Retracing a mother's journey with grandparents.

Delacre, Lulu. *Salsa Stories.* Scholastic, 2000. **(COL)** Ages 11–14. Family stories from various Latin American countries.

Doyle, Eugene. *Stray Voltage.* Front Street, 2002. Ages 9–13. Coping with abandonment by mother, Vermont farm life.

Flake, Sharon G. *Money Hungry.* Hyperion, 2001. Ages 12–18. Inner-city life, homelessness, poverty, single mother and daughter relationship.

Fleischman, Paul. *Seek.* Cricket, 2001. Ages 14–18. Search for biological father.

Fogelin, Adrian. *Anna Casey's Place in the World.* Peachtree, 2001. Ages 10–13. Dealing with homelessness and a foster home.

—————. *The Big Nothing.* Peachtree, 2004. Ages 11–14. Dealing with parental marital problems and teen anxiety.

—————. *Sister Spider Knows All.* Peachtree, 2003. Ages 11–14. Flea market culture, developing an extended family.

Fusco, Kimberly Newton. *Tending to Grace.* Knopf, 2004. Ages 12–15. Finding a home, mother/daughter relationship, stuttering.

Giff, Patricia Reilly. *Pictures of Hollis Woods.* Wendy Lamb, 2002. Ages 10–14. Coping with abandonment, foster homes.

Griffin, Adele. *The Other Shepards.* Hyperion, 1998. Ages 11–14. Parents dealing with loss and grief, two sisters seeking parental affection.

Holt, Kimberly Willis. *Keeper of the Night.* Holt, 2003. Ages 11–15. Family dealing with the suicide of a parent, Guam.

Horvath, Polly. *The Canning Season.* Farrar, 2003. Ages 12–18. Finding a family, extended family. Humor.

—————. *Everything on a Waffle.* Farrar, 2001. Ages 9–14. Finding a family, foster home.

—————. *The Trolls.* Farrar, 1999. Ages 9–13. Eccentric aunt babysitter, storyteller. Humor.

Jiménez, Francisco. *The Circuit: Stories from the Life of a Migrant Child.* Scholastic, 2000/1997. **(COL)** Ages 12–18. Life of migrant farmworkers, poverty, Mexican-Americans.

Jocelyn, Marthe. *Would You.* Random, 2008. Ages 15–18. Coping with a sister's accident and coma.

Johnson, Angela. *Heaven.* Simon & Schuster, 1998. Ages 11–16. Discovery of being adopted, seeking one's identity.

Johnston, Tony. *Any Small Goodness: A Novel of the Barrio.* Illustrated by Raoúl Colón. Scholastic, 2001. Ages 10–15. Mexican family life in a Los Angeles barrio.

Jones, Kimberly K. *Sand Dollar Summer.* Simon & Schuster, 2006. Ages 11–15. Family adjustment to a new home in Maine.

Keehn, Sally M. *The First Horse I See.* Philomel, 1999. Ages 12–15. Training an abused racehorse, coping with the death of a mother.

Koertge, Ron. *Mariposa Blues.* Joy Street, 1991. Ages 11–15. Training and racing horses, father–son relationship.

—————. *Tiger, Tiger, Burning Bright.* Orchard, 1994. Ages 12–16. Grandfather–grandson relationship. Humor.

Koss, Amy Goldman. *The Ashwater Experiment.* Dial, 1999. Ages 10–14. Craft shows, frequent family relocations.

Lawrence, Iain. *The Lightkeeper's Daughter.* Delacorte, 2002. Ages 15–18. Dealing with family guilt, reconciliation.

Leavitt, Martine. *Heck, Superhero.* Front Street, 2004. Ages 12–15. Gifted artist dealing with a missing mother and homelessness.

Lynch, Chris. *Gypsy Davey.* HarperCollins, 1994. Ages 14–18. Coping with a dysfunctional mother and sister, single-parent family.

Mackler, Carolyn. *The Earth, My Butt, and Other Big Round Things.* Candlewick, 2003. Ages 13–18. Disillusionment with not feeling part of the family, weight control, and self-image.

McEwan, Ian. *The Daydreamer.* HarperCollins, 1994. Ages 10–13. Family life, imagination.

McKay, Hilary. *The Exiles in Love.* Simon & Schuster, 1998. Ages 10–14. Grandmother–granddaughter relationship. Humor.

—————. *Indigo's Star.* Simon & Schuster, 2004. Ages 11–14. Unorthodox English family, dealing with bullies at school. Humor.

————. *Saffy's Angel*. Simon & Schuster, 2002. Ages 9–12. Unorthodox English family life, discovery of being adopted. Humor.

Meldrum, Christina. *Madapple*. Knopf, 2008. Ages 15–18. A family mystery and court trial involve murder and a virgin birth.

Nelson, Theresa. *Ruby Electric*. Simon & Schuster, 2003. Ages 10–13. Father–daughter relationship, single-parent family life.

O'Connor, Barbara. *Moonpie and Ivy*. Farrar, 2001. Ages 10–13. Daughter coping with abandonment by her mother.

Paterson, Katherine. *The Same Stuff as Stars*. Clarion, 2002. Ages 10–13. Abandonment, dysfunctional family.

Peck, Richard. *Strays Like Us*. Dial, 1998. Ages 11–15. Drug addiction, extended family.

Rice, David. *Crazy Loco*. Dial, 2001. (COL) Ages 12–18. Nine short stories about growing up Latino/a, devoted to family and tradition, in southern Texas.

Rocklin, Joanne. *Strudel Stories*. Delacorte, 1999. (COL) Ages 10–14. Stories of a Jewish family's history.

Saldaña, René. *The Jumping Tree*. Delacorte, 2001. Ages 11–14. Set in a Texas border town, Mexican-American family.

Smith, Hope Anita. *Keeping the Night Watch*. Illustrated by E. B. Lewis. Holt, 2008. Ages 11–15. Relationships within an African-American family. Free verse and sonnets. Reluctant readers.

————. *The Way a Door Closes*. Illustrated by Shane Evans. Holt, 2003. Ages 11–15. A contemporary African-American family. Verse novel.

Sones, Sonya. *One of Those Hideous Books Where the Mother Dies*. Simon & Schuster, 2004. Ages 13–18. Father–daughter relationship, homosexual father. Free verse.

Testa, Maria. *Becoming Joe DiMaggio*. Illustrated by Scott Hunt. Candlewick, 2002. Ages 10–14. Italian-American grandfather. Story told in narrative poems.

Tolan, Stephanie S. *Surviving the Applewhites*. HarperCollins, 2002. Ages 12–15. Finding a home with an eccentric family, home schooling, juvenile delinquency. Humor.

Twice Told: Original Stories Inspired by Original Artwork. Illustrated by Scott Hunt. Dutton, 2006.

(COL) Ages 12–16. Pairs of popular and acclaimed young adult authors responding to illustrations on many topics, some fantastic, most realistic.

Walter, Virginia. *Making Up Megaboy*. Illustrated by Katrina Roecklein. DK Ink, 1998. Ages 11–15. Gun violence, psychological withdrawal, comic book culture.

Werlin, Nancy. *The Rules of Survival*. Dial, 2006. Ages 14–18. Child abuse at the hands of a mentally disturbed mother in a suspenseful thriller.

Williams, Lori Aurelia. *Shayla's Double Brown Baby Blues*. Simon & Schuster, 2001. Ages 13–18. Parental neglect, support of extended family.

Wolff, Virginia Euwer. *True Believer*. Atheneum, 2001. Ages 12–18. Single-parent family, poverty, friendship. Free verse.

Woodson, Jacqueline. *Behind You*. Putnam, 2004. Ages 14–18. Parents and friends coping with the death of a teenaged boy. Alternating voices.

————. *Hush*. Putnam, 2002. Ages 11–16. Teenager in a witness protection program, family life.

————. *Locomotion*. Putnam, 2003. Ages 9–14. Free verse. Surviving family death due to a fire.

PEERS

Brashares, Ann. *The Sisterhood of the Traveling Pants*. Delacorte, 2001. Ages 12–15. Four teenage girlfriends coping with being separated over the summer, and a pair of jeans. Sequels available.

Brooks, Martha. *True Confessions of a Heartless Girl*. Farrar, 2003. Ages 14–18. Marriage, death, Canadian prairie town.

Castellucci, Cecil. *The Plain Janes*. Illustrated by Jim Rugg. DC Comics, 2007. (GR) Ages 14–18. Forming a secret club in a new school and home in suburbia.

DiCamillo, Kate. *Because of Winn-Dixie*. Candlewick, 2000. Ages 9–12. Adjusting to small-town life, love for a dog, making friends.

————. *The Tiger Rising*. Candlewick, 2001. Ages 10–13. Coping with the death of a parent, treatment of animals, friendship.

Dowell, Frances O'Roark. *Chicken Boy*. Atheneum, 2005. Ages 9–13. Adjusting to the death of a mother, learning to fit in, making a new friend.

Fine, Anne. *Up on Cloud Nine.* Delacorte, 2002. Ages 10–14. Attempted suicide, friendship.

Fogelin, Adrian. *Crossing Jordan.* Peachtree, 2000. Ages 11–14. Overcoming racial prejudice, running.

Frank, E. R. *Friction.* Simon & Schuster, 2003. Ages 13–18. Teacher–student relationships, peer pressure.

Frost, Helen. *Keesha's House.* Farrar, 2003. Ages 11–18. Seven teens leaving home and looking for shelter when facing problems. Monologues in poetic verse forms.

Griffin, Adele. *Amandine.* Hyperion, 2001. Ages 12–15. Manipulative relationship between two teenagers.

Grove, Vicki. *Reaching Dustin.* Putnam, 1998. Ages 10–13. Farm life, school relationships.

Gutman, Dan. *The Homework Machine.* Simon & Schuster, 2006. Ages 9–12. A boy inventor and the social dynamics that result from his invention. First person narration by four characters.

Hautman, Pete. *Godless.* Simon & Schuster, 2004. Ages 14–18. Creating a new religion that takes on a power of its own among friends.

Hemphill, Stephanie. *Things Left Unsaid.* Hyperion, 2004. Ages 14–18. Teenage girl seeking her own identity, a friend's attempted suicide. Free verse.

Henkes, Kevin. *Bird Lake Moon.* HarperCollins, 2008. Ages 9–12. Alternating perspectives between two boys, neighbors at summer homes in Wisconsin.

Koertge, Ron. *Margaux with an X.* Candlewick, 2004. Ages 14–18. Unexpected friendship, friends helping each other.

Lubar, David. *Sleeping Freshmen Never Lie.* Dutton, 2005. Ages 13–16. High school freshmen life, first dates, and walking in the halls. Humor.

Lyga, Barry. *The Astonishing Adventures of Fanboy and Goth Girl.* Houghton, 2006. Ages 14–18. Coping with bullying by writing a graphic novel.

Moriarty, Jaclyn. *The Year of Secret Assignments.* Scholastic, 2004. Ages 14–18. Pen pals, romance. Humor.

Myers, Walter Dean. *What They Found: Love on 145th Street.* Wendy Lamb, 2007. **(COL)** Ages 13–18. Fifteen interrelated stories exploring different aspects of love.

Oates, Joyce Carol. *Big Mouth and Ugly Girl.* HarperCollins, 2002. Ages 14–18. Unlikely friendship, finding the courage to fight the system, integrity.

O'Connor, Barbara. *Fame and Glory in Freedom, Georgia.* Farrar, 2003. Ages 9–13. Friendship, school contest, visual impairment.

Paulsen, Gary. *Harris and Me: A Summer Remembered.* Harcourt, 1993. Ages 11–15. Episodic adventures on a farm with a cousin. Humor.

Perkins, Lynne Rae. *All Alone in the Universe.* Greenwillow, 1999. Ages 11–15. False friends, adjusting to change.

———. *Criss Cross.* Greenwillow, 2005. Ages 11–15. Missed communications with different outcomes, contemplative moments among friends.

Randle, Kristen D. *Breaking Rank.* Morrow, 1999. Ages 14–18. High school peer tutor, gang member. Alternating points of view.

Rapp, Adam. *33 Snowfish.* Candlewick, 2003. Ages 16–18. Sexually abused runaways, homelessness, drug addiction.

Salisbury, Graham. *Island Boyz: Short Stories.* Wendy Lamb, 2002. **(COL)** Ages 13–16. Ten short stories set in Hawaii about bullying, peer pressure, and other topics.

Schusterman, Neal. *Antsy Does Time.* Dutton, 2008. Ages 11–14. A boy helping out a dying friend by giving a month of his own life. Humor.

Stauffacher, Sue. *Donuthead.* Knopf, 2003. Ages 9–14. Unlikely friendship.

Wayland, April Halprin. *Girl Coming in for a Landing.* Illustrated by Elaine Clayton. Knopf, 2002. Ages 12–16. A year in the life of a teenage girl. Free verse, humor, wide appeal.

Wild, Margaret. *Jinx.* Walker, 2002. Ages 15–18. Dealing with the death of friends. Free verse.

ROMANCE AND SEXUALITY

Anderson, Laurie Halse. *Speak.* Farrar, 1999. Ages 14–18. Social outcast, calling the police, date rape.

Bennett, Veronica. *Cassandra's Sister.* Candlewick, 2007. Ages 15–18. A mix of fiction and literary biography of Jane Austen.

Burgess, Melvin. *Doing It.* Holt, 2004. Ages 14–18. Sexual urges and anxieties of three teenage boys.

Deak, Erzsi, and Kristin Embry Litchman, editors. *Period Pieces.* HarperCollins, 2003. **(COL)**

Ages 10–14. Girls' experiences as they begin to menstruate.

Dessen, Sarah. *Someone Like You.* Viking, 1998. Ages 13–18. Teenaged girls dealing with romance and pregnancy.

Draper, Sharon. *Romiette and Julio.* Atheneum, 1999. Ages 12–18. Falling in love on the Internet, objections to interracial dating.

Ferris, Jean. *Love among the Walnuts.* Harcourt, 1998. Ages 13–18. Love and crime. Humor.

Freitas, Donna. *The Possibilities of Sainthood.* Farrar, 2008. Ages 14–16. Experiences of first love and family feuds in a Catholic school and an immigrant family.

Freymann-Weyr, Garret. *My Heartbeat.* Houghton, 2002. Ages 14–18. Teen bisexual love. A coming-of-age novel.

Gonzalez, Julie. *Wings.* Delacorte, 2005. Ages 14–18. Falling in love with the wrong people. Two parallel narrators.

Hartinger, Brent. *Geography Club.* HarperTempest, 2003. Ages 14–18. Mutual support among gay and lesbian teenagers in high school.

————. *Split Screen: Attack of the Soul-Sucking Brain Zombies.* HarperTempest, 2007. Ages 14–18. Two books in one about friends, one gay and one bisexual, facing romantic troubles.

Johnson, Angela. *The First Part Last.* Simon & Schuster, 2003. Ages 14–18. Teenage father raising an infant daughter.

Koertge, Ron. *The Arizona Kid.* Little, Brown, 1988. Ages 14–18. A gay uncle, a summer job at a racetrack, falling in love. Humor.

Koja, Kathie. *Talk.* Farrar, 2005. Ages 14–18. Discovering sexual orientation, high school play, self-perception.

Larochelle, David. *Absolutely, Positively Not.* Scholastic, 2005. Ages 12–18. Hilarious coming-out story told as a first-person narrative.

Lawrence, Iain. *Ghost Boy.* Delacorte, 2000. Ages 12–16. Running away to the circus, unrequited love.

Levithan, David. *Boy Meets Boy.* Knopf, 2003. Ages 14–18. Accepting others and their sexual orientations. Humor.

Lockhart, E. *The Disreputable History of Frankie Landau-Banks.* Hyperion, 2008. Ages 15–18. Romance, gender, and power questioned by a girl in an elite boarding school.

Lynch, Chris. *Inexcusable.* Simon & Schuster, 2005. Ages 14–18. Football player rationalizing his actions, date rape.

Myers, Walter Dean. *Street Love.* HarperCollins, 2006. Ages 15–18. Hope, love, and anger across social class lines in Harlem. Verse novel suitable for readers' theatre.

Naylor, Phyllis Reynolds. *The Grooming of Alice.* Simon & Schuster, 2000. Ages 12–15. Dating and boyfriends, worrying about body image.

Orff, Joel. *Waterwise.* Alternative Comics, 2004. **(GR)** Ages 16–18. Recalling the past and life choices with old childhood friends.

Peters, Julie Anne. *Luna.* Little, Brown, 2004. Ages 15–18. Dealing with identity and a transsexual sibling.

Resau, Laura. *Red Glass.* Delacorte, 2007. Ages 13–18. First romance on a trip through Mexico and northern Guatemala.

Sanchez, Alex. *Getting It.* Simon & Schuster, 2006. Ages 15–18. Gay and straight friends helping one another.

Sones, Sonya. *What My Mother Doesn't Know.* Simon & Schuster, 2001. Ages 12–16. The delightful surprise of falling in love. Free verse. Wide appeal.

Spinelli, Jerry. *Stargirl.* Knopf, 2000. Ages 11–15. Courage of nonconformity, first love, and rejection.

Tashjian, Janet. *The Gospel According to Larry.* Holt, 2001. Ages 13–16. Opposing consumerism on a website, romantic attraction.

Van Draanen, Wendelin. *Flipped.* Knopf, 2001. Ages 11–14. Romance told in alternate chapters by opposite sex friends.

Wild, Margaret. *One Night.* Knopf, 2004. Ages 14–18. Dealing with teen pregnancy and single motherhood. Free verse.

Williams, Lori Aurelia. *When Kambia Elaine Flew in from Neptune.* Simon & Schuster, 2001. Ages 12–18. Dealing with sexual abuse and poverty.

Wilson, Martin. *What They Always Tell Us.* Delacorte, 2008. Ages 14–18. High school student exploring issues of sexual identity, suicide attempt.

Winick, Judd. *Pedro and Me: Friendship, Loss, and What I Learned.* Holt, 2000. **(GR)** Ages 14–18. AIDS patient, cartoons and comics.

Wittlinger, Ellen. *Hard Love.* Simon & Schuster, 1999. Ages 15–18. Emotional chaos, falling in love with a free spirit, lesbian friend.

———. *Parrotfish.* Simon & Schuster, 2007. Ages 14–18. A transgendered high school student adjusting to his new identity as a male.

Wolff, Virginia Euwer. *Make Lemonade.* Holt, 1993. Ages 12–18. Coping with teenage parenthood. Free verse.

Woodson, Jacqueline. *From the Notebooks of Melanin Sun.* Scholastic, 1995. Ages 12–18. Being raised by a lesbian parent, race relations.

———. *I Hadn't Meant to Tell You This.* Delacorte, 1994. Ages 12–16. Dealing with parental sexual abuse, friendship.

———. *If You Come Softly.* Putnam, 1998. Ages 13–18. Biracial love, coping with people's reactions.

Young, Karen Romano. *The Beetle and Me: A Love Story.* Greenwillow, 1999. Ages 13–16. Struggling for independence, romance.

Zarr, Sara. *Story of a Girl.* Little, 2007. Ages 15–18. A girl's reputation and self-worth ruined by premarital sex with a boyfriend.

———. *Sweethearts.* Little, 2008. Ages 15–18. Two teens confronting a shared abusive sexual situation from seven years earlier.

COMING OF AGE

Bauer, Joan. *Rules of the Road.* Putnam, 1998. Ages 12–16. Summer job driving the owner of a chain shoestore. Humor.

Bedard, Michael. *Stained Glass.* Tundra, 2001. Ages 12–18. Piecing together the past of a homeless girl.

Brooks, Kevin. *Lucas.* Scholastic, 2003. Ages 14–17. Dealing with prejudice and bigotry, father–daughter relationship.

Cart, Michael, editor. *Rush Hour: Face; A Journal of Contemporary Voices* (Volume 3). Delacorte, 2005. **(COL)** Ages 15–18. Broad theme of "face" explored in this short story collection in a variety of forms and genres.

———. *Rush Hour: Reckless; A Journal of Contemporary Voices* (Volume 4). Delacorte, 2006. **(COL)** Ages 14–18. Stories dealing with the psychology of recklessness in teenagers.

Chambers, Aidan. *Postcards from No Man's Land.* Dutton, 2002. Ages 14–18. Finding parallels between the past of World War II and the present.

Curtis, Christopher Paul. *Bucking the Sarge.* Random, 2004. Ages 13–18. Mother–son relationship, welfare system fraud. Humor.

Dorfman, Ariel, and Joaquin Dorfman. *Burning City.* Random, 2005. Ages 15–18. Delivering messages by bicycle in Manhattan. Sophisticated and cosmopolitan.

Fleischman, Paul. *Breakout.* Cricket, 2003. Ages 15–18. Runaway, dealing with foster homes.

———. *Whirligig.* Holt, 1998. Ages 14–18. Atoning for a drunk driving accident. A nonlinear narrative.

French, Simon. *Where in the World.* Peachtree, 2003. Ages 10–14. Adjusting to a new country, relationship between a boy and his grandfather.

Green, John. *An Abundance of Katherines.* Dutton, 2006. Ages 14–18. A former child prodigy seeking direction to his life while on a road trip.

———. *Paper Towns.* Dutton, 2008. Ages 15–18. Quentin, age 17, trying to understand the mystery of his longtime next-door neighbor, Margo.

Henkes, Kevin. *Olive's Ocean.* Greenwillow, 2003. Ages 11–15. First romance, dealing with a death of a classmate. Journal entries.

Jacobson, Jennifer Richard. *Stained.* Atheneum, 2005. Ages 15–18. Dealing with religious and sexual identities, love, and death in small-town New Hampshire.

Johnson, Maureen. *The Key to the Golden Firebird.* HarperCollins, 2004. Ages 13–18. Sisters struggling with their father's death, dealing with drugs, alcohol, and sex.

Johnson, R. Kikuo. *Night Fisher.* Fantagraphics, 2005. **(GR)** Ages 15–18. Disaffected teens at a prep school on Maui.

Kephart, Beth. *Undercover.* HarperCollins, 2007. Ages 14–18. Personal insights for a girl who ghostwrites love messages for her friends.

Koertge, Ron. *Boy Girl Boy.* Harcourt, 2005. Ages 14–18. An evolving friendship among three teens approaching adulthood.

Lynch, Chris. *Slot Machine.* HarperCollins, 1995. Ages 13–16. Dealing with obesity, gaining acceptance. Humor. Also, *Extreme Elvin* (1999) and *Me, Dear Dad & Alcatraz* (2005) continue Elvin's life as an outsider growing up. Humor.

Myers, Walter Dean. *Monster.* Scholastic, 1999. Ages 12–18. Being on trial as a murder accomplice, narrated from jail cell and courtroom. TV script form.

Oates, Joyce Carol. *Small Avalanches and Other Stories.* HarperCollins, 2003. **(COL)** Ages 14–18. Twelve stories featuring teenage girls' experiences.

Saldaña, René, Jr. *Finding Our Way: Stories.* Wendy Lamb, 2003. **(COL)** Ages 13–18. Twelve short stories about Latino experiences.

Snell, Gordon, editor. *Thicker Than Water: Coming-of-Age Stories by Irish and Irish-American Writers.* Delacorte, 2001. **(COL)** Ages 14–18. Twelve stories by well-known writers for young adults.

Sonnenblick, Jordan. *Notes from the Midnight Driver.* Scholastic, 2006. Ages 15–18. A teenage boy's legal problems and his community service at a nursing home. First person narrative, humor.

Tamaki, Mariko. *Emiko Superstar.* Illustrated by Steve Rolston. Minx, 2008. **(GR)** Ages 14–18. An Asian-Canadian teen returning home and reflecting on her time in the spotlight as a superstar.

———. *Skim.* Illustrated by Jillian Tamaki. Groundwood, 2008. **(GR)** Ages 14–18. After losing her only friend, a misfit faces questions of life, death, identity, and friendship.

Wieler, Diana. *Drive.* Douglas & McIntyre, 1998. Ages 15–18. A teenage boy's struggle to support his family, a blues guitarist.

Williams-Garcia, Rita. *No Laughter Here.* HarperCollins, 2004. Ages 12–16. Female circumcision in Nigeria.

Wynne-Jones, Tim. *Rex Zero, The King of Nothing.* Farrar, 2007. Ages 10–13. Concern about adult behaviors at home and school by middle school boy. Humor.

Yolen, Jane, and Bruce Coville. *Armageddon Summer.* Harcourt, 1998. Ages 14–18. Two teenaged siblings' doubts about a religious cult. Chapters alternate between male and female protagonists.

PHYSICAL, EMOTIONAL, MENTAL, AND BEHAVIORAL CHALLENGES

Burgess, Melvin. *Smack.* Holt, 1998. Ages 15–18. Heroin addiction.

Creech, Sharon. *Granny Torrelli Makes Soup.* Illustrated by Chris Raschka. HarperCollins, 2003. Ages 9–12. Friendship, visual impairment.

Crutcher, Chris. *Staying Fat for Sarah Byrnes.* Greenwillow, 1993. Ages 14–18. Being an outsider, obesity, facial scars, friendship.

Frank, E. R. *America.* Simon & Schuster, 2002. Ages 15–18. Suicide attempt, drug addiction, racial rejection.

Gantos, Jack. *I Am Not Joey Pigza.* Farrar, 2007. Ages 10–13. Hyperactive Joey adjusting to reentry of his father into his life.

———. *Joey Pigza Loses Control.* Farrar, 2000. Ages 9–13. Living with attention deficit/hyperactivity.

———. *Joey Pigza Swallowed the Key.* Farrar, 1998. Ages 9–14. Living with attention deficit/hyperactivity.

———. *What Would Joey Do?* Farrar, 2002. Ages 10–12. Dysfunctional parent, coping with attention deficit/hyperactivity.

George, Madeleine. *Looks.* Viking, 2008. Ages 12–18. An unlikely friendship between two high school girls, one anorexic, one obese.

Going, K. L. *Fat Kid Rules the World.* Putnam, 2003. Ages 14–18. Friendship, dealing with obesity, drug abuse.

Hautman, Pete. *Invisible.* Simon & Schuster, 2005. Ages 12–18. Friendship between two high school boys, deteriorating mental health.

Hobbs, Valerie. *Defiance.* Farrar, 2005. Ages 11–14. Dealing with cancer and cancer treatments, gaining strength through a friendship with an elderly poet.

Koertge, Ron. *The Brimstone Journals.* Candlewick, 2001. Ages 13–18. Teens speaking about problems, such as gang pressures and sexual abuse. Poetic monologues.

———. *Stoner and Spaz.* Candlewick, 2002. Ages 15–18. Relationship between a drug abuser and a person with cerebral palsy.

Koller, Jackie French. *The Falcon.* Simon & Schuster, 1998. Ages 13–18. Coping with emotional problems, living in a psychiatric ward.

Konigsburg, E. L. *Silent to the Bone.* Simon & Schuster, 2000. Ages 11–15. Elective mutism as a result of emotional trauma, friendship.

Mazer, Harry. *The Wild Kid.* Simon & Schuster, 1998. Ages 10–13. Runaway with Down syndrome, encounter with a reform-school escapee.

McCormick, Patricia. *Cut.* Front Street, 2000. Ages 13–18. Dealing with self-mutilation and elective mutism, living in a psychiatric hospital.

Rapp, Adam. *Under the Wolf, Under the Dog.* Candlewick, 2004. Ages 16–18. Living in a therapeutic facility for suicidal and drug-addicted teens.

Rosen, Renee. *Every Crooked Pot.* St. Martin's, 2007. Ages 15–18. Growing up with a disfiguring birthmark and an overly protective father.

Schumacher, Julie. *Black Box.* Delacorte, 2008. Ages 15–18. First person account of a younger sister trying to help her older sister cope with severe depression.

Sones, Sonya. *Stop Pretending: What Happened When My Big Sister Went Crazy.* HarperCollins, 1999. Ages 12–16. Coping with emotions about a sister's mental illness. Free verse.

Trueman, Terry. *Stuck in Neutral.* HarperCollins, 2000. Ages 12–18. Living with cerebral palsy, euthanasia.

Vaught, Susan R. *Big Fat Manifesto.* Bloomsbury, 2008. Ages 13–19. Overweight high school senior writing in her school newspaper about being fat in a thin society.

Vizzini, Ned. *It's Kind of a Funny Story.* Hyperion, 2006. Ages 15–18. A teenage boy battling depression, resorting to drugs, and eventually developing self-awareness.

Weeks, Sarah. *So B. It.* HarperCollins, 2004. Ages 10–14. Dealing with agoraphobia, developmental disability, seeking family origins.

Wolff, Virginia Euwer. *Probably Still Nick Swansen.* Holt, 1988. Ages 12–17. Coping with a learning disability, self-acceptance.

Wood, June Rae. *About Face.* Putnam, 1999. Ages 9–12. Having a disfiguring birthmark.

COMMUNITIES

Abelove, Joan. *Go and Come Back.* DK Ink, 1998. Ages 13–18. Peruvian tribe in the Amazon jungle, cultural anthropologists.

Anderson, Laurie Halse. *Prom.* Viking, 2005. Ages 14–18. An ordinary high school senior dealing with friendship, dating, and the hypocrisies of high school life.

Cameron, Ann. *Colibrí.* Farrar, 2003. Ages 11–16. Kidnapping, coming of age in Guatemala.

Carlson, Lori Marie, editor. *Moccasin Thunder: American Indian Stories for Today.* HarperCollins, 2005.

(COL) Ages 14–18. Ten stories depict the everyday traditions and struggles of Native Americans and their communities.

Craig, Colleen. *Afrika.* Tundra, 2008. Ages 12–15. Understanding apartheid cruelty while living in South Africa.

Creech, Sharon. *Love That Dog.* HarperCollins, 2001. Ages 9–12. Writing poetry in school. Free verse.

Danticat, Edwidge. *Behind the Mountains.* Orchard, 2002. Ages 11–15. Immigration to Brooklyn from rural Haiti. Diary entry format.

Fleischman, Paul. *Seedfolks.* HarperCollins, 1997. Ages 11–15. Gardening as an impetus for urban renewal in a community.

Frost, Helen. *Spinning through the Universe: A Novel in Poems from Room 214.* Farrar, 2004. Ages 11–14. Considering school and family by a teacher and her students. In poetic forms, explained at the end.

Going, K. L. *Saint Iggy.* Harcourt, 2006. Ages 15–18. New York City housing projects, school suspensions, drug use, 16-year-old Iggy's struggles.

Howe, James. *The Misfits.* Simon & Schuster, 2001. Ages 10–14. Coping with bullies, school elections. Humor.

Ives, David. *Voss.* Putnam, 2008. Ages 10–16. In the form of letters home to a friend, an illegal immigrant from Slobovia describing job hunting and other challenges in an American city. Humorous.

Kurtz, Jane. *The Storyteller's Beads.* Harcourt, 1998. Ages 10–14. Famine, political strife, and religious persecution in Ethiopia.

McDonald, Janet. *Chill Wind.* Farrar, 2002. Ages 14–18. (COL) Teenage African-American mother in urban housing projects, dropping out of school.

———. *Spellbound.* Farrar, 2001. Ages 13–18. Living in urban housing projects, teenage African-American mothers, dropping out of school. Humor.

———. *Twists and Turns.* Farrar, 2003. Ages 13–18. Living in an urban housing project, teenage African-American sisters struggling to run a business.

Myers, Walter Dean. *145th Street.* Delacorte, 2000. (COL) Ages 12–18. Ten short stories about the people of Harlem in New York City.

Na, An. *A Step from Heaven.* Front Street, 2001. Ages 14–18. Immigration from Korea to the United States, adjusting to a new community.

Naidoo, Beverley. *The Other Side of Truth.* Harper-Collins, 2001. Ages 11–16. Exposing corruption in Nigeria, living as political refugees.

————. *Out of Bounds: Seven Stories of Conflict and Hope.* HarperCollins, 2003. **(COL)** Ages 11–15. Effects of apartheid in South Africa from 1940 to 2000.

Ochoa, Annette, Betsy Franco, and Tracy L. Gourdine, editors. *Night Is Gone, Day Is Still Coming: Stories and Poems by American Indian Teens and Young Adults.* Candlewick, 2003. **(COL)** Ages 12–18. Poems and stories speaking of the past, present, and future.

Olsen, Sylvia. *The Girl with a Baby.* Sono Nis, 2004. Ages 13–18. A Native American girl living in British Columbia coping with pregnancy and a new baby.

————. *White Girl.* Sono Nis, 2005. Ages 13–18. An outsider adjusting to an Indian reserve in Canada.

Park, Linda Sue. *Project Mulberry.* Clarion, 2005. Ages 10–13. A Korean-American family dealing with prejudice and learning tolerance while adjusting to life in Illinois.

Paulsen, Gary. *Sisters/Hermanas.* Translated into Spanish by Gloria de Aragón Andújar. Harcourt, 1993. Ages 14–18. A bilingual novella about class and racial differences, prostitution, a Texas community.

Quintana, Anton. *The Baboon King.* Translated from the Dutch by John Niewenhuizen. Walker, 1999. Ages 13–16. Living in the wild of East Africa as a cultural outcast.

Resau, Laura. *What the Moon Saw.* Delacorte, 2006. Ages 10–15. Summer with grandparents in a remote village of Mexico.

Staples, Suzanne Fisher. *Haveli: A Young Woman's Courageous Struggle for Freedom in Present-Day Pakistan.* Knopf, 1993. Ages 12–18. Sequel to *Shabanu.* Life as a second wife in an arranged marriage.

————. *Shabanu: Daughter of the Wind.* Knopf, 1989. Ages 12–18. Life of a young woman in the present-day Cholistan desert of Pakistan, arranged marriage.

————. *Shiva's Fire.* Farrar, 2000. Ages 13–18. Finding a career as a dancer in present-day India.

————. *Under the Persimmon Tree.* Farrar, 2005. Ages 12–16. Surviving in war from northern Afghanistan to Pakistan after 9/11.

Stine, Catherine. *Refugees.* Delacorte, 2005. Ages 14–18. Dealing with alienation by an Afghan teen and an American teen after the September 11 attack. Told through phone calls and e-mails.

Stratton, Allan. *Chanda's Secrets.* Annick, 2004. Ages 14–18. Living with AIDS in sub-Saharan Africa.

Whelan, Gloria. *Homeless Bird.* HarperCollins, 2000. Ages 10–13. Arranged marriage in India, coping with widowhood without family support.

Yang, Gene Luen. *American Born Chinese.* First Second, 2006. **(GR)** Ages 14–18. Three intertwined stories about growing up Chinese American. Mixed genre.

Yumoto, Kazumi. *The Spring Tone.* Translated from the Japanese by Cathy Hirano. Farrar, 1999. Ages 12–16. Coping with the death of a grandmother in Japan.

Zemser, Amy Bronwen. *Beyond the Mango Tree.* Greenwillow, 1998. Ages 11–15. Seeing life in Liberia through an American girl's eyes, friendship.

Zenatti, Valérie. *When I Was a Soldier.* Bloomsbury, 2005. Ages 14–18. A recent 18-year-old immigrant, in Israel, struggling to adjust to required military service.

ADVENTURE AND SURVIVAL

Bauer, Joan. *Backwater.* Putnam, 1999. Ages 13–16. A mountain adventure, seeking family genealogy.

Booth, Coe. *Tyrell.* Scholastic, 2006. Ages 14–18. New York City's South Bronx, homelessness, welfare fraud, struggle of 15-year-old Tyrell. First person, fast-paced.

Couloumbis, Audrey. *The Misadventures of Maude March, or, Trouble Rides a Fast Horse.* Random, 2005. Ages 10–13. Sisters in a zany Wild West adventure. Humor. Good read-aloud.

Creech, Sharon. *The Wanderer.* HarperCollins, 2000. Ages 11–14. Sea adventure, coping with the death of parents, adjusting to an adoptive family. Dual points of view.

Doctorow, Cory. *Little Brother.* Tor, 2008. Ages 14–18. Questions about civil liberties when 17-year-old Marcus is held by Homeland Security.

Doyle, Roddy. *Wilderness.* A. A. Levine, 2007. Ages 12–16. A dual narrative involving a reunion in

Dublin with a long-absent mother and a dogsledding adventure in Finland.

Ellis, Sarah. *The Several Lives of Orphan Jack.* Illustrated by Bruno St.-Aubin. Groundwood, 2003. Ages 9–12. An orphan's adventure on the road. Language play.

Hobbs, Will. *The Maze.* Morrow, 1998. Ages 13–18. Running away from a youth detention center, conservation of an endangered species.

———. *Wild Man Island.* HarperCollins, 2002. Ages 13–18. Alaskan kayaking adventure, archeological discoveries.

Jennings, Richard W. *The Great Whale of Kansas.* Houghton, 2001. Ages 10–13. Discovery of the fossils of a prehistoric fish and a whale. Humor.

Key, Watt. *Alabama Moon.* Farrar, 2006. Ages 11–15. Raised by an antigovernment radical father in rural Alabama, a teenage boy facing civilization and reform school. Appeals to reluctant readers.

Lee, Tanith. *Piratica: Being a Daring Tale of a Singular Girl's Adventure Upon the High Seas.* Dutton, 2004. Ages 11–14. Melodramatic, tongue-in-cheek pirate's story. Presented in three acts.

McCaughrean, Geraldine. *The White Darkness.* HarperTempest, 2007. Ages 14–18. Survival thriller on an Antarctic expedition.

Mikaelsen, Ben. *Touching Spirit Bear.* HarperCollins, 2001. Ages 13–18. Coping with anger, rehabilitation of a juvenile delinquent.

Myers, Walter Dean. *Scorpions.* Harper, 1988. Ages 11–15. Effects of gangs on young people, survival in an urban environment.

Paulsen, Gary. *Hatchet.* Bradbury, 1987. Ages 9–12. Airplane crash, survival in Canadian wilderness.

———. *Woodsong.* Bradbury, 1990. Ages 12–16. Northern Minnesota dogsledding, Iditarod race.

Rosoff, Meg. *How I Live Now.* Random, 2004. Ages 15–18. An enemy invasion in England, survival, relationship with cousins.

Stewart, Trenton Lee. *The Mysterious Benedict Society.* Little, 2007. Ages 10–14. Four gifted children recruited for a society planning a takeover of the world.

———. *The Mysterious Benedict Society and the Perilous Journey.* Little, 2008. Ages 10–14. Four gifted children, a scavenger hunt, and the missing Mr. Benedict.

SPORTS

Coy, John. *Crackback.* Scholastic, 2005. Ages 13–18. High school football player overcoming criticism by his new coach and his father.

Crutcher, Chris. *Athletic Shorts: Six Short Stories.* Greenwillow, 1991. **(COL)** Ages 14–18. The power of sports in the lives of six teenagers.

Deans, Sis. *Racing the Past.* Holt, 2001. Ages 10–14. Dealing with anger and bullying, running.

de la Peña, Matthew. *Ball Don't Lie.* Delacorte, 2005. Ages 14–18. A talented basketball player dealing with foster homes and struggling to survive in an urban environment.

Deuker, Carl. *Gym Candy.* Houghton, 2007. Ages 13–18. High school football player, steroid use.

———. *Runner.* Houghton, 2005. Ages 12–18. A solitary teen runner dealing with an alcoholic father and crime in an action-packed story.

Feinstein, John. *Vanishing Act.* Knopf, 2006. Ages 11–18. Mysterious disappearance of a female Russian tennis player at the U.S. Open.

FitzGerald, Dawn. *Soccer Chick Rules.* Roaring Brook, 2006. Ages 10–14. A tax levy needed for a winning soccer team's future.

Hautman, Pete. *Rash.* Simon & Schuster, 2006. Ages 14–18. A 16-year-old runner in a futuristic society dealing with male aggression, artificial intelligence.

Jenkins, A. M. *Damage.* HarperCollins, 2001. Ages 16–18. Coping with depression, playing football, sexual relationship.

———. *Out of Order.* HarperCollins, 2003. Ages 14–18. High school baseball player trying to cope with academic problems.

Johnson, Scott. *Safe at Second.* Philomel, 1999. Ages 13–18. Overcoming adversity as a result of a baseball injury.

Juby, Susan. *Another Kind of Cowboy.* HarperTeen, 2007. Ages 14–18. Two teenage dressage riders, a rich girl, and a closeted 16-year-old boy seeking identity.

Koertge, Ron. *Shakespeare Bats Cleanup.* Candlewick, 2003. Ages 12–15. Coping with an inability to play baseball due to illness. Diary in poetic forms.

Lipsyte, Robert. *Yellow Flag.* HarperTeen, 2007. Ages 14–18. Teen struggling with mixed emotions about his choice: NASCAR racer or trumpet player?

Lupica, Mike. *Heat.* Philomel, 2006. Ages 11–15. Cuban-American Little League ballplayer, his family, his dreams. Humor.

Lynch, Chris. *Iceman.* HarperCollins, 1994. Ages 14–18. Coping with out-of-control anger on the ice hockey rink, parent–son relationship.

————. *Shadow Boxer.* HarperCollins, 1993. Ages 14–18. Coping with the death of a father, sibling rivalry in the boxing ring.

Powell, Randy. *Run If You Dare.* Farrar, 2001. Ages 13–18. Father–son relationship, high school track team.

Ritter, John H. *The Boy Who Saved Baseball.* Philomel, 2003. Ages 10–14. Saving the town baseball field.

————. *Choosing Up Sides.* Philomel, 1998. Ages 10–14. Father–son relationship, baseball, left-handedness.

————. *Under the Baseball Moon.* Philomel, 2006. Ages 11–14. A bond between a softball player and a jazz musician.

Roberts, Kristi. *My Thirteenth Season.* Holt, 2005. Ages 10–14. A girl struggling with her mother's death and challenging a cruel coach who dislikes having a girl baseball player.

Strum, James. *The Golem's Mighty Swing.* Drawn and Quarterly, 2001. **(GR)** Ages 12–18. Prohibition-era baseball teams of the 1920s; ethnic relations.

Wallace, Rich. *One Good Punch.* Knopf, 2007. Ages 14–18. Captain of the track team, marijuana found in his locker.

————. *Playing without the Ball: A Novel in Four Quarters.* Knopf, 2000. Ages 15–18. Overcoming loneliness and gaining confidence playing basketball.

Weaver, Will. *Hard Ball: A Billy Baggs Novel.* HarperCollins, 1998. Ages 12–18. Coping with paternal expectations, baseball rivalry.

MYSTERIES

Abrahams, Peter. *Down the Rabbit Hole.* HarperCollins, 2005. Ages 11–15. Amateur actress/story protagonist caught in the middle of a murder mystery.

Allison, Jennifer. *Gilda Joyce: Psychic Investigator.* Dutton, 2005. Ages 10–14. A young detective uncovering the truth behind a family tragedy. Humor.

Alphin, Elaine Marie. *The Perfect Shot.* Carolrhoda, 2005. Ages 13–18. A grieving witness struggling with his responsibilities. Told in flashbacks interspersed with facts from the study of American judicial history.

Balliett, Blue. *Chasing Vermeer.* Illustrated by Brett Helquist. Scholastic, 2004. Ages 10–14. Student detectives searching for a missing painting.

————. *The Wright 3.* Illustrated by Brett Helquist. Scholastic, 2006. Ages 9–14. Art crime, a Frank Lloyd Wright house, three young sleuths.

Box, C. J. *Open Season.* Putnam, 2001. Ages 13–18. Wyoming game warden, endangered species, oil pipeline.

————. *Savage Run.* Putnam, 2002. Ages 13–18. Opposing environmental activism by violence.

Cormier, Robert. *The Rag and Bones Shop.* Delacorte, 2001. Ages 14–18. Questioning a murder suspect by a police detective.

DeFelice, Cynthia. *Death at Devil's Bridge.* Farrar, 2000. Ages 10–13. Summer job on a fishing boat, illegal drugs, suspicion of murder. Coming-of-age story.

Dowd, Siobhan. *Bog Child.* Random, 2008. Ages 14–18. Discovery of a preserved child's body in Ireland leads to the exposure of two mysteries, one ancient and one more recent. Magical realism.

————. *A Swift Pure Cry.* Random, 2007. Ages 14–18. Family questioned when a dead baby is found.

Ehrenhaft, Daniel. *Drawing a Blank; or How I Tried to Solve a Mystery, End a Feud, and Land the Girl of My Dreams.* Illustrated by Trevor Ristow. HarperCollins, 2006. Ages 13–18. New England prep school, kidnapping, Scotland. Alternating chapters of first person narratives and superhero comic-strip episodes. Humor.

Fleischman, Sid. *Bo & Mzzz Mad.* Greenwillow, 2001. Ages 10–13. Family feud, a missing map for gold treasure. Humor.

Hiaasen, Carl. *Hoot.* Knopf, 2003. Ages 10–14. Protecting the environment, owl habitat. Humor.

Hobbs, Will. *Ghost Canoe.* Morrow, 1997. Ages 11–14. Life of the Makah people of the northwest coast of Washington; finding buried treasure, footprints, and a shipwreck.

Jennings, Richard W. *Mystery in Mt. Mole.* Houghton, 2003. Ages 9–12. Mysterious disappearance of a vice principal. Humor.

Jinks, Catherine. *Evil Genius.* Harcourt, 2007. Ages 12–15. A suspenseful thriller with a child prodigy who hacks into computer systems.

Morgenroth, Kate. *Jude.* Simon & Schuster, 2004. Ages 14–18. Murder, drugs, and mystery; a coming-of-age story.

Peacock, Shane. *Eye of the Crow.* Tundra, 2007. Ages 11–16. First in a new mystery series imagining Sherlock Holmes as a teenage sleuth in London in the 1860s.

Petrucha, Stefan. *Nancy Drew: The Demon of River Heights.* Papercutz, 2005. **(GR)** Ages 9–14. Favorite girl detective in a graphic novel with manga-style art.

Plum-Ucci, Carol. *The Body of Christopher Creed.* Harcourt, 2000. Ages 14–18. Mysterious disappearance of a social outcast.

Riordan, Rick. *The Maze of Bones.* Scholastic, 2008. Ages 9–13. The first book in a new ten-book mystery series, the 39 Clues, featuring card collecting and online gambling in a dangerous global adventure.

Sachar, Louis. *Holes.* Farrar, 1998. Ages 11–15. Dealing with adversity in a juvenile detention camp, finding a real friend. Humor.

————. *Small Steps.* Delacorte, 2006. Ages 11–14. A focus on two of the secondary characters after the closing of Camp Green Lake. Sequel to *Holes* (1998).

Sorrells, Walter. *Fake I.D.* Dutton, 2005. Ages 14–18. A missing mother, changing identities, suspense thriller.

Valentine, Jenny. *Me, the Missing, and the Dead.* HarperTeen, 2008. Ages 15–18. Mysterious discoveries about a missing father. Humor.

Van Draanen, Wendelin. *Sammy Keyes and the Hotel Thief.* Knopf, 1998. Ages 10–13. Investigating a robbery. Others in this detective series with a female protagonist: *Sammy Keyes and the Sisters of Mercy* and *Sammy Keyes and the Search for Snake Eyes.*

Werlin, Nancy. *Black Mirror.* Dial, 2001. Ages 13–18. Investigating a death in a boarding school.

————. *Double Helix.* Dial, 2004. Ages 15–18. Suspenseful mystery involving genetic engineering, family secrets, and arguments.

————. *The Killer's Cousin.* Delacorte, 1998. Ages 13–18. Acquittal of murder, facing the past.

————. *Locked Inside.* Delacorte, 1998. Ages 13–18. Kidnapping by a teacher, plotting an escape.

Westerfeld, Scott. *So Yesterday.* Penguin, 2004. Ages 15–18. Market-research-trends thriller set in New York City, finding the next "cool thing."

Zusak, Markus. *I Am the Messenger.* Knopf, 2005. Ages 15–18. A cab driver receiving mysterious messages that turn him into a hero. Who is the sender?

RELATED FILMS, VIDEOS, AND DVDS

Note: **MS** *refers to middle school;* **HS** *refers to high school.*

Baby (2000). Author: Patricia MacLachlan (1993). 93 minutes. MS, HS

Because of Winn-Dixie (2005). Author: Kate DiCamillo (2000). 106 minutes. MS

Beloved (1998). Author: Toni Morrison (1987). 172 minutes. HS

Bridge to Terabithia (2007). Author: Katherine Paterson (1977). 96 minutes. MS

Can a Guy Say No? (1986). Author: Todd Strasser, *A Very Touchy Subject* (1985). 60 minutes. HS

The Clique (2008). Author: Lisi Harrison (2004). 87 minutes. MS

Clowning Around (1991). Author: David Martin, *Clowning Sim* (1988). 183 minutes. MS

Confessions of a Teenage Drama Queen (2004). Author: Dyan Sheldon (1999). 89 minutes. HS

A Cry in the Wild (1990). Author Gary Paulsen, *Hatchet* (1987). 82 minutes. MS

The Day They Came to Arrest the Book (1987). Author: Nat Hentoff (1982). 47 minutes. HS

Election (1999). Author: Tom Perrotta (1998). 103 minutes. HS—11th and 12th grade

Ellen Foster (1997). Author: Kaye Gibbons (1987). 108 minutes. HS

The Face on the Milk Carton (1995). Author: Caroline B. Cooney (1993). 120 minutes. HS

Finding Buck McHenry (2000). Author: Alfred Slote (1991). 94 minutes. MS

Friday Night Lights (1999). Author: H. G. Bissinger (1990). 118 minutes. HS

Fried Green Tomatoes (1991). Author: Fannie Flagg, *Fried Green Tomatoes at the Whistle Stop Café* (1987). 137 minutes. HS

Holes (2003). Author: Louis Sachar (1998). 117 minutes. MS

Homecoming (1996). Author: Cynthia Voigt (1996). 105 minutes. MS, HS

Homeward Bound (1993). Author: Sheila Burnford, *The Incredible Journey* (1961). 84 minutes. MS

Hoot (2006). Author: Carl Hiaasen (2004). 91 minutes. MS

Iron Will (1993). Author: John Reynolds Gardiner, *Stone Fox* (1980). 109 minutes. MS

Lemony Snicket's A Series of Unfortunate Events (2004). Author: Daniel Handler, *The Bad Beginning* (1999). 107 minutes. MS, HS

Maniac Magee (1992). Author: Jerry Spinelli (1990). 30 minutes. MS

The Martian Child (2007). Author: David Gerrold (2002). 106 minutes. HS

The Mighty (1998). Author: Rodman Philbrick, *Freak the Mighty* (1993). 100 minutes. MS

The Nanny Diaries (2007). Authors: Emma Laughlin and Nicola Kraus (2002). 106 minutes. HS

Nick & Norah's Infinite Playlist (2008). Authors: Rachel Cohn and David Levithan (2006). 90 minutes. HS

Oliver Twist (2005). Author: Charles Dickens (1838). 130 minutes. HS

The Power of One (1992). Author: Bryce Courtenay (1989/1980). 127 minutes. HS

Pride and Prejudice (2005). Author: Jane Austen (1813). 129 minutes. HS

P.S. I Love You. (2007). Author: Cecelia Ahern (2003). 126 minutes. HS

Rabbit-Proof Fence (2002). Author: Doris Pilkington (2002). 93 minutes. MS, HS

The River Kings Collection (1991). Author: Max Fatchen (1966). 201 minutes. MS

Seal Morning (1995). Author: Rowena Farre (1957). 103 minutes. MS

Shiloh (1997) and *Shiloh 2* (1999). Author: Phyllis Reynolds Naylor, *Shiloh* (1991) and *Shiloh Season* (1996). 93 minutes, 96 minutes. MS

The Sisterhood of the Traveling Pants (2005) and *The Sisterhood of the Traveling Pants 2* (2008). Author: Ann Brashares (2001, 2005). 117 minutes; 119 minutes. MS, HS

Snow Falling on Cedars (1996). Author: David Guterson (1994). 128 minutes. HS

Speak (2004). Author: Laurie Halse Anderson (1999). 89 minutes. HS

Summer of the Monkeys (1998). Author: Wilson Rawls (1976). 101 minutes. MS

Whale Rider (2002). Author: Witi Ihimaera (2003/1987). 101 minutes. MS, HS

Where the Heart Is (2000). Author: Billie Letts (1995). 120 minutes. HS

Where the Red Fern Grows (2003). Author: Wilson Rawls (1961). 86 minutes. MS

SOURCES FOR FILMS, VIDEOS, AND DVDS

The Video Source Book. Syosset, NY: National Video Clearinghouse, 1979–. Published by Gale Research, Detroit, MI. An annual reference work that lists media and provides sources for purchase and rental.

Websites of large video distributors

www.libraryvideo.com

www.knowledgeunlimited.com

chapter FOUR

MODERN FANTASY

Many revered works of literature for young people fall into the genre of modern fantasy. *Gulliver's Travels, Twenty Thousand Leagues under the Sea, The Adventures of Pinocchio, Alice's Adventures in Wonderland, A Wrinkle in Time,* and *The Hobbit* immediately come to mind. The creation of stories that are highly imaginative— yet believable—is the hallmark of this genre.

EFINITION AND DESCRIPTION

Modern fantasy refers to stories written by known authors in which the events, settings, or characters are outside the realm of possibility. A fantasy is a story that cannot happen in the real world, and for this reason this genre has been called the literature of the fanciful impossible. In modern fantasy stories animals talk, inanimate objects come to life, imaginary worlds exist, and ghosts and other supernatural phenomena interact with or act upon human characters, often in stories of suspense and mystery. Most horror stories fall into this category as well as the highly popular vampire stories. An example is Stephenie Meyer's Twilight Saga. The first book in the suspenseful vampire romance saga, *Twilight,* published in 2005, became a best-seller and has since been made into a popular movie. Another category subsumed under this definition of modern fantasy is science fiction, a subgenre that often features scientifically plausible or technologically possible future developments that were only imaginary at the time of publication. Although in some cases, certain elements of some science fiction works have later been shown to be possible, these novels and short stories are still categorized as modern fantasy.

Modern fantasy has its roots in traditional folk literature, from which motifs, characters, stylistic elements, and, at times, themes have been drawn. The authors of modern fantasies are known, and this fact distinguishes the genre from traditional folktales, whose authors are unknown. *Folktales* (or *traditional fantasy*) include the entire body of stories passed down from ancient times by oral traditions. Folklorists are intrigued by the startling similarity of traditional tales around the world. One explanation is that the first humans created these stories and took them along as they populated the globe, the theory of *monogenesis* or "single origin." The other theory, called *polygenesis* or "many origins," holds that early humans had similar urges, needs, doubts, and motives, and created similar stories in response to them and the world around them. Both theories have merit; the facts lie hidden in ancient prehistory. Regardless of origins, traditional fantasy provides background for understanding and appreciating many types of modern fantasy. Magic, mythical creatures, quests, and personified animals found in traditional fantasies are also encountered in modern fantasies. Knowledge of traditional fantasy can provide students with a deeper understanding of and greater appreciation for modern fantasy.

In modern fantasy the *cycle format,* in which one book is linked to another through characters, settings, or both, is especially prevalent. Elleman (1987) states, "Events in [fantasy] cycle books are often strung out over three or four volumes. Authors attempt to make each novel self-contained, with varying degrees of success, but usually readers need the entire series for full impact" (p. 418). The cycle format appeals to readers who become attached to certain characters and then delight in reading the next book in the series. An example of the cycle format can be found in the Prydain Chronicles, a series of quest adventures based on Welsh legends by Lloyd Alexander.

EVALUATION AND SELECTION OF MODERN FANTASY

The usual standards for fine fiction must also be met by authors of modern fantasy. Believable and well-rounded characters that develop and change, well-constructed plots, well-described settings with

EARLY IMPORTANT WORKS *of* MODERN FANTASY

Date	Literary Work	Significance
1726	*Gulliver's Travels* by Jonathan Swift (England)	An adult novel prototype of an adventure story read by young people
1835	*Fairy Tales* by Hans Christian Andersen (Denmark)	First modern folktales
1864	*Journey to the Center of the Earth* by Jules Verne (France)	First science fiction (written for adults)
1865	*Alice's Adventures in Wonderland* by Lewis Carroll (England)	First children's masterpiece of modern fantasy
1897	*Dracula* by Bram Stoker (England)	An adult novel that helped popularize vampires in literature
1910	*Tom Swift and His Airship* by Victor Appleton (United States)	First juvenile science fiction novel
1926	*Amazing Stories,* science fiction magazine, begun (United States)	Recognition of science fiction as a literary genre
1937	*The Hobbit* by J. R. R. Tolkien (England)	Quest adventure with a cult following
1950	*The Lion, the Witch, and the Wardrobe* by C. S. Lewis (England)	First book of the quest adventure series Chronicles of Narnia, told with religious overtones
1954	*The Fellowship of the Ring* by J. R. R. Tolkien (England)	First book in the Lord of the Rings trilogy
1962	*A Wrinkle in Time* by Madeleine L'Engle (United States)	Classic science fiction novel for young readers
1964	*The Book of Three* by Lloyd Alexander (United States)	First book in the Prydain Chronicles based on medieval Welsh tales
1968	*A Wizard of Earthsea* by Ursula Le Guin (United States)	Classic work about a boy wizard facing evil
1968	*Dragonflight* by Anne McCaffrey (United States)	First in a series of novels about Pern, a colony of Earth, threatened by spores that devour organic matter
1974	*Carrie* by Stephen King (United States)	An adult horror novel featuring a young girl with special powers; this novel and others by King became popular with young adults

internal consistency, a style appropriate to the story, and worthy themes are elements to be expected in all fiction. In addition, the following criteria apply specifically to modern fantasy:

- Authors of modern fantasy have the challenge of persuading readers to believe that unreal, strange, whimsical, or magical events nevertheless have an internal logic and consistency. Sometimes, authors will accomplish this purpose by beginning the story in a familiar, ordinary setting with typical contemporary human beings as characters. A transition is then made to the fantasy world, as exemplified in C. S. Lewis's *The Lion, the Witch and the Wardrobe,* in which the siblings in the story enter a wardrobe in an old house only to discover that the back of the wardrobe leads into the land of Narnia, a fantasy world with unusual characters. Other fantasies begin in the imagined world but manage, through well-described settings and consistent, well-rounded characters, to make this new world believable. Either way, the plot, characters, and setting must be so well developed that the reader is able to suspend disbelief and accept the impossible as real for the duration of the story.

- For modern fantasy to be truly imaginative, the author usually provides a unique setting. In some stories, the setting may move beyond the realistic in both time (moving to the past, future, or holding still) and place (imagined worlds); in other stories only one of these elements (place or time) will go beyond reality.

TYPES OF MODERN FANTASY

In modern fantasy, as in other genres, the distinctions between types are not totally discrete. The types of modern fantasy in the sections that follow are a starting point for thinking about the variety of fantastic stories, motifs, themes, and characters that gifted authors have created. Additional types could be listed, and you will find that some stories may fit appropriately in more than one type. For example, Mary Hoffman's *Stravaganza: City of Masks* has been discussed as a historical fantasy because of its authentic historical setting, but its inclusion of spirits from the past also makes it a story of the supernatural.

Modern Folktales

Modern folktales, or *literary folktales* as they are also called, are tales told in a form similar to that of a traditional tale with the incorporation of some traditional folktale elements: strong, overt conflict; a fast-moving plot with a sudden resolution; a vague setting; and, in some cases, magical elements. Some traditional tales have been expanded into full-length novels, but a known, identifiable author has written these tales in their present form. In other words, these stories did not spring from the cultural heritage of a group of people through the oral tradition but rather from the mind of one creator. This distinction does not matter at all to young readers, who enjoy these recent tales as much as they do folktales. The tales of Hans Christian Andersen are the earliest and best known of modern folktales. More recently, other authors, including Donna Jo Napoli (*Bound* and *Zel*) and Robin McKinley (*Beauty* and *Spindle's End*), have become known for their modern folktales.

Magical Realism

Magical realism, a blend of fantasy and realism, is a term applied to a trend in literature that began to appear in the 1950s and 1960s. Magical realism "once thought of only in relation to certain Latin American literary works can now be found in a variety of works from around the world. It has even

NOTABLE   *Authors of Modern Fantasy*

David Almond, British writer noted for magical realism novels for young adults. *Skellig,* Carnegie Medal winner; *Kit's Wilderness; The Fire-Eaters.* www.davidalmond.com

Peter Dickinson, British author of modern fantasies including science fiction novels. *Eva; The Ropemaker; The Tears of the Salamander.* www.peterdickinson.com

Nancy Farmer, author known for unusual settings and issue-driven plots, as in *The House of the Scorpion,* a science fiction novel, winner of the National Book Award for young people's literature. *The Ear, the Eye, and the Arm; The Sea of Trolls.* www.nancyfarmerwebsite.com

Cornelia Funke, German author of popular dragon stories including *Dragon Rider, The Thief Lord,* and *Inkheart.* www.corneliafunkefans.com

Margaret Peterson Haddix, an author of fantasies including science fiction and mysteries with supernatural elements. *Found; Running out of Time; Double Identity; Just Ella; Turnabout.* www.haddixbooks.com

Shannon Hale, an author of many modern folktales, including *The Goose Girl; Princess Academy; Book of a Thousand Days;* and *Rapunzel's Revenge,* the first in a series of graphic novel retellings with her husband Dean Hale. www.squeetus.com

Ursula K. LeGuin, author of the well-known Earthsea quest adventure series and a more recent series about an enslaved town, Annals of the West Shore, including *Gifts; Voices;* and *Powers.* www.ursulakleguin.com

Lois Lowry, winner of the Newbery Medal for *The Giver,* a popular work of science fiction about an apparent utopia. *Gathering Blue; The Messenger.* www.loislowry.com

Donna Jo Napoli, author noted for her modern folktales, including *Bound,* a novel-length retelling of the Chinese Cinderella story. *Crazy Jack; Zel.* www.donnajonapoli.com

Terry Pratchett, British author of the Discworld series that includes *The Wee Free Men.* Winner of the Carnegie Medal for *The Amazing Maurice and His Educated Rodents,* a work of humorous animal fantasy. www.terrypratchettbooks.com

Philip Pullman, British creator of His Dark Materials, a trilogy comprising *The Golden Compass, The Subtle Knife,* and *The Amber Spyglass.* www.philippullman.com

J. K. Rowling, British author of the popular bestselling series about Harry Potter, a child wizard. *Harry Potter and the Sorcerer's Stone.* www.jkrowling.com

emerged in works of fiction for young adults" (Latham, 2006, 2007). Magical realism has the appearance of a work of realism, but gradually introduces the fantastic as an integral, and necessary, part of the story. The fantastic is merged into these stories such that the distinction between realism and fantasy is blurred, often leaving the reader in some doubt as to what is real and what is fantasy. Magical realism stories have the feel of realism, but the magical elements cause them to fall outside the definition of realistic fiction.

Faris (2004) identifies the characteristics associated with magical realism: an unresolved element of magic, placement in the realistic world, doubt remaining for the reader whether what occurred was real or not, a closeness of two worlds, the real and the magical, and disruptions of time, space, and identity. An example is Isabel Allende's works, including her adult and young adult novels, such as *City of the Beasts.* Young adult authors recognized for magical realism include Francesca Lia Block (*Weetzie Bat* and its sequels) and David Almond (*Skellig* and *The Fire-Eaters,* among others). For discussion on David Almond's works and magical realism, see Latham (2006).

Stories of the Supernatural

The supernatural, a force more powerful than nature, provides the backdrop for many recent works of fantasy for young adults. In these stories events occur that cannot be explained scientifically. Popular types of supernatural tales are mysteries in which supernatural events occur, stories with supernatural characters, stories involving psychic powers, and horror stories.

In *mysteries* a serious crime has usually been committed, after which clues are gradually revealed by the protagonist. Many characters appear to be possible suspects until one suspect turns out to be the perpetrator of the crime. Many authors write mysteries for young people in which the solution to the crime is partially supernatural or arrived at with supernatural assistance. A ghost may appear in the story as the murder victim who returns from the dead to help the protagonist find the killer and to prevent future murders, as occurs in *The Ghost of Fossil Glen* by Cynthia DeFelice. Other times the ghosts may be evil influences or fearful threats that try to prevent discovery of the truth, as is the case in Eve Bunting's *The Presence: A Ghost Story.*

Modern fantasies for young adults include stories with a myriad of *supernatural characters* in addition to ghosts, such as vampires, witches, wizards, goblins, elves, trolls, werewolves, sorcerers, and devils. Nancy Farmer's Viking hero tale set in Scandinavia, *The Sea of Trolls,* has mysterious Norns and trolls as characters. Mythical creatures such as dragons, unicorns, and mermaids, believed to have lived long ago, also play roles in stories of the supernatural. In Eva Ibbotson's *Island of the Aunts* the need to care for mythical creatures from the sea, such as mermaids, is the story motive. In Stephenie Meyer's vampire novel, *Twilight,* a teenage girl falls in love at her new school with a handsome, though tortured, vampire.

Witches are often portrayed as broom-wielding villains of both traditional and modern tales, as in the Russian stories about Baba Yaga. Witchcraft in young adult literature has been a focus of adult criticism because of an upsurge of sects whose members refer to themselves as witches and because of an increase in fundamentalist religious groups. Some parent groups have attempted to censor young adult books featuring witches and other elements of the occult. Chapter 11 has a discussion on censorship and schools' responsibilities in these situations.

Psychic powers can provide a character with special knowledge that is sometimes dangerous and frightening. Psychic powers include telepathic abilities, extrasensory perception, the ability to communicate with the dead or cross into other worlds, extraordinary mental ability, and clairvoyance. For example, in Joan Lowery Nixon's *Spirit Seeker* a murder is solved through the help of a psychic with clairvoyance.

Horror stories present the struggle against evil and portray tragic and often violent events that are shocking, revolting, and terrifying. Although horror stories may appear to portray reality at its worst, the stories are more about evil that goes beyond natural human behavior and so have an element of the supernatural. The resolution of such stories usually solves the crime, explains how it occurred, and reassures the reader. Stephen King, especially recognized for a large body of horror stories, has avid teenage fans for works such as *Carrie* (1974) and *Firestarter* (1980), which have young protagonists. His books are not included in the Recommended Books because they are adult literature.

Special Fantasy Situations

Writers of *personified animal stories* create knowledgeable animals who perform unusual feats, manifest human emotions, and establish organized communities. An example is *The Amazing Maurice and His Educated Rodents* by Terry Pratchett. A recent animal fantasy by Tor Seidler, *Gully's Travels,* relates the adventures of a lhasa apso told from the dog's perspective.

Small or giant people provide yet another special situation around which to build a story. *Gulliver's Travels,* the eighteenth-century novel, has inspired many stories of people of an unusual size. Terry Pratchett's recent *The Wee Free Men* portrays the adventures of a clan of six-inch-tall men who struggle to ward off an invasion of fairies.

Characters who do not seem to belong and feel like misfits can be found in stories in which the protagonist is *half-human and half-pixie.* In such an unusual situation the protagonist finds it difficult to fit well in the world of either parent. Examples can be found in *The Moorchild* by Eloise McGraw and *Cold Tom* by Sally Prue. *The Moorchild* also features a changeling, a child switched at birth for another child.

Historical Fantasy

Historical fantasy is similar to historical fiction in that the setting, both in time and place, is fully and authentically developed; in addition, an important and usually obvious fantastic element underlies these mixed-genre stories. In the **time-warp fantasy,** a present-day protagonist goes back in time to a different era. A contrast between the two time periods is shown to readers through the modern-day protagonist's astonishment with earlier customs. In Jeanette Winterson's *Tanglewreck* the element of time is explored through past and present travel adventures in a quest for an ancient Egyptian clock. Historical fantasy may also encompass **stories with an animal narrator** in which the narration of a historical event is related through the thoughts of an intelligent animal, as found in Roland Smith's *The Captain's Dog: My Journey with the Lewis and Clark Tribe*.

Quest Adventures

Quest adventures are stories with a search motif. The quest may have a lofty purpose, such as justice or love, or a rich reward, such as a magical power or a hidden treasure. Many of these novels are set in medieval times and are reminiscent of the search for the holy grail. In a quest adventure, the author depicts an imaginary otherworld complete with its society, history, family trees, geographic location, population, religion, customs, and traditions. Often, characters are drawn from traditional myths and legends. The conflict in these tales usually centers on the struggle between good and evil. The protagonist is engaged in a struggle against external forces of evil and internal temptations or weaknesses. Thus the quest usually represents a journey of self-discovery and personal growth for the protagonist, in addition to the search for the reward. *The Hobbit,* written by J. R. R. Tolkien in 1937, is one of the earliest quest fantasies. Because of the complex adventures and heroism of these novels, they have a strong allure for students in middle school and high school. Good examples are Ursula Le Guin's Earthsea trilogy and J. K. Rowling's Harry Potter series.

Science Fiction

Science fiction is a form of imaginative literature that projects the future of humankind based on scientifically described discoveries or changes in the earth's environment; it also imagines life on other planets. Therefore, story elements in science fiction must have the appearance of scientific plausibility or technical possibility. Hypotheses presented in science fiction appear believable to the reader because settings and events are built on extensions of known technologies and scientific concepts.

In novels of science fiction such topics as mind control, genetic engineering, space technologies and travel, visitors from outer space, and future political and social systems all seem possible to readers. These novels especially fascinate young people because they feature characters who must learn to adjust to change and become new people, two aspects of living that adolescents also experience. In addition, science fiction stories attempt to portray the world, or ideas about it, that young people will one day inhabit; for this reason, science fiction is often called *futuristic fiction.*

Utopias and *dystopias* are occasionally found in science fiction novels for young adults. A utopian novel presents an imaginary future of ideal social and governmental perfection, whereas a dystopian novel depicts a future place whose people live in fearful, wretched conditions. Both story types are set in a future based on technology and describe planned environments. In young adult novels such as Lois Lowry's *The Giver, Gathering Blue,* and *The Messenger,* the story opens in what seems to be a utopian village, but rather soon this perfect world is shown to have gone wrong. In this sense the reader is moved into a dystopian world that the protagonist must save or flee from. M. T. Anderson's *Feed* portrays a dystopian society in which everyone has a computer brain implant that provides immediate access to entertainment, personal communications, and corporate advertising. Dystopias are also found in L. J. Adlington's *Cherry Heaven* and in Suzanne Collins' *The Hunger Games.*

Science fiction is important because of its popularity among young adults. Those who are reluctant to read science fiction or who have never read it may want to start with books by Margaret Peterson Haddix (*Double Identity; Turnabout*), Lois Lowry (*The Giver*), or Nancy Farmer (*The House of the Scorpion*). Lower-level readers may want to begin with Sylvia Waugh (*Earthborn; Space Race*) or Nancy Etchemendy (*The Power of Un*).

Modern fantasy has appeal for persons with nonliteral minds, for people who go beyond the letter of a story to its spirit. Young adults with lively imaginations are especially open to reading fantasies. The many types and topics within this genre offer a breadth of inspiring and delightful entertainment. Since the level of conceptual difficulty varies considerably in this genre, modern fantasy offers excellent stories for all young adults.

REFERENCES

Elleman, B. (1987). Current trends in literature for children. *Library Trends, 35*(3), 413–426.

Faris, W. B. (2004). *Ordinary enchantments: Magical realism and the remystification of narrative.* Nashville, TN: Vanderbilt Press.

King, S. (1974). *Carrie.* Garden City, NY: Doubleday.

———. (1980). *Firestarter.* New York: New American Library.

Latham, D. (2006). *David Almond: Memory and magic.* Lanham, MD: Scarecrow.

———. (2007). The cultural work of magical realism in three young adult novels. *Children's Literature in Education, 38*(1), 59–70.

Tolkien, J. R. R. (1937). *The hobbit.* Boston: Houghton Mifflin.

RECOMMENDED MODERN FANTASY BOOKS

Ages indicated refer to concept and interest levels. Formats other than novels are coded as follows:

(GR)   *Graphic novel*
(PI)   *Picture book*
(COL)   *Short story collection*

MODERN FOLKTALES

Curtis, Christopher Paul. *Mr. Chickee's Funny Money.* Random, 2005. Ages 9–13. Humorous tall tale, a rollicking plot with a touch of magic and intrigue. Good read-aloud, may appeal to resistant readers.

Geras, Adèle. *Ithaka.* Harcourt, 2006. Ages 15–18. A reimagining of *The Odyssey* through young protagonists. Also, *Troy* (Harcourt, 2001) retells *The Iliad* with coming-of-age experiences of two orphaned sisters.

Gruber, Michael. *The Witch's Boy.* HarperCollins, 2005. Ages 11–14. Literary fairy tale of a witch who takes an abandoned infant into her home.

Haddix, Margaret Peterson. *Just Ella.* Simon & Schuster, 1999. Ages 12–18. A continuation of the Cinderella story.

Hale, Shannon. *Book of a Thousand Days.* Bloomsbury, 2007. Ages 12–15. Retelling of a little known tale by the Grimms, Maleen Maid.

———. *The Goose Girl.* Bloomsbury, 2003. Ages 12–16. Retold fairy tale featuring a betrayed princess and human–animal communication.

———. *Princess Academy.* Bloomsbury, 2005. Ages 10–14. Unusual talents discovered while attending an academy for potential princesses.

———. *River Secrets.* Bloomsbury, 2006. Ages 10–15. Razo, a character from Hale's *The Goose Girl,* and his adventures as a spy.

Hale, Shannon, and Dean Hale. *Rapunzel's Revenge.* Illustrated by Nathan Hale. Bloomsbury, 2008. **(GR)** Ages 10–14. Teaming up Rapunzel and Jack of beanstalk fame in an adventure tale.

McCaughrean, Geraldine. *Not the End of the World.* HarperCollins, 2005. Ages 14–18. A thoughtful retelling of the biblical story of Noah's Ark.

McKinley, Robin. *Beauty: A Retelling of the Beauty and the Beast.* Harper, 1978. Ages 12–18.

———. *Spindle's End.* Putnam, 2000. Ages 12–18. A retelling of Sleeping Beauty.

Michaelis, Antonia. *Tiger Moon.* Translated from the German by Anthea Bell. Abrams, 2008. Ages 14–18. Set in India at the beginning of the twentieth century, the stories of a young bride and a young thief intertwined.

Murdock, Catherine Gilbert. *Princess Ben.* Houghton, 2008. Ages 11–16. A melange of fairy tale favorites including Cinderella, Snow White, and Saint George and the Dragon in novel form.

Napoli, Donna Jo. *Bound.* Simon & Schuster, 2004. Ages 12–18. A retelling of the Chinese version of Cinderella, set in northern China.

———. *Crazy Jack.* Delacorte, 1999. Ages 11–14. A retelling of Jack and the Beanstalk.

———. *Zel.* Dutton, 1996. Ages 12–16. A retelling of Rapunzel from various characters' points of view.

Pattou, Edith. *East.* Harcourt, 2003. Ages 12–16. A retelling of East o' the Sun and West o' the Moon.

Pullman, Philip. *The Scarecrow and His Servant.* Illustrated by Peter Bailey. Knopf, 2005. Ages 9–13. A modern fairy tale and full-length novel of a scarecrow and an orphan boy.

Reeve, Philip. *Here Lies Arthur.* Scholastic, 2008. Ages 14–18. A brutal recreation of the Arthurian legend exposing the dark side of Camelot.

Spiegelman, Art, and Françoise Mouly, editors. *Folklore and Fairy Tale Funnies.* HarperCollins, 2000. Ages 14–18. **(COL, GR)** Part of the Little Lit series. Fifteen original fractured folktales in graphic format.

Stanley, Diane. *Bella at Midnight.* Illustrated by Bagram Ibatoulline. HarperCollins, 2006. Ages 10–14. A new, original Cinderella story.

MAGICAL REALISM

Allende, Isabel. *City of the Beasts.* HarperCollins, 2002. Ages 14–18. Trying to locate the legendary Beast in the Amazon jungle.

Almond, David. *Clay.* Delacorte, 2006. Ages 11–18. An ordinary altar boy in a small English town and his new friend, a gifted and mysterious artist.

————. *The Fire-Eaters.* Delacorte, 2004. Ages 12–18. Antiwar novel set in 1962 in northern England during the Cuban Missile Crisis.

————. *Heaven Eyes.* Delacorte, 2001. Ages 10–16. Escape and adventure on a raft, orphans.

————. *Kit's Wilderness.* Delacorte, 2000. Ages 12–18. English coal-mining families, ancestral ghosts.

————. *Skellig.* Delacorte, 1999. Ages 10–16. Mysterious stranger in a garage and grave illness.

Bedard, M. *Stained Glass.* Tundra, 2001. Ages 13–18. A broken stained-glass window, a homeless girl, searching for home, set in Canada.

Block, Francesca Lia. *Blood Roses.* Joanna Cotler, 2008. Ages 15–18. Nine short stories depicting girls seeking love, sex, and self-awareness.

————. *Cherokee Bat and the Goat Guys.* HarperCollins, 1992. Ages 15–18. Third in the Weetzie books, four friends forming a rock band.

————. *Weetzie Bat.* Harper & Row, 1989. Ages 14–18. Wild adventures in Los Angeles for Weetzie Bat and her friends.

————. *Witch Baby.* HarperCollins, 1991. Ages 14–18. Adventures in Los Angeles's frenetic pop world while searching for identity.

Brooks, Kevin. *Lucas.* Scholastic, 2003. Ages 13–18. Mysterious boy and his effects on the inhabitants of an island.

Clarke, Judith. *Kalpana's Dream.* Front Street, 2005. Ages 11–15. Unusual occurrences in response to an essay assignment, Indian culture, set in Australia.

Hoffman, Alice. *Green Angel.* Scholastic, 2003. Ages 13–18. Survival in the face of the tragic loss of the entire family.

Lester, Julius. *The Old African.* Illustrated by Jerry Pinkney. Dial, 2005. **(PI)** Ages 9–12. Overcoming oppression in a novella-length allegory based on a slave legend.

Richardson, Nigel. *The Wrong Hands.* Knopf, 2006. Ages 12–18. A thrilling mystery set in London merges technology and magical realism.

STORIES OF THE SUPERNATURAL

Avi. *Midnight Magic.* Scholastic, 1999. Ages 10–14. Magicians, ghosts in 1400s.

Barry, Dave, and Ridley Pearson. *Peter and the Star-catchers.* Hyperion, 2004. Ages 9–13. A humorous magical adventure told a... a play by J. M. Barrie, firs... published in 1928.

Bedard, Michael. *The Painte... Tales.* Tundra, 2003. **(COL...** of twenty-three brief stor... a seventeenth-century Chinese Shandong scholar; ghosts, magicians, and haunted monasteries.

Bell, Hilari. *Flame.* Simon & Schuster, 2003. Ages 12–18. A war adventure set in the mythical land of Farsala, partly drawn from Persian legends, ability to control fire, human sacrifice.

————. *The Goblin Wood.* HarperCollins, 2003. Ages 11–16. Witches, goblins, and a knight versus the religious Hierarch.

Bunting, Eve. *The Presence: A Ghost Story.* Clarion, 2003. Ages 12–18. Communication with the dead, dealing with guilt.

Carey, Janet Lee. *Dragon's Keep.* Harcourt, 2007. Ages 12–16. A princess fulfilling Merlin's prophecy.

Constable, Kate. *The Singer of All Songs.* Scholastic, 2004. Ages 12–16. Priestess of ice magic versus a sorcerer.

Coville, Bruce, editor. *A Glory of Unicorns.* Scholastic, 1998. **(COL)** Ages 10–13. Short stories about unicorns.

DeFelice, Cynthia. *The Ghost of Fossil Glen.* Farrar, 1998. Ages 9–13. Ghost of a murdered girl unraveling the mystery of her death.

Delaney, Joseph. *Revenge of the Witch: The Last Apprentice,* Book 1. Illustrated by Patrick Arrasmith. Greenwillow, 2005. Ages 10–14. Horror and thrills for the apprentice of the local Spook in England of long ago. Accessible to many readers.

Dickinson, Peter. *The Ropemaker.* Delacorte, 2001. Ages 12–18. A perilous journey to restore protective magic powers.

————. *The Tears of the Salamander.* Random, 2003. Ages 11–15. Sorcerer uncle, fire salamanders, volcano, eighteenth-century Italy and Sicily.

Dixon, Chuck. *Nightwing: On the Razor's Edge.* Illustrated by Greg Land and Drew Geraci. DC Comics, 2005. **(GR)** Ages 13–18. Superhero Nightwing and various villains.

Farmer, Nancy. *The Ear, the Eye, and the Arm.* Orchard, 1994. Ages 11–15. An adventure of three kidnapped children and the mutant detectives who seek them. Humor.

———. *The Sea of Trolls*. Atheneum, 2004. Ages 9–14. A Scandinavian hero tale with magic, trolls, and mysterious Norns.

Funke, Cornelia. *The Dragon Rider*. Translated from the German by Anthea Bell. Scholastic, 2004. Ages 9–14. An orphan's quest to find a dragon's home.

———. *Inkheart*. Translated from the German by Anthea Bell. Scholastic, 2003. Ages 12–18. Abduction by fictional characters brought to life in this adventure tale. *Inkspell* (Scholastic, 2005) is a strong sequel, with quotes from notable authors as chapter headings.

———. *The Thief Lord*. Translated from the German by Oliver Latsch. Scholastic, 2002. Ages 10–14. Orphaned brothers in a magical Venice adventure.

Hahn, Mary Downing. *The Old Willis Place: A Ghost Story*. Clarion, 2004. Ages 9–13. Mystery featuring alternating points of view in a diary and in a character's narration.

Haptie, Charlotte. *Otto and the Flying Twins*. Holiday, 2004. Ages 11–15. Magic, dealing with prejudices.

Hardinge, Frances. *Well Witched*. HarperCollins, 2008. Ages 10–13. Ancient spirit, powers to fulfill wishes made at a wishing well.

Hurston, Zora Neale. *The Skull Talks Back and Other Haunting Tales*. Adapted by Joyce Carol Thomas. Illustrated by Leonard Jenkins. HarperCollins, 2004. **(PI)** Ages 9–13. An illustrated retelling of six of Hurston's supernatural folktales.

Ibbotson, Eva. *Island of the Aunts*. Illustrated by Kevin Hawkes. Dutton, 2000. Ages 9–13. Kidnapped children care for mythical sea creatures, such as mermaids and dragons.

Jones, Diana Wynne. *Dark Lord of Derkholm*. Greenwillow, 1998. Ages 13–18. A wizard and his unconventional magical family, satirical fantasy. Sequel: *Year of the Griffin*.

Klause, Annette Curtis. *Blood and Chocolate*. Delacorte, 1997. Ages 15–18. Teenage werewolf who loves a human boy.

Lanagan, Margo. *Black Juice*. HarperCollins, 2005. **(COL)** Ages 15–18. Ten fantasy stories set just outside of reality. Good for class discussions and introduction to fantasy.

Larbalestier, Justine. *Magic or Madness*. Penguin, 2005. Ages 14–18. The Australian protagonist re-sists witchcraft, but is transported to New York City.

McKinley, Robin. *The Stone Fey*. Illustrated by John Clapp. Harcourt, 1998. **(PI)** Ages 13–18. A mountain fey, romance, a family farm.

McKinley, Robin, and Peter Dickinson. *Water: Tales of Elemental Spirits*. Putnam, 2002. **(COL)** Ages 12–16. A six-story fantasy collaboration with an aquatic theme.

Melling, O. R. *The Hunter's Moon*. Abrams/Amulet, 2005. Ages 14–18. First in a trilogy that blends Irish mythology and geography with a teenage female protagonist.

Meyer, Stephenie. *Twilight*. Little, Brown, 2005. Ages 14–18. Romance with a tormented vampire.

Nixon, Joan Lowery. *The Haunting*. Delacorte, 1998. Ages 12–16. Mystery and evil surrounding a Louisiana plantation house.

———. *Spirit Seeker*. Delacorte, 1995. Ages 12–16. Double murder of parents, mysterious psychic, clairvoyance.

Noyes, Deborah, editor. *Gothic!: Ten Original Dark Tales*. Candlewick, 2004. **(COL)** Ages 14–18. Mystery, terror, witches, vampires, demons; payment for the crimes of the past. Good read-alouds.

Pullman, Philip. *Clockwork*. Illustrated by Leonid Gore. Scholastic, 1998. Ages 9–14. A storyteller, a clockmaker's failed apprentice, an evil clockmaker, and a Faustian tale within a tale.

Rylant, Cynthia. *God Went to Beauty School*. HarperCollins, 2003. Ages 12–18. God's discovery of pains and joys in the world. Humor, free verse.

Slade, Arthur. *Dust*. Random, 2003. Ages 12–16. Children missing from Saskatchewan, Canada; mysterious visitor.

Stine, R. L., editor. *Beware!: R. L. Stine Picks His Favorite Scary Stories*. HarperCollins, 2002. **(COL)** Ages 9–14. Nineteen horror stories, poems, and cartoons.

———. *The Haunting Hour*. HarperCollins, 2001. **(COL)** Ages 9–14. Ten short stories with a horror theme.

Vande Velde, Vivian. *Never Trust a Dead Man*. Harcourt, 1999. Ages 12–16. Murder mystery, burial cave, and a medieval witch.

Werlin, Nancy. *Impossible.* Dial, 2008. Ages 14–18. A family curse and a pregnancy after a rape on prom night. Mixed genre.

Wooding, Chris. *The Haunting of Alaizabel Cray.* Scholastic, 2004. Ages 12–18. Horror tale set in an alternative Victorian London.

SPECIAL FANTASY SITUATIONS

Anderson, M. T. *Whales on Stilts!* Harcourt, 2005. Ages 10–14. Wacky, over-the-top fantasy adventure with laser-wielding whales. Humor.

Avi. *Strange Happenings: Five Tales of Transformation.* Harcourt, 2006. (COL) Ages 10–15. Five short stories including shape-changers and other bizarre events. Good read-aloud.

Billingsley, Franny. *The Folk Keeper.* Simon & Schuster, 1999. Ages 10–14. Orphaned girl posing as a boy, half-human/half-seafolk.

Briggs, Raymond. *Ug: Boy Genius of the Stone Age.* Knopf, 2002. (PI) Ages 9–16. A disgruntled but inventive Stone Age dweller.

Clement-Davies, David. *Fire Bringer.* Dutton, 2000. Ages 12–18. Personified red deer epic fantasy set in Scotland in the 1300s.

Crutcher, Chris. *The Sledding Hill.* Ages 11–18. Greenwillow, 2005. Postmodern novel in which the author plays a role and a narrator speaks from beyond the grave, censorship and intellectual freedom, tragic deaths.

Czekaj, Jef. *Grampa and Julie: Shark Hunters.* Top Shelf, 2004. (GR) Ages 10–15. Hunting sharks, meeting monkeys. Humor.

Fleischman, Paul. *Weslandia.* Illustrated by Kevin Hawkes. Candlewick, 1999. (PI) Ages 9–14. Growing a strange crop as a basis for a new civilization.

Gaiman, Neil. *Coraline.* HarperCollins, 2008. **(GR)** Ages 10–15. A graphic adaptation of Gaiman's 2002 horror novel.

———. *The Graveyard Book.* Illustrated by Dave McKean. HarperCollins, 2008. Ages 11–16. An orphaned baby eluding capture cared for by a caring but dead couple. Reluctant readers.

———. *The Wolves in the Walls.* Illustrated by Dave McKean. HarperCollins, 2003. (GR) Ages 9–14. Nightmarish wolves commandeer a home.

Gonzalez, Julie. *Wings.* Delacorte, 2005. Ages 13–18. A young man's belief in his ability to sprout wings and fly.

Harper, Charisse Mericle. *Fashion Kitty.* Hyperion, 2005. (GR) Ages 9–13. Helping kittens with their wardrobe dilemmas and peer interactions.

Harris, James S. *Shades of Blue,* vol. 1. Illustrated by Cal Slayton. DDP, 2005. (GR) Ages 12–16. Female superhero with power to conduct electricity.

Irwin, Jane, and Jeff Verndt. *Vögelein: A Clockwork Faerie.* Fiery Studio, 2003. (GR) Ages 11–16. First five issues of *Vögelein* about a mechanical fairy created in the seventeenth century.

Johnson, D. B. *Henry Builds a Cabin.* Houghton, 2002. (PI) Ages 9–13. Personified animal story and Henry David Thoreau's philosophy of housing. Others in the series, *Henry Climbs a Mountain,* about nature, politics, and Thoreau; and *Henry Hikes to Fitchburg,* about Thoreau's philosophy on naturalism versus materialism.

McGraw, Eloise. *The Moorchild.* Simon & Schuster, 1996. Ages 9–15. Neither human nor folk, a changeling seeks her identity.

Nilsson, Per. *You & You & You.* Translated from the Swedish by Tara Chace. Front Street, 2005. Ages 15–18. Three cerebral misfits crossing paths in a sexually graphic novel, strong language.

Palatini, Marge. *The Web Files.* Illustrated by Richard Egielski. Hyperion, 2001. (PI) Ages 9–12. Humorous personified animal mystery.

Pratchett, Terry. *The Amazing Maurice and His Educated Rodents.* HarperCollins, 2001. Ages 12–16. Cats, rats in a Pied Piper swindle.

———. *The Wee Free Men.* HarperCollins, 2003. Ages 10–14. A witch-to-be, a clan of six-inch men, and a Fairyland invasion. Sequels include *A Hat Full of Sky* (2004) and *Wintersmith* (2006).

Prue, Sally. *Cold Tom.* Scholastic, 2003. Ages 12–16. Half-human boy, rejection by his Elfin tribe.

Rodi, Rob. *Crossovers.* CrossGeneration, 2003. (GR) Ages 11–18. Suburban family with an alien collaborator, a superhero, a vampire slayer, and a warrior princess.

Sala, Richard. *Maniac Killer Strikes Again: Delirious, Mysterious Stories.* Fantagraphics, 2004. (COL, GR) Ages 14–18. Stories of monsters and secret societies, villains and mad scientists. Humor.

Schusterman, Neal. *The Schwa Was Here*. Dutton, 2005. Ages 11–15. A friend's ability to appear and disappear, feeling unnoticed. Humor, especially for boys.

Seidler, Tor. *Gully's Travels*. Illustrated by Brock Cole. Scholastic, 2008. Ages 9–12. An adventure story told from the perspective of Gully, a pampered lhasa apso.

Sfar, Joann. *Little Vampire Does Kung Fu!* Translated from the French by Mark and Alexis Siegel. Simon & Schuster, 2003. **(GR)** Ages 12–16. French comics format, bullying, strange monsters, body humor, space travel, and kung fu.

Tan, Shaun. *The Arrival*. Illustrated by author. Scholastic, 2007. **(GR)** Ages 12–18. A lone immigrant's journey and adjustment to an unknown fantasy world. Wordless graphic novel.

———. *Tales from Outer Suburbia*. Scholastic, 2009. **(COL)** Ages 10–18. Fifteen illustrated tales filled with emotional complexities.

Westerfeld, Scott. *Peeps*. Razorbill, 2005. Ages 15–18. A medical thriller: a vampire and a vampire hunter interspersed with descriptions of actual parasites.

Zevin, Gabrielle. *Elsewhere*. Farrar, 2005. Ages 12–18. An afterlife where aging occurs in reverse.

HISTORICAL FANTASY

Beckman, Thea. *Crusade in Jeans*. Front Street, 2003. Ages 11–15. Time travel to Middle Ages, Children's Crusade.

Branford, Henrietta. *Fire, Bed, and Bone*. Candlewick, 1998. Ages 10–14. England, peasants' rebellion in 1381; told from the point of view of a hunting dog.

Cooper, Susan. *King of Shadows*. Simon & Schuster, 1999. Ages 12–16. A child actor, time travel, Shakespeare's London, 1599.

Curry, Jane Louise. *The Black Canary*. Simon & Schuster, 2005. Ages 11–15. Time-travel adventure, Elizabethan England, with a biracial protagonist.

———. *Dark Shade*. McElderry, 1998. Ages 12–16. Time-travel adventure, Pennsylvania, 1758.

Gardner, Sally. *I, Coriander*. Dial, 2005. Ages 11–15. A blend of time and place for a fairy princess, back to seventeenth-century London.

Haddix, Margaret Peterson. *Found*. Simon & Schuster, 2008. Ages 10–14. A mystery involving time travel and two opposing forces.

Hoffman, Mary. *Stravaganza: City of Masks*. Bloomsbury, 2002. Ages 13–18. Adventures in a parallel world similar to sixteenth-century Venice. Sequel: *Stravaganza II: City of Stars*. Time travel to sixteenth-century Sienna, Italy.

Meyer, Kai. *The Water Mirror*. Translated from the German by Elizabeth D. Crawford. Simon & Schuster, 2005. Ages 10–14. Two orphans apprenticed in medieval Venice to a magical mirror maker.

Myers, Laurie. *Lewis and Clark and Me: A Dog's Tale*. Illustrated by Michael Dooling. Holt, 2002. Ages 9–13. Seaman, Meriwether Lewis's Newfoundland dog, describes Lewis and Clark's expedition, which he accompanied from St. Louis to the Pacific Ocean.

Smith, Roland. *The Captain's Dog: My Journey with the Lewis and Clark Tribe*. Harcourt, 1999. Ages 12–16. First-person account by Lewis's dog of the 1804–1806 expedition to explore the western wilderness.

Thal, Lilli. *Mimus*. Translated from the German by John Brownjohn. Annick, 2005. Ages 13–18. An apprenticeship to a court jester, depiction of the barbarity of the Middle Ages. Humor.

Winterson, Jeannette. *Tanglewreck*. Bloomsbury, 2006. Ages 10–15. An adventure to find a lost mystical Timekeeper involving time warps and psychic powers.

QUEST ADVENTURES

Alexander, Lloyd. *The Book of Three*. Holt, 1964. Ages 10–14. An assistant pig keeper's quest to save his land from evil, based on medieval Welsh myths. Others in the Prydain Chronicles include *The Black Cauldron, The Castle of Llyr, The High King,* and *Taran Wanderer*.

———. *The Golden Dreams of Carlo Chuchio*. Holt, 2007. Ages 10–14. A treasure map adventure by a young daydreamer.

Bass, L. G. *Sign of the Qin*. Hyperion, 2004. Ages 13–18. A young Starlord's quest to save mankind from destruction by demonic hordes, based on Chinese mythology.

Cashore, Kristin. *Graceling*. Harcourt, 2008. Ages 14–18. The adventure of young Lady Katsa possessing a superhuman gift of killing and a young man whose own gift causes her to seek justice.

Collins, Suzanne. *Gregor the Overlander.* Scholastic, 2003. Ages 9–14. A strange underworld quest foretold by an epic battle and an ancient prophecy.

Crossley-Holland, Kevin. *The Seeing Stone: Arthur Trilogy,* Book 1. Scholastic, 2001. Ages 12–18. King Arthur and the Crusades, Middle Ages. Others in the series include *At the Crossing Places* and *King of the Middle March.*

Divakaruni, Chitra Banerjee. *The Conch Bearer.* Millbrook, 2003. Ages 10–14. The return of a magical conch shell to its home in the Himalayan mountains of India.

Flanagan, John. *The Ruins of Gorlan.* Philomel, 2005. Ages 11–16. A group of five orphans, assignments as apprentices, saving the kingdom. First in a series from Australia.

Gavin, Jamila. *The Blood Stone.* Farrar, 2005. Ages 12–16. A search for a father from Europe to Arabia to the Mogul Empire in the seventeenth century.

Ibbotson, Eva. *The Secret of Platform 13.* Dutton, 1998. Ages 9–13. Rescue of a stolen young prince by a wizard, a fey, and an ogre.

———. *Which Witch?* Dutton, 1999. Ages 10–14. A great wizard and a marriage competition among witches.

Le Guin, Ursula K. *Gifts.* Harcourt, 2004. Ages 13–16. A parallel world of conflict between occupiers and occupied cultures. Also: *Voices.* Harcourt, 2006. Ages 13–16. *Powers.* Harcourt, 2007. Ages 13–16.

———. *A Wizard of Earthsea.* Parnassus, 1968. Ages 11–18. Apprentice wizard Ged, a quest for self-identity. Others in this series include *The Farthest Shore, The Tombs of Atuan,* and *Tehanu: The Last Book of Earthsea.*

Lewis, C. S. *The Lion, the Witch and the Wardrobe.* Illustrated by Pauline Baynes. Macmillan, 1950. Ages 9–14. Good versus evil in a Christian allegory featuring four children, an evil witch, and a lion. Others in the Chronicles of Narnia series include *The Horse and His Boy, The Last Battle, The Magician's Nephew, Prince Caspian, The Silver Chair,* and *The Voyage of the* Dawn Treader.

Morpurgo, Michael. *Sir Gawain and the Green Knight.* Illustrated by Michael Foreman. Candlewick, 2004. Ages 11–14. A retelling of the medieval tale set in King Arthur's court.

Oppel, Kenneth. *Airborn.* HarperCollins, 2004. Ages 11–14. A search for mysterious winged mammals, pirates.

Paterson, Katherine. *Parzival: The Quest of the Grail Knight.* Lodestar, 1998. Ages 10–16. A retelling of the Arthurian legend of the Knight Parzival.

Pierce, Meredith Ann. *Treasure at the Heart of the Tanglewood.* Viking, 2001. Ages 12–16. A healer maiden, animal companions, and a quest to conquer an evil wizard.

Pratchett, Terry. *Nation.* HarperCollins, 2008. Ages 12–15. An alternative nineteenth century setting for this adventure on an archipelago after a shipwreck caused by a tsunami. Humor.

Pullman, Philip. *The Golden Compass.* Knopf, 1996. Ages 12–18. Abduction of children in an alternate world in which reason and magic vie for power. Others in the His Dark Materials trilogy include *The Subtle Knife* and *The Amber Spyglass.*

Reeve, Philip. *Larklight: A Rousing Tale of Dauntless Pluck in the Farthest Reaches of Space.* Illustrated by David Wyatt. Bloomsbury, 2006. Ages 10–15. A pirate space adventure set in 1851. Humor.

Riordan, Rick. *The Lightning Thief.* Hyperion, 2005. Ages 10–15. Campy, heroic quest with deities and demigods from Greek mythology. Humor.

Rodda, Emily. *Rowan of Rin.* Greenwillow, 2002. Ages 9–12. Villagers' quest to restore their water supply. Others in the series include *Rowan and the Zebak* and *Rowan and the Travelers.*

Rowling, J. K. *Harry Potter and the Sorcerer's Stone.* Scholastic, 1998. Ages 10–16. A neglected boy with a great destiny as a wizard. Others in the series include *Harry Potter and the Chamber of Secrets, Harry Potter and the Prisoner of Azkaban, Harry Potter and the Goblet of Fire, Harry Potter and the Order of the Phoenix, Harry Potter and the Half-Blood Prince,* and *Harry Potter and the Deathly Hallows.*

Stroud, Jonathan. *The Amulet of Samarkand.* Hyperion, 2003. Ages 12–16. Adventures of an apprentice magician and a demon while seeking an amulet. Others in the Bartimaeus Trilogy are *The Golem's Eye* (2004) and *Ptolemy's Gate* (2005).

Tolkien, J. R. R. *The Hobbit.* Houghton, 1937. Ages 12–18. Adventures of Bilbo Baggins and the wizard Gandalf in Middle Earth.

Wein, Elizabeth E. *The Lion Hunter: The Mark of Solomon,* Book One. Viking, 2007. Ages 12–16. An embattled hero faces betrayal and abuse in a saga about a sixth-century Ethiopian dynasty.

Yolen, Jane. *Sword of the Rightful King: A Novel of King Arthur.* Harcourt, 2003. Ages 12–16. A variation of the King Arthur legend.

SCIENCE FICTION

Adlington, L. J. *Cherry Heaven.* Greenwillow, 2008. Ages 14–18. Dystopian novel that takes place in a troubled society different, but reminiscent of our own. Alternating narratives.

————. *The Diary of Pelly D.* Greenwillow, 2005. Ages 13–18. Dystopian novel featuring Holocaust-like events. Could be paired with historical fiction and nonfiction works about the Holocaust.

Anderson, M. T. *Feed.* Candlewick, 2002. Ages 15–18. Dystopian novel featuring a collapsing environment and technology overload.

Bawden, Nina. *Off the Road.* Clarion, 1998. Ages 9–13. Close family bonds in a dystopian world.

Bell, Hilari. *A Matter of Profit.* HarperCollins, 2001. Ages 12–18. Mystery and adventure, theme of understanding alien races with unique characteristics.

Card, Orson Scott. *Ender's Game.* Starscape, 2002/1977. Reissue. Ages 14–18. Genetic engineering, war games.

————. *Ender's Shadow.* TOR, 1999. Ages 14–18. Alien invasion, homeless children.

————. *Shadow of the Hegemon.* TOR, 2001. Ages 14–18. World control, kidnappers.

Cart, Michael, editor. *Tomorrowland: Ten Stories about the Future.* Scholastic, 1999. **(COL)** Ages 11–16. Futuristic stories by well-known authors, many suitable as read-alouds.

Clements, Andrew. *Things Not Seen.* Putnam/Philomel, 2002. Ages 11–16. Mystery involving an invisible boy and his blind friend.

Collins, Suzanne. *The Hunger Games.* Scholastic, 2008. Ages 15–18. A North American dystopia set in the near future.

Crew, Gary. *The Watertower.* Illustrated by Steven Woolman. Crocodile, 1998. **(PI)** Ages 10–15. Alien presence, transformation.

DuPrau, Jeanne. *City of Ember.* Random, 2003. Ages 10–15. Futuristic, disintegrating society and dwindling supplies.

Etchemendy, Nancy. *The Power of Un.* Front Street, 2000. Ages 10–14. A magical device to go back in time and alter events.

Farmer, Nancy. *The House of the Scorpion.* Simon & Schuster, 2002. Ages 13–18. A futuristic, corrupt drug empire between Mexico and the United States, ethics of cloning.

Haddix, Margaret Peterson. *Double Identity.* Simon & Schuster, 2005. Ages 10–14. Suspenseful revelations of family secrets and cloning.

————. *Turnabout.* Simon & Schuster, 2000. Ages 9–13. Injections to reverse the aging process.

Kostick, Conor. *Epic.* Viking, 2007. Ages 13–18. A future society in which success means winning in the gaming world.

Lowry, Lois. *Gathering Blue.* Houghton, 2000. Ages 11–16. A talented young weaver's struggles to survive in a cruel, futuristic society.

————. *The Giver.* Houghton, 1993. Ages 11–16. Struggle of conscience for a newly appointed receiver of memories in a utopian society.

————. *The Messenger.* Houghton, 2004. Ages 11–16. A young, gifted hero's sacrifice to restore his utopian village.

Mackel, Kathy. *Can of Worms.* Avon, 1999. Ages 10–14. Humor, extraterrestrial creatures, reptilian invaders.

Rapp, Adam. *Decelerate Blue.* First Second, 2006. **(GR)** Ages 15–18. Dystopian graphic novel.

Reeve, Philip. *Mortal Engines.* HarperCollins, 2003. Ages 12–16. A violent future world, movable and moving cities consume small towns. First of the Hungry Cities Chronicles.

Strahan, Jonathan. *The Starry Rift: Tales of New Tomorrows.* Viking, 2008. **(COL)** Ages 14–18. Sixteen science fiction stories by well-known writers.

Waugh, Sylvia. *Earthborn.* Delacorte, 2002. Ages 10–14. Girl's dilemma in deciding to remain on Earth or leave with her parents.

————. *Space Race.* Delacorte, 2000. Ages 10–14. Father and son aliens on Earth, missing spaceships.

Westerfeld, Scott. *Uglies.* Simon & Schuster, 2005. Ages 12–18. An apparent utopia focused on invasive "nip and tuck," image-obsessed customs.

RELATED FILMS, VIDEOS, AND DVDS

Note: **MS** *refers to Middle School;* **HS** *refers to high school.*

Aquamarine (2006). Author: Alice Hoffman (2001). 104 minutes. MS

Beowulf (2007). Northern European mythology. 114 minutes. HS

Big and Hairy (1998). Author: Brian Daly (1994). 94 minutes. MS

The Chronicles of Narnia: Prince Caspian (2008). Author: C. S. Lewis (1962). 150 minutes. MS

The Chronicles of Narnia: The Lion, the Witch, and the Wardrobe (2005). Author: C. S. Lewis (1950). 140 minutes. MS, HS

City of Ember (2008). Author: Jeanne DuPrau (2003). 95 minutes. MS, HS

Coraline (2009). Author: Neil Gaiman (2002). 100 minutes. MS, HS

Ella Enchanted (2004). Author: Gail Carson Levine (1997). 96 minutes. MS

Eragon (2006). Author: Christopher Paolini (2003). 104 minutes. MS

Escape to Witch Mountain (1995). Author: Alexander Key (1968). 97 minutes. MS

The Golden Compass (2007). Author: Philip Pullman (1996). 113 minutes. MS, HS

Harry Potter and the Chamber of Secrets (2002). Author: J. K. Rowling (1999). 161 minutes. MS, HS

Harry Potter and the Goblet of Fire (2005). Author: J. K. Rowling (2000). 157 minutes. MS, HS

Harry Potter and the Order of the Phoenix (2007). Author: J. K. Rowling (2003). 138 minutes. MS, HS

Harry Potter and the Prisoner of Azkaban (2004). Author: J. K. Rowling (1999). 142 minutes. MS, HS

Harry Potter and the Sorcerer's Stone (2001). Author: J. K. Rowling (1998). 152 minutes. MS, HS

The Hobbit (1991). J. R. R. Tolkien (1937). 76 minutes. MS

Inkheart (2008). Author: Cornelia Funke (2003). 106 minutes. MS

Iron Giant (1999). Author: Ted Hughes, *The Iron Giant* (1969, 1999). 85 minutes. MS

Journey to Watership Down (2003). Author: Richard Adams, *Watership Down* (1974). 44 minutes. MS, HS

Lord of the Rings (2001). Author: J. R. R. Tolkien (1954–1955). 208 minutes. MS, HS

Redwall: Friends or Foes? (1999). Author: Brian Jacques (1987). 90 minutes. MS, HS

The Seeker: The Dark Is Rising (2007). Author: Susan Cooper (1973). 99 minutes. MS

Stardust (2007). Author: Neil Gaiman (1999). 127 minutes. HS

Thief Lord (2006). Author: Cornelia Funke (2002). 98 minutes. MS

Tuck Everlasting (2002). Author: Natalie Babbitt (1975). 88 minutes. MS, HS

Twilight (2008). Author: Stephenie Meyer (2005). 122 minutes. HS

The Water Horse (2007). Author: Dick King-Smith. 112 minutes. MS

A Wrinkle in Time (2003). Author: Madeleine L'Engle (1962). 128 minutes. MS, HS

SOURCES FOR FILMS, VIDEOS, AND DVDS

The Video Source Book. Syosset, NY: National Video Clearinghouse, 1979–. Published by Gale Research, Detroit, MI. An annual reference work that lists media and provides sources for purchase and rental.

Websites of large video distributors

www.libraryvideo.com
www.knowledgeunlimited.com

chapter FIVE

HISTORICAL FICTION

Historical fiction brings history to life by placing appealing characters in accurately described historical settings. By telling the stories of these characters' everyday lives as well as presenting their triumphs and failures, authors of historical fiction provide young readers with the human side of history, making it more real and more memorable.

DEFINITION AND DESCRIPTION

Historical fiction is realistic fiction set in a time remote enough from the present to be considered history. Stories about events that occurred at least one generation (defined as twenty years or more) prior to the date of the original publication have been included in this chapter and categorized as historical fiction.

Although historical fiction stories are imaginary, the events and characters' actions must be within the realm of the possible. In these stories, actual historical events, authentic period settings, and real historical figures blend with fictional characters and plots in an imaginary story constructed around the facts. In *A Reference Guide to Historical Fiction for Children and Young Adults*, Adamson (1987) states:

> Historical fiction recreates a particular historical period with or without historical figures as incidental characters. It is generally written about a time period in which the author has not lived or no more recently than one generation before its composition. For example, fiction written in 1987 must be set, at the latest, in 1967, to be considered historical. Fiction written in 1930 but set in 1925 does not fulfill this criterion for legitimate historical fiction. (p. ix)

In the most common form of historical fiction, the main characters of the story are imaginary, but some secondary characters may be actual historical figures. These stories usually depict a *significant historical event,* such as a war, an economic depression, or a natural disaster. An example is the 1944 Newbery Medal winner, *Johnny Tremain* by Esther Forbes. Set in the U.S. Revolutionary War period, this story tells of Johnny, a fictitious character, apprenticed to a silversmith. In the course of the story, Samuel Adams, John Hancock, and Paul Revere are introduced as minor characters.

In another form of historical fiction, the past is described complete with an accurate reconstruction of the physical location and the *social traditions, customs, morals, and values of the period,* but with no mention of an actual historical event or actual historical figures as characters. An example of this story type is *The Witch of Blackbird Pond* by Elizabeth George Speare. The Puritan way of life in Connecticut in the 1600s is depicted in this story about young Kit from Barbados who becomes involved in a witchcraft trial.

Another type of historical story is one in which elements of fantasy are found, and therefore the story does *not* qualify as historical fiction. For example, time warps and other supernatural features may be found in Mary Hoffman's *Stravaganza: City of Masks.* These stories are categorized as *historical fantasy* and are included in Chapter 4, "Modern Fantasy."

EVALUATION AND SELECTION OF HISTORICAL FICTION

Historical fiction must first be evaluated for its story strength. It must tell an engaging story. The author of historical fiction must also present historical facts with as much accuracy and objectivity as books of history. Historical fiction is also judged on other aspects of presentation:

- *Setting.*   A setting must be described in sufficient detail to provide an authentic sense of a specific time and place without overwhelming the story. Details such as hair and clothing styles, architecture and furnishings, foods and food preparation, and modes of transportation must be subtly woven into the story to provide a convincing, authentic period setting. The characters must act within the traditions and norms of their times.

- *Language.*   Expressing the language or dialect of the period presents a particular challenge to the author of historical stories. Dialogue that occurs within the text often becomes problematic for the writer. If the language being spoken or the speech of the period is greatly different from that of today, then the author faces a decision: remain true to the language of the time but cause readers difficulties in comprehending, or present the language in today's dialect but lose the flavor and authenticity of the language of the period. Patricia Reilly Giff in *Nory Ryan's Song* introduces some Irish words at the beginning of the story and uses them throughout the novel to provide a flavor of the language without losing meaning. In any case, it seems important that the language not jar the reader by its obvious inappropriateness or lose the reader by its extreme difficulty. Most authors for young adults strive to attain the middle ground—some flavor of a language difference but modified to be understandable to the modern reader. Young adults adapt easily to dialects and may even find occasion to use dialect to lend flavor to their subsequent writing.

- *Bias.*   Many adults today are unaware that the history they learned many years ago may have been biased or one-sided. Some authors attempt to include more modern interpretations of historical events in historical fiction by setting the record straight or adding a minority or female presence to the story. However, as was previously mentioned, care must be taken that the characters behave in a historically accurate fashion.

Many educators are convinced of the benefits students gain from the integration of history and literature as part of the social studies curriculum. Smith, Monson, and Dobson (1992) found in their study that students in fifth-grade classrooms in which historical novels were used along with textbooks recalled more historical facts and indicated greater enjoyment in their social studies classes than the students in classrooms that had a similar curriculum without the addition of historical novels. We believe the same holds true with middle school and high school students.

The Scott O'Dell Award, established in 1981 by the author Scott O'Dell, honors what is judged to be the most outstanding work of children's historical fiction published in the previous year. The work must be written by a U.S. citizen and be set in the New World. The Scott O'Dell Award winners (www.scottodell.com) can be a source for selecting outstanding historical fiction for use with students. The National Council of Social Studies publishes a list of the most notable trade books in the field of social studies from the preceding year in the April/May issue of its journal, *Social Education*. This list, which is available online at www.cbcbooks .org, includes many works of historical fiction and is a useful source for recent books of the genre.

TOPICS OF HISTORICAL FICTION

Two ways of presenting historical fiction novels are through selecting and grouping books by *universal themes* or through setting up book sets according to the *historical periods* in which the books are set.

NOTABLE *Authors of Historical Fiction*

M. T. Anderson, U.S. author and illustrator of children's and young adult books. Noted for the historical fiction series on slavery, *The Astonishing Life of Octavian Nothing,* Volume I: *The Pox Party* and Volume II: *The Kingdom on the Waves.* Also: *Feed; Whales on Stilts.*

Avi [Wortis], author noted for historical fiction novels set in the United States and the British Isles. *Crispin: The Cross of Lead; The True Confessions of Charlotte Doyle; The Fighting Ground; The Barn.* www.avi-writer.com

Christopher Paul Curtis, author of realistic and historical fiction novels depicting African-American characters who live in or near Flint, Michigan. *The Watsons Go to Birmingham 1963; Bud, Not Buddy; Elijah of Buxton.* www.christopherpaulcurtis.com

Karen Cushman, author of acclaimed historical novels set in the Middle Ages. *Catherine, Called Birdy; The Midwife's Apprentice; Matilda Bone.* Also, *Rodzina.* www.karencushman.com

Cynthia DeFelice, author of many novels with an emphasis on historical fiction with U.S. settings and ghost stories. *Weasel; Bringing Ezra Back; The Ghost of Fossil Glen.* www.cynthiadefelice.com

Karen Hesse, author of the free-verse novel *Out of the Dust,* set in Oklahoma in the 1930s. Also noted for World War II historical books: *Letters from Rifka; The Cats in Krasinski Square.*

Kimberly Willis Holt, author of novels about characters with disabilities and living in small towns of the American South. *My Louisiana Sky; When Zachary Beaver Came to Town; Dancing in Cadillac Light.* www.kimberlywillisholt.com

Catherine Jinks, Australian author of books for young adults including The Pagan Chronicles, a historical fiction series about the medieval crusades. www.catherinejinks.com

Iain Lawrence, Canadian author of historical novels including the high-seas adventure trilogy *The Wreckers, The Smugglers,* and *The Buccaneers.* Also, *Lord of the Nutcracker Men,* a World War I novel.

Geraldine McCaughrean, British author of *Stop the Train!,* set in Oklahoma in 1893; *The Kite Rider,* set in thirteenth-century China; and *The Pirate's Son,* eighteenth-century England to Madagascar. www.geraldinemccaughrean.co.uk

Katherine Paterson, author of historical fiction novels set in Japan: *The Sign of the Chrysanthemum; The Master Puppeteer.* Also, author of historical fiction novels set in New England: *Jip, His Story; Preacher's Boy.* www.terabithia.com

Richard Peck, U.S. author of realistic fiction and historical fiction set in rural Illinois and Indiana in the nineteenth and early twentieth centuries. *A Long Way from Chicago; The River between Us; The Teacher's Funeral: A Comedy in Three Parts.* www.richardpeck.smartwriters.com

Ann Rinaldi, writer noted for historical fiction novels about early U.S. history. *A Break with Charity: A Story about the Salem Witch Trials; A Stitch in Time; An Acquaintance with Darkness; Numbering All the Bones.* www.annrinaldi.net

Laurence Yep, author of historical fiction about Chinese Americans and their adjustments to life in the United States. *Dragonwings; Dragon's Gate; The Traitor.* Also, *Hiroshima: A Novella.*

EARLY IMPORTANT WORKS *of* HISTORICAL FICTION

Date	Literary Work/Event	Significance
1888	*Otto of the Silver Hand* by Howard Pyle	One of the first works of historical fiction to be widely recognized
1929	Newbery Medal given to *The Trumpeter of Krakow* by Eric Kelly	National recognition for a work of historical fiction
1932–1943	Publication of the first eight books in the Little House series by Laura Ingalls Wilder	Classic historical fiction series for children
1944	Newbery Medal given to *Johnny Tremain* by Esther Forbes	National recognition for a work of historical fiction
1949–1960	Many historical novels published including *The Door in the Wall* by Marguerite de Angeli, *The Witch of Blackbird Pond* by Elizabeth George Speare, and *The Lantern Bearers* by Rosemary Sutcliff	Dramatic increase in the quality and quantity of historical novels for children and young adults
1961	Newbery Medal given to *Island of the Blue Dolphins* by Scott O'Dell	Landmark historical novel with a strong female protagonist from a minority culture
1971	*Journey to Topaz* by Yoshiko Uchida	Early historical work by and about a minority (Japanese-American)
1975	*The Song of the Trees* by Mildred Taylor	First in a series of books about an African-American family's struggle starting in rural Mississippi after the Civil War
1984	*The Sign of the Beaver* by Elizabeth George Speare given the first Scott O'Dell Award	The Scott O'Dell Award is established to bring recognition to historical novels set in North America
1989	Elizabeth George Speare receives the Laura Ingalls Wilder Award for her outstanding works of historical fiction	Recognition of an author of historical fiction for her substantial contribution to literature for young people

Universal Themes in Historical Fiction

Common themes that extend across time and place in historical stories can be an approach for selecting historical fiction for classroom use. For example, a theme such as seeking new frontiers could be explored using a group of four to six novels set in different times and places. Some examples of themes are presented in the following lists, along with books that might be selected for study of the theme. You will discover other themes when you read historical fiction novels and consider their commonalities.

EFFECTS OF WAR

Caged Eagles by Eric Walters
Bat 6 by Virginia Euwer Wolff
Hiroshima: A Novella by Laurence Yep
An Innocent Soldier by Josef Holub
Red Moon at Sharpsburg by Rosemary Wells
Weedflower by Cynthia Kadohata
Yellow Star by Jennifer Roy
Someone Named Eve by Joan M. Wolf

FAMILY CLOSENESS IN TIMES OF ADVERSITY

Fever 1793 by Laurie Halse Anderson
Nory Ryan's Song by Patricia Reilly Giff
Water Street by Patricia Reilly Giff
Out of the Dust by Karen Hesse
A Small White Scar by K. A. Nuzum
The Porcupine Year by Louise Erdrich

SEEKING REFUGE AND OPPORTUNITY THROUGH IMMIGRATION

The Cuckoo's Child by Suzanne Freeman
Fire in the Hills by Anna Myers
Good Night, Maman by Norma Fox Mazer
Secrets in the Fire by Henning Mankell
Flight to Freedom by Ana Veciana-Suarez
Beyond the Western Sea: The Escape from Home by Avi
Two Suns in the Sky by Miriam Bat-Ami
Elijah of Buxton by Christopher Paul Curtis
The Braid by Helen Frost

ECONOMIC CHALLENGES

The Traitor by Laurence Yep
Bud, Not Buddy by Christopher Paul Curtis
Esperanza Rising by Pam Muñoz Ryan
Little Audrey by Ruth White
Hattie Big Sky by Kirby Larson

Periods of History in Fiction

The natural relationship of historical fiction stories to the study of history and geography suggests integrating historical fiction novels into units on periods of both world and U.S. history. Seven historical periods in which historical fiction novels can be placed are reviewed in capsule form in the following subsections, in order to give you an idea of focus points for these units. Works of historical fiction set during these eras can be selected from the lists at the end of this chapter. Biographies of individuals from the same era are found in the lists at the end of Chapter 6, "Nonfiction," where you will find the books also organized by historical periods.

BEGINNINGS OF CIVILIZATION UP TO 3000 B.C.   The period preceding 3000 B.C. represents prehistoric cultures and civilizations. Early peoples (Java, Neanderthals, Cro-Magnons) and their civilizations in the Middle East and Asia are included. Egyptians, Syrians, and Phoenicians developed civilizations, and Hebrews produced a religious faith, Judaism, that resulted in the Old Testament. The subcontinent of India was the site of Aryan civilizations. Chinese dynasties were responsible for excellent works of art and agricultural systems of irrigation. An example of a historical novel set in this time period is Peter Dickinson's *A Bone from a Dry Sea.*

CIVILIZATIONS OF THE ANCIENT WORLD, 3000 B.C. TO A.D. 600   The era of the Greek city-states was followed by a period of Roman rule in Western Europe. Christianity was founded in Jerusalem by Jesus of Nazareth and spread throughout Europe. Ancient Asia was the site of enduring civilizations that bred two remarkable men born about 560 B.C.: the Indian religious leader Buddha and the Chinese philosopher Confucius. Both have had a lasting influence on their civilizations. One novel set in this time period, Sonia Levitin's *Escape from Egypt,* retells the story of Moses leading his people from Egypt to the promised land.

CIVILIZATIONS OF THE MEDIEVAL WORLD, 600 TO 1500   The eastern part of the Roman Empire, ruled from the capital of Constantinople, maintained its stability and preserved the civilization. This civilization, the Byzantine Empire, created a distinct culture and branch of the Christian Church—the Orthodox Church—which influenced Russia to adopt both the religion and the culture. Following the fall of the Roman Empire, Western Europe dissolved into isolated separate regions without strong governments. Many of the responsibilities of government were carried out by the Christian Church. The church dominated the economic, political, cultural, and educational life of the Middle Ages in Western Europe. These feudal societies eventually gave rise to the separate nations of modern Europe. During this era, early African and American civilizations arose independently. The great civilizations of China, Korea, and Japan continued to flourish throughout these centuries. Avi's *Crispin: The Cross of Lead* and K. M. Grant's *Blue Flame* portray medieval life in England and France.

EMERGENCE OF MODERN NATIONS, 1500 TO 1800   The Renaissance was a literary and artistic movement that swept Western Europe. Other important developments of this period include the invention of the printing press, a new emphasis on reason, a reformation of the Christian Church, and advances in science. During this same period, central governments throughout Europe increased their power. Spain, and then France, dominated Europe in the 1500s and 1600s. In the 1700s, Russia, Austria, and Prussia rose to power. This was also a time when Europeans explored and settled in Africa, India, and the Americas. The Portuguese and Spanish took the lead in explorations and acquired many foreign colonies. England, the Netherlands, France, and Russia also colonized and influenced East Asia, India, Africa, and the Americas.

Revolutions created new governments and new nations. The American Revolution (1776–1781) created a new nation; the French Revolution in 1789 affected the direction of governments toward democracy in all of Europe. Two historical novels that capture the political conflicts that gave rise to the U.S. Revolutionary War are Anna Myers' *The Keeping Room* and Janet Lunn's *The Hollow Tree.*

Napoleon built an empire across Europe, but lost it when European nations united in their efforts to defeat him. The nations of Latin America began to gain their independence. China expanded gradually under the Ming and Ch'ing dynasties. Japan prospered under the Tokugawa shogunate. The United States and Canada were the sites of rapid population increases due to immigration. The settlements in North America were predominantly along the eastern coasts, but some westward expansion began in the United States and Canada.

DEVELOPMENT OF INDUSTRIAL SOCIETY, 1800 TO 1914   Near the beginning of the century in the War of 1812 the United States declared war on the British Empire to protest trade restrictions imposed by the British on U.S. trade with France. Also, the United States objected to British military support of American Indians who were fighting U.S. settlements in the Indian wars.

The 1800s were marked by a rapid shift from agricultural societies to industrial societies. Great Britain was an early site for this change. The factory system developed and prospered, while working and living conditions deteriorated for the worker. Two stories about life as a mill worker in this period are Katherine Paterson's *Bread and Roses, Too* and James Lincoln Collier and Christopher Collier's *The Clock*. New technology—railroad trains, steamboats, the telegraph, and telephone—affected transportation and communications. Advances in science and medicine helped to explain the world and improved the quality of life. Education developed into an important institution in Western Europe and North America. Europe underwent revolutions that readjusted boundaries and eventually led to the establishment of new nations.

The westward movement in North America was fully realized as pioneers settled across the United States and Canada. The building of railroads hastened the establishment of new settlements. Massive immigration from European countries and China contributed to this rapid development. Native Americans struggled for survival in the face of these massive population shifts. Black slavery had existed in the American colonies from the earliest days, but in the 1800s slavery became a social and economic issue resulting in the Civil War (1861–1865). Slavery was abolished and the Union was preserved at the cost of 600,000 lives and a major rift between the North and the South. Rosemary Wells' *Red Moon at Sharpsburg* interweaves war stories from both the North and the South.

The United States grew in economic and political strength. An age of imperialism resulted in firm control of large areas of the world by other world powers such as England, France, and Belgium. Great Britain dominated India and parts of Africa and continued its influence over Canada, Australia, and New Zealand, while Japan became a powerful force in eastern Asia.

WORLD WARS IN THE TWENTIETH CENTURY, 1914 TO 1945   The 1914–1945 period includes World War I (1914–1918) in Europe, in which the United States and Canada joined forces with the Allies (Great Britain, France, Russia, Greece, and Romania) against Germany; the between-wars period that included the Great Depression; Hitler's rise to power in 1933; and World War II (1939–1945) in Europe and Asia, in which Canada and the United States joined forces with England, France, and the Soviet Union to battle Germany, Italy, and Japan. In 1917 the Bolshevik Revolution established a Communist government in Russia. In 1931, Great Britain recognized Canada, Australia, New Zealand, and South Africa as completely independent. However, these nations declared their loyalty to the British monarch and continued their cultural ties with Great Britain. The Holocaust during World War II—the persecution and killing of Jewish and other people by the Nazi regime—stands out as one of the most atrocious periods in modern history. Edith Baer's *Walk the Dark Streets* recounts the effects of Hitler's rise to power on a small German town. World War II ended shortly after the United States dropped nuclear devices on Hiroshima and Nagasaki, Japan. Eleanor Coerr's *Mieko and the Fifth Treasure,* Toshi Maruki's *Hiroshima, No Pika,* Theodore Taylor's *The Bomb,* and Laurence Yep's *Hiroshima: A Novella* provide moving accounts of the effects of atomic warfare.

POST–WORLD WAR II ERA, 1945 TO 1980S   During the postwar era, the United States and Western European nations were involved in a struggle for world influence against the Communist nations, particularly the Soviet Union and China. A massive arms buildup, including nuclear weapons, was undertaken by the major nations of both sides. The Korean War (1950–1953) and the Vietnam War (1965–1973) were major conflicts in which the United States fought to contain Communist expansion. The Korean War, combined with the postwar economic recovery of Japan, drew attention to the growing importance of East Asia in world affairs. *Sonny's War* by Valerie Hobbs and *The Purple Heart* by Marc Talbert describe the Vietnam War era. The Soviet Union launched a series of satellites, beginning with Sputnik 1 on October 4, 1957, inaugurating the space age. An enormous increase in scientific knowledge occurred as a result of massive spending for weapons development and space exploration. The 1950s and 1960s have been described as the Cold War decades because of the hostility between the Soviet Union and the United States. In the 1970s public pressure mounted in the United States to reduce the nation's external military commitments.

During the 1960s a strong civil rights movement, led by Martin Luther King Jr. and other prominent figures of the era, fought for equal treatment of African-Americans. The movement led to desegregation of schools, restaurants, transportation, and housing. Equal rights for women were also sought during the feminist movement in the 1970s. An example of a book set in the 1960s is Christopher Paul Curtis's *The Watsons Go to Birmingham—1963,* a story about the civil rights struggle in the U.S. South.

Many fine works of historical fiction for young readers can now be found. Young adults have an opportunity to learn by living vicariously the lives of people from long ago—people from different cultures and from different parts of the world.

REFERENCES

Adamson, L. G. (1987). *A reference guide to historical fiction for children and young adults.* Westport, CT: Greenwood Press.

Smith, J. A., Monson, J. A., & Dobson, D. (1992). A case study on integrating history and reading instruction through literature. *Social Education, 56,* 370–375.

RECOMMENDED HISTORICAL FICTION BOOKS

Ages indicated refer to content appropriateness and conceptual and interest levels. Formats other than novels are coded as follows:

(GR)	*Graphic novel*
(PI)	*Picture book*
(COL)	*Short story collection*

BEGINNINGS OF CIVILIZATION UP TO 3000 B.C.

Brennan, J. H. *Shiva*. Lippincott, 1990. Ages 11–15. Prehistoric Europe, Neanderthal and Cro-Magnon tribes. Sequels are *Shiva Accused: An Adventure of the Ice Age* and *Shiva's Challenge: An Adventure of the Ice Age*.

Cowley, Marjorie. *Anooka's Answer*. Clarion, 1998. Ages 10–15. Southern France, Upper Paleolithic era.

———. *Dar and the Spear-Thrower*. Clarion, 1994. Ages 10–15. Southeastern France, Cro-Magnon era.

Craig, Ruth. *Malu's Wolf*. Orchard, 1995. Ages 9–13. Stone Age Europe, prehistory, domestication of wolves.

Denzel, Justin. *Boy of the Painted Cave*. Philomel, 1988. Ages 10–14. Prehistory, Stone Age, France and Spain, cave paintings.

———. *Return to the Painted Cave*. Philomel, 1997. Ages 10–14. Prehistory, Stone Age, France and Spain, cave paintings.

Dickinson, Peter. *A Bone from a Dry Sea*. Delacorte, 1993. Ages 11–15. Story of a prehistoric tribe spun from an archaeological dig.

———. *The Kin*. Putnam, 2003. Ages 10–16. Prehistoric clans of Africa. The Kin series, including *Po's Story, Suth's Story, Mana's Story*, and *Noli's Story*, is now published in one volume.

Levin, Betty. *Thorn*. Front Street, 2005. Ages 12–16. Prehistoric times, birth defects.

CIVILIZATIONS OF THE ANCIENT WORLD, 3000 B.C. TO A.D. 600

Hunter, Mollie. *The Stronghold*. Harper, 1974. Ages 9–14. British Isles, 100 B.C.

Lawrence, Caroline. *The Thieves of Ostia: A Roman Mystery*. Millbrook, 2002. Ages 11–14. Roman port city Ostia in A.D. 79.

Levitin, Sonia. *Escape from Egypt*. Little, Brown, 1994. Ages 14–18. Jews, 1200 B.C.

Sutcliff, Rosemary. *Frontier Wolf*. Dutton, 1981. Ages 10–16. Young Roman army officer in northern England facing invading tribes, before A.D. 409.

———. *The Light beyond the Forest: The Quest for the Holy Grail*. Dutton, 1980. Ages 12–18. Recreation of the times of King Arthur and his knights, c. A.D. 520.

CIVILIZATIONS OF THE MEDIEVAL WORLD, 600 TO 1500

Alder, Elizabeth. *The King's Shadow*. Farrar, 1995. Ages 12–18. England, end of Saxon era, pre-1066.

Avi. *Crispin: The Cross of Lead*. Hyperion, 2002. Ages 11–15. England, 1300s.

———. *Crispin: At the Edge of the World*. Hyperion, 2006. Ages 10–16. England, 1377. Minstrels Crispin, Bear, and Troth, a shunned girl, joining forces in fourteenth-century England, with a foray into Brittany. Sequel to *Crispin: The Cross of Lead*, 2002.

Branford, Henrietta. *The Fated Sky*. Candlewick, 1999. Ages 11–16. Norway, Iceland, early Viking era.

Cadnum, Michael. *The Book of the Lion*. Viking, 2000. Ages 13–18. Knights in the Crusades, England, 1100s.

———. *Raven of the Waves*. Orchard, 2001. Ages 13–18. England, Norsemen in England, A.D. 794.

Cushman, Karen. *Catherine, Called Birdy*. Clarion, 1994. Ages 12–16. England, manor life, 1290s.

———. *Matilda Bone*. Clarion, 2000. Ages 12–16. Medical practitioner, England, Middle Ages.

———. *The Midwife's Apprentice*. Clarion, 1995. Ages 12–16. England, Middle Ages.

Grant, K. M. *Blue Flame*. Walker, 2008. Ages 12–15. Tangled moral, religious, and land disputes in 1242 in Languedoc region of France.

———. *Blood Red Horse*. Walker, 2005. Ages 12–16. Crusades, A.D. 1185–1193.

Heuston, Kimberley Burton. *Dante's Daughter*. Front Street, 2003. Ages 14–18. Writer Dante's family, Italy in the fourteenth century.

Jinks, Catherine. *Pagan's Crusade*. Candlewick, 2003. Ages 12–18. A squire with the Templar Knights of Jerusalem, 1187. Sequels: *Pagan in Exile* (2004); *Pagan's Vows* (2004); *Pagan's Scribe* (2005).

Love, D. Anne. *The Puppeteer's Apprentice*. Simon & Schuster, 2003. Ages 9–12. England in the Middle Ages.

McCaughrean, Geraldine. *The Kite Rider.* HarperCollins, 2002. Ages 12–16. China, seaport city, Kublai Khan, 1200s.

Napoli, Donna Jo. *Breath.* Atheneum, 2003. Ages 14–18. Germany, late 1200s.

———. *Daughter of Venice.* Random, 2002. Ages 11–15. Venice, Italy, 1500s.

Newth, Mette. *The Transformation.* Translated by Faith Ingwarsen. Farrar, 2000. Ages 13–18. Greenland, Inuit girl, 1400s.

Park, Linda Sue. *A Single Shard.* Clarion, 2001. Ages 9–14. Korean village, 1100s.

Paterson, Katherine. *The Sign of the Chrysanthemum.* Crowell, 1973. Ages 11–14. Political unrest, Japan, 1100s.

Sedgwick, Marcus. *The Dark Horse.* Random, 2003. Ages 13–18. Ancient Britain, Viking tribes.

Shulevitz, Uri. *The Travels of Benjamin of Tudela: Through Three Continents in the Twelfth Century.* Farrar, 2005. (PI) Ages 9–14. A journey across southern Europe and the Middle East beginning in 1159.

Tingle, Rebecca. *The Edge on the Sword.* Putnam, 2001. Ages 12–16. Feudal England, late 800s.

Yolen, Jane, and Robert Harris. *Girl in a Cage.* Putnam, 2002. Ages 11–15. England, invasion of Scotland, 1306.

EMERGENCE OF MODERN NATIONS, 1500 TO 1800

Anderson, Laurie Halse. *Chains.* Simon & Schuster, 2008. Ages 12–18. Two enslaved teenage sisters sold in 1776 to rich loyalists in New York City.

———. *Fever 1793.* Simon & Schuster, 2000. Ages 12–18. Philadelphia, yellow fever epidemic, freed slaves' role, 1793.

Anderson, M. T. *The Astonishing Life of Octavian Nothing, Traitor to the Nation:* Volume I: *The Pox Party.* Candlewick, 2006. Ages 14–18. Pre-Revolutionary slavery in New England. Volume II: *The Kingdom on the Waves.* Ages 14–18. Candlewick, 2008. Enlistment in the Royal Ethiopian Regiment to obtain freedom from slavery.

Avi. *The Fighting Ground.* Lippincott, 1984. Ages 10–14. U.S. Revolutionary War era, 1770s.

Bruchac, Joseph. *The Arrow over the Door.* Dial, 1998. Ages 9–12. Quaker boy and Abenaki Indian boy, in United States, 1777.

Duble, Kathleen Benner. *The Sacrifice.* Simon & Schuster, 2005. Ages 11–15. U.S. Colonial era, Salem witch hunts, 1692.

Forbes, Esther. *Johnny Tremain.* Houghton, 1943. Ages 10–13. U.S. Revolutionary War era, 1770s.

Hearn, Julie. *The Minister's Daughter.* Atheneum, 2005. Ages 14–18. Christianity and old beliefs, pregnancy and witchcraft, in an English village in 1645.

Hesse, Karen. *Stowaway.* Simon & Schuster, 2000. Ages 10–14. British sailing ship, Captain Cook's voyage, 1768–1771.

Ketchum, Liza. *Where the Great Hawk Flies.* Clarion, 2005. Ages 10–14. Relationships between white settlers and Pequot Indians, intermarriage, in Vermont, 1782.

Lawrence, Iain. *The Wreckers.* Delacorte, 1998. Ages 10–14. Adventures on the high seas; pirates, treasure, mystery in the 1800s. The trilogy includes *The Smugglers* (1999) and *The Buccaneers* (2001).

Lunn, Janet. *The Hollow Tree.* Viking, 2000. Ages 11–15. U.S. Revolutionary War, 1777.

McCaughrean, Geraldine. *The Pirate's Son.* Scholastic, 1998/1996. Ages 12–16. Pirates, England to Madagascar, early 1700s.

McCully, Emily Arnold. *Beautiful Warrior.* Arthur A. Levine, 1998. (PI) Ages 9–12. Kung fu, two seventeenth-century Chinese women near the end of the Ming dynasty.

Meyer, Carolyn. *Mary, Bloody Mary.* Harcourt, 1999. Ages 11–15. Mary Tudor and the court of her father Henry VIII of England, 1600s.

Myers, Anna. *The Keeping Room.* Walker, 1997. Ages 10–13. South Carolina, U.S. Revolutionary War era, 1770s.

Paterson, Katherine. *The Master Puppeteer.* Crowell, 1975. Ages 12–16. Poverty and discontent in Osaka, Japan, 1700s.

Rees, Celia. *Pirates!* Bloomsbury, 2003. Ages 13–18. Swashbuckling adventure on the high seas, 1725.

Rinaldi, Ann. *A Break with Charity: A Story about the Salem Witch Trials.* Harcourt, 1992. Ages 12–18. Salem witch trials, 1692.

————. *A Stitch in Time.* Scholastic, 1994. Ages 12–18. Salem, Massachusetts, family saga, 1788–1791.

Rockwell, Anne. *They Called Her Molly Pitcher.* Illustrated by Cynthia Von Buhler. Knopf, 2002. **(PI)** Ages 9–12. Revolutionary War, 1778.

Speare, Elizabeth George. *The Witch of Blackbird Pond.* Houghton, 1958. Ages 10–14. U.S. colonial era, 1680s.

Taylor, Mildred. *The Land.* Phyllis Fogelman, 2001. Ages 11–15. Mixed-race young man in the South, post–U.S. Civil War, 1870s.

Van Leeuwen, Jean. *Hannah's Helping Hands.* Phyllis Fogelman, 1999. Ages 9–12. U.S. Revolutionary War, Connecticut, 1779.

DEVELOPMENT OF INDUSTRIAL SOCIETY, 1800 TO 1914

Auch, Mary Jane. *Ashes of Roses.* Holt, 2002. Ages 14–18. Fire in New York City shirtwaist factory in 1911.

————. *Frozen Summer.* Holt, 1998. Ages 11–15. Unromanticized depiction of pioneer family life in western New York, 1816. Others in this family trilogy: *Journey to Nowhere* (1997) and *Road to Home* (2000).

Avi. *The Barn.* Orchard, 1994. Ages 9–13. Hardships of farm life in Oregon in the 1850s.

————. *Beyond the Western Sea: The Escape from Home.* Orchard, 1996. Ages 11–14. Ireland, 1851.

————. *Silent Movie.* Illustrated by C. B. Mordan. Atheneum, 2003. **(PI)** Ages 8–12. Swedish immigrants, fledgling film industry, New York City, early 1900s.

————. *The True Confessions of Charlotte Doyle.* Orchard, 1990. Ages 11–15. England, United States, 1830s.

Bartoletti, Susan Campbell. *No Man's Land: A Young Man's Story.* Blue Sky, 1999. Ages 11–15. Confederate Army, Georgia Okefenokee Regiment, U.S. Civil War, 1860s.

Blackwood, Gary. *Second Sight.* Dutton, 2005. Ages 11–15. Civil War backdrop, 1864.

Boling, Katharine. *January 1905.* Harcourt, 2004. Ages 9–13. Child labor, U.S. mill town, 1905.

Bruchac, Joseph. *The Winter People.* Dial, 2002. Ages 12–16. French and Indian War, Abenaki village, 1759.

Byars, Betsy. *Keeper of the Doves.* Viking, 2002. Ages 9–13. Kentucky in 1899.

Cadnum, Michael. *Blood Gold.* Viking, 2004. Ages 12–18. Adventure, California Gold Rush, 1849.

Collier, James Lincoln, and Christopher Collier. *The Clock.* Delacorte, 1992. Ages 11–15. Connecticut mill life, early 1800s.

Curtis, Christopher Paul. *Elijah of Buxton.* Scholastic, 2007. Ages 11–14. Freed slaves in a refuge house, Canada, 1849.

Cushman, Karen. *Rodzina.* Clarion, 2003. Ages 10–14. Orphan train, Chicago to California, 1881.

DeFelice, Cynthia. *Bringing Ezra Back.* Farrar, 2006. Ages 9–13. Dealing with evil, Ohio frontier, 1830s. Sequel to *Weasel* (1990).

————. *Weasel.* Macmillan, 1990. Ages 9–13. Ohio frontier, 1830s.

Donnelly, Jennifer. *A Northern Light.* Harcourt, 2003. Ages 14–18. Mystery and suspense in upstate New York, 1906.

Draper, Sharon M. *Copper Sun.* Atheneum, 2006. Ages 14–18. Ashanti girl, slave trade and plantation life, Carolinas, early 1800s.

Erdrich, Louise. *The Game of Silence.* HarperCollins, 2005. Ages 10–14. White settlers' threats to the Ojibwe way of life. Northern Wisconsin, 1850.

————. *The Porcupine Year.* HarperCollins, 2008. Ages 10–14. Displaced by the U.S. Government, the Ojibwe family seeking a home, 1852. Sequel to *The Birchbark House* (1999) and *The Game of Silence* (2005).

Fleischman, Sid. *Bandit's Moon.* Illustrated by Joseph A. Smith. Greenwillow, 1998. Ages 10–13. Mexican bandit Joaquin Murieta, California Gold Rush era, mid-1800s.

Frost, Helen. *The Braid.* Farrar, 2006. Ages 12–16. Scottish teenage sisters separated when one goes to Canada, 1850s. Verse novel.

Giff, Patricia Reilly. *Maggie's Door.* Random, 2003. Ages 9–13. Ireland, potato famine, immigration, 1840s.

————. *Nory Ryan's Song.* Delacorte, 2000. Ages 9–13. Ireland, potato famine, 1845.

————. *Water Street.* Random, 2006. Ages 10–14. Irish American immigrants, 1875. Sequel to *Nory Ryan's Song* and *Maggie's Door.*

Hill, Kirkpatrick. *Minuk: Ashes in the Pathway.* Illustrated by Patrick Faricy. Pleasant Company, 2002. Ages 10–14. Eskimo village in Alaska, 1890.

Holub, Josef. *An Innocent Soldier.* Translated from the German by Michael Hofmann. Scholastic, 2005. Ages 14–18. Napoleon's Russian campaign, 1812.

Hurst, Carol Otis. *Through the Lock.* Houghton, 2001. Ages 10–14. Farm community, Connecticut, 1800s.

Ibbotson, Eva. *Journey to the River Sea.* Dutton, 2002. Ages 11–14. Brazil, 1910.

———. *The Star of Kazan.* Illustrated by Kevin Hawkes. Dutton, 2004. Ages 10–14. Abandoned child mystery, Germany and Austria, late 1800s.

LaFaye, A. *Worth.* Simon & Schuster, 2004. Ages 10–14. Orphan train, Nebraska, late 1900s.

Lester, Julius. *Day of Tears: A Novel in Dialogue.* Hyperion, 2005. Ages 12–18. Account of the biggest slave auction in American history. Savannah, Georgia, 1859.

Lewis, J. Patrick. *The Brothers' War: Civil War Voices in Verse.* National Geographic, 2007. Ages 10–14. Poems honoring historical and fictional heroes of the U.S. Civil War.

Lowry, Lois. *The Silent Boy.* Houghton, 2003. Ages 10–14. Developmental disability, New England town, 1908–1911.

Lyons, Mary E. *Dear Ellen Bee: A Civil War Scrapbook of Two Union Spies.* Simon & Schuster, 2000. Ages 10–14. Richmond, Virginia, U.S. Civil War, 1860s.

Major, Kevin. *Ann and Seamus.* Illustrated by David Blackwood. Groundwood, 2004. Ages 11–18. Adventure and love story in Newfoundland in 1828. Free verse.

McCaughrean, Geraldine. *Stop the Train!* HarperCollins, 2003. Ages 11–15. Railroad, homesteading in Enid, Oklahoma, in 1893.

McMullan, Margaret. *How I Found the Strong.* Houghton, 2004. Ages 11–15. A 10-year-old boy witnessing Civil War battlefield slaughter while searching for his father.

Myers, Anna. *Assassin.* Walker, 2005. Ages 11–15. Alternating narratives by John Wilkes Booth and an assistant seamstress in the White House, assassination of Abraham Lincoln, 1865.

Paterson, Katherine. *Bread and Roses, Too.* Clarion, 2006. Ages 11–15. Mill workers' strike, Massachusetts, 1912.

———. *Jip, His Story.* Dutton, 1996. Ages 10–15. Vermont poor farm, 1850s.

———. *Preacher's Boy.* Clarion, 1999. Ages 10–14. Christian life, Vermont, late 1800s.

Paulsen, Gary. *Soldier's Heart: A Novel of the Civil War.* Delacorte, 1998. Ages 11–16. Minnesota farm boy, 1860s.

Pearsall, Shelley. *Trouble Don't Last.* Knopf, 2002. Ages 11–15. Northern Kentucky, slavery, 1859.

Peck, Richard. *Fair Weather.* Dial, 2001. Ages 9–13. Rural Illinois and Chicago, 1893. Humor.

———. *The River between Us.* Dial, 2003. Ages 13–18. Southern Illinois town, race relations, early Civil War era, 1861. Humor.

———. *The Teacher's Funeral: A Comedy in Three Parts.* Dial, 2004. Ages 10–14. Rural Indiana, 1904. Humor.

Place, François. *The Old Man Mad about Drawing: A Tale of Hokusai.* Translated from the French by William Rodarmor. Godine, 2003. Ages 10–14. Artist Hokusai, the customs of his age, Japan, 1800s.

Rinaldi, Ann. *Numbering All the Bones.* Hyperion, 2002. Ages 12–15. U.S. Civil War, Andersonville prison in southwest Georgia, slavery, 1864.

Robinet, Harriette Gillem. *Forty Acres and Maybe a Mule.* Atheneum, 1998. Ages 8–12. Reconstruction era, South Carolina and Georgia, treatment of former slave families, 1865.

———. *Missing in Haymarket Square.* Atheneum, 2001. Ages 10–15. Exploitative working conditions, Chicago, 1886.

Schmidt, Gary. *Lizzie Bright and the Buckminster Boy.* Clarion, 2004. Ages 12–18. Race relations, Christian life, Maine, 1912.

Siegelson, Kim. *Trembling Earth.* Putnam, 2004. Ages 12–18. Survival story, Okefenokee Swamp, Georgia, U.S. Civil War era, 1860s.

Snyder, Zilpha Keatley. *Gib Rides Home.* Delacorte, 1998. Ages 9–13. Nebraska orphanage and farm life, early 1900s. Sequel: *Gib and the Gray Ghost.*

Stolz, Joëlle. *The Shadows of Ghadames.* Translated from the French by Catherine Temerson. Delacorte, 2004. Ages 12–15. Muslim traditions, sex roles, Libya, late 1800s.

Tal, Eve. *Double Crossing: A Jewish Immigration Story.* Cinco Puntos, 2005. Ages 11–15. Emigration from the Ukraine in 1905.

Thomas, Joyce Carol. *I Have Heard of a Land.* Illustrated by Floyd Cooper. HarperCollins, 1998. **(PI)** Ages 8–12. Homesteading, African-American woman, Oklahoma territory, 1800s.

Wells, Rosemary. *Red Moon at Sharpsburg.* Viking, 2007. Ages 12–15. Civil War stories interwoven from both sides, North and South. Battle of Antietam, Virginia, 1862.

Whelan, Gloria. *Angel on the Square.* HarperCollins, 2001. Ages 11–16. St. Petersburg, Russia, fall of the Russian Empire, 1913.

Wilson, Diane Lee. *Black Storm Comin'.* Simon & Schuster, 2005. Ages 12–16. Mixed-race family traveling from Missouri to California; Pony Express; Civil War backdrop, 1860.

Winthrop, Elizabeth. *Counting on Grace.* Random, 2006. Ages 10–15. Laboring in a Vermont mill, 1910.

Yep, Laurence. *Dragon's Gate.* HarperCollins, 1993. Ages 12–16. Sierra Nevada, transcontinental railroad, 1867.

———. *Dragonwings.* Harper, 1979. Ages 10–15. Chinese immigrants, California, early 1900s.

———. *The Traitor.* Farrar, 2003. Ages 12–16. Chinese and Western coal miners in the Wyoming Territory, 1885.

Yin. *Coolies.* Illustrated by Chris Soentpiet. Philomel, 2001. **(PI)** Ages 8–12. Chinese Americans, transcontinental railroad, 1860s.

WORLD WARS IN THE TWENTIETH CENTURY, 1914 TO 1945

Adler, David. *The Babe and I.* Illustrated by David Widener. Harcourt, 1999. **(PI)** Ages 9–13. Depression era in the Bronx, New York.

Baer, Edith. *Walk the Dark Streets.* Farrar, 1998. Ages 13–18. Effects of Hitler's rise to power in a small German town, 1933–1940.

Bat-Ami, Miriam. *Two Suns in the Sky.* Front Street, 1999. Ages 13–18. New York state, relations among European refugees and U.S. citizens, World War II era.

Coerr, Eleanor. *Mieko and the Fifth Treasure.* Putnam, 1993. Ages 9–13. Nagasaki bombardment during World War II, Japan, 1945.

Cormier, Robert. *Frenchtown Summer.* Delacorte, 1999. Ages 11–14. Massachusetts, 1938. Free verse.

———. *Heroes.* Delacorte, 1998. Ages 14–18. Revenge seeking by a disfigured hero upon return from World War II.

Curtis, Christopher Paul. *Bud, Not Buddy.* Delacorte, 1999. Ages 9–14. Michigan, Depression era, 1930s.

Disher, Garry. *The Divine Wind: A Love Story.* Scholastic, 2002. Ages 14–18. Racism, love, family conflict, Australia, before and during World War II, 1930s and 1940s.

Doucet, Sharon Arms. *Fiddle Fever.* Clarion, 2000. Ages 9–14. Cajun life in southern Louisiana, World War I, 1914–1918.

Dowell, Frances O'Roark. *Dovey Coe.* Atheneum, 2000. Ages 9–14. Murder trial, North Carolina, 1928.

Glatsheyn, Yankev. *Emil and Karl.* Translated from the Yiddish by Jeffrey Shandler. Roaring Brook, 2006. Ages 10–15. Two boys, one Christian and one Jewish, growing up in pre–World War II Vienna.

Hartnett, Sonya. *Thursday's Child.* Candlewick, 2002. Ages 14–18. Australia, Depression era, 1930s.

Havill, Juanita. *Eyes Like Willy's.* Illustrated by David Johnson. HarperCollins, 2004. Ages 12–16. Austrian and French friends on opposite sides, World War I era.

Hesse, Karen. *The Cats in Krasinski Square.* Illustrated by Wendy Watson. Scholastic, 2004. **(PI)** Ages 9–12. Nazi occupation of Warsaw, Jewish ghetto, World War II era. Free verse.

———. *Letters from Rifka.* Holt, 1992. Ages 9–12. Russian immigration to the United States, 1919.

———. *Out of the Dust.* Scholastic, 1997. Ages 11–14. Oklahoma, dust bowl, drought, 1930s. Free verse.

———. *Witness.* Scholastic, 2001. Ages 11–15. Ku Klux Klan, Vermont, 1924. Free verse in five acts.

Hughes, Dean. *Soldier Boys.* Atheneum, 2001. Ages 13–18. An American and a German in World War II era. Chapters alternate point of view.

Janeczko, Paul B. *Worlds Afire.* Candlewick, 2004. Ages 12–15. Hartford, Connecticut, fire in 1944. Narrative poems.

Kadohata, Cynthia. *Weedflower.* Simon & Schuster, 2006. Ages 10–14. An internment camp in Arizona desert, Japanese-American family, World War II era.

Kerr, M. E. *Slap Your Sides.* HarperCollins, 2001. Ages 14–18. Quaker and conscientious objector in World War II.

———. *Your Eyes in Stars.* HarperCollins, 2006. Ages 14–18. Small town in upstate New York during the Depression, relationships between Germans and Americans, Jews and Gentiles.

Larson, Kirby. *Hattie Big Sky.* Delacorte, 2006. Ages 12–16. Homesteading in Montana, discrimination toward Germans during World War I, 1918.

Lawrence, Iain. *B for Buster.* Delacorte, 2004. Ages 12–18. Canadian Air Force, World War II, deployment to England for raids over Germany, 1943.

———. *Lord of the Nutcracker Men.* Delacorte, 2001. Ages 10–14. England and France, World War I era.

Lisle, Janet Taylor. *The Art of Keeping Cool.* Simon & Schuster, 2000. Ages 10–13. United States and Canada, World War II.

Maguire, Gregory. *The Good Liar.* Clarion, 1999. Ages 9–13. Occupied France, World War II era.

Maruki, Toshi. *Hiroshima No Pika.* Lothrop, 1980. Ages 9–15. Bombardment of Hiroshima, 1945.

Mazer, Norma Fox. *Good Night, Maman.* Harcourt, 1999. Ages 10–14. Holocaust survivors, Jewish refugees in Oswego, New York, World War II era.

Mikaelsen, Ben. *Petey.* Hyperion, 1998. Ages 11–15. Cerebral palsy and its treatment, 1920s.

Morpurgo, Michael. *Private Peaceful.* Scholastic, 2004. Ages 13–18. England and France during World War I era.

Myers, Anna. *Fire in the Hills.* Walker, 1996. Ages 12–16. Rural Oklahoma, German immigrant family, World War I era.

Myers, Walter Dean. *Harlem Summer.* Scholastic, 2007. Ages 14–18. Harlem Renaissance and Prohibition era, New York City, 1925.

Park, Linda Sue. *When My Name Was Keoko: A Novel of Korea in World War II.* Clarion, 2002. Ages 10–14. Japanese occupation of Korea, 1940s.

Parkinson, Siobhan. *Kathleen: The Celtic Knot.* Pleasant Company, 2003. Ages 10–14. Ireland, poverty in Dublin, 1937.

Peck, Richard. *A Long Way from Chicago.* Dial, 1998. Ages 10–15. Southern Illinois, 1930s. Humor.

———. *A Year Down Yonder.* Dial, 2000. Ages 10–15. Southern Illinois, Depression era, 1937. Humor.

Peck, Robert Newton. *Horse Thief.* HarperCollins, 2002. Ages 13–18. Florida, Depression era, 1930s.

Polacco, Patricia. *The Butterfly.* Philomel, 2000. (PI) Ages 9–12. French Resistance, persecution of Jews, World War II.

Ray, Delia. *Ghost Girl: A Blue Ridge Mountain Story.* Clarion, 2003. Ages 10–14. Virginia, Depression era, 1929–1932.

Roy, Jennifer. *Yellow Star.* Marshall Cavendish, 2006. Ages 10–15. Nazi occupation of the Lodz ghetto, Poland, 1939–1945.

Ryan, Pam Muñoz. *Esperanza Rising.* Scholastic, 2000. Ages 9–14. Mexico and United States, Depression era, 1930s.

Salisbury, Graham. *Eyes of the Emperor.* Random, 2005. Ages 12–18. Japanese Americans in World War II, prejudice, training scout dogs.

Spinelli, Jerry. *Milkweed.* Random, 2003. Ages 13–18. Warsaw, persecution of Jews, 1940s.

Taylor, Theodore. *The Bomb.* Harcourt, 1995. Ages 12–18. Atomic weapons testing, western Pacific Ocean, 1946.

Walters, Eric. *Caged Eagles.* Orca, 2000. Ages 11–15. Canada, internment of Japanese Canadians, World War II era.

———. *War of the Eagles.* Orca, 1998. Ages 11–15. Canada, internment of Japanese Canadians, World War II era.

Wells, Rosemary. *Wingwalker.* Illustrated by Brian Selznick. Hyperion, 2002. Ages 9–13. Depression-era Oklahoma, a move to Minnesota, 1930s.

Wolf, Joan M. *Someone Named Eve.* Clarion, 2007. Ages 11–16. A Czechoslovakian child survivor with Aryan features placed in a German family, World War II, 1942.

Yep, Laurence. *Hiroshima: A Novella.* Scholastic, 1995. Ages 9–14. Dropping of the atomic bomb, Japan, 1945.

Zusak, Markus. *The Book Thief.* Knopf, 2006. Ages 15–18. A German foster girl in a working class family during World War II. Narrated by Death.

POST–WORLD WAR II ERA, 1945 TO 1980S

Clinton, Catherine. *A Stone in My Hand.* Candlewick, 2002. Ages 12–18. Palestine, 1980s.

Curtis, Christopher Paul. *The Watsons Go to Birmingham—1963.* Delacorte, 1995. Ages 8–12. Flint, Michigan, to Birmingham, Alabama, U.S. Civil Rights movement.

Cushman, Karen. *The Loud Silence of Francine Green.* Clarion, 2006. Ages 11–15. McCarthyism in Los Angeles, 1950s.

Freeman, Suzanne. *The Cuckoo's Child.* Greenwillow, 1996. Ages 10–13. Beirut to Tennessee, 1962.

Grimes, Nikki. *Jazmin's Notebook.* Dial, 1998. Ages 12–16. Harlem, 1960s.

Guterson, David. *Snow Falling on Cedars.* Harcourt, 1994. Ages 15–18. A Japanese American and a German American, both veterans of World War II, a murder trial in Washington state, 1950s.

Hobbs, Valerie. *Sonny's War.* Farrar, 2002. Ages 12–16. Vietnam War era, California, 1966.

Houston, Julian. *New Boy.* Houghton, 2005. Ages 13–18. Civil rights struggle, blatant racism, first black student in a Connecticut boarding school, late 1950s.

Johnston, Tony. *Bone by Bone by Bone.* Roaring Brook, 2007. Ages 11–16. A risky friendship between two boys, one black, one white, in Tennessee in the 1950s.

Kadohata, Cynthia. *Kira-Kira.* Simon & Schuster, 2004. Ages 12–18. Japanese Americans, small-town Georgia in the late 1950s.

Lawrence, Iain. *Ghost Boy.* Delacorte, 2000. Ages 13–18. Death of a parent in World War II, an outcast, joining a circus, late 1940s.

Levine, Ellen. *Catch a Tiger by the Toe.* Viking, 2005. Ages 10–14. Father caught up in McCarthy witch-hunt hearings, Communism, issues of freedom of expression, 1953.

Lyon, George Ella. *Sonny's House of Spies.* Simon & Schuster, 2004. Ages 12–15. Family secrets, homosexual father, Alabama, 1940s and 1950s.

Mah, Adeline Yen. *Chinese Cinderella: The True Story of an Unwanted Daughter.* Delacorte, 1999. Ages 12–18. China, 1940s and 1950s.

Mankell, Henning. *Secrets in the Fire.* Translated from the Swedish by Anne Connie Stuksrud. Annick, 2003. Ages 11–14. Land mines, poverty, Mozambique civil war, southern Africa, 1970s and 1980s.

Martin, Ann M. *Belle Teal.* Scholastic, 2001. Ages 9–12. Rural South, 1962.

———. *A Corner of the Universe.* Scholastic, 2002. Ages 9–13. Mental disability, U.S. small-town life, 1960.

Nuzum, K.A. *A Small White Scar.* HarperCollins, 2006. Ages 12–15. Caring for a twin brother with Down syndrome in Colorado in the 1940s.

Park, Frances, and Ginger Park. *My Freedom Trip: A Child's Escape from North Korea.* Illustrated by Debra Reid Jenkins. Boyds Mills, 1998. **(PI)** Ages 8–11. Crossing the 38th parallel prior to the Korean War, late 1940s.

Sharenow, Robert. *My Mother the Cheerleader.* HarperTeen, 2007. Ages 13–16. A white family's protest of the court-ordered integration of their daughter's school, New Orleans, 1960.

Talbert, Marc. *The Purple Heart.* HarperCollins, 1992. Ages 10–13. Father–son relationship, Vietnam War era, 1967.

Veciana-Suarez, Ana. *Flight to Freedom.* Orchard, 2002. Ages 11–18. Cuban immigration to Miami, 1967.

White, Ruth. *Belle Prater's Boy.* Farrar, 1996. Ages 10–15. Loss of mother, extended family, friendship, Virginia, 1950s.

———. *Little Audrey.* Farrar, 2008. Ages 10–14. Poverty and hunger in a Virginia coal mining camp, 1948. First person narrative.

———. *Memories of Summer.* Farrar, 2000. Ages 13–18. Life in Virginia and Michigan, 1950s.

———. *The Search for Belle Prater.* Farrar, 2005. Ages 10–15. Sequel to *Belle Prater's Boy.* Looking for a missing mother in rural Virginia in 1950s.

———. *Tadpole.* Farrar, 2003. Ages 10–15. Appalachian mountains, 1950s.

Wolff, Virginia Euwer. *Bat 6.* Scholastic, 1998. Ages 11–15. California, Japanese Americans, post–World War II adjustments, 1948.

RELATED FILMS, VIDEOS, AND DVDS

Note: **MS** *refers to middle school;* **HS** *refers to high school.*

The Boy in the Striped Pajamas (2008). Author: John Boyne (2006). 90 minutes. MS, HS

Cry, the Beloved Country (1995). Author: Alan Paton (1951). 106 minutes. HS

The December Boys (2007). Author: Michael Noonan (1990/2008). 105 minutes. MS

The Devil's Arithmetic (1999). Author: Jane Yolen (1988). 97 minutes. MS, HS

In the Time of Butterflies (2001). Author: Julia Alvarez (1994). 95 minutes. HS

Jakob the Liar (1999). Author: Jurek Becker (1969). 120 minutes. HS

Lyddie (1995). Author: Katherine Paterson (1991). 90 minutes. MS, HS

A Midwife's Tale (1997). Author: Laurel Ulrich (1990). 88 minutes. MS, HS

My Louisiana Sky (2001). Author: Kimberly Willis Holt (1998). 98 minutes. MS, HS

The Other Boleyn Girl (2008). Author: Philippa Gregory (2001). 115 minutes. HS

A Picture of Freedom (1999). Author: Patricia McKissack (1997). Dear America Series. 30 minutes. MS

Seabiscuit (2003). Author: Laura Hildenbrand (2001). 141 minutes. MS, HS

A Separate Peace (2004). Author: John Knowles (1959). 91 minutes. HS

Skylark (1999). Author: Patricia MacLachlan (1994). 98 minutes. MS, HS

So Far from Home (1999). Author: Barry Denenberg (1997). Dear America Series. 30 minutes. MS

Sounder (2003). Author: William H. Armstrong (1969). 96 minutes. MS

Standing in the Light (1999). Author: Mary Pope Osborne (1998). Dear America Series. 30 minutes. MS

Winter of the Red Snow (1999). Author: Kristiana Gregory (1996). Dear America Series. 30 minutes. MS

SOURCES FOR FILMS, VIDEOS, AND DVDS

The Video Source Book. Syosset, NY: National Video Clearinghouse, 1979–. Published by Gale Research, Detroit, MI. An annual reference work that lists media and provides sources for purchase and rental.

Websites of large video distributors

www.libraryvideo.com
www.knowledgeunlimited.com

chapter SIX

NONFICTION: BIOGRAPHY *and* INFORMATIONAL BOOKS

As young people mature they develop their own particular tastes, including their tastes in reading material. Some prefer to read about the real world and real people. For them, nonfiction is ideal. Today's innovative and inviting works of nonfiction are an excellent source of information for young people and the adults who guide their learning.

DEFINITION AND DESCRIPTION

Nonfiction is usually classified to include biography and informational books. *Biography* gives factual information about the lives of actual people, including their experiences, influences, accomplishments, and legacies. *Autobiography* is similar in every respect to biography, except that the author tells about his or her own life. *Memoir*, though related to autobiography in that it deals with an event or events in the author's life, must also have an element of retrospection, or reflection, on the events' meaning to the author (Barrington, 1997). The point of memoirs is the authors' revelations of what events in their lives meant to them, not the events themselves. Laminack and Bell (2004) point out the similarity of first person narratives and memoirs and note that, without an author's note, a reader may not be able to tell whether the events actually happened to the author. *Informational books* can be written on any aspect of the social or natural world, including what is known of outer space.

Nonfiction can best be defined in terms of emphasis: the content emphasis of nonfiction is documented fact about the natural world, human behavior, and society. Its primary purpose is to inform. In contrast, the content of fictional literature is largely, if not wholly, a product of the imagination, and its purpose is to entertain. Nonfiction writing is often referred to as *expository* writing, or writing that explains, whereas fiction writing is called *narrative* writing, or writing that tells a story.

Although the roots of nonfiction can be traced to the seventeenth century, much of the growth and development of this genre occurred in the last half of the twentieth century. Early works of nonfiction helped define this genre. Some of these works are found in the feature Early Important Works of Nonfiction.

EARLY IMPORTANT WORKS *of* NONFICTION

Date	Literary Work/Event	Significance
1657	*Orbis Pictus* (The World in Pictures) by John Amos Comenius	First known work of nonfiction for young people
1922	*The Story of Mankind* by Hendrik Van Loon	First book to win the Newbery Medal; lively style and creative approach greatly influenced subsequent books for young people
1940	*Daniel Boone* by James H. Daugherty	First biography to win the Newbery Medal
1948	*Story of the Negro* by Arna Bontemps	First book for young people by an African American to win a Newbery Honor
1952	*Diary of a Young Girl* by Anne Frank	Autobiography that raised the public's awareness of the power of this genre; helped many to understand the tragedy of the Jewish holocaust

ELEMENTS OF NONFICTION

Understanding the parts, or elements, of nonfiction and how they work together is helpful in becoming more analytical about this kind of literature. Teachers who can explain nonfiction writing and help students read it more skillfully can also help them improve their reading of other expository texts, including textbooks! Likewise, teachers can use this knowledge to evaluate and select textbooks as well as nonfiction for their students.

Biography, which is more narrative than expository in nature, more closely resembles fiction than nonfiction in its elements. For the elements of fiction, refer to Chapter 2.

Structure

Structure has to do with how the author organizes the information to be presented. Most informational literature is structured in one or more of the following ways.

- *Description.* The author gives the characteristics of the topic (e.g., *The Octopus: Phantom of the Sea* by Mary Cerullo and Jeffrey Rotman, photographer).
- *Sequence.* The author describes items or events in order, usually chronologically or numerically (e.g., *The Incredible Journey of Lewis and Clark* by Rhoda Blumberg).
- *Comparison.* The author juxtaposes two or more entities or stances on issues and lists their similarities and differences (e.g., *The War on Terrorism (Opposing Viewpoints)* edited by Karen F. Balkin).
- *Cause and effect.* The author relates an action and then shows the effect, or result, of this action (e.g., *Blizzard! The Storm That Changed America* by Jim Murphy).
- *Problem and solution* (also referred to as *question and answer*). The author states a problem and its solution or solutions (e.g., *Understanding the Holy Land: Answering Questions about the Israeli–Palestinian Conflict* by Mitch Frank).

Some works of nonfiction will employ a single text structure; others, particularly longer works, will employ several.

Theme

Theme in nonfiction is the main point made in the work. Though a work of nonfiction may communicate hundreds of facts about a topic, the theme of the work will answer the question, What's the point? (Colman, 1999, p. 221). Sometimes the theme will be a cognitive concept, such as the way viruses multiply; in other cases, it will be an emotional insight, such as a new or deepened awareness of the strength of the human spirit to endure social injustice, as in Schoschana Rabinovici's biography *Thanks to My Mother.*

Style

Style is how authors and illustrators, with their readers in mind, express themselves in their respective media. Sentence length and complexity, word choice, and formal versus conversational tone are stylistic components that writers of nonfiction share with writers of fiction. Technical vocabulary, captions, and graphic elements such as tables, charts, illustrations, photographs, diagrams, maps, and indexes are associated mostly with nonfiction. How authors use these devices is part of their individual style. James Cross Giblin's conversational tone and use of period photographs and political cartoons, quotes, and source notes in his book *The Life and Death of Adolf Hitler* demonstrate how style can make nonfiction more interesting.

Teachers should not assume that their students understand the elements of nonfiction simply because they can read. Explaining these structures in textbooks and trade books when they appear helps students learn how to read expository writing more effectively.

EADING AND UNDERSTANDING NONFICTION

Throughout this text we emphasize the importance of selecting books that match students' interests. This particularly applies to selection of nonfiction, because of its appeal to teenage boys (Jones, 1998; Sullivan, 2004; Scieszka, 2005), the group most likely to become disenchanted with reading. (See Chapter 10 for a discussion of resistant readers.) While girls are more likely to accept and read works of fiction tradition- ally assigned or offered as reading options in school, boys' reading preferences often run to nontraditional subjects and formats found most frequently in nonfiction (e.g., *recreational literature* such as how-to topics; books about sports, films, and computer games; or *books with highly visual pages* featuring many illustrations, boxes or lists of information, and pages reminiscent of television or computer screens).

Research studies indicate that young people in the United States have trouble reading and writing expository texts, partly because of lack of early classroom experience with nonfiction (Campbell, Kapi- nus, & Beatty, 1995; Duke, 2000; Mullis, Martin, Gonzalez, & Kennedy, 2003). Such studies reveal that *it is only with repeated experience with a specific genre that one learns how to read or write that genre.*

ORMATS OF NONFICTION FOR YOUNG ADULTS

Biographies and informational books for young people are currently being produced in the following most common distinct formats:

- *Nonfiction chapter book.* Graphics and illustrations are common in more recent nonfiction chap- ter books but are still less important than the text. Examples include *Blizzard! The Storm That Changed America* by Jim Murphy and *Columbus and the World around Him* by Milton Meltzer.

Strategies to Promote Nonfiction and Motivate Students to Read It

- Booktalk works of nonfiction regularly.
- Prominently display appealing works of nonfiction, singly or in themed sets.
- Include nonfiction as options for required independent reading and required in-class reading.
- Read aloud brief passages from excellent informational books to pique students' interest in the books; occasionally, read aloud an entire short work of nonfiction.
- In all of the above, include some nonfiction on topics of interest to males.

Strategies to Improve Students' Comprehension of Nonfiction

BEFORE READING

Ask questions to discover **students' current schemata** on the subject treated in the text.

Example: Before reading a work of nonfiction set in Europe during World War II, ask someone to locate Europe on the world map and ask questions such as the following:

- What countries comprise Europe? Locate them on the map.
- Which countries formed the Allied Forces? Which countries formed the Axis Forces? With which group did the United States side?
- What were the causes of World War II?
- When did World War II take place?
- What else do you know about World War II?

Based on students' responses, **provide background information and vocabulary needed to comprehend the text** to be read.

DURING READING

Display for student reference the **strategies that good readers use to prepare for reading:**

- Skim the text before reading it to get the gist of the material; note **headings, tables, captions, bold-font vocabulary, chapter titles.**
- **Divide reading into sections;** check comprehension of each section before proceeding to the next by:
  1. **Retelling the information** after reading each section.
  2. **Writing down main ideas** as an aid to remembering them.
  3. **Formulating questions** about what you do not understand.

Display for student reference the following **strategies that good readers use when they do not understand a passage:**

- **Reread the passage**
- **Slow down your reading speed**
- **Visualize what is read**
- If comprehension difficulties persist, **identify unknown words and find their meanings**
- **Review prior passages**

AFTER READING

Organize ways for students to **review and clarify new information** such as discussion groups, oral presentations, and short written responses on the topic.

Provide students with an opportunity to **translate their new information into different forms,** such as team-written news articles or class debates.

- *Series* nonfiction—several books published around a common theme. Series nonfiction for readers in grades 6 to 12 falls into three categories: personal interests, high-low (high interest, lower reading level), and curriculum-related topics aimed at high achievers (Lemke, 2004). See the Life Balance series (Watts) for younger teens about maintaining physical and mental health and, for older teens, the Opposing Viewpoints series about controversial topics such as gangs, domestic violence, and drug abuse (Greenhaven).

- *Nonfiction picture book for older readers.* Large, uncomplicated illustrations help to convey the information. Examples include *Leonardo da Vinci* by Diane Stanley and *A Long and Uncertain Journey: The 27,000-Mile Voyage of Vasco da Gama* by Joan Goodman, illustrated by Tom McNeely.

- *Photoessay and photobiography.* Presentation of information is equally balanced between text and illustration. Examples include *Lincoln: A Photobiography* by Russell Freedman, *Murals: Walls That Sing* by George Ancona, and *Inventing the Future: A Photobiography of Thomas Alva Edison* by Marfé F. Delano.

- *Fact books.* Presentation of information is mainly through lists, charts, and tables. Examples include almanacs, sports trivia and statistics books, and books of world records such as *The Guinness Book of World Records.*

EVALUATION AND SELECTION OF NONFICTION

Every work of nonfiction need not fulfill all of the following criteria to be worthy. Moreover, no one book can cover a topic completely. By offering students a variety of satisfactory books on the same topic to be read and compared, a teacher or librarian compensates for the shortcomings of a good-but-not-great book.

- Nonfiction must be written in a clear, direct, easily understandable style.
- Captions and labels must be clearly written and informative.
- Facts must be accurate and current.
- Nonfiction must distinguish between fact, theory, and opinion.
- The author's qualifications to write on the subject should be clearly stated.
- *Personification*—attributing human qualities to animals, material objects, or natural forces—is to be avoided, because the implication is factually inaccurate. *Teleology*—giving humanlike purpose to natural phenomena—is another rhetorical device to be avoided in nonfiction.
- Works of nonfiction must be attractive to young people. Intriguing covers, impressive illustrations, and less dense text make nonfiction inviting.
- Presentation of information should be from known to unknown, general to specific, or simple to more complex.
- Subheadings make text easier to read and comprehend.
- Reference aids (tables of contents, indexes, pronunciation guides, glossaries, maps) make information in works of nonfiction easier to find and understand.

- Stereotyping must be avoided.

Selecting the best nonfiction for young adults can be a challenge. Many teachers and librarians find the following professional review sources helpful in identifying outstanding biographies and informational books.

"Outstanding Science Trade Books for Students K–12": An annual annotated list of notable books in the field of science coproduced by the National Science Teachers Association and the Children's Book Council (www.cbcbooks.org)

"Notable Social Studies Trade Books for Young People": An annual annotated list of notable books in the field of social studies coproduced by the National Council for the Social Studies and the Children's Book Council (www.cbcbooks.org)

In addition, NCTE's Orbis Pictus Award for Nonfiction (www.ncte.org) and the American Library Association's Robert F. Sibert Informational Book Award (www.ala.org), two annual nonfiction award programs, frequently identify outstanding works of nonfiction for young adults.

NOTABLE *Authors of Nonfiction*

Susan Campbell Bartoletti, author whose books explore the impact of broad social movements on young people. *Growing Up in Coal Country; Kids on Strike; The Boy Who Dared.* www.scbartoletti.com

Rhoda Blumberg, author of books about important explorations in U.S. history. *Shipwrecked: The True Adventures of a Japanese Boy; York's Adventures With Lewis and Clark: An African-American's Part in the Great Expedition.*

Dennis B. and **Judith B. Fradin,** coauthors of biographies of civil rights activists. *Ida B. Wells: Mother of the Civil Rights Movement; The Power of One: Daisy Bates and the Little Rock Nine.*

Russell Freedman, author of photobiographies of famous Americans and of informational books about U.S. history. *Lincoln: A Photobiography; The Voice That Challenged a Nation: Marian Anderson and the Struggle for Equal Rights.*

James Cross Giblin, author of biographies and informational books about the social implications of cultural developments and inventions.

When Plague Strikes: The Black Death, Smallpox, AIDS; The Life and Death of Adolf Hitler.

Jan Greenberg and **Sandra Jordan,** coauthors of picture book biographies about renowned artists and their works. *Vincent Van Gogh: Portrait of an Artist; Chuck Close, Up Close; Action Jackson.*

David Macaulay, author-illustrator of several mixed-genre books about construction of monumental buildings and informational picture books for older readers. *Cathedral; Building Big; Mosque.* www.davidmacaulay.com

Jim Murphy, author of informational chapter books about events in U.S. history. *Blizzard! The Storm That Changed America; An American Plague: The True and Terrifying Story of the Yellow Fever Epidemic of 1793.* www.jimmurphybooks.com

Diane Stanley, author-illustrator of picture book biographies for older readers. *Leonardo da Vinci; Michelangelo.* www.dianestanley.com

YPES OF BIOGRAPHIES

In adult nonfiction, biographies must be completely documented to be acceptable. In biographies for young people, more latitude is allowed, and biographers use some invention. This invention ranges from choosing what aspect of the subject the biographer wants to emphasize as the theme of the book (e.g., great energy or love of freedom) to inventing situations and conversation. Biographies can be classified by degree of documentation, as described in the following subsections.

Authentic Biography

In *authentic biography,* all factual information is documented through eyewitness accounts, written documents, letters, diaries, and, more recently, audio and video recordings. Details in the lives of people who lived long ago, such as conversations, are often difficult to document, however. So, for the sake of art, biographers must use such devices as interior monologue (telling what a person probably thought based on known actions), indirect discourse (reporting the gist of what someone said without using quotation marks), attribution (interpretation of known actions to determine probable motives), and inference to make their stories lively and appealing and worth the readers' time. It is advisable to read and compare several biographies of a subject, if possible, to counteract any bias an author might have. *York's Adventures with Lewis and Clark: An African-American's Part in the Great Expedition* by Rhoda Blumberg is an example of authentic biography.

Fictionalized Biography

Fictionalized biography is also based on careful research, but the author creates dramatic episodes from known facts by using imagined conversation. The conversation is, of course, carefully structured around the pertinent facts that are known, but the actual words are invented by the author. An early example of fictionalized biography of interest to mathematics students is *Carry On, Mr. Bowditch* by Jean Lee Latham. A recent example is *The Boy Who Dared* by Susan Campbell Bartoletti.

Biographies can also be classified by coverage of the subject's life—complete or partial. In evaluating biographies for young people, you will want to look for a balance between the need for adequate coverage and the tolerance that the target audience has for detail. Also, more attention to the subject's childhood and teen years makes these works more appealing to young people.

OPICS OF INFORMATIONAL BOOKS

Nonfiction is by far the largest single genre in literature in that everything known to humankind is a conceivable topic. Organization of such an enormous variety of topics could, of course, be done in a variety of ways. We have chosen to organize this world of knowledge into three categories: the natural sciences, the social sciences, and the humanities. Under each of these broad divisions, we have further organized by *topics of interest and relevance to young people*, believing that these are the subjects young people will be most interested in and most likely to read about. Note that titles in the Recommended Nonfiction Books list at the end of this chapter are organized accordingly, both for ease in locating titles by subject and for finding sets of books for classroom instruction. Examples of books about each topic are given in parentheses in the following lists.

Natural Sciences

The natural sciences deal with the study of the natural world. This includes biological science (the study of living organisms) and physical science (the study of nonliving materials), as well as practical applications of pure science such as medicine, architecture, and engineering.

NATURAL SCIENCE TOPICS OF INTEREST AND RELEVANCE TO YOUNG PEOPLE

- **The Human Body and Health** (*Chew on This: Everything You Didn't Want to Know about Fast Food* by Eric Schlosser and Charles Wilson)
- **Sex and Sexuality, including Pregnancy, Teenage Parents, Abstinence, Contraception, and Abortion** (*Dating, Relationships, and Sexuality: What Teens Should Know* by Wendy H. Beckman)
- **Nature: Earth's Ecosystems, Forces, and Life Forms** (*Forces of Nature: The Awesome Power of Volcanoes, Earthquakes, and Tornadoes* by Catherine Grace)
- **Careers and Practical Applications in Natural Science, including Space Exploration** (*Gorilla Doctors: Saving Endangered Great Apes* by Pamela S. Turner)

Social Sciences

The social sciences are concerned with the systematic study of human behavior and society.

SOCIAL SCIENCE TOPICS OF INTEREST AND RELEVANCE TO YOUNG PEOPLE

- **Human and Civil Rights Issues** (e.g., Child Labor, Gangs, GLBTQs, Immigrants, the Poor) (*Child Labor Today: A Human Rights Issue* by Wendy Herumin)
- **War and History** (*Who Was First? Discovering the Americas* by Russell Freedman)
- **Cultural and Ethnic Diversity** (*Islam: Understanding the History, Beliefs, and Culture* by Julie Williams)
- **Money and Money Management** (*The Complete Idiot's Guide to Money for Teens* by Susan Shelley)
- **School-Related Issues** (*Bullying: How to Deal with Taunting, Teasing, and Tormenting* by Kathleen Winkler)
- **Sports** (*Let Me Play: The Story of Title IX: The Law that Changed the Future of Girls in America* by Karen Blumenthal)
- **Jobs and Careers** (*Choosing a Career* by Linda Aksomitis)

Humanities

The humanities include the visual arts of drawing, filmmaking, painting, and sculpture; the performing arts of dance, music, and acting; and the communicative art of writing (literature and poetry).

HUMANITIES-RELATED TOPICS OF INTEREST AND RELEVANCE TO YOUNG PEOPLE

- Music and Making Music (*Should Music Lyrics Be Censored for Violence and Exploitation?* by Roman Espejo)
- Film, Acting, and Making Films (*Filmmaking for Teens: Pulling Off Your Shorts* by Troy Lanier and Clay Nichols)
- Art, including Book Illustration (*Making Comics: Storytelling Secrets of Comics, Manga and Graphic Novels* by Scott McCloud)
- Dance (*Hip-Hop and Urban Dance* by Tamsin Fitzgerald)
- Writing (*What It Is* by Lynda Barry)

In the late twentieth century, as the stature of nonfiction rose and more top-flight authors and illustrators were engaged in its production, the quality of research, writing, and art in these books improved. A lighter, yet factual, tone balanced with high-quality, informative illustrations and graphics emerged as the preferred nonfiction style beginning in the 1980s (Elleman, 1987). The trend toward more illustrations and less text in nonfiction makes this genre particularly appealing to today's visually oriented young people.

REFERENCES

Barrington, J. (1997). *Writing the memoir: From truth to art.* Portland, OR: Eighth Mountain Press.

Campbell, J. R., Kapinus, B., & Beatty, A. S. (1995). Interviewing children about their literacy experiences. Data from NAEP's integrated reading performance record at grade 4. Washington, DC: U.S. Department of Education.

Colman, P. (1999). Nonfiction is literature, too. *The New Advocate, 12*(3), 215–223.

Duke, N. K. (2000). 3.6 minutes a day: The scarcity of informational texts in first grade. *Reading Research Quarterly, 35*(2), 202–225.

Elleman, Barbara. (1987). Current trends in literature for children. *Library Trends, 35*(3), 413–426.

Jones, P. (1998). *Connecting young adults and libraries* (2nd ed.). New York: Neal-Schuman.

Laminack, L. L., & Bell, B. H. (2004). Stretching the boundaries and blurring the lines of genre. *Language Arts, 81*(3), 248–253.

Lemke, S. D. (2004, October 15). Taking stock of series nonfiction for teens. *Booklist,* p. 416.

Mullis, I. V. S., Martin, M. O., Gonzalez, E. J., & Kennedy, A. M. (2003). *PIRLS 2001 international report: IEA's study of reading literacy achievement in primary grades.* Chestnut Hill, MA: Boston College.

Scieszka, J. (2005). *Guys write for guys read.* New York: Viking.

Sullivan, M. (2004). Why Johnny won't read. *School Library Journal, 50*(8), 36–39.

RECOMMENDED NONFICTION BOOKS

Ages indicated refer to approximate ages of students for which the book is suitable. Book formats other than novels are coded as follows:

(GR)   *Graphic novel*
(PI)   *Picture book*
(COL) *Short story collection*

Biographies are organized by the same historical eras as works of historical fiction (Chapter 5), except prior to 3000 B.C., so that books in these two genres can be matched.

Biography

CIVILIZATIONS OF THE ANCIENT WORLD, 3000 B.C. TO A.D. 600

Bankston, John. *The Life and Times of Alexander the Great.* Lane, 2004. Ages 11–13. Fourth century B.C. king of Macedonia.

Demi. *Muhammad.* Simon & Schuster, 2003. (PI) Ages 11–13. Seventh-century Arabian prophet, founder of the Muslim religion.

Freedman, Russell. *Confucius: The Golden Rule.* Illustrated by Frédéric Clément. Scholastic, 2002. (PI) Ages 11–14. Fifth-century B.C. (approximately) Chinese philosopher.

Lasky, Kathryn. *The Librarian Who Measured the Earth.* Illustrated by Kevin Hawkes. Little, Brown, 1994. Ages 11–12. (PI) Second-century B.C. Greek geographer and astronomer Eratosthenes.

Zannos, Susan. *The Life and Times of Socrates.* Lane, 2004. Ages 11–14. Fifth-century B.C. Athenian philosopher.

CIVILIZATIONS OF THE MEDIEVAL WORLD, 600 TO 1500

Demi. *Marco Polo.* Marshall Cavendish, 2008. (PI) Ages 10–13. Picture book biography of the thirteenth-century Venetian's fantastic trip to China.

Doak, Robin S. *Galileo: Astronomer and Physicist.* Compass Point Books, 2005. Ages 11–15. Life of the Italian astronomer who defended the Copernican theory and invented the telescope.

Freedman, Russell. *The Adventures of Marco Polo.* Illustrated by Bagram Ibatoulline. Scholastic, 2006. Ages 11–16. Biography of the thirteenth-century Venetian explorer.

Meltzer, Milton. *Columbus and the World around Him.* Watts, 1990. Ages 12–17. Sixteenth-century Genoese (Italian) explorer.

Shulevitz, Uri. *The Travels of Benjamin of Tudela: Through Three Continents in the Twelfth Century.* Farrar, 2005. Ages 11–14. Fourteen-year journey of a Spanish Jew in twelfth-century Europe and the Middle East.

Sís, Peter. *Starry Messenger.* Farrar, 1996. (PI) Ages 11–14. Seventeenth-century Italian astronomer and physicist Galileo.

Stanley, Diane. *Joan of Arc.* Morrow, 1998. (PI) Ages 11–14. Fifteenth-century French heroine and saint.

THE EMERGENCE OF MODERN NATIONS, 1500 TO 1800

Adler, David A. *B. Franklin, Printer.* Holiday, 2001. Ages 11–13. Eighteenth-century American statesman, scientist, inventor, and author Benjamin Franklin.

Anderson, M. T. *Handel, Who Knew What He Liked.* Illustrated by Kevin Hawkes. Candlewick, 2001. (PI) Ages 10–13. Eighteenth-century German-born English composer Handel.

Aronson, Marc. *Sir Walter Ralegh and the Quest for El Dorado.* Clarion, 2000. Ages 12–17. Seventeenth-century English navigator, courtier, and statesman.

Dash, Joan. *The Longitude Prize.* Illustrated by Dušan Petričić. Farrar, 2000. Ages 12–18. Life and times of the eighteenth-century clockmaker who invented a way of measuring longitude at sea.

Fleming, Candace. *Ben Franklin's Almanac: Being a True Account of the Good Gentleman's Life.* Atheneum, 2003. Ages 11–14. Eighteenth-century

American statesman, scientist, inventor, and author Benjamin Franklin.

Fritz, Jean. *The Great Little Madison*. Putnam, 1989. Ages 11–14. James Madison, fourth president of the United States.

Giblin, James Cross. *The Amazing Life of Benjamin Franklin*. Illustrated by Michael Dooling. Scholastic, 2000. **(PI)** Ages 10–13. Eighteenth-century American statesman, scientist, inventor, and author.

———. *Thomas Jefferson: A Picture Book Biography*. Illustrated by Michael Dooling. Scholastic, 1994. **(PI)** Ages 10–13. Third president of the United States.

Lasky, Kathryn. *The Man Who Made Time Travel*. Illustrated by Kevin Hawkes. Farrar, 2003. **(PI)** Ages 10–13. Eighteenth-century British clockmaker John Harrison, who solved the problem of tracking longitude in shipboard navigation.

Marrin, Albert. *George Washington and the Founding of a Nation*. Dutton, 2001. Ages 11–17. Statesman and first president of the United States.

Murphy, Jim. *The Real Benedict Arnold*. Clarion, 2007. Ages 12–16. Evenhanded, authentic biography of the eighteenth-century Revolutionary general best known for his treason.

Nelson, Marilyn. *The Freedom Business: Including a Narrative of the Life and Adventures of Venture, a Native of Africa*. Illustrated by Deborah Dancy. Boyds Mills/Wordsong, 2008. Ages 14–18. Eighteenth-century slave Venture Smith's own narrative paralleled with Nelson's poems.

Reich, Susanna. *Painting the Wild Frontier: The Art and Adventures of George Catlin*. Clarion, 2008. Ages 12–18. Biography of the eighteenth-century painter of Native American life.

Rosen, Michael. *Shakespeare: His Work and His World*. Candlewick, 2001. Ages 11–14. Seventeenth-century British dramatist and poet.

Stanley, Diane, and Peter Vennema. *Bard of Avon: The Story of William Shakespeare*. Illustrated by Diane Stanley. Morrow, 1992. **(PI)** Ages 11–13. Seventeenth-century British dramatist and poet.

———. *Leonardo da Vinci*. Morrow, 1996. **(PI)** Ages 11–14. Sixteenth-century Italian painter.

———. *Michelangelo*. HarperCollins, 2000. **(PI)** Ages 11–14. Sixteenth-century Italian painter and sculptor.

———. *Saladin: Noble Prince of Islam*. HarperCollins, 2002. **(PI)** Ages 11–14. Twelfth-century Sultan of Egypt.

THE DEVELOPMENT OF INDUSTRIAL SOCIETY, 1800 TO 1914

Bennett, Veronica. *Cassandra's Sister: Growing Up Jane Austen*. Candlewick, 2007. Ages 14–18. A fictionalized biography of the famed British writer (1775–1817).

Blumberg, Rhoda. *The Incredible Journey of Lewis and Clark*. Lothrop, 1987. Ages 11–14. Partial biography of the leaders of the 1803–1806 expedition to the American West.

———. *York's Adventures with Lewis and Clark: An African-American's Part in the Great Expedition*. HarperCollins, 2004. Ages 11–15. Clark's slave and member of the Corps of Discovery.

Bolden, Tonya. *Maritcha: A Nineteenth-Century American Girl*. Abrams, 2005. Ages 11–15. A free black child's experiences in New York City before, during, and after the Civil War.

Bruchac, Joseph. *Sacajawea: The Story of Bird Woman and the Lewis and Clark Expedition*. Silver Whistle, 2000. Ages 13–18. William Clark and a Shoshoni Indian interpreter and guide alternate in describing their experiences on the Lewis and Clark expedition.

Chang, Ina. *A Separate Battle: Women and the Civil War*. Lodestar, 1991. **(COL)** Documented survey of women's many roles in this bloody conflict.

Dennenberg, Barry. *Lincoln Shot: A President's Life Remembered*. Illustrated by Christopher Bing. Feiwel & Friends, 2008. Ages 10–15. Large-format biography of Lincoln.

Fleischman, Sid. *The Trouble Begins at 8: A Life of Mark Twain in the Wild, Wild West*. HarperCollins, 2008. Ages 10–15. Partial biography of the nineteenth-century writer focusing on the seven years he traveled in the Wild West.

Fleming, Candace. *The Lincolns: A Scrapbook Look at Abraham and Mary*. Random, 2008. Ages 11–15. Biography of the Lincolns, including Mary Lincoln's life after the president's assassination.

Fradin, Dennis B., and Judith B. Fradin. *Ida B. Wells: Mother of the Civil Rights Movement*. Clarion, 2000. Ages 11–17. Former slave who fought for racial equality.

Freedman, Russell. *Lincoln: A Photobiography*. Clarion, 1987. Ages 11–14. Sixteenth president of the United States.

————. *The Wright Brothers: How They Invented the Airplane*. Holiday, 1991. Ages 11–14. History of early aviation and its founders in words and period photographs.

Giblin, James. *Good Brother, Bad Brother: The Story of Edwin Booth and John Wilkes Booth*. Clarion, 2005. Ages 12–18. The very different lives of the Booth brothers—one the preeminent actor of his day, the other an assassin.

Greenberg, Jan, and Sandra Jordan. *Vincent Van Gogh: Portrait of an Artist*. Delacorte, 2001. Ages 11–18. Nineteenth-century Dutch painter.

Hamilton, Virginia. *Many Thousand Gone: African Americans from Slavery to Freedom*. Illustrated by Leo and Diane Dillon. Random, 1993. **(COL)** Ages 11–14. Lives of African Americans who lived as slaves from the earliest days of slavery in America to 1865.

Johnson, Dolores. *Onward: A Photobiography of African-American Polar Explorer Matthew Henson*. National Geographic, 2005. Ages 11–14. Henson's important role in Robert Peary's successful expedition to the North Pole in 1909.

Kerley, Barbara. *The Dinosaurs of Waterhouse Hawkins*. Illustrated by Brian Selznick. Scholastic, 2001. **(PI)** Ages 11–14. Nineteenth-century British artist and lecturer who was one of the first to sculpt life-sized dinosaurs from fossil records.

Kraft, Betsy H. *Theodore Roosevelt: Champion of the American Spirit*. Clarion, 2003. Ages 11–14. Twenty-sixth president of the United States.

Krull, Kathleen. *Lives of the Musicians: Good Times, Bad Times (and What the Neighbors Thought)*. Illustrated by Kathryn Hewitt. Harcourt, 1993. **(COL)** Ages 10–14. Snapshot biographies of sixteen musical greats from classical to ragtime.

————. *Lives of the Writers: Comedies, Tragedies (and What the Neighbors Thought)*. Illustrated by Kathryn Hewitt. Harcourt, 1994. **(COL)** Ages 10–13. Brief histories of twenty classic writers.

Latham, Jean Lee. *Carry On, Mr. Bowditch*. Houghton, 1955. Ages 11–18. Self-taught American navigator and mathematician.

Marrin, Albert. *Sitting Bull and His World*. Dutton, 2000. Ages 11–18. Chief of the Dakota Sioux.

McClafferty, Carla K. *Something Out of Nothing: Marie Curie and Radium*. Farrar, 2006. Ages 12–16. Life (1867–1934) of the great Polish research scientist and winner of two Nobel Prizes.

Nelson, Marilyn. *Fortune's Bones: The Manumission Requiem*. Front Street, 2004. Ages 12–18. A slave's life and death story told in six poems.

Reich, Susanna. *Clara Schumann: Piano Virtuoso*. Clarion, 1999. Ages 11–14. German composer and performer.

Rosen, Michael. *Dickens: His Work and His World*. Illustrated by Robert Ingpen. Candlewick, 2005. Ages 11–14. The nineteenth-century British author's childhood, influences, and works.

Sandler, Martin W. *Lincoln through the Lens: How Photography Revealed and Shaped an Extraordinary Life*. Walker, 2008. Ages 10–15. Early history of photography and how it affected Lincoln's life and era.

Sís, Peter. *The Tree of Life: Charles Darwin*. Farrar, 2003. **(PI)** Ages 12–14. English evolutionist.

Stanley, Diane, and Peter Vennema. *Charles Dickens: The Man Who Had Great Expectations*. Illustrated by Diane Stanley. Morrow, 1993. **(PI)** Ages 11–14. English novelist.

Wilson, Janet. *The Ingenious Mr. Peale: Painter, Patriot, and Man of Science*. Atheneum, 1996. Ages 11–14. American portrait painter.

Wishinsky, Frieda. *What's the Matter with Albert? A Story of Albert Einstein*. Illustrated by Jacques Lamontagne. Maple Tree Press, 2002. **(PI)** Ages 9–13. Vignettes in picture-book format of Albert Einstein's childhood, told from the viewpoint of a young newspaper reporter interviewing Einstein.

WORLD WARS OF THE TWENTIETH CENTURY, 1914 TO 1945

Bartoletti, Susan Campbell. *The Boy Who Dared.* Scholastic, 2008. Ages 11–18. Fictionalized biography of German teenager Helmuth Hübener, executed for his resistance to the Nazis.

————. *Hitler Youth: Growing Up in Hitler's Shadow.* Scholastic, 2005. Ages 11–15. Twelve individuals tell of their experiences as members of the Hitler Youth Organization.

Bausum, Ann. *Dragon Bones and Dinosaur Eggs: A Photobiography of Explorer Roy Chapman Andrews.* National Geographic, 2000. Ages 11–16. American paleontologist known for finding dinosaur fossils in China.

Bernier-Grand, Carmen T. *Frida: Viva la vida! Long Live Life!* Illustrated by Frida Kahlo. Marshall Cavendish, 2007. Ages 12–18. Biography in free verse poems of the twentieth-century Mexican painter.

Britton-Jackson, Livia. *I Have Lived a Thousand Years: Growing Up in the Holocaust.* Simon & Schuster, 1997. Ages 12–18. Autobiographical account of life in a Nazi concentration camp.

Delano, Marfé F. *Inventing the Future: A Photobiography of Thomas Alva Edison.* National Geographic, 2002. Ages 11–14. American inventor.

Engle, Margarita. *The Poet Slave of Cuba: A Biography of Juan Francisco Manzano.* Illustrated by Sean Qualls. Holt, 2006. **(PI)** Ages 12–14. Partial biography (age 6–16) of the nineteenth-century Cuban poet.

Fleischman, Sid. *Escape! The Story of the Great Houdini.* Greenwillow, 2006. Ages 11–15. Biography of the world-famous magician who lived from 1874 to 1926.

Fleming, Ann M. *The Magical Life of Long Tack Sam.* Riverhead, 2007. **(GR)** Ages 13–16. Memoir of the author's Chinese great-grandfather who was born in 1885 in China and became a world-class magician.

Fradin, Judith B., and Dennis B. Fradin. *Jane Addams: Champion of Democracy.* Clarion, 2006. Ages 11–18. Biography of American activist and founder of Chicago's Hull House.

Frank, Anne. *Anne Frank: The Diary of a Young Girl, The Definitive Edition.* Translated from the Dutch by Susan Massotty. Doubleday, 1995. Ages 11–18. Netherlands. Autobiography written by German-born Jewish girl while in hiding from Nazis.

Giblin, James C. *Charles A. Lindbergh: A Human Hero.* Clarion, 1997. Ages 11–14. American aviator.

————. *The Life and Death of Adolf Hitler.* Clarion, 2002. Ages 13–18. Austrian-born German dictator and chancellor, and architect of the Jewish holocaust.

Jiménez, Francisco. *Breaking Through.* Houghton, 2001. Ages 11–14. Partial autobiography of a Mexican itinerant farm laborer in California in the 1950s and 1960s.

Katin, Miriam. *We Are on Our Own.* Drawn & Quarterly, 2006. **(GR)** Ages 14–18. Author's memoir about escaping from Nazi-occupied Hungary during World War II.

Krinitz, Esther N., and Bernice Steinhardt, *Memories of Survival.* Hyperion, 2005. Ages 12–18. A holocaust survival story in embroidered panels and captions.

Lear, Linda. *Beatrix Potter: A Life in Nature.* St. Martin's, 2007. Ages 15 and up. Life of the beloved British author, illustrator, and environmentalist.

Lobel, Anita. *No Pretty Pictures: A Child of War.* Greenwillow, 1998. Ages 11–18. Partial autobiography (ages 5–10) of the Czechoslovakian-born American children's author-illustrator.

Lutes, Jason, and Nick Bertozzi. *Houdini: The Handcuff King.* Hyperion, 2007. **(GR)** Ages 11–15. Portrait of the American magician and showman.

Maurer, Richard. *The Wright Sister.* Millbrook, 2003. Ages 12–14. Orville and Wilbur Wright's sister and "third member of the team," Katherine.

McClafferty, Carla K. *In Defiance of Hitler: The Secret Mission of Varian Fry.* Farrar, 2008. Ages 12–18. How Fry helped 2,000 refugees escape Nazi-occupied France.

Millman, Isaac. *Hidden Child.* Farrar, 2005. **(PI)** Ages 11–14. Picture-book autobiography of the author's struggle for survival as a child in Nazi-occupied France.

Nelson, Marilyn. *Carver: A Life in Poems.* Front Street, 2000. Ages 12–14. African-American scientist, educator, and author.

Partridge, Elizabeth. *Restless Spirit: The Life and Work of Dorothea Lange.* Viking, 1998. Ages 11–14.

American photographer of the Great Depression and World War II eras.

———. *This Land Was Made for You and Me: The Life and Songs of Woody Guthrie.* Viking, 2002. Ages 11–14. American songwriter and folksinger.

Poole, Josephine. *Anne Frank.* Illustrated by Angela Barrett. Knopf, 2005. **(PI)** Ages 11–13. Excellent introduction to the famous author and her diary.

Rabinovici, Schoschana. *Thanks to My Mother.* Translated from the German by James Skofield. Dial, 1998. Ages 12–17. Autobiographical account of a Lithuanian Jew's life in Nazi concentration camps.

Reef, Catherine. *e. e. cummings: A Poet's Life.* Clarion, 2006. Ages 12–18. Biography of the unconventional twentieth-century (1894–1962) American poet.

Spillebeen, Geert. *Kipling's Choice.* Translated from the French by Terese Edelstein. Houghton, 2005. Originally published in Belgium, this fictionalized biography of Rudyard Kipling's son ends with his first battle in World War I.

Sullivan, George. *Berenice Abbott, Photographer: An Independent Vision.* Clarion, 2005. Ages 11–15. Life of the twentieth-century American pioneer in photography.

Weatherford, Carole B. *Becoming Billie Holiday.* Illustrated by Floyd Cooper. Boyds Mills/Wordsong, 2008. Ages 13–18. A fictionalized memoir in verse of the famous African-American jazz singer.

POST–WORLD WAR II ERA, 1945 TO 2000

Barakat, Ibtisam. *Tasting the Sky: A Palestinian Childhood.* Farrar, 2007. A Palestinian woman's memoir of her childhood experience during the Six Days' War (1967).

Bausum, Ann. *Freedom Riders: John Lewis and Jim Zwerg on the Front Lines of the Civil Rights Movement.* National Geographic, 2005. Ages 11–15. Dual biographies of a black man (Lewis) and a white man (Zwerg) who were activists in the civil rights movement.

Beah, Ishmael. *A Long Way Gone: Memoirs of a Boy Soldier.* Farrar, 2007. Ages 16–18. Experiences of a 12-year-old recruited as a soldier in Sierra Leone's brutal civil war in the 1990s.

Bechdel, Alison. *Fun Home: A Family Tragicomic.* Houghton, 2006. **(GR)** Ages 14–18. Author's autobiography featuring her quirky family.

Bridges, Ruby, and Margo Lundell. *Through My Eyes.* Scholastic, 1999. Ages 11–14. Memoir of the first black child to integrate a New Orleans public elementary school (1960).

Brimner, Larry D. *We Are One: The Story of Bayard Rustin.* Boyds Mills, 2007. Ages 11–16. Biography of the architect of the civil rights movement.

Delano, Marfé F. *Genius: A Photobiography of Albert Einstein.* National Geographic, 2005. Ages 11–14. Einstein's life, personal thoughts, and theories presented with numerous large photographs.

Dendy, Leslie, and Mel Boring. *Guinea Pig Scientists: Bold Self-Experimenters of Science and Medicine.* Holt, 2005. **(COL)** Ages 11–18. Collected biography of people who served as subjects in scientific studies.

Ellis, Deborah. *Our Stories, Our Songs: African Children Talk About AIDS.* Fitzhenry & Whiteside (Canada), 2005. Ages 12–18. Autobiographical vignettes of many African youths whose lives have been changed by AIDS.

Fradin, Dennis Brindell. *With a Little Luck: Surprising Stories of Amazing Discovery.* Dutton, 2006. Collected biography of eleven scientists who lived during the last four centuries.

Fradin, Dennis B., and Judith B. Fradin. *The Power of One: Daisy Bates and the Little Rock Nine.* Clarion, 2004. Ages 14–18. Mentor of the African-American students who integrated Central High School in Little Rock in 1957.

Freedman, Russell. *Babe Didrikson Zaharias: The Making of a Champion.* Clarion, 1999. Ages 10–18. Preeminent woman athlete of the twentieth century.

———. *Martha Graham: A Dancer's Life.* Clarion, 1998. Ages 11–18. American dancer, choreographer, and teacher.

———. *The Voice That Challenged a Nation: Marian Anderson and the Struggle for Equal Rights.* Clarion, 2004. Ages 11–18. African-American singer.

Gantos, Jack. *Hole in My Life.* Farrar, 2002. Ages 12–18. Partial autobiography (teen years) of noted American children's author.

Greenberg, Jan. *Romare Bearden: Collage of Memories.* Abrams, 2003. Ages 11–14. African-American collage artist.

———. *Frank O. Gehry: Outside In.* DK Ink, 2000. Ages 11–14. American architect.

———. *Runaway Girl: The Artist Louise Bourgeois.* Abrams, 2003. Ages 12–18. American sculptor.

———, and Sandra Jordan. *Andy Warhol: Prince of Pop.* Delacorte, 2004. Ages 13–18. Life and work of the pop art icon.

———, and Sandra Jordan. *Chuck Close, Up Close.* DK Ink, 1998. Ages 11–14. American artist who creates oversized portraits despite paralysis.

Hemphill, Stephanie. *Your Own, Sylvia.* Knopf, 2007. Ages 14–18. Fictionalized biography of Sylvia Plath told in poems.

Jiménez, Francisco. *Reaching Out.* Houghton, 2008. Ages 12–18. Fictionalized autobiography of the Mexican-American author's college days in the 1960s.

Lat. *Kampung Boy.* Roaring Brook, 2006. **(GR)** Ages 13–17. Autobiography of the Malaysian cartoonist.

Levine, Ellen. *Rachel Carson.* Viking, 2007. Ages 12–16. Part of the Up Close series; a biography of the environmental pioneer.

Lewis, J. Patrick. *Black Cat Bone.* Illustrated by Gary Kelley. Creative, 2006. **(PI)** Ages 12–18. Picture book biography of blues guitarist Robert Johnson, told in poems.

Li, Moying. *Snow Falling in Spring: Coming of Age in China during the Cultural Revolution.* Farrar, 2008. Ages 12–18. Author's memoir of her harrowing fourteen years living in China during the brutal Cultural Revolution.

Medicine Crow, Joseph, and Herman Viola. *Counting Coup: Becoming a Crow Chief on the Reservation and Beyond.* National Geographic, 2006. Ages 12–18. Autobiography of this twentieth-century Native American's life.

Myers, Walter Dean. *Bad Boy: A Memoir.* Amistad, 2001. Ages 12–18. Growing up in Harlem in the 1940s and 1950s.

Myrick, Leland. *Missouri Boy.* Roaring Brook, 2006. Partial autobiography of the author's early years living in a small Midwestern town.

Partridge, Elizabeth. *John Lennon: All I Want Is the Truth.* Viking, 2005. Ages 15–18. Honest but non-judgmental biography of the influential twentieth-century musician.

Peters, Craig. *Bill Gates: Software Genius of Microsoft.* Enslow, 2003. Ages 14–18. Profile of Microsoft founder and computer-technology visionary Bill Gates. One of the Internet Biographies series.

Rembert, Winfred. *Don't Hold Me Back: My Life and Art.* Cricket, 2003. **(PI)** Ages 11–13. Autobiography of the African-American artist.

Rosen, Renee. *Every Crooked Pot.* St. Martin's, 2007. Ages 15–18. Memoir of Nina Goldman and the effects of her port-wine facial birthmark and her father on her life.

Roy, Jennifer. *Yellow Star.* Marshall Cavendish, 2006. Ages 10–15. The story of Syvia Perlmutter, one of the twelve children to survive the Lodz ghetto in Poland during World War II.

Rubin, Susan G. *Delicious: The Life and Art of Wayne Thiebaud.* Chronicle, 2007. Ages 11–14. Life of the contemporary painter of everyday objects.

Satrapi, Marjane. *Persepolis: The Story of a Childhood.* Pantheon, 2003. **(GR)** Ages 15–18. An autobiographical graphic novel of the author's childhood in Iran during the Islamic Revolution.

———. *Persepolis 2: The Story of a Return.* Pantheon, 2004. **(GR)** Ages 15–18. The author's teen years in Vienna and her return to fundamentalist Iran.

Siegal, Siena C. *To Dance: A Ballerina's Graphic Novel.* Illustrated by Mark Siegel. Simon & Schuster, 2006. **(GR)** Ages 10–14. A ballerina's memoir.

Silverstein, Ken. *The Radioactive Boy Scout: The True Story of a Boy and His Backyard Nuclear Reactor.* Random, 2004. Ages 14–18. In the mid-1990s a teenager secretly builds a hazardous nuclear reactor.

Sís, Peter. *The Wall: Growing Up behind the Iron Curtain.* Farrar, 2007. Ages 12–16. **(PI/GR)** Autobiographical account of growing up in Czechoslovakia under Soviet rule.

Zenatti, Valérie. *When I Was a Soldier.* Translated from the French by Adriana Hunter. Bloomsbury, 2005. Ages 14–18. Memoir of a French immigrant's coming of age and beginning to question the politics of war as a result of her required two-year military service in the Israeli army, 1988–1990.

Informational Books

NATURAL SCIENCES

The Human Body and Health

Austin, James. *Underage Drinking*. Greenhaven, 2007. Ten essays for reluctant readers on various aspects of underage drinking such as bingeing and parental responsibility.

Davidson, Sue, and Ben Morgan. *Human Body Revealed*. DK, 2002. Ages 10–14. How various parts of the human body fit together; uses doublepage illustrations, photos, and overlays.

Dillon, Eric. *Obesity*. Greenhaven, 2006. Ages 12–16. Eight essays presenting varying viewpoints on health risks, causes, and emotional impact of obesity in young people.

Egendorf, Laura K. *Smoking*. Greenhaven, 2007. Ages 12–16. Fifteen essays for reluctant readers on various aspects of smoking such as secondhand smoke, factors contributing to teen smoking, and government regulation.

Farrell, Jeanette. *Invisible Allies: Microbes That Shape Our Lives*. Farrar, 2005. Ages 12–18. Human dependence on microbes.

————. *Invisible Enemies: Stories of Infectious Disease*. Farrar, 2005. Ages 12–18. Seven dreaded human diseases and efforts made to avoid or cure them.

Fleischman, John. *Phineas Gage: A Gruesome but True Story about Brain Science*. Houghton, 2002. Ages 12–14. How a freak accident played an important role in the development of our knowledge of the brain.

Gay, Kathlyn. *Am I Fat? The Obesity Issue for Teens*. Enslow, 2006. Ages 13–18. Causes of the epidemic and ways people combat obesity.

Giblin, James Cross. *When Plague Strikes: The Black Death, Smallpox, AIDS*. Illustrated by David Frampton. HarperCollins, 1995. Ages 12–18. History and unfortunate parallels of three epidemics.

Hawcock, David. *The Amazing Pull-Out Pop-Up Body in a Book*. DK Publishing, 1997. Ages 11–14. Unfolds to a 5-foot-high 3D wall poster of a human body.

Hinds, Maureen J. *Fighting the AIDS and HIV Epidemic: A Global Battle*. Enslow, 2007. Ages 13–18. Explanation of the virus; ways to prevent and treat it; its impact on the world.

Levin, Judith. *Anxiety and Panic Attacks*. Rosen, 2008. Ages 12–16. Causes, symptoms, and management of mental disorders related to anxiety.

Macaulay, David, with Richard Walker. *The Way We Work: Getting to Know the Amazing Human Body*. Houghton, 2008. Ages 12–18. Fully illustrated guide to the human body and its systems.

Murphy, Jim. *An American Plague: The True and Terrifying Story of the Yellow Fever Epidemic of 1793*. Clarion, 2003. Ages 11–18. The history, science, and politics of Philadelphia's harrowing ordeal.

Palid, Thea. *Mixed Messages: Interpreting Body Image and Social Norms*. ABDO, 2008. Ages 11–15. Case studies, critical thinking questions, professional advice, and support for girls.

Rebman, Renée C. *Addictions and Risky Behaviors: Cutting, Bingeing, Snorting and Other Dangers*. Enslow, 2006. Ages 13–18. Causes and characteristics of specific addictions and help for dealing with them.

Schlosser, Eric, and Charles Wilson. *Chew on This: Everything You Didn't Want to Know about Fast Food*. Houghton/Graphia, 2006. Ages 11–18. The dangers of eating too much fast food.

Shivack, Nadia. *Inside Out: Portrait of an Eating Disorder*. Atheneum, 2007. **(GR)** Ages 14–18. A memoir of the author's battles with anorexia and bulimia.

Simon, Seymour. *Guts: Our Digestive System*. HarperCollins, 2005. Ages 9–14. Photoessay about the workings of the human digestive system.

Williams, Heidi. *Body Image*. Greenhaven, 2008. Essays on various aspects of teen concepts on body image.

Wolf, Bernard. *HIV Positive*. Dutton, 1997. Ages 11–18. Photoessay. A single mother with AIDS.

Sex and Sexuality, including Pregnancy, Teenage Parents, Abstinence, Contraception, and Abortion

Beckman, Wendy H. *Dating, Relationships, and Sexuality: What Teens Should Know*. Enslow, 2006. Ages 13–18. How roles and relationships have changed over time; body image, popularity, communication, and gender identity.

Bell, Ruth. *Changing Bodies, Changing Lives: A Book for Teens on Sex and Relationships* (3rd ed.). Three Rivers, 1998. Ages 13–18. A thorough discussion of sexual and emotional changes during the teen years.

Brynie, Faith. *101 Questions About Sex and Sexuality: With Answers for the Curious, Cautious, and Confused.* 21st Century, 2003. Ages 11–18. Actual questions collected from middle school and high school students.

Currie-McGhee, Leanne. *Sexually Transmitted Diseases.* ReferencePoint, 2008. Ages 15–18. Current information on the topic with color illustrations and drawings. See others in the Compact Research: Diseases and Disorders Series.

Daldry, Jeremy. *The Teenage Guy's Survival Guide: The Real Deal on Girls, Growing Up and Other Guy Stuff.* Little, Brown, 1999. Ages 12–18. Advice and reassurance on girls, body changes, and sexuality.

Forssberg, Mann. *Sex for Guys.* Groundwood, 2007. Ages 14–18. Part of the Groundwork Guides Series. An overview of the social issues related to teen males and sex.

Gravelle, Karen. *What's Going on Down There? Answers to Questions Boys Find Hard to Ask.* Illustrated by Robert Leighton. Walker, 1998. Ages 11–18. Guide to puberty and sex-related matters for boys.

Haney, Johannah. *The Abortion Debate: Understanding the Issues.* Enslow, 2008. Ages 13–18. Explanation of terms and issues; impact of the issue on politics.

Harris, Robie H. *It's Perfectly Normal: A Book about Changing Bodies, Growing Up, Sex, and Sexual Health.* Illustrated by Michael Emberley. Candlewick, 1994. Ages 11–18.

———. *It's So Amazing! A Book about Eggs, Sperm, Birth, Babies and Families.* Illustrated by Michael Emberley. Candlewick, 1999. Ages 11–18.

Jukes, Mavis. *It's a Girl Thing: How to Stay Healthy, Safe, and in Charge.* Illustrated by Debbie Tilley. Knopf, 1996. Ages 11–18. Discussion of puberty and sexuality for girls.

Nilsson, Lennart, and Lars Hamberger. *A Child Is Born.* Delacorte, 2003. **(PI)** Ages 11–18. Fetal development within the womb from a few weeks after conception to birth; spectacular microphotography.

Stoppard, Miriam (Dr.). *Sex Ed.* Illustrated by Sally Artz. DK, 1997. Ages 13–18. Masturbation, contraception, homosexuality, orgasm, safe sex, STDs, and pregnancy.

Weston, Carol. *Private and Personal: Questions and Answers for Girls Only.* HarperCollins, 2000. Ages 11–18. Advice for preteen and teen girls on growing up today.

Nature: Earth's Ecosystems, Forces, and Life Forms

Cerullo, Mary M. *The Octopus: Phantom of the Sea.* Photography by Jeffrey L. Rotman. Cobblehill, 1997. Ages 11–14. Life and habits of one of the sea's most intelligent creatures.

Collard, Sneed B. *The Prairie Builders: Reconstructing America's Lost Grasslands.* Houghton, 2005. Ages 11–14. Present-day recreation of the tallgrass prairie in Iowa.

Desonie, Dana. *Oceans: How We Use the Seas.* Chelsea House, 2007. Ages 13–18. A detailed introduction to ocean science and conservation.

Devlin, Keith. *The Math Instinct: Why You're a Mathematical Genius (along with Lobsters, Birds, Cats and Dogs).* Thunder's Mouth Press, 2005. Ages 14–18. Intuitive math solutions by animals to problems of counting, trajectory, motion, and patterns.

Fridell, Ron. *Earth-Friendly Energy.* Lerner, 2008. Ages 10–14. Multiple aspects of the topic with maps, charts, photos. See others in the Saving Our Earth Series.

Gamlin, Linda, editor. *Eyewitness: Evolution.* DK Publishing, 2000. Ages 10–13. The theory of evolution and how new species develop.

Gore, Al, and Jane O'Connor. *An Inconvenient Truth: The Crisis of Global Warming.* Viking, 2007. Ages 11–18. Adapted from the documentary, an investigation of the climate issues threatening our planet.

Grace, Catherine. *Forces of Nature: The Awesome Power of Volcanoes, Earthquakes, and Tornadoes.* National Geographic, 2004. Ages 11–14. Causes of these phenomena, their scale, and capacity for destruction.

Hoose, Phillip. *The Race to Save the Lord God Bird.* Farrar, 2004. Ages 11–18. History of the ivory-billed woodpecker.

Koppes, Steven. *Killer Rocks from Outer Space: Asteroids, Comets, and Meteorites.* Carolrhoda, 2003. Ages 11–14. Information about past and future cosmic collisions.

Kurlansky, Mark. *The Cod's Tale.* Illustrated by S. D. Schindler. Penguin, 2001. Ages 11–18. The role of the Atlantic cod in the history of North America and Europe.

Lynch, Wayne. *Prairie Grasslands.* NorthWord, 2006. Ages 11–15. A study of this ecosystem and the interconnectedness of living things to their surroundings. See also *Rocky Mountains,* NorthWord, 2006.

Murphy, Jim. *Blizzard! The Storm That Changed America.* Scholastic, 2000. Ages 11–18. The 1888 snowstorm that paralyzed the northeastern United States for four days.

Orenstein, Ronald. *New Animal Discoveries.* Millbrook, 2001. Ages 11–14. New animal discoveries within the last two decades, with photographs.

Relf, Pat. *A Dinosaur Named Sue: The Story of the Colossal Fossil: The World's Most Complete T. Rex.* Scholastic, 2000. Ages 11–14. Sensation surrounding Sue's discovery, ownership, and mounting for museum display.

Singer, Marilyn. *Venom.* Darby Creek, 2007. Ages 11–14. Presentation of creatures that use venom for attack and defense.

Sloan, Christopher. *The Human Story: Our Evolution from Prehistoric Ancestors to Today.* Photography by Kenneth Garrett. Illustrated by Alfons Kennis and Adrie Kennis. National Geographic, 2004. Ages 11–18. Facts and theories of paleoanthropology (including natural selection); richly illustrated.

Sussman, Art. *Dr. Art's Guide to Planet Earth: For Earthlings Ages 12 to 120.* Illustrated by Emiko-Rose Koike. Chelsea Green, 2000. Ages 11–18. How our planet works and what can happen when the balance of nature is upset.

Tanaka, Shelley. *Climate Change.* Groundwood, 2006. Ages 14–18. Part of the Groundwork Guides Series. An overview of the social and political issues related to climate change.

Treaster, Joseph B. *Hurricane Force: In the Path of America's Deadliest Storms.* Kingfisher, 2007. Ages 12–16. A scientific and socioeconomic photoessay about hurricanes.

Turner, Pamela S. *Life on Earth—and Beyond: An Astrobiologist's Quest.* Charlesbridge, 2008. Ages 10–13. NASA scientist Christopher McKay's study of bacteria that live in extreme climatic conditions.

Webster, Stephen. *The Kingfisher Book of Evolution.* Kingfisher, 2000. Ages 11–14. Beliefs concerning animal and human origins; theory of evolution; history of life on Earth; evolution of behavior; evolution of humans; future of evolution.

Young, Mitchell, editor. *Garbage and Recycling.* Gale, 2007. Ages 15–18. Part of the Opposing Viewpoints series, this volume focuses on issues of waste disposal.

Careers and Practical Applications in Natural Science, including Space Exploration

Abadzis, Nick. *Laika.* Roaring Brook/FirstSecond, 2007. **(GR)** Ages 12–15. The story of the first dog in space.

Angelo, Joseph A. Frontiers in Space Series. Facts on File. Ages 14–18. Includes *Robot Spacecraft* (2006); *Rockets* (2006); *Spacecraft for Astronomy* (2006); *Life in the Universe* (2007); *Satellites* (2006).

Ball, Johnny. *Go Figure! A Totally Cool Book about Numbers.* DK Publishing, 2005. Ages 10–14. Filled with facts, figures, and brainteasers including geometry, predictability, and logic.

Bishop, Nic. *Digging for Bird Dinosaurs: An Expedition to Madagascar.* Houghton, 2000. Ages 11–14. Photoessay about paleontologist Cathy Forster at work.

Carson, Mary Kay. *Exploring the Solar System.* Chicago Review, 2006. Ages 10–14. Space and space exploration.

Gardner, Robert. *Chemistry Projects with a Laboratory You Can Build.* Enslow, 2007. Ages 11–15. Part of the Build-a-Lab! Science Experiments Series.

———, and Barbara G. Conklin. *Chemistry Science Fair Projects Using French Fries, Gumdrops, Soap, and Other Organic Stuff.* Enslow, 2004. Ages 11–14. Twenty-nine organic chemistry experiments.

Hakim, Joy. *Einstein Adds a New Dimension.* Smithsonian, 2007. Ages 12–18. An account of the development of quantum theory and modern cosmology.

Innes, Brian. *DNA and Body Evidence.* M. E. Sharpe, 2007. Ages 14–18. History and evolution of DNA and blood analysis and fingerprinting. Part of the four-volume Forensic Evidence Series. See also: *Fingerprints and Impressions* (Innes, Brian, 2007); *Fire and Explosives* (Wright, John D., 2007); *Hair and Fibers* (Wright, John D., 2007).

Macaulay, David. *Building Big.* Houghton, 2000. **(PI)** Ages 12–18. Design and construction of notable bridges, tunnels, skyscrapers, domes, and dams.

———. *Castle.* Houghton, 1977. **(PI)** Ages 11–18. Assembly of a thirteenth-century British castle.

———. *Cathedral: The Story of Its Construction.* Houghton, 1973. (PI) Ages 11–18. Building a French Gothic cathedral in the thirteenth century.

———. *Mosque.* Houghton, 2003. **(PI)** Ages 11–18. Building a mosque in sixteenth-century Istanbul.

———. *The Way Things Work.* Houghton, 1988. Ages 11–14. **(PI)** [CD-ROM version: Dorling Kindersley, 1994.] (1998 updated version titled *The New Way Things Work.*) A guide to the workings of machines, including (in updated edition) digital ones.

Markle, Sandra. *Measuring Up! Experiments, Puzzles, and Games Exploring Measurement.* Atheneum, 1995. Ages 10–13. Measurement-related challenges requiring problem-solving skills.

Maurer, Richard. *Rocket! How a Toy Launched the Space Age.* Crown, 1995. Ages 11–14. Trials and errors of pioneers in modern rocketry.

Montgomery, Sy. *Quest for the Tree Kangaroo: An Expedition to the Cloud Forest of New Guinea.* Illustrated by Nic Bishop. Houghton, 2006. Ages 11–15. Another in the author's excellent series showing scientists at work.

———. *Search for the Golden Moon Bear: Science and Adventure in the Asian Tropics.* Houghton, 2004. Ages 11–18. Account of a scientific expedition to Southeast Asia in search of a mysterious golden bear.

———. *The Tarantula Scientist.* Photography by Nic Bishop. Houghton, 2004. Ages 11–14. Facts about tarantulas and the exciting life of one scientist.

Platt, Richard. *Forensics.* Houghton, 2005. Ages 12–16. What the forensic scientist does: evidence collection, DNA analysis, fingerprinting, and more.

Rubin, Susan Goldman. *There Goes the Neighborhood: Ten Buildings People Loved to Hate.* Holiday House, 2001. Ages 12–18. How "architectural eyesores become icons."

Severance, John. *Skyscrapers: How America Grew Up.* Holiday, 2000. Ages 11–14. A history of American skyscrapers and the technologies that enabled their construction.

Sullivan, George. *Built to Last: Building America's Amazing Bridges, Dams, Tunnels, and Skyscrapers.* Scholastic, 2005. Ages 11–16. Engineering and construction of major structures like the Golden Gate Bridge and Sears Tower described in text and illustrations.

Turner, Pamela S. *Gorilla Doctors: Saving Endangered Great Apes.* Houghton, 2005. Ages 11–14. Veterinarians' efforts to save mountain gorillas in Rwanda and Uganda exemplify scientific field work.

Walker, Sally M. *Fossil Fish Found Alive: Discovering the Coelacanth.* Carolrhoda, 2002. Ages 10–14. Behind-the-scenes look at oceanographers' research and discoveries.

———. *Secrets of a Civil War Submarine: Solving the Mysteries of the H. L. Hunley.* Carolrhoda, 2005. Ages 12–18. The archaeological process seen through the excavation of a Civil War submarine from Charleston Harbor.

SOCIAL SCIENCES

Human and Civil Rights Issues (e.g., Child Labor, Gangs, GLBTQs, Immigrants, the Poor)

Altman, Linda J. *Bioethics: Who Lives, Who Dies, and Who Decides?* Enslow, 2006. Ages 13–18. Such topics as assisted reproduction and abortion, allocation of medical resources, and end-of-life issues.

———. *Genocide: The Systematic Killing of People* (revised and expanded). Enslow, 2008. Ages 13–18. Historic and recent examples of genocide, causes, and ways to avert it in the future.

Bales, Kevin, and Rebecca Cornell. *Slavery Today.* Groundwood, 2008. Part of the Groundwork Guides Series. An overview of child slavery today and related social issues.

Bartoletti, Susan C. *Black Potatoes: The Story of the Great Irish Famine, 1845–1850.* Houghton, 2001. Ages 11–18. Impact of the famine on Ireland and the United States.

———. *Growing Up in Coal Country.* Houghton, 1996. Ages 11–14. Photoessay chronicling the harsh lives of young boys who worked as Pennsylvania coal miners prior to child labor laws.

———. *Kids on Strike.* Houghton, 1999. Ages 11–18. Roles of children and young adults in American labor strikes during the nineteenth and early twentieth centuries.

Bial, Raymond. *Tenement: Immigrant Life on the Lower East Side.* Houghton, 2002. Ages 11–18. Photoessay describing the gritty life in New York tenements from the early 1800s to 1930.

Daniels, Peggy. *Gangs.* Greenhaven, 2007. Ages 12–16. Fourteen essays addressing the problem with gangs, girls in gangs, immigrants in gangs, and gang intervention.

Freedman, Russell. *In Defense of Liberty: the Story of America's Bill of Rights.* Holiday, 2003. Ages 11–18. Discussion of the Constitution and civil liberties.

———. *Kids at Work: Lewis Hine and the Crusade against Child Labor.* Photos by Lewis Hine. Clarion, 1994. Ages 11–18. Child labor in America during the early 1900s.

Haynes, Charles C., Sam Chaltain, and Susan M. Glisson. *First Freedoms: A Documentary History of the First Amendment Rights in America.* Oxford, 2006. Ages 12–18. History, issues, and people pertinent to the developing notion of free speech.

Herumin, Wendy. *Child Labor Today: A Human Rights Issue.* Enslow, 2007. Ages 12–18. Part of the Issues in Focus Today Series. Current facts about and portraits of the 218,000,000 children forced to work in harsh conditions worldwide.

Hinojosa, Maria. *Crews: Gang Members Talk to Maria Hinojosa.* Photography by German Perez. Harcourt, 1995. Ages 14–18. Interviews with seven young Queens, New York, gang members.

Hopkinson, Deborah. *Shutting Out the Sky: Life in the Tenements of New York 1880–1924.* Scholastic, 2003. Ages 11–14. The lives of five immigrants living in New York City's tenements.

Kuklin, Susan. *No Choirboy: Murder, Violence, and Teenagers on Death Row.* Holt, 2008. Ages 15–18. A look at prisons, young prisoners, punishment, and the concept of justice in the United States.

Levithan, David, and Billy Merrill, editors. *The Full Spectrum: A New Generation of Writing about Gay, Lesbian, Bisexual, Transgender, Questioning, and Other Identities.* Knopf, 2006. **(COL)** Ages 13–17. Forty nonfiction pieces by writers under the age of 23.

MacDonald, Joan V. *Religion and Free Speech Today: A Pro/Con Debate.* Enslow, 2008. Ages 13–18. Opposing views about the place of religion in public life; the constitutional issues involved.

McWhorter, Diane. *A Dream of Freedom: The Civil Rights Movement from 1954 to 1968.* Scholastic, 2004. Ages 10–18. Heroism, idealism, and political turmoil surrounding the civil rights movement.

Nathan, Debbie. *Pornography.* Groundwood, 2007. Ages 14–18. Part of the Groundwork Guides Series. An overview of the social issues related to pornography and young people.

Nelson, Marilyn. *A Wreath for Emmett Till.* Illustrated by Philippe Lardy. Houghton, 2005. Ages 15–18. Poems chronicling the racially motivated lynching of black teenager Emmett Till in 1955.

Stokes, John A. with Lois Wolfe and Herman Viola. *Students on Strike: Jim Crow, Civil Rights, Brown, and Me.* National Geographic, 2008. Ages 11–16. First person account of the student strike in Virginia in 1951 that was part of the 1954 Brown decision.

War and History

Allen, Thomas B. *George Washington, Spymaster: How the Americans Outspied the British and Won the Revolutionary War.* National Geographic, 2004. Ages 11–14. The roles of intelligence and counterintelligence in the Revolutionary War.

Ambrose, Stephen E. *The Good Fight: How World War II Was Won.* Atheneum, 2001. Ages 11–14. Fact-filled photo survey of America's involvement in World War II.

Anderson, Dale, and Jane Bingham, Peter Chrisp, Christopher Gavett, Steven Maddocks, editors. *Exploring the Middle Ages.* Marshall Cavendish, 2005. Eleven-volume encyclopedia offering an international survey of global events that occurred between A.D. 500 and 1500.

Aronson, Marc. *The Real Revolution: The Global Story of American Independence.* Clarion, 2005. Ages 13–18. The global social, political, and economic underpinnings of this country's move to independence from Great Britain.

Balkin, Karen F., editor. *The War on Terrorism (Opposing Viewpoints).* Greenhaven, 2004. Ages 14–18. Twenty-eight authors take pro/con stances on various aspects of terrorism.

Frank, Mitch. *Understanding the Holy Land: Answering Questions about the Israeli–Palestinian Conflict.* Viking, 2005. Ages 12–18. Presenting the facts about the Israeli-Palestinian conflict using a question-and-answer format.

Freedman, Russell. *Children of the Great Depression.* Clarion, 2005. Ages 11–18. Photoessay about the causes of the economic disaster of the 1920s and 1930s and life during this time.

————. *Who Was First? Discovering the Americas.* Clarion, 2007. Ages 12–15. A look at various ideas about the discovery of the Americas.

Goodman, Joan Elizabeth. *A Long and Uncertain Journey: The 27,000-Mile Voyage of Vasco da Gama.* Illustrated by Tom McNeely. Mikaya/Firefly, 2001. **(PI)** Ages 11–14. The Portuguese explorer's epic journey of 1497–1499.

Greenfeld, Howard. *After the Holocaust.* Greenwillow, 2001. Ages 12–18. Post–World War II experiences of eight Jewish holocaust survivors (oral histories).

Hampton, Wilborn. *War in the Middle East: A Reporter's Story: Black September and the Yom Kippur War.* Candlewick, 2007. Ages 13–18. Issues and events of the 1970 Jordanian conflict and the 1973 Israeli conflict.

Hopkinson, Deborah. *Up Before Daybreak: Cotton and People in America.* Scholastic, 2006. Ages 9–14. How cotton production affected the lives of Americans from the Industrial Revolution to the 1950s.

Hoose, Phillip. *We Were There, Too! Young People in U.S. History.* Farrar, 2001. Ages 11–14. Contributions of dozens of young people who helped shape our nation.

Kaufman, Michael T. *1968.* Roaring Brook, 2009. Ages 14–18. Argument that the events of 1968 and their impact on people made this a watershed year.

Lewis, J. Patrick. *The Brothers' War: Civil War Voices in Verse.* National Geographic, 2007. Ages 12–18. Poems about those who fought in the American Civil War illustrated with historical photographs.

Murphy, Jim. *The Boys' War: Confederate and Union Soldiers Talk about the Civil War.* Clarion, 1990. Ages 11–18. Military roles of underage soldiers, often in their own words.

————. *A Young Patriot: The American Revolution as Experienced by One Boy.* Clarion, 1996. Ages 11–18. Based on the memoirs of Joseph Plumb Martin who enlisted in the Continental Army in 1776 at 15.

Oppenheim, Joanne. *Dear Miss Breed: True Stories of the Japanese American Incarceration during World War II and a Librarian Who Made a Difference.* Scholastic, 2006. Ages 12–16.

Philip, Neil. *The Great Circle: A History of the First Nations.* Clarion, 2006. Ages 11–15. An explanation of the historical relationship between Native Americans and white settlers.

Rogasky, Barbara. *Smoke and Ashes: The Story of the Holocaust* (expanded edition). Holiday, 2002. Ages 12–18. Nonfiction about anti-Semitism and hate groups from World War II to present.

Springer, Jane. *Genocide.* Groundwood, 2006. Ages 14–18. Part of the Groundwork Guides Series. A history of recent genocides and related political and social issues.

Cultural and Ethnic Diversity

Barber, Nicola. *Afghanistan.* Arcturus, 2008. Ages 10–14. Basic facts, history, recent social, political, economic, and environmental changes, and current issues of this country. See others in the Changing World Series.

Friedman, Lauri S. *Discrimination.* Greenhaven, 2007. Ages 12–16. Seventeen essays for reluctant readers with varying opinions about racial discrimination and profiling, ethnic team names, gay marriage, race-based humor, and affirmative action.

Gaskins, Pearl Fuyo, editor. *What Are You? Voices of Mixed-Race Young People.* Holt, 1999. Ages 13–18. Interviews, essays, and poetry by forty young adults relating their experiences growing up in the United States.

The Guinness Book of World Records. Guinness Media, Inc. Published annually. Ages 11–14. Annual update on human achievement.

Hill, Laban C. *Harlem Stomp! A Cultural History of the Harlem Renaissance.* Little, Brown, 2004. Ages 11–18. Early twentieth-century African-American migration north; 1920s Harlem.

Saddiqui, Haroon. *Being Muslim.* Groundwood, 2006. Ages 14–18. An exploration of current political, religious, and secular aspects of being Muslim. Part of the Groundwork Guides Series.

Sloan, Christopher. *Bury the Dead: Tombs, Corpses, Mummies, Skeletons and Rituals.* National Geographic, 2002. Ages 11–18. Funeral rites across time and culture.

Weaver, Janice. *From Head to Toe: Bound Feet, Bathing Suits, and Other Bizarre and Beautiful Things.* Illustrated by Francis Blake. Tundra, 2003. Ages 10–14. Cross-cultural exploration of fashion.

Williams, Julie. *Islam: Understanding the History, Beliefs, and Culture.* Enslow, 2008. Ages 13–18. History, questions, and current events relating to the fastest-growing religion in the world.

Money and Money Management

Denega, Danielle. *Smart Money: How to Manage Your Cash.* Franklin Watts, 2008. Ages 12–15. Overview of money management, including getting a job, budgeting, paying taxes, and investing.

Monteverde, Matt. *Frequently Asked Questions about Budgeting and Money Management.* Rosen, 2008. Ages 12–18. Facts, risky behaviors, and advice on personal finances. See others in the FAQ: Teen Life Series.

Shelley, Susan. *The Complete Idiot's Guide to Money for Teens.* Alpha, 2001. Ages 12–18. A guide to earning, budgeting, saving, investing, keeping track of, and spending money.

School-Related Issues

Daniels, Peggy. *Zero Tolerance Policies in Schools.* Greenhaven, 2008. Ages 12–16. Fourteen essays presenting the pros and cons of the effectiveness and fairness of zero tolerance policies, including their effect on schools, minorities, and students generally.

Francis, Barbara. *Other People's Words: What Plagiarism Is and How to Avoid It.* Enslow, 2005. Ages 12–18. Explanation for why plagiarism is wrong and how people can avoid it in their work.

Gordon, Sherrie M. *Downloading Copyrighted Stuff from the Internet: Stealing or Fair Use?* Enslow, 2006. Ages 12–18. How file-sharing works; what is fair and what is not.

Hamilton, Jill. *Bullying and Hazing.* Greenhaven, 2008. Ages 12–16. Fourteen essays presenting varying opinions about bullying, including female, Internet, and homophobic. Aimed at reluctant readers.

———. *Dress Codes in School.* Greenhaven, 2008. Ages 12–16. Eleven essays for reluctant readers on the pros and cons of dress codes, including dress codes for teachers.

———. *Electronic Devices in Schools.* Greenhaven, 2007. Ages 12–16. Sixteen essays for reluctant readers on the pros and cons of iPods, cell phones, camera phones, YouTube, laptops, and PDAs in schools.

Williams, Heidi. *Plagiarism.* Greenhaven, 2008. Ages 12–16. Twelve essays on the current status of plagiarism, its causes, the impact of the Internet, and policies that seek to prevent it.

Winkler, Kathleen. *Bullying: How to Deal with Taunting, Teasing, and Tormenting.* Enslow, 2005. Ages 12–18. What bullying is, why it happens, and what kids and communities can do to prevent it.

Sports

Blumenthal, Karen. *Let Me Play: The Story of Title IX: The Law that Changed the Future of Girls in America.* Atheneum, 2005. Ages 12–18. The legislation that gave girls and women equal access to physical education classes, gymnasiums, universities, and graduate schools.

Macy, Sue. *Swifter, Higher, Stronger: A Photographic History of the Summer Olympics.* National Geographic, 2004. Ages 11–18. Fascinating facts, history, controversies, and tragedies surrounding the games.

Nelson, Kadir. *We Are the Ship: The Story of Negro League Baseball.* Hyperion, 2008. **(PI)** Ages 11–15. History, challenges, personalities, and facts surrounding the days of the Negro League.

Willett, Edward. *Frequently Asked Questions about Exercise Addiction.* Rosen, 2008. Ages 12–18. Facts, risky behaviors, and advice for both genders.

Wiseman, Blaine. *Extreme Skateboarding.* Weigl, 2008. Ages 10–14. Overview of the sport, equipment, venues, and stand-out athletes. See others in the Extreme Series.

Zahensky, Barbara A. *Frequently Asked Questions About Athletes and Eating Disorders.* Rosen, 2008. Ages 12–18. Facts and advice concerning professional athletes as role models and students' trying to please coaches.

Jobs and Careers

Aksomitis, Linda. *Choosing a Career.* Greenhaven, 2008. Ages 12–16. Twelve essays for reluctant readers on various aspects of careers: planning, careers for the disabled, nontraditional careers, the military, internships and apprenticeships.

Blackwell, Amy H. *Personal Care Services, Fitness, and Education.* Ferguson, 2008. Ages 15–18. Twelve occupations that require a high school diploma only. See others in the Great Careers with a High School Diploma Series.

Camelo, Wilson. *The U.S. Airforce and Military Careers.* Ages 12–16. Enslow, 2006. Part of the Armed Forces and Military Careers Series. History and career information about the U.S. Air Force.

Ferguson Publications. *Careers in Focus* (53-volume series). Up-to-date information presented in sixteen to twenty-five articles profiling jobs within each field. Examples: *Film* (2006) covers nineteen jobs in this industry; *Automotives* (2009) covers nineteen careers for car enthusiasts; *Child Care* (2006) covers eighteen jobs in the field.

———. *Top Careers in Two Years* (11-volume series). Ages 15–18. Profiles of jobs requiring an associate's degree, comparable certification, or work/life experience.

———. *Top 100: The Fastest Growing Careers for the 21st Century.* Ferguson, 2000. Ages 15–18. Profiles of jobs likely to offer employment in the future, including requirements (education, tools, skills) and average salaries.

———. *25 Jobs That Have It All.* Ferguson, 2001. Ages 12–18. Profiles of the jobs that will pay the most, grow quickest, and hire the greatest number of people in the future, based on Department of Labor statistics.

Rosen Publishing. Careers and Opportunities Series; Career Resource Library Series; Careers in the New Economy Series; and Cool Careers without College Series. Ages 13–18.

HUMANITIES

Music and Making Music

Espejo, Roman. *Should Music Lyrics Be Censored for Violence and Exploitation?* Greenhaven, 2008. Ages 13–18. Twelve essays on the pros and cons of censorship, whether lyrics are harmful, whether there is violence in hip-hop and rap music, and whether advisory labeling is effective. Part of the At Issue Series.

Helsby, Genevieve. *Those Amazing Musical Instruments!* Sourcebooks, 2007. Ages 9–15. A guide to musical instruments.

Merino, Noel. *Rap Music.* Greenhaven, 2008. Ages 13–18. Fourteen essays presenting opposing viewpoints on the cultural and political impact of rap music, its effect on black women, and the claim that it promotes violence.

Film, Acting, and Making Films

Hamlett, Christina. *Screenwriting for Teens: The 100 Principles of Screenwriting Every Budding Writer Must Know.* Michael Wiese Productions, 2006. Ages 13–18. A guide to completing a first short film, including exercises, examples, and a recommended reading list.

Lanier, Troy, and Clay Nichols. *Filmmaking for Teens: Pulling Off Your Shorts.* Michael Wiese Productions, 2005. Ages 13–18. A guide to making one's first film.

Art, Including Book Illustration

Amara, Philip. *So, You Wanna Be a Comic Book Artist?* Beyond Words, 2001. Ages 10–14. A career guide to being a comic book artist.

Ancona, George. *Murals: Walls That Sing.* Marshall Cavendish, 2003. Ages 10–14. How wall paintings represent their communities.

Evans, Dilys. *Show and Tell: Exploring the Fine Art of Children's Book Illustration.* Chronicle, 2008. Ages 12–18. A behind-the-scenes look at how twelve children's book illustrators ply their craft.

McCloud, Scott. *Making Comics: Storytelling Secrets of Comics, Manga and Graphic Novels.* Harper, 2006. How to make drawings become a story and how cartooning choices communicate meaning to readers.

Sayre, Henry. *Cave Paintings to Picasso: The Inside Scoop on 50 Art Masterpieces.* Chronicle, 2004. Ages 11–14. Art history from 22,000 B.C. to 1964.

Dance

Fitzgerald, Tamsin. *Hip-Hop and Urban Dance.* Heinemann, 2008. Ages 11–14. Choreography, clothes, fashion, and culture of hip-hop.

Writing

Barry, Lynda. *What It Is.* Drawn & Quarterly, 2008. Ages 14–18. A lavish guide to writing and exploring one's creativity.

Bodden, Valerie. *Creating the Character: Dialogue and Characterization.* Creative Education, 2008.

Ages 12–18. Advice, exercises, and examples from classic and contemporary works. See also in this series *Painting the Picture: Imagery and Description; Setting the Style: Wording and Tone; Telling the Tale: Narration and Point of View* (all 2008).

Marcus, Leonard S., editor. *The Wand in the Word: Conversations with Writers of Fantasy.* Candlewick, 2006. Ages 12–18. Interviews with thirteen writers of fantasy for young people.

Wolf, Allan. *Immersed in Verse: An Informative, Slightly Irreverent and Totally Tremendous Guide to Living the Poet's Life.* Illustrated by Tuesday Mourning. Lark Books, 2006. Ages 12–14.

RELATED FILMS, VIDEOS, AND DVDS

Note: **MS** *refers to Middle School;* **HS** *refers to high school.*

Anne Frank: The Whole Story (2001). Author: Anne Frank, *Anne Frank: The Diary of a Young Girl* (1952). 189 minutes. MS, HS

Castle (2002); *Cathedral* (1987); *Pyramid* (2000); *Roman City* (1991). Author: David Macaulay. 60 minutes each. MS

Fast Food Nation (2006). Author: Eric Schlosser, *Fast Food Nation: The Dark Side of the All-American Meal* (2001). 116 minutes. MS, HS

Malcolm X (1992). Author: Malcolm X, *The Autobiography of Malcolm X* (1965). 202 minutes. HS

October Sky (1999). Author: Homer H. Hickman, *Rocket Boys: A Memoir* (1998). 108 minutes. MS, HS

Persepolis (2007). Author: Marjane Satrapi, *Persepolis: The Story of a Childhood* (2003). 96 minutes. HS

SOURCES FOR FILMS, VIDEOS, AND DVDS

The Video Source Book. Syosset, NY: National Video Clearinghouse, 1979–. Published by Gale Research, Detroit, MI. An annual reference work that lists media and provides sources for purchase and rental.

Websites of large video distributors

www.libraryvideo.com
www.knowledgeunlimited.com

chapter SEVEN

POETRY

Poetry is an enjoyable literary form for all ages. Poems that relate to any and every subject, event, mood, and emotion can be found and shared throughout the school day, providing a flash of humor or a new perspective on a topic. We hope you will read and reread favorite poems to your students each day and also encourage them to read and write poetry.

Throughout the secondary school years, poetry can be shared orally during the school day. The poetry section of your school library media center is worth perusing for interesting poetry books to use in your classroom. Although more poetry for young people is being written and published and many teachers and their students are enjoying this genre of literature, some teachers report that they do not share poetry because of their uncertainty about poetry and how to share it. By learning more about poetry and some of the best-loved and most respected poets, a teacher can become more skillful at selecting and presenting good and enjoyable poems for students.

DEFINITION AND DESCRIPTION

Poetry is the concentrated expression of ideas and feelings through precise and imaginative words selected for their sonorous and rhythmic effects. Originally, poetry was oral; minstrels once traversed the countryside, reciting poetry and singing songs to listeners of all ages. The musicality of poetry makes it especially suitable for teachers and students to read aloud and, at times, to put to music.

Students often believe that rhyme is an essential ingredient of poetry; yet some types of poetry do not rhyme. What, then, distinguishes poetry from prose? The concentration of thought and feeling expressed in succinct, exact, and beautiful language, and an underlying pulse or rhythm are the traits that most strongly set poetry apart from prose.

Not all rhyming, rhythmical language merits the label of poetry. *Verse* is a language form in which simple thoughts or stories are told in rhyme with a distinct beat or meter. Mother Goose and nursery rhymes are good examples of well-known, simple verses. And of course, we are all too aware of the *jingle,* a catchy repetition of sounds heard so often in commercials. The lyrics of many popular songs also are examples of verse. The most important features of verses and jingles are their strong rhyme and rhythm with frequent word repetition. Content is light or even silly. Although verses and jingles can be enjoyable and have a place in the classroom, poetry can enrich students' lives by giving them new insights and fresh views on life's experiences and by eliciting strong emotional responses.

Novels in verse for young adults are appearing with greater frequency and represent another instance of the blending of genres. Novels in verse are not dicussed in this chapter but in the appropriate genre chapters according to the nature of the story. The annotations indicate the form used, such as free verse. Some noteworthy examples of such novels are Virginia Euwer Wolff's *True Believer,* Ron Koertge's *Shakespeare Bats Cleanup* and *The Brimstone Journals,* and Walter Dean Myers' *Street Love.*

TYPES OF POETRY BOOKS

A wide variety of poetry books is available today for students and teachers. Selecting books of poetry for use in the classroom as bridges between classroom activities, as materials for reading, and as literature for enjoyment will require teachers to review and evaluate the many types of poetry books, from anthologies and books of poems on special topics and by favorite poets to single illustrated poems in picture book formats.

Anthologies of Poetry

A large, comprehensive *anthology* of poetry is a useful tool in the classroom. The better anthologies are organized by subjects for easy retrieval of poems appropriate for almost any occasion. In addition, indexes of poets and titles, or first lines, are usually provided in these books. Works by both contemporary and traditional poets that appeal to a wide age range and use many poetic forms can be found in most anthologies. An example is *The Invisible Ladder: An Anthology of Contemporary American Poems for Young Readers,* edited by Liz Rosenberg.

Poetry collections should be judged on the quality of the poetry choices. If you decide that the poetry is well selected, consider the illustrations and the appearance of the book. The beauty of illustrations is secondary to the quality of the poems.

Poetry Books by a Single Poet

Types of books

A collection of poems by one poet may include the complete works or may focus on poems on a particular topic. *Poetry books by a single poet* can be enjoyable for students who are beginning to understand and appreciate the works of a particular poet. Mel Glenn's *Class Dismissed! High School Poems,* with photographs by Michael J. Bernstein, has been a favorite of many young adults. Sara Holbrook's poetry books, including *By Definition: Poems of Feelings* and *I Never Said I Wasn't Difficult,* also address the concerns and feelings of young adults. Adolescents who are identifying favorite poets particularly appreciate poetry books of this kind.

Thematic Poetry Books

Thematic poetry books feature poems on one topic, for one age group, or of one poetic form. These specialized collections become important materials for teachers and young people who come to love certain kinds of poetry. Beautifully illustrated thematic collections are available and seem to be especially enjoyed by some students for independent reading. An example is *I Feel a Little Jumpy around You: A Book of Her Poems and His Poems Collected in Pairs,* selected collaboratively by Naomi Shihab Nye and Paul B. Janeczko.

Single Illustrated Poetry Books

Single illustrated poems of medium length are now being presented frequently in picture book formats. The poems are usually narrative in nature. These editions make poetry more appealing and accessible to many students, but in some cases the illustrations may remove the opportunity for students to form their own mental images from the language created by poets. A publication of Ernest L. Thayer's *Casey at the Bat: A Ballad of the Republic Sung in the Year 1888* is illustrated by C. F. Payne in mixed-media paintings in a humorous, exaggerated style.

ELEMENTS OF POETRY

Just as with a work of fiction, the elements of a poem should be considered if the reader is to understand and evaluate the poem. Each of these parts—meaning, rhythm, sound patterns, figurative language, and sense imagery—is treated in the following discussion.

- *Meaning.* Meaning is the underlying idea, feeling, or mood expressed through the poem. As with other literary forms, poetry is a form of communication; it is the way a particular writer chooses to express emotions and thoughts. Thus the meaning of the poem is the expressed or implied message the poet conveys.

- *Rhythm.* Rhythm is the beat or regular cadence of the poem. Poetry, a form of literature meant to be read aloud and heard, relies on rhythm to help communicate meaning. A fast rhythm is effected through short lines, clipped syllables, sharp, high vowel sounds, such as the sounds represented by *a, e,* and *i,* and abrupt consonant sounds, such as the sounds represented by *k, t,* and *p.* A fast rhythm can provide the listener with a feeling of happiness, excitement, drama, or even tension and suspense. A slow rhythm is effected by longer lines, multisyllabic words, full or low vowel sounds such as the sounds represented by *o, oo,* and *u,* and resonating consonant sounds such as represented by *m, n,* and *l.* A slow rhythm can evoke languor, tranquillity, inevitability, and harmony, among other feelings. A change in rhythm during a poem signals the listener to a change in meaning.

- *Sound patterns.* Sound patterns are made by repeated sounds and combinations of sounds in the words. Words, phrases, or lines are sometimes repeated in their entirety. Also, parts of words may be repeated, as with rhyme, the most recognized sound device. *Rhyme* occurs when the ends of words (the last vowel sound and any consonant sound that may follow) have the same sounds. Examples of rhyming words are *vat, rat, that, brat,* and *flat,* as well as *hay, they, flay, stray,* and *obey. Assonance* is another pattern poets use for effect. The same vowel sound is heard repeatedly within a line or a few lines of poetry, as exemplified in the words *hoop, gloom, moon, moot,* and *boots. Alliteration* is a pattern in which initial consonant sounds are heard frequently within a few lines of poetry—for example, *ship, shy,* and *shape. Consonance* is similar to alliteration but usually refers to a close juxtaposition of similar final consonant sounds, as in *flake, chuck,* and *stroke. Onomatopoeia* is the use of words that imitate real-world sounds. Examples are *buzz* for the sound of a bee and *hiss* for snakes.

- *Figurative language.* Figurative language, which can take many different forms, involves comparing or contrasting one object, idea, or feeling with another one. A *simile* is a direct comparison, typically using *like* or *as* to point out the similarities. For example, "The house was *like* a fortress." A *metaphor* is an implied comparison without a signal word to evoke the similarities. For example, "The house was a fortress." *Personification* is the attribution of human qualities to animate nonhuman beings or to inanimate objects for the purpose of drawing a comparison between the animal or object and human beings, as in "The *house glared* down haughtily at passersby." *Hyperbole* is an exaggeration to highlight reality or to point out ridiculousness. Middle schoolers especially enjoy hyperbole because it appeals to their strong sense of the absurd. An example of hyperbole can be seen in "The house, painted a blinding shade of red, fairly vibrated."

- *Sense imagery.* Poets play on one or more of the five senses in descriptive and narrative language. *Sight* may be awakened through the depiction of beauty; *hearing* may be evoked by the sounds of a city street; *smell* and *taste* may be recalled through the description of a fish left too long in the sun; and finally, *touch* can be sensitized through describing the gritty discomfort of a wet swimsuit caked with sand from the beach. After listening to a poem, students can be asked to think about which of the senses the poet is appealing to.

These elements of poetry may be used by teachers as criteria for selecting poems and grouping them for presentation. However, teaching each of these elements as separate items to be memorized and used to analyze poems has caused many students to dislike poetry. To help your students come to appreciate poetry, it is far better for you to be enthusiastic, select wisely, read aloud well, and provide your students with many opportunities to read and enjoy it.

EVALUATION AND SELECTION OF POETRY

The criteria to keep in mind when evaluating a poem for use with students are as follows:

- The ideas and feelings expressed are worthy, fresh, and imaginative.
- The expression of the ideas and feelings is unique and likely to cause the reader to perceive ordinary things in new ways.
- The poem is appropriate to the experiences and age of the students and does not preach to them or pander to their baser instincts.
- The poem presents the world through a young person's perspective and focuses on young people's lives and activities or on activities to which people of all ages can relate.

Since students in intermediate and middle grades report a preference for narrative poems (Kutiper, 1985; Abrahamson, 2002), including narrative poems among those you select to share with students is advisable. Although certain poets may be favored by your students, they will likely enjoy the poetry of many other writers if exposed to them. Be sure to share with your students poems by a variety of authors.

The findings from a survey of poetry preferences of students in grades 4 to 6 (Terry, 1974) can be helpful to teachers in selecting poems for a new group of students at the middle school level. In this study students preferred narrative poems over lyric poems. In fact, limericks were the favored poetic form in this study. Free verse and haiku were not well liked. Students preferred poems that had pronounced sound patterns of all kinds, but especially enjoyed poems that rhymed. Rhythm was also an important element to these students; they preferred poems with regular, distinctive beats. Imagery and figurative language were not as well received; students reported that they did not always understand poems with considerable figurative language. In this same study students reported a preference for the realistic content of humorous poems, poems about animals, and poems about enjoyable familiar experiences. A study of poetry preferences of students in grades 7 to 9 (Kutiper, 1985) found similar preferences to those of the younger students. In Kutiper's study, poems by Shel Silverstein and Jack Prelutsky were found to be highly popular and were among those rated most highly.

Abrahamson's (2002) review of earlier studies of poetry preferences of young adults had similar results. Students in grades 7 to 12 liked narrative poems, humorous poems, and the elements of rhythm and rhyme in poetry. Older students preferred more subtle humor, and figurative language was less appreciated by younger students in that it interfered with their understanding. In reviewing Kutiper's 1985 study, Abrahamson also pointed out that the mode of poetry presentation, whether listening to it read aloud, listening to it read aloud while reading it, or reading it only, made a difference to students. In the majority of the poems other than the most popular ones (where presentation did not matter), the students who listened to the poems while reading them at the same time usually gave the poems the lowest ratings, suggesting that this format may not be the best way to share poetry in the classroom. Students especially enjoyed short rhyming poems read aloud and preferred that serious poems or poems without rhyme or obvious rhythm be experienced through reading them silently.

A study by Kutiper and Wilson (1993) was conducted to determine whether an examination of school library circulation records in elementary and middle schools would confirm the findings of the earlier poetry preference studies. The findings indicated that the humorous contemporary poetry of Shel Silverstein and Jack Prelutsky dominated the students' choices. Collections of poetry by poetry award winners did not circulate widely, nor were they widely available in the school libraries studied, even though these poets reflect a higher quality of language and usage than in the light verse so popular with students.

Kutiper and Wilson state that real interest in poetry must go beyond Prelutsky and Silverstein. This interest needs to be developed by teachers who provide an array of poetry that builds on students' natural interests. A good selection of rhyming narrative poems with distinct rhythms about humorous events and well-liked familiar experiences is a good starting point for students who have little experience with poetry.

Students' appreciation of poetry can be broadened and deepened by a good teacher. Poetry collections should include a balance of poems and anthologies that reflect both females and males as complex human beings and avoid gender-biased stereotypes. In studying the portrayals of gender in young adult poetry, Johnson and McClanahan, with Mertz (1999), read approximately twenty volumes of poetry for young adults and discussed gender representation in five of the collections they viewed as rich. They recommend open and honest discussions of the portrayals of gender in poetry in an environment that is safe and where alternative views can be presented.

In selecting poems to read to students, the list of notable poets and the list of poets who have won the National Council of Teachers of English Excellence in Poetry for Children Award are good starting points. The NCTE Award was established in 1977 in the United States to honor living U.S. poets whose poetry has contributed substantially to the lives of young people.

NCTE EXCELLENCE IN POETRY FOR CHILDREN AWARD WINNERS

1977	David McCord	1991	Valerie Worth
1978	Aileen Fisher	1994	Barbara Juster Esbensen
1979	Karla Kuskin	1997	Eloise Greenfield
1980	Myra Cohn Livingston	2000	X. J. Kennedy
1981	Eve Merriam	2003	Mary Ann Hoberman
1982	John Ciardi	2006	Nikki Grimes
1985	Lilian Moore	2009	Lee Bennett Hopkins
1988	Arnold Adoff		

This award, now given every three years, is for a poet's entire body of writing for children ages 3 through 13. Although the age range does not cover the entire young adult period, most of these poets have some poetry that is age appropriate for young adults.

A reference book, *Young Adult Poetry: A Survey and Theme Guide* (Schwedt & DeLong, 2002) is a useful tool for students and teachers in middle school and high school for locating poems to support the curriculum and to address student interests. This bibliography annotates 198 poetry books and identifies themes in more than 6,000 poems.

OETRY TYPES AND FORMS

Poetry can be classified in many ways; one way is to consider two main types that generally differ in purpose: lyric and narrative poetry. *Lyric poetry* captures a moment, a feeling, or a scene, and is descriptive in nature, whereas *narrative poetry* tells a story or includes a sequence of events. From this definition, you will recognize the following selection to be a lyric poem.

THE LEOPARD OF LONELINESS

Loneliness, the leopard,
Stalks the heart;
He captures his prey
And tears it apart.

When he is through,
He goes for the bone;
When he is full,
He leaves you—alone.

— CHARLES GHIGNA

Lyric

NOTABLE *Authors of Poetry*

Paul Fleischman, poet noted for his collections of poems composed and printed for two or more readers to read in unison and solo. *Big Talk: Poems for Four Voices; Joyful Noise: Poems for Two Voices.* www.paulfleischman.net

Nikki Giovanni, a poet known for her free verse about African Americans. *Ego-Tripping and Other Poems for Young People; The Selected Poems of Nikki Giovanni; Quilting the Black-Eyed Pea.* www.nikki-giovanni.com

Mel Glenn, a poet whose poems embody the speech of young adults from diverse backgrounds; many narrative poems are included in his body of work. *Class Dismissed! High School Poems; Foreign Exchange: A Mystery in Poems; Jump Ball: A Basketball Season in Poems; Split Image: A Story in Poems; Who Killed Mr. Chippendale? A Mystery in Poems.* www.melglenn.com

Sara Holbrook, known as a poet and a performer of poetry that appeals to adolescents. *By Definition: Poems of Feelings; I Never Said I Wasn't Difficult; Walking on the Boundaries of Change: Poems of Transition.* www.saraholbrook.com

Paul B. Janeczko, a poet and anthologist known for his many collections of poems that appeal to young adults. *Postcard Poems; Pocket Poems: Selected for a Journey; That Sweet Diamond: Baseball Poems; Worlds Afire; A Poke in the I; Stone Bench in an Empty Park.* www.paulb janeczko.com

J. Patrick Lewis, a poet recognized for his poems illuminating history: *The Brothers' War: Civil War Voices in Verse; A Celebration of Outstanding Women; Monumental Verses.* Also, collaborated with Paul B. Janeczko: *Birds on a Wire.* www.jpatricklewis.com

Naomi Shihab Nye, a Palestinian-American poet and anthologist whose meditative poems offer global perspectives and whose edited collections include Mexican, Native American, and Middle Eastern poetry. *Come with Me: Poems for a Journey; This Same Sky: A Collection of Poems from around the World.*

Liz Rosenberg, poet and anthologist of poetry collections for young adults who includes poems by adult poets in her collections. *Earth-Shattering Poems; Light-Gathering Poems; Roots and Flowers: Poets and Poems on Family; The Invisible Ladder: An Anthology of Contemporary American Poems for Young Readers.*

Joyce Sidman, a poet especially known for vivid poems that explore ecosystems and provide science information. *Butterfly Eyes and Other Secrets of the Meadow; Song of the Water Boatman and Other Pond Poems.* www.joycesidman.com

Gary Soto, a writer whose poetry captures the experiences of growing up in a Mexican neighborhood in California's Central Valley. *A Fire in My Hands; Neighborhood Odes; Worlds Apart: Traveling with Fernie and Me.* www.garysoto.com

The next selection is an example of a narrative poem.

EVOLUTION

*TV came
out of radio,
free verse
came out of rhyme.
I am
coming out of middle school,
changing all the time.
It's time
to lose the water wings,
crawl out of this lagoon.
I want to stand upright.
Get on my feet.
I want it soon.*

— SARA HOLBROOK

Narrative

Poetry can also be categorized by its *poetic form,* which refers to the way the poem is structured or put together. *Couplets, tercets, quatrains,* and *cinquains* refer to the number (two, three, four, and five) of lines in a stanza—a set of lines of poetry grouped together. Couplets, tercets, quatrains, and cinquains usually rhyme, though the rhyme schemes may vary; these poetic forms may constitute an entire poem, or a poem may comprise a few stanzas of couplets, tercets, and so on.

Other specific forms frequently found in poetry for young adults are limericks, ballads, haiku, free verse, and concrete poetry. Two recent collections of poetry, *Poems from Homeroom: A Writer's Place to Start* by Kathi Appelt and *A Kick in the Head* edited by Paul B. Janeczko, feature poems written in many different poetic forms. These collections may be of interest to teachers who wish to encourage students to think about form and how best to express their emotions and thoughts in poetry.

A *limerick* is a humorous one-stanza, five-line verse form (usually narrative), in which lines 1, 2, and 5 rhyme and are of the same length and lines 3 and 4 rhyme and are of the same length but shorter than the other lines. The following example is a limerick by Edward Lear, the poet who popularized this poetic form in the nineteenth century.

A YOUNG LADY OF NORWAY

*There was a Young Lady of Norway
Who casually sat in a doorway;
    When the door squeezed her flat,
    She exclaimed, "What of that?"
This courageous Young Lady of Norway.*

— EDWARD LEAR

limerick

A *sonnet* is a fourteen-line poem in two stanzas, an octave and a sestet, or sometimes printed in a single fourteen-line stanza. Sonnets generally rhyme, though the rhyme schemes may vary. A clear break in emotion or thought occurs between the two stanzas or after the middle of the sonnet. Sonnets are often poems of argument or persuasion intended to convince, whether about politics, religion, or love. Sonnets are often thought of as poems of love, and many love sonnets have been written. In the following poem by Christina Rossetti the speaker asks to be remembered.

SONNET

Remember me when I am gone away,
*   Gone far away into the silent land;*
*   When you can no more hold me by the hand,*
Nor I half turn to go yet turning stay.
Remember me when no more day by day
*   You tell me of our future that you planned:*
*   Only remember me; you understand*
It will be late to counsel then or pray.

Yet if you should forget me for a while
*   And afterwards remember, do not grieve;*
*   For if the darkness and corruption leave*
*   A vestige of the thoughts that once I had,*
Better by far that you should forget and smile
*   Than that you should remember and be sad.*

— CHRISTINA ROSSETTI

A *ballad* is a fairly long narrative poem of popular origin, usually adapted to singing. These traditional story poems are often romantic or heroic. "The Outlandish Knight," a thirteen-stanza ballad, tells the tale of the clever young woman who tricks the man who deceived her.

THE OUTLANDISH KNIGHT

An outlandish knight came out of the North,
*   To woo a maiden fair,*
He promised to take her to the North lands,
*   Her father's only heir.*

"Come, fetch me some of your father's gold
*   And some of your mother's fee;*
And two of the best nags out of the stable,
*   Where they stand thirty and three."*

She fetched him some of her father's gold
*   And some of her mother's fee;*
And two of the best nags out of the stable,
*   Where they stood thirty and three.*

He mounted her on her milk-white steed,
*   He on the dapple grey;*
They rode till they came unto the sea-side,
*   Three hours before it was day.*

"Light off, light off thy milk-white steed,
  And deliver it unto me;
Six pretty maids have I drowned here,
  And thou the seventh shall be."

"Pull off, pull off thy silken gown,
  And deliver it unto me;
Methinks it looks too rich and too gay
  To rot in the salt sea."

"Pull off, pull off thy silken stays,
  And deliver them unto me;
Methinks they are too fine and gay
  To rot in the salt sea."

"Pull off, pull off the Holland smock
  And deliver it unto me;
Methinks it looks too rich and gay
  To rot in the salt sea."

"If I must pull off my Holland smock,
  Pray turn thy back unto me,
For it is not fitting that such a ruffian
  A woman unclad should see."

He turned his back towards her,
  And viewed the leaves so green;
She catch'd him round the middle so small,
  And tumbled him into the stream.

He dropped high, and he dropped low,
  Until he came to the tide—
"Catch hold of my hand, my pretty maiden,
  And I will make you my bride."

"Lie there, lie there, you false-hearted man,
  Lie there instead of me;
Six pretty maidens have you drowned here,
  And the seventh has drowned thee."

She mounted on her milk-white steed,
  And led the dapple grey;
She rode till she came to her father's hall,
  Three hours before it was day.

— TRADITIONAL

  Haiku is a lyric unrhymed poem of Japanese origin with seventeen syllables, usually arranged in three lines with a syllable count of five, seven, and five. Haiku is highly evocative poetry that frequently espouses harmony with and appreciation of nature. Here is an example.

Haiku

*from the tar papered
    tenement roof, pigeons
        hot-foot it into flight.*
— A N I T A   W I N T Z

5
7
5

There are two lesser-known verse forms similar to haiku. *Renga* is a Japanese verse form in which poets alternate turns playing off the previous verse, usually beginning with three lines, followed by two lines in response to start a poetic chain. Examples can be found in *Birds on a Wire,* or, *A Jewel Tray of Stars,* by Paul B. Janeczko and J. Patrick Lewis. *Sijo* is an ancient Korean poetic form with three lines, each fourteen to sixteen syllables, not focused solely on nature, and often with a surprise ending. Examples are found in Linda Sue Park's *Tap Dancing on the Roof: Sijo.*

Free verse is unrhymed poetry with little or light rhythm. Sometimes words within a line will rhyme. The subjects of free verse are often abstract and philosophical; they are always reflective.

Free Verse

E V E N   W H E N
*I close my eyes
    the light that was
        you
            burns
                against my lids.*
— C H R I S T I N E   H E M P

Concrete poetry is written and printed in a shape that signifies the subject of the poem. Concrete poems are a form that must be seen to be fully appreciated. These poems do not usually have rhyme or definite rhythm; they rely mostly on the words, their meanings and shapes, and the way the words are arranged on the page to evoke images. In "A Weak Poem" the positioning of the words helps convey the meaning and the humor.

Concrete

A   W E A K   P O E M
(to be read lying down)

Oh dear, this poem is very weak

It can hardly stand up straight

Which comes from eating junk food

And going to bed too late.

— R O G E R   M c G O U G H

POETRY IN THE CLASSROOM

Poetry is enjoyable and enhances students' literacy development. Teachers and librarians can entice students into a lifelong love for poetry by making available a well-balanced collection of poetry books and by providing many positive experiences with poetry.

Students Listening to and Saying Poems

Experience

Teachers and librarians can begin by providing students with many opportunities to hear and say poems. Later, when students have developed a love of poetry and an affinity for the language play in poems, they can read poetry by fine poets and poems by their classmates and then begin to write poems themselves. In other words, poetry needs to be shared in both oral and written forms.

Poetry should be shared with students often by reading it aloud. As discussed earlier, poetry was originally an oral form of literature; it still relies heavily on the auditory perceptions of listeners. Moreover, oral language is the basis of literacy. These two facts combine nicely to make listening to poetry and saying poems a natural introduction to poetry.

Reading Poetry Aloud to Students

Experience

Poetry should be read aloud to students often. Brief, positive encounters with one or two poems at a time are best. Too many poems in one sitting may overwhelm students or make the reading tedious. The following points will help you read poetry well.

- Introduce the poem to the class before reading it aloud, either by tying the poem in with something else or by briefly telling why you have chosen to read this poem aloud. Then state the title of the poem and begin to read. After reading the poem, be sure to announce the name of the poet so that students discover the writers they especially enjoy.

- Poetry should be read for its meaning. Read aloud a poem just as you read aloud prose. Avoid unnatural intonations and follow the punctuation clues. Often, poetry is phrased in such a way that you must continue past the end of the line to the next before pausing. In other words, the breaks must be determined by the meaning units of the poem, not by the lines.

- A corollary of the preceding rule is that a reader should not force or overemphasize the beat of the poem, which can result in an annoying singsong effect. The natural rhythm of the poem will be felt in a more interesting way if you read naturally and let the poetic language provide the rhythm.

- Poetry should be enunciated clearly. Each sound and each syllable of a poem must be heard to be appreciated. Therefore, you will often need to slow down your normal reading pace to give full value to each sound.

- Poetry needs to be performed and dramatized. Take some chances and try out different effects (using different voices, elongating words, singing, shouting, whispering, pausing dramatically, and so on) as you read poems aloud. Your voice is a powerful tool: You may change it from louder to softer to only a whisper; you may start at a deep, low pitch and rise to a medium and eventually high pitch; you may speak very quickly in a clipped fashion and then slow down and drawl out the words. Holbrook's *Wham! It's a Poetry Jam: Discovering Performance Poetry* (2002) offers good suggestions for performing poetry and even for running a poetry contest.

- Some poems may need to be read aloud a number of times before their many meanings are perceived. In addition, people just enjoy hearing their favorite poems again and again.

- Consider recording audios of poems and making them available along with the poem in print for students to listen to and read. Individual students may enjoy recording a favorite poem for other students' listening. Commercially made CDs with popular poets reading their works, accompanied by music, are available and quite popular. Live recordings are also available online. Some teachers have asked school volunteers who are good readers to peruse a poetry anthology, select a favorite poem, and then read the poem on audio for use by individual students.

- After reading a poem aloud, some form of response is occasionally enjoyed. Sometimes the response students have to a poem is simply the desire to hear it again. Other times, students need just a few moments to reflect silently on the poem. Some poems warrant discussion, and students can take the opportunity to tell how the poem made them feel or what it made them think about.

Choral Poetry

A time-honored technique for saying and hearing poems over and over again, *choral poetry* consists of interpreting and saying a poem together as a group. Students may practice and recite a poem aloud from memory or rehearse and read it aloud. Students enjoy this way of experiencing poetry because they can participate within the safety of a group. The following sections explain how to select choral poems and teach them to students.

1. Selection
At first, select short poems (from one to four stanzas) until your students develop some skill with choral reading. Poems that work best as choral readings generally have straightforward meaning and are upbeat and humorous. Poems that contain dialogue or that are composed of couplets and have relatively short lines readily lend themselves to choral arrangements. Later, you will want to experiment with longer, more complex poems.

2. Rehearsal
For most choral presentations, the first step is for the teacher to read aloud the selected poem, phrasing it as it should be read. Then each line or pair of lines is said by the teacher and repeated by the students until they know them. It is preferable for the students to repeat the lines after the teacher and for the teacher to avoid reciting with the class, so that the students will speak without waiting for the teacher's voice. Once the entire poem is learned in this way, variations can be added for performing the poem.

3. Arrangements
Options for reading a poem chorally include unison, two or three parts, solo voices, cumulative buildup, and simultaneous voices.

- In unison choral speaking, the students learn the poem and recite it together as a group.
- Two-part or three-part choral poetry is usually based on arranging students into voice types (for example, high, medium, and low) to achieve different effects and by selecting lines of the poem for each group to recite or read.

- Solo voices can be added to either of these presentations and are sometimes used for asking a question or making an exclamation.
- Some poems lend themselves to cumulative buildup presentations, in which, for example, only two voices say the first line, then two more join in on the second, and then two more, gradually building to a crescendo until the entire class says the last line or stanza.
- Poetry collections arranged for dramatic choral readings can be found. Paul Fleischman's *Joyful Noise: Poems for Two Voices; I Am Phoenix: Poems for Two Voices;* and *Big Talk: Poems for Four Voices* are well-known examples. These poems are written in a manner that is already suitable for choral reading. Pairs or groups of four students can each take a different poem from one of these collections for presentation.

Many other variations can be developed for use in choral presentations. As soon as young people learn that poems do not have to be read sedately through exactly as written, they will begin to find excitement and deeper meaning in poetry and quickly become adept at arranging poems inventively.

4. *Performance*

Incorporating action, gestures, body movements, and facial expressions can produce more interesting presentations. Allowing various interpretations of the same poem is an excellent way to encourage more original and insightful interpretations. Students truly enjoy this nonthreatening way of sharing poetry. Occasionally performing a well-honed choral poem for an audience can bring pride to students. The class next door, the principal, another teacher, the librarian, the custodian, or a visiting parent make good audiences.

In addition to performing choral poetry, teachers can encourage individual students to voluntarily learn a poem by heart and then recite the poem in a small group or as part of a group performance, perhaps around a theme. For example, a small group of interested students might each select a poem about space as part of their study about space in science. Douglas Florian's collection of space poems, *Comets, Stars, the Moon, and Mars: Space Poems and Paintings,* could be a resource for this activity.

Students Reading Poems

Experience

Students can enjoy reading poetry both silently and aloud to others, especially serious poems (Abrahamson, 2002). Teachers should have available one or two comprehensive poetry anthologies for students to browse through for general purposes. In addition, some specialized collections by a single poet, such as *A Fury of Motion: Poems for Boys* by Charles Ghigna, and another two or three books of poems on a single topic, such as *Revenge and Forgiveness: An Anthology of Poems,* selected by Patrice Vecchione, are needed as well. Bringing in new poetry books occasionally over the course of the school year will spark renewed interest in reading poetry. Students can also be encouraged to make copies of their favorite poems from various collections to develop personal, individual anthologies. Many students choose to illustrate these and arrange the poems in new and inventive ways. The following strategies have also been proven to encourage students to read poetry.

- Place students in pairs to take turns reading favorite poems to one another. Make videos or audios of these readings and permit students to listen to or watch their own and other students' readings.

Teachers have found that when students listen to their own reading of poetry, they begin to note singsong readings and learn to avoid them.

- Place students in pairs with two or three books of poems for each pair. Provide fifteen to twenty minutes for students to read the poems in the books and then select one to read aloud to the class. During the reading time the teacher circulates and encourages and assists students in preparing to read poems aloud.

- Ask each student to select three poems by one poet and find something out about the poet; then place students in small groups of five or six to tell briefly about the poet and read the three poems aloud. Janeczko's *The Place My Words Are Looking For: What Poets Say about and through Their Work* (1990) is an excellent resource for this purpose. The author's comments on the work of more than forty poets and examples of their poetry can assist students in this activity.

- Have students find three poems on the same topic, such as hurt feelings, independence, popularity, or friendship, and then read them aloud in pairs or small groups.

- Students may also find poems that are of the same poetic form—cinquains, limericks, and so forth; or poems that exhibit similar poetic elements—rhyme, alliteration, or onomatopoeia; or poems that have fast or slow rhythms. These poems can then be read aloud and compared over a day or week.

Students Writing Poems

A rich poetry environment stimulates young people's interest in writing their own poems. A book about teaching poetry, *Just People and Other Poems for Young Readers and Paper/Pen/Poem: A Writer's Way to Begin* (Appelt, 1997), may be a natural starting place for helping students to think about poetry and writing poetry. Other books that provide suggestions on how to include poetry in the classroom are *Wordplaygrounds: Reading, Writing, and Performing Poetry in the English Classroom* (O'Connor, 2004); *Give Them Poetry! A Guide for Sharing Poetry with Children K–8* (Sloan, 2003); *Poems Please! Sharing Poetry with Children* (Booth & Moore, 2003); *Awakening the Heart: Exploring Poetry in Elementary and Middle School* (Heard, 1999); and *Opening a Door: Reading Poetry in the Middle School Classroom* (Janeczko, 2003).

Teachers often start poetry writing as a collaborative effort. The class brainstorms for ideas, then composes the poem orally as the teacher writes it on the board, on a chart, or on an overhead transparency. As students become comfortable with writing group poetry, they can branch off and begin composing poems in pairs or individually. Collections of poems written by young adults can appeal to students and encourage them in their own writing efforts. Poetry books by students from 12 to 18 years old, such as Franco's edited collections, *You Hear Me? Poems and Writing by Teenage Boys* (2000) and *Things I Have to Tell You: Poems and Writing by Teenage Girls* (2001), could be introduced as an extension to a writing lesson.

Students should be reminded that poetry is a form of communication and that they should think of an idea, feeling, or event to write about in their poems. They should be reminded that poetry does not have to rhyme and that they should write about something of interest to them. Poetry for young adults follows no absolute rules; perfection of form should not be a goal. Other suggestions to foster poetry writing include the following:

- Have students compile personal and class anthologies of their own poems or their favorite poems.
- Design bulletin boards with poetry displays of students' own poems as well as copies of poems by favorite poets.
- Let students rework a narrative poem into a different genre, such as a newspaper article or a letter. In turn, students may attempt the reverse—taking a newspaper article and putting it to verse.
- Suggest to students that they design posters, individually or in groups, to illustrate a favorite poem. Posters are then displayed in the classroom for a few weeks.
- Encourage students to use the works of professional poets as models, by attempting imitation of a whole poem or of specific techniques.
- Read aloud several poems of one poetic form; then assist the students in identifying the form to reveal the characteristics of its structure. Quatrains, cinquains, haiku, concrete poems, and limericks can all be used as writing models with students once they have an appreciation for poetry and for specific poetic forms.

Some poets have suggested other models and patterns for students to follow in writing poetry. Koch's *Wishes, Lies, and Dreams* (1999); Hopkins' *Pass the Poetry, Please!* (1987); Janeczko's *How to Write Poetry* (1999) and *Seeing the Blue Between: Advice and Inspiration for Young Poets* (2002); Fagin's *The List Poem: A Guide to Teaching and Writing Catalog Verse* (2000); and Katz and Thomas's *The Word in Play: Language, Music, and Movement in the Classroom* (2004) are useful resources for teachers who want to encourage students to compose poems.

Poetry and Technology

The website www.ReadWriteThink.org is a partnership of the International Reading Association, the National Council of Teachers of English, and the Verizon Foundation to provide educators with access to high-quality practices and resources through free Internet-based content. Lessons and Web resources to support the lessons are provided according to grade bands (6–8 or 9–12, for example) and areas of literacy.

Two lesson plans from this website with useful ideas for teaching poetry in grade 6 to 8 classrooms are *In the Poet's Shoes: Performing Poetry and Building Meaning* by Beth O'Connor and *Astronomy Poetry: Combining Poetry with Content Areas* by Che-Mai Gray. Through dramatic readings and exploration of Internet resources students develop their own interpretations of a poem's meaning as part of *In the Poet's Shoes*. Students also give an oral performance of their own poetry as part of this set of lessons. In *Astronomy Poetry* students listen to and discuss poetry that pertains to the study of astronomy and write their own poems to enhance their knowledge and appreciation of the subject. As part of this set of lessons students compose original poetry books about astronomy by using the website's printing press resource.

The website www.ReadWriteThink.org also has lesson plans for grades 9 to 12. The lesson plan *A Poem of Possibilities: Thinking about the Future* by Susanne Rubinstein combines poetry writing and publication as a way to help students process the pressures of change in their lives. Inspired by

readwritethink.org

a published poem, each student develops a poem presenting who he or she will be and the life being led five years in the future. Online resources are indicated for research on the poem and the poet, and assignment sheets are provided for teachers. In *Stairway to Heaven: Examining Metaphor in Popular Music* by Sue Carmichael, a set of lessons about popular culture is used to help students in grades 9 to 12 connect to classical texts being studied in school. Students explore how lyrics of popular songs contain the same literary elements, such as metaphor, simile, and symbolism, used in the literary texts read in class. With a "literary graffiti tool" provided as part of the lesson students develop their own literary graffiti pictures.

REFERENCES

Abrahamson, R. F. (2002). Poetry preference research: What young adults tell us they enjoy. *Voices from the Middle, 10*(2), 20–22.

Appelt, K. (1997). *Just people and other poems for young readers & Paper/pen/poem: A young writer's way to begin.* Houston, TX: Absey.

Booth, D., & Moore, B. (2003). *Poems please! Sharing poetry with children.* Markham, ON: Pembroke.

Fagin, L. (2000). *The list poem: A guide to teaching & writing catalog verse.* New York: Teachers and Writers Collaborative.

Franco, B. (Ed.). (2001). *Things I have to tell you: Poems and writing by teenage girls.* Photos by N. Nickels. Cambridge, MA: Candlewick.

———. (Ed.). (2000). *You hear me? Poems and writing by teenage boys.* Cambridge, MA: Candlewick.

Ghigna, C. (2003). The leopard of loneliness. In C. Ghigna, *A fury of motion: Poems for boys.* Honesdale, PA: Boyds Mills.

Heard, G. (1999). *Awakening the heart: Exploring poetry in elementary and middle school.* Portsmouth, NH: Heinemann.

Hemp, C. (1993). Even when. In P. B. Janeczko, Ed., *Looking for your name.* New York: Orchard.

Holbrook, S. (2002). *Wham! It's a poetry jam: Discovering performance poetry.* Honesdale, PA: Boyds Mills.

———. (2003). Evolution. In S. Holbrook, *By definition: Poems of feelings.* Honesdale, PA: Boyds Mills.

Hopkins, L. B. (1987). *Pass the poetry please!* New York: Harper & Row.

Janeczko, P. B. (1990). *The place my words are looking for: What poets say about and through their work.* New York: Bradbury.

———. (Ed.). (1999). *How to write poetry.* New York: Scholastic.

———. (Ed.). (2002). *Seeing the blue between: Advice and inspiration for young poets.* Cambridge, MA: Candlewick.

———. (2003). *Opening a door: Reading poetry in the middle school classroom.* New York: Scholastic Professional.

———. (Ed.). (2005). *A kick in the head.* Illustrated by C. Raschka. Cambridge, MA: Candlewick.

Johnson, A. B., & McClanahan, L. G., with Mertz, M. P. (1999). Gender representation in poetry for young adults. *ALAN Review, 26*(3), 39–44.

Katz, S. A., & Thomas, J. A. (2004). *The word in play: Language, music, and movement in the classroom.* Baltimore: P. H. Brookes.

Koch, K. (1999/1970). *Wishes, lies and dreams: Teaching children to write poetry.* New York: Random.

Kutiper, K. (1985). Survey of the adolescent poetry preferences of seventh, eighth, and ninth graders. Ph.D. dissertation, University of Houston.

Kutiper, K., & Wilson, P. (1993). Updating poetry preferences: A look at the poetry children really like. *The Reading Teacher, 47*(1), 28–35.

Lear, E. (1946). A young lady of Norway. In *The complete nonsense book.* New York: Dodd, Mead.

McGough, R. (1997). A weak poem. In R. McGough, *Bad, bad cats.* New York: Puffin.

O'Connor, J. S. (2004). *Word playgrounds: Reading, writing, and performing poetry in the English classroom.* Urbana, IL: National Council of Teachers of English.

Rossetti, C. (1998). Sonnet. In M. Rosen, *Classic poetry: An illustrated collection.* Illustrated by Paul Howard. Cambridge, MA: Candlewick.

Schwedt, R., & DeLong, J. (2002). *Young adult poetry: A survey and theme guide.* Westport, CT: Greenwood.

Sloan, G. (2003). *Give them poetry! A guide for sharing poetry with children K–8.* New York: Teachers College Press.

Terry, A. C. (1974). *Children's poetry preferences: A national survey of upper elementary grades.* Urbana, IL: National Council of Teachers of English.

Wintz, A. (2000). From the tar papered. In P. B. Janeczko, Ed., *Stone bench in an empty park.* Photographs by H. Silberman. New York: Orchard.

RECOMMENDED POETRY BOOKS

Ages indicated refer to content appropriateness and conceptual and interest levels. Book formats other than novels are coded as follows:

(GR) *Graphic novel*
(PI) *Picture book*
(COL) *Short story collection*

ANTHOLOGIES OF POETRY

Booth, David, editor. *'Til All the Stars Have Fallen.* Illustrated by Kady Denton. Viking, 1990. Ages 10–13. A Canadian collection of seventy-six poems from a variety of sources.

Driscoll, Michael. *A Child's Introduction to Poetry.* Illustrated by Meredith Hamilton. Black Dog & Leventhal, 2003. Ages 10–14. Discusses poetic forms and individual poets, with examples.

Ferris, Helen, compiler. *Favorite Poems Old and New!* Illustrated by Leonard Weisgard. Doubleday, 1957. Ages 6–14. Not illustrated but an excellent and large anthology of older poems at a moderate price.

Hall, Donald, editor. *The Oxford Illustrated Book of American Children's Poems.* Oxford University, 2001/1999. Ages 9–13. Poems arranged chronologically by historical periods.

Harrison, Michael, and Christopher Stuart-Clark, editors. *The New Oxford Treasury of Children's Poems.* Oxford, 1987. Ages 9–12. Good illustrated selection of contemporary and classic poems, many of British origin.

———. *The Oxford Treasury of Classic Poems.* Oxford, 1996. Ages 12–18. A collection of famous traditional poems by mostly British poets.

Morris, Jackie, compiler and illustrator. *The Barefoot Book of Classic Poems.* Barefoot Books, 2006. Ages 9–14. Seventy-four familiar poems by well-known British and American poets.

Philip, Neil, editor. *A New Treasury of Poetry.* Illustrated by John Lawrence. Stewart, Tabori, & Chang, 1990. Ages 11–15. Favorite English classic poems.

Rosenberg, Liz, editor. *The Invisible Ladder: An Anthology of Contemporary American Poems for Young Readers.* Holt, 1996. Ages 12–18. Includes commentary by poets with ideas for writing.

SPECIALIZED POETRY BOOKS

(Poetry books by a single poet and thematic poetry books are included.)

Adoff, Arnold, editor. *I Am the Darker Brother: An Anthology of Modern Poems by African Americans.* Drawings by Benny Andrews. Simon & Schuster, 1997/1968. Ages 13–18. This revised edition includes twenty-one new poems and nineteen additional poets.

Agard, John. *Half-Caste and Other Poems.* Hodder, 2005. Ages 14–18. A collection of forty-five poems that address race and identity. Humor.

Appelt, Kathi. *Poems from Homeroom: A Writer's Place to Start.* Holt, 2002. Ages 12–18. Poems about the experiences of young people. A bibliography of books on writing poems and stories, and various poetic forms exemplified.

Carlson, Lori M., editor. *Cool Salsa: Bilingual Poems on Growing Up Latino in the United States.* Holt, 1994. Ages 13–18. A collection of poems that express Latino youth culture.

———. *Red Hot Salsa: Bilingual Poems on Life, Love, and Victory.* Holt, 2005. Ages 12–18. Another collection of poems about the Latino experience by well-known and emerging poets.

Clinton, Catherine, editor. *I, Too, Sing America: Three Centuries of African-American Poetry.* Illustrated by Stephen Alcorn. Houghton, 1998. Ages 11–18. A chronological arrangement of twenty-five African-American poets, a brief biography, and one or more poems for each.

———, editor. *A Poem of Her Own: Voices of American Women Yesterday and Today.* Illustrated by Stephen Alcorn. Abrams, 2003. Ages 11–18. Poems from twenty-five American women poets with a biography of each.

Crisler, Curtis L. *Tough Boy Sonatas.* Illustrated by Floyd Cooper. Boyds Mills, 2007. Ages 14–18. Voices of African-American males growing up in Gary, Indiana.

Cullinan, Bernice E., editor. *A Jar of Tiny Stars: Poems by NCTE Award-Winning Poets.* Boyds Mills, 1995. Ages 9–12. A collection of favorite poems by NCTE Award poets.

Dunbar, Paul Laurence. *Jump Back, Honey: The Poems of Paul Laurence Dunbar.* Hyperion, 1999. Ages 10–13. A collection of the best known of the late-nineteenth-century writer's poems.

Fleischman, Paul. *Big Talk: Poems for Four Voices.* Illustrated by Beppe Giacobbe. Candlewick, 2000. Ages 9–14. Poems to be read aloud by four people, with color-coded text to indicate the reader.

———. *I Am Phoenix: Poems for Two Voices.* Illustrated by Eric Beddows. Harper, 1985. Ages 9–14. Poems about birds; to be read aloud by two readers.

———. *Joyful Noise: Poems for Two Voices.* Illustrated by Eric Beddows. Harper, 1988. Ages 9–14. Poems about insects; to be read aloud by two readers.

Florian, Douglas. *Comets, Stars, the Moon, and Mars: Space Poems and Paintings.* Harcourt, 2007. Ages 9–13. Twenty poems about space.

Ghigna, Charles. *A Fury of Motion: Poems for Boys.* Boyds Mills, 2003. Ages 12–18. Poems to appeal to boys and some girls.

Giovanni, Nikki. *Ego-Tripping and Other Poems for Young People.* Illustrated by George Ford. Hill Books, 1993. Ages 11–14. Poems about ordinary people.

———, editor. *Grand Fathers: Reminiscences, Poems, Recipes, and Photos of the Keepers of Our Traditions.* Holt, 1999. Ages 14–18. Tributes to grandfathers.

———, editor. *Grand Mothers: Reminiscences, Poems, Recipes, and Photos of the Keepers of Our Traditions.* Holt, 1994. Ages 14–18. Tributes to grandmothers.

Glaser, Isabel Joshlin, editor. *Dreams of Glory: Poems Starring Girls.* Simon & Schuster, 1995. Ages 10–13. A collection of thirty poems about girls.

Glenn, Mel. *Class Dismissed! High School Poems.* Photographs by Michael J. Bernstein. Clarion, 1982. Ages 12–18. Seventy poems about the emotional lives of high school students.

———. *Foreign Exchange: A Mystery in Poems.* Morrow, 1999. Ages 12–18. A realistic portrayal of a small town, its residents, and high school. Free verse.

———. *Jump Ball: A Basketball Season in Poems.* Dutton, 1997. Ages 12–18. A realistic look at an urban high school basketball team.

Grandits, John. *Blue Lipstick: Concrete Poems.* Clarion, 2007. Ages 10–18. A humorous collection of thirty-four concrete poems featuring teenage life.

———. *Technically, It's Not My Fault.* Clarion, 2004. Ages 9–13. Two dozen funny concrete poems with the point of view of an 11-year-old boy.

Greenberg, Jan. *Heart to Heart: New Poems Inspired by Twentieth Century American Art.* Abrams, 2001. Ages 12–18. A collection of poems by Americans writing about American art.

———, collector. *Side by Side: New Poetry Inspired by Art from around Our World.* Abrams, 2008. Ages 14–18. Thirty international poems with the art that inspired them.

Grimes, Nikki. *A Dime a Dozen*. Pictures by Angelo. Dial, 1998. Ages 11–15. Coming-of-age poems.

Heard, Georgia. *Songs of Myself*. Mondo, 2000. Ages 8–13. Twelve poems and a traditional song reflecting how children feel about themselves.

Holbrook, Sara. *By Definition: Poems of Feelings*. Boyds Mills, 2003. Ages 10–13. Poems about early adolescence.

————. *I Never Said I Wasn't Difficult*. Boyds Mills, 1996. Ages 10–14. Poems that capture the emotions experienced while growing up.

————. *Walking on the Boundaries of Change*. Boyds Mills, 1998. Ages 11–18. A collection of poems that capture adolescents' feelings about social life.

Holbrook, Sara, and Allan Wolf. *More Than Friends: Poems from Him and Her*. Boyds Mills, 2008. Ages 11–16. Alternating voices of a boy and a girl in the throes of affection. The various poetic forms used are identified and explained in an addendum.

Hopkins, Lee Bennett. *America at War*. Illustrated by Stephen Alcorn. Simon & Schuster, 2008. Ages 10–16. A reflection on many American experiences during wartime.

————. *Got Geography!: Poems*. Illustrated by Philip Stanton. Greenwillow, 2006. Ages 9–14. Sixteen poems by traditional and contemporary poets celebrating many facets of geography.

————, editor. *My America: A Poetry Atlas of the United States*. Illustrated by Stephen Alcorn. Simon & Schuster, 2000. Ages 9–14. Poems evocative of seven geographical regions of the United States.

Janeczko, Paul B., selector. *Dirty Laundry Pile: Poems in Different Voices*. Illustrated by Melissa Sweet. HarperCollins, 2001. Ages 10–13. Animate beings and inanimate objects express themselves in these poems.

————, selector. *A Kick in the Head: An Everyday Guide to Poetic Forms*. Illustrated by Chris Raschka. Candlewick, 2005. Ages 9–14. A collection of poems of various forms with brief explanations of each form.

————, selector. *Looking for Your Name: A Collection of Contemporary Poems*. Orchard, 1993. Ages 13–18. Poems of social and political conflict.

————, selector. *A Poke in the I: A Collection of Concrete Poems*. Illustrated by Chris Raschka. Candlewick, 2001. Ages 10–14. A collection of concrete poems.

————, selector. *Stone Bench in an Empty Park*. Photographs by Henri Silberman. Orchard, 2000. Ages 10–13. A collection of haiku.

————. *That Sweet Diamond: Baseball Poems*. Atheneum, 1998. Ages 10–14. Nineteen free-verse poems about baseball.

Janeczko, Paul B., and J. Patrick Lewis. *Birds on a Wire, or, A Jewel Tray of Stars*. Illustrated by Gary Lippincott. Wordsong, 2008. Ages 8–15. Small town life in springtime described using the ancient Japanese verse form called renga, in which two or more poets take turns.

Johnson, Angela. *The Other Side: Shorter Poems*. Orchard, 1998. Ages 11–16. Poems about growing up as an African-American girl in Alabama.

Kennedy, Caroline, editor. *My Favorite Poetry for Children*. Illustrated by Jon J. Muth. Hyperion, 2005. Ages 9–12. A varied selection of old and new poems.

Knudson, R. R., and May Swenson, editors. *American Sports Poems*. Orchard, 1996/1988. Ages 11–18. A collection of 158 poems about various sports from a spectator point of view.

Lawson, JonArno. *Black Stars in a White Night Sky*. Wordsong, 2008. Ages 10–15. Serious, funny, and imaginative poems on a wide range of topics for adolescents who want to explore more complex poetry.

Lewis, J. Patrick. *The Brothers' War: Civil War Voices in Verse*. National Geographic, 2007. Ages 12–18. Poems honoring historical and fictional heroes.

————. *Monumental Verses*. National Geographic, 2005. Ages 10–15. Poems paying tribute to famous American monuments.

————. *Vherses: A Celebration of Outstanding Women*. Illustrated by Mark Summers. Creative, 2005. Ages 9–14. Literary portraits of fourteen women.

Liu, Siyu, and Orel Protopopescu. *A Thousand Peaks: Poems from China*. Illustrated by Siyu Liu. Pacific View Press, 2001. Ages 12–18. Classical Chinese poetry and a brief cultural history of China.

Merriam, Eve. *The Inner City Mother Goose*. Illustrated by David Diaz. Simon & Schuster, 1996/1969. Ages 14–18. Poems depicting the grim reality of inner-city life.

Morrison, Lillian, compiler. *Way to Go! Sports Poems.* Illustrated by Susan Spellman. Boyds Mills, 2001. Ages 9–14. Forty-two poems about a variety of sports.

Myers, Walter Dean. *Blues Journey.* Illustrated by Christopher Myers. Holiday, 2003. Ages 10–14. Original poems honoring the blues and its themes.

————. *Here in Harlem: Poems in Many Voices.* Holiday, 2004. Ages 13–18. Poems presenting the people of Harlem.

————. *Jazz.* Illustrated by Christopher Myers. Holiday, 2006. Ages 8–12. Fifteen poems celebrating the stages of jazz.

Nye, Naomi Shihab. *A Maze Me: Poems for Girls.* Illustrated by Terre Maher. Greenwillow, 2005. Ages 12–18. A collection of more than seventy free verse poems, newly published, about everyday experiences girls will understand.

————, editor. *Is This Forever, or What? Poems & Paintings from Texas.* Greenwillow, 2004. Ages 12–18. A collection of poems about Texas.

————, editor. *The Space between Our Footsteps: Poems and Paintings from the Middle East.* Simon & Schuster, 1998. Ages 13–18. Poems from the Middle East and North Africa.

————, editor. *This Same Sky: A Collection of Poems from Around the World.* Four Winds, 1992. Ages 11–18. Poems from sixty-nine different countries.

————, editor. *What Have You Lost?* Photographs by Michael Nye. Greenwillow, 1999. Ages 12–18. Poems about different kinds of loss.

Nye, Naomi Shihab, and Paul B. Janeczko, editors. *I Feel a Little Jumpy around You: A Book of Her Poems and His Poems Collected in Pairs.* Simon & Schuster, 1996. Ages 13–18. Pairs of poems that offer insight to how men and women look at the world.

Park, Linda Sue. *Tap Dancing on the Roof: Sijo.* Illustrated by Istvan Banyai. Clarion, 2007. Ages 10–16. Sijo poems, a three-line traditional Korean poetic form, with lighthearted examples.

Peters, Lisa Westberg. *Earthshake: Poems from the Ground Up.* Illustrated by Cathie Felstead. Greenwillow, 2003. Ages 10–13. Poems about geology.

Rochelle, Belinda. *Words with Wings: A Treasury of African-American Poetry and Art.* Harper-Collins/Amistad, 2001. Ages 10–16. Each of twenty poems is facing a painting in this large-format collection.

Rosenberg, Liz, and Deena November, editors. *I Just Hope It's Lethal: Poems of Sadness, Madness, and Joy.* Houghton, 2005. Ages 14–18. A collection of ninety-one poems about emotions, especially depression and related emotions.

Rylant, Cynthia. *Boris.* Harcourt, 2005. Ages 11–16. Poems speaking to a cat about his life and the life of the narrator. Free verse.

Sidman, Joyce. *Butterfly Eyes and Other Secrets of the Meadow.* Houghton, 2006. Ages 9–12. An ecosystem of a meadow captured in poems combining riddles and science information.

————. *Song of the Water Boatman and Other Pond Poems.* Illustrated by Beckie Prange. Houghton, 2005. Ages 9–12. Poems about pond life reveal science facts.

————. *This Is Just to Say: Poems of Apology and Forgiveness.* Illustrated by Pamela Zagarenski. Houghton, 2007. Ages 10–16. Fictional students' "sorry" poems with responses from the fictional recipients of the poems.

————. *The World According to Dog: Poems and Teen Voices.* Houghton, 2003. Ages 13–18. Poems about dogs and essays by teens about their dogs.

Singer, Marilyn. *Central Heating: Poems about Fire and Warmth.* Illustrated by Meilo Su. Knopf, 2005. Ages 10–14. Fire poems evoke comfort and power.

Soto, Gary. *Worlds Apart: Traveling with Fernie and Me.* Illustrated by Greg Clarke. Putnam, 2005. Ages 9–13. Two friends on imaginary global adventures.

Vecchione, Patrice, editor. *The Body Electric: An Anthology of Poems.* Holt, 2002. Ages 13–18. Poems about body image.

————, editor. *Faith and Doubt.* Holt, 2007. Ages 13–18. A themed anthology exploring many facets of faith and doubt in poems from celebrated poets around the world.

————. *Revenge and Forgiveness: An Anthology of Poems.* Holt, 2004. Ages 14–18. Poems about human nature and human emotions.

————. *Truth and Lies.* Holt, 2000. Ages 15–18. A multicultural anthology of seventy poems on the theme of the title.

Worth, Valerie. *Animal Poems.* Illustrated by Steve Jenkins. Farrar, 2007. Ages 9–14. Posthumous collection of twenty-three poems, each capturing a creature in its singularity.

SINGLE ILLUSTRATED POEMS

Longfellow, Henry Wadsworth. *Paul Revere's Ride: The Landlord's Tale.* Illustrated by Charles Santore. HarperCollins, 2003. Ages 9–14. Dramatic illustrations accompany this classic poem.

Myers, Walter Dean. *Harlem.* Illustrated by Christopher Myers. Scholastic, 1997. Ages 11–15. A poem celebrating Harlem.

Nelson, Marilyn. *Fortune's Bones: The Manumission Requiem.* Front Street, 2004. **(PI)** Ages 11–16. An illustrated memorial through a series of poems of an enslaved man who died in 1798.

———. *A Wreath for Emmett Till.* Illustrated by Philippe Lardy. Houghton, 2005. **(PI)** Ages 14–18. An illustrated memorial to the lynched teen through interlocking sonnets.

Service, Robert W. *The Cremation of Sam McGee.* Illustrated by Ted Harrison. Greenwillow, 1987. Ages 10–14. A narrative Yukon adventure poem. Humor.

———. *The Shooting of Dan McGrew.* Illustrated by Ted Harrison. Godine, 1988. Ages 10–14. Another of Service's classic adventure poems. Humor.

Shange, Ntozake. *Ellington Was Not a Street.* Illustrated by Kadir Nelson. Simon & Schuster, 2004. Ages 10–13. Memories of a Harlem childhood are captured in this illustrated poem.

Thayer, Ernest L. *Casey at the Bat: A Ballad of the Republic Sung in the Year 1888.* Illustrated by C. F. Payne. Simon & Schuster, 2003. Ages 9–13. Humorous illustrated version of the classic ballad.

chapter EIGHT

LITERATURE *for a* DIVERSE SOCIETY

This chapter is presented in three parts. The first part, Culturally Responsive Instruction, focuses on ways teachers can make their teaching relevant to their students and to the world their students will inhabit. The second and third parts, Multicultural Literature and International Literature, identify literature that supports culturally responsive instruction.

CULTURALLY RESPONSIVE INSTRUCTION

Background

A serious mismatch exists in today's schools in the United States. On the one hand, school curricula present predominantly mainstream Euro-American perspectives. Moreover, public and private secondary school teachers in this country are predominantly (86.6% in 2003–2004) from Euro-American, suburban backgrounds (U.S. Department of Education, 2003–2004) and have been trained to teach in ways that work best with people like themselves. Many teachers have not had close, sustained relationships with individuals from different ethnic or cultural or lower socioeconomic backgrounds (Schmidt, 2005). On the other hand, school populations in the United States have become increasingly diverse, as evidenced by the U.S. Department of Education's prediction that school-aged minority populations will become the majority populations by 2010 (U.S. Department of Education, 2002b).

The resulting mismatch has contributed to an education system that is not working for many students. The Office of National Assessment for Educational Progress, for instance, since its inception in 1992, has reported a continuing reading achievement gap between whites on the one hand and Native Americans, Latinos, and African Americans on the other. In 2005 the average reading scores for eighth-grade whites was 271 versus 249 for Native Americans, 246 for Latinos, and 243 for African Americans (U.S. Department of Education, 2005). Other evidence of the problem is the school dropout rates of some minority populations. As reported by the National Center for Educational Statistics (U.S. Department of Education, 2002a), the high school dropout rate in 2000 for Latinos was 27.8 percent and 13.1 percent for African Americans, as compared to 3.8 percent for Asian Americans, and 6.9 percent for whites. Clearly, teachers and school administrators need to become more familiar with the realities of culture and its impact on teaching and learning (Ford & Moore, 2004, p. 34).

Some within the field of education are exploring more responsive ways to address this problem. *Culturally responsive instruction* is grounded in making the school experience relevant to all students by (1) reshaping school curricula to encompass the perspectives of *all* cultures represented in the student body while adhering to standards of achievement and (2) employing teaching strategies that suit the learning styles of *all* students. The goal is to make connections with students' backgrounds, interests, and experiences so that all students will feel part of the school experience, remain engaged, and experience success in learning (Schmidt, 2005). In the next section we address teaching strategies that take into consideration students' cultural differences, particularly as they relate to literacy learning and achievement.

Teaching Strategies and Literature

Schmidt (2005) outlines several characteristics of culturally responsive instruction, most of which can be understood as strategies that can be directly related to literature. These strategies are discussed along with examples of their application in the following section:

HIGH EXPECTATIONS—SUPPORTING STUDENTS AS THEY DEVELOP THE LITERACY APPROPRIATE TO THEIR AGES AND ABILITIES   All students need support in literacy acquisition, but our focus here is on providing that support to young people who have traditionally not received it in full measure—members of

strategy

certain ethnic minorities and resistant readers, two groups that often overlap. As discussed in Chapter 10, resistant readers often cite irrelevance of teacher-selected reading materials to their lives and instructional practices as reasons for not reading. The following strategies can help teachers actively support the literacy development of those who reject reading:

- *Find reading material for independent reading and reading aloud that is relevant to students' lives.* Believing that all students can achieve is closely connected to becoming acquainted with students personally and finding ways to help them achieve, including being knowledgeable about literature that is culturally relevant to them. For minority students this may be literature about young people whose lives and cultures are similar to their own. For males this will be reading material appealing to males. For second language learners this may be bilingual literature in English and the student's native tongue, to make learning English easier.

- *Insure that school and classroom literature collections reflect the cultural diversity of the classrooms, schools, and communities.* In cases where schools and communities are culturally homogeneous, librarians and teachers should nonetheless select books that reflect the diversity of the greater world their students will live in.

- *Give students a choice in reading material.* Teachers and librarians may need to broaden the scope of what they consider appropriate reading material to include less conventional formats—picture books, graphic novels, nonfiction such as automotive manuals and cookbooks, magazines, and audiobooks. Giving students a choice in what they read acknowledges them and shows that their teachers and librarians are interested in them and care that they learn.

- *Conference with students about their reading as often as possible.* One-on-one discussions give teachers an opportunity to learn about students' individual reading interests and needs, to supply pinpoint reading instruction as needed, to express interest in what students are currently reading, and to suggest other books they might like to read.

- *Establish routines, many of which can be literature-related.* Routines help stabilize the school day and give students something to look forward to. A simple but important daily routine is giving each student a friendly greeting at the classroom door. In addition, teachers can start or end the day (or class) with a poem, being sure that the poems reflect the cultures represented in their classes. Collections such as Lori M. Carlson's *Red Hot Salsa: Bilingual Poems on Being Young and Latino in the United States* or Naomi Shihab Nye's *The Space between Our Footsteps: Poems and Paintings from the Middle East* would be ideal for sharing with young people. A good follow-up to reading poems aloud is to post copies of the poems on the bulletin board for students to reread later.

Like this

Examples of other literature-related routines include (1) regular times to read aloud to students and to devote to independent reading; (2) students listing in their journals the titles of books read independently; (3) students recommending books to other students either during a once-weekly open forum or by listing recommended books on a permanent wall chart for all to see.

CURRICULUM RESHAPED BY CULTURAL SENSITIVITY AND MEDIATED FOR CULTURALLY VALUED KNOWLEDGE—CONNECTING WITH THE STANDARDS-BASED CURRICULUM AS WELL AS INDIVIDUAL

STUDENTS' CULTURAL BACKGROUNDS   A reshaped curriculum will be more inclusive than the traditional one. Social studies and history curricula, for example, will include perspectives of those long neglected—Native Americans, African Americans, Asian Americans, and Latinos to name a few. Science curricula will include important contributions made by minority scientists. Reading and literature curricula will include works by minority or foreign authors. For example, a literature unit could focus on a notable minority author such as Francisco Jiménez, a Mexican American whose works describe the struggles of immigrants and their families who work in the California fields. Likewise, a literature unit could focus on the works of Walter Dean Myers, whose works of contemporary fiction describe situations and problems experienced by many urban African Americans. Generally teachers will choose one of the featured author's works to read aloud and others for students to read in literature circles. The Lists of Notable Authors found in Chapters 3 to 7 include some minority authors. In this chapter there are two Lists of Notable Authors, Multicultural and International, to consider for author choices.

The goal of those who write, publish, and promote multicultural and international young adult literature is to help young people learn about, understand, and, ultimately, accept those different from themselves, thus breaking the cycles of prejudice between peoples of different ethnicities, religions, or languages. Progress toward this goal in the United States may well begin when young people read or listen to works of multicultural or international literature and realize how *similar* they are to those of different cultures and how *interesting* their differences are. These books help build bridges and erase borders between people of different nationalities and cultures, to use the metaphors of Jella Lepman (1964/2002) and Hazel Rochman (1993).

Ideas for bringing works of multicultural and international literature to your students' attention, facilitating their reading or listening to them, and integrating the books into the school curricula include the following strategies:

- Match or pair works of multicultural or international literature with similar works (in genre, theme, or topic) by mainstream authors and illustrators, saying, "If you liked this [mainstream] book, you would probably like this [multicultural or international] book, too."

- Use lists of character names, if unusual or numerous, or maps of story settings as story aids, if warranted. These lists or maps can be kept in view as a story is read.

- Integrate multicultural and international books into instructional or thematic units. In social studies and history units, these books can lend an authentic "I was there" flavor to the learning experience.

- Encourage students to search for further information about a culture or country represented in a book, either as an individual or a whole-class effort and done either as the book is being read or after it is finished. Encourage students to chart the similarities and differences between their cultures and the other culture or country.

- Operate from the conviction that international books are for everyone, not just for "gifted" students.

- Post titles of other books written or illustrated by a current favorite multicultural or international author or illustrator.

strategy!

ACTIVE TEACHING METHODS—INVOLVING STUDENTS IN A VARIETY OF READING, WRITING, LISTENING, SPEAKING, AND VIEWING BEHAVIORS THROUGHOUT THE LESSON PLAN   Throughout this textbook we have encouraged independent reading and reading aloud to students as often as possible. We have also included lists of literature-related films in each genre chapter to encourage the use of this medium. Chapter 9, "Teaching Strategies," is devoted to ways to enhance all students' experiences with literature. To make these activities culturally relevant, teachers and librarians need to select as material for reading or study a balanced selection of literature by and about the ethnic, religious, or language groups represented in their classrooms, schools, and communities. As a start, teachers and librarians can booktalk and display culturally diverse books regularly along with mainstream books (see Chapter 9 discussion of "booktalking") and include culturally relevant books in text sets for classroom study or independent reading. A collection of multicultural and international books to booktalk on the subject of growing up or coming of age might include

The Absolutely True Diary of a Part-Time Indian by Sherman Alexie (Spokane Indian)
American Born Chinese (GR) by Gene Luen Yang (Chinese American)
Climbing the Stairs by Padma Venkatraman (Indian)
Re-Gifters (GR) by Mike Carey, Sonny Liew, Marc Hempel (Korean American)
Strange Relations by Sonia Levitin (Jewish)
Tough Boy Sonatas (poetry) by Curtis L. Crisler (African American)
What the Moon Saw by Laura Resau (Mexican American)

INSTRUCTION AROUND GROUPS AND PAIRS—COMPLETING ASSIGNMENTS INDIVIDUALLY, BUT USUALLY IN SMALL GROUPS OR PAIRS WITH TIME TO SHARE IDEAS AND THINK CRITICALLY ABOUT THE WORK   The reason culturally relevant instruction promotes students working in groups and pairs is to decrease anxiety students experience when left on their own. Advantages specific to shared reading activities are that more able students give less able ones insights into how good readers get meaning from a text, various interpretations of the text are shared, and discussions and predictions ensue, all leading to a fuller understanding of what is read.

Response to literature can also be a group effort. Choice, planning, preparation, and presentation of the response can all be done in pairs or small groups. Of course, some methods of response work better than others as group efforts. Responses particularly well suited to pairs or small groups include rewriting part of the book into a skit, radio play, or readers' theatre piece and performing it, or creating a jackdaw (explained in Chapter 9) around the book's setting. *Cyrano* by Geraldine McCaughrean, a retelling of the classic French play, for example, lends itself to being interpreted through readers' theatre.

POSITIVE RELATIONS WITH FAMILIES AND COMMUNITY—DEMONSTRATING CLEAR CONNECTIONS WITH STUDENT FAMILIES AND COMMUNITIES IN TERMS OF CURRICULUM CONTENT AND RELATIONSHIPS   Regular contact between school personnel and those most involved with a young person's education at the present time—whether parents or members of the student's extended family—keeps lines of communication open and also sends the message that students and their families are valued by the educational establishment. Positive exchanges can be in the form of responses to literature that lead students back to their families or communities. For individuals this may involve interviewing an older family member about family history after reading a work of historical fiction. Such interviews can be the basis for writing family stories that can be collected into a class anthology. For a whole class it may be a civic action project like improvement of housing for migrant workers in their community stemming from their reading of a work of multicultural literature, such as Beth Atkin's *Voices from the Fields: Children of Migrant Farmworkers Tell Their Stories.*

We have built a case for culturally responsive instruction and for the fact that good literature relevant to students' lives is central to such instruction. Next we will define and discuss two bodies of literature that support culturally responsive instruction—multicultural and international literature. *Multicultural literature and international literature are not separate genres, but occur in all genres.*

You will have noted many references to multicultural and international books and authors throughout the previous chapters in discussions of trends and issues, notable author and illustrator lists, and end-of-chapter recommended booklists. In an ideal culturally integrated world, such inclusion would be sufficient. But the groups and perspectives represented in multicultural literature have, until recently, been totally absent from or misrepresented in books for young people and remain underrepresented today. Furthermore, neither multicultural nor international literature is well known or fully recognized by the educational mainstream. Changing demographics in this country and globalization of our society require school curricula and materials that will prepare young people to live in a changing and ever more diverse world.

ULTICULTURAL LITERATURE

Definition and Description

Multicultural literature is defined in various ways within the educational community. Some define it broadly as *all* books about people and their individual or group experiences, originating both in this country and in other countries. Some define it more narrowly as literature by and about groups in this country that have been overshadowed and to various degrees disregarded by the dominant Euro-American culture. This definition includes all racial, ethnic, religious, and language group minorities; those living with physical or mental disabilities; gays, lesbians, and bisexuals; and the poor. Examples of multicultural literature used in this section emphasize literature by and about the racial, religious, and language groups in the United States that have created a substantial body of young adult literature. This includes literature by and about African Americans; Asian Americans (including people of Chinese, Hmong, Japanese, Korean, and Vietnamese decent); Latinos (including Cuban Americans, Mexican Americans, Puerto Ricans, and others of Spanish descent); religious cultures (including Buddhist, Hindu, Jewish, and Muslim); and Native Americans (a general term referring to the many tribes of American Indians). Examples of books about other marginalized groups are to be found throughout the genre chapters, especially in the recommended books listed at the end of each genre chapter.

Unfortunately, many of the groups mentioned continue to experience social oppression, discrimination, or loss of civil rights. Some schools have responded by adapting their curricula to include *social justice education,* the "conscious and reflexive blend of content and process intended to enhance equity across multiple social identity groups, foster critical perspectives, and promote social action" (Carlisle, Jackson, & George, 2006, p. 56). An important content component of social justice education is the young adult literature that documents the history and stories of the disenfranchised, presents their perspectives, and allows members of these groups to be heard. Those who read these works are introduced to information not always presented in textbooks and have the opportunity to forge relationships, albeit vicarious, with people or cultural groups they would not otherwise know.

Early multicultural books helped define this body of literature. Some of these works are highlighted in the Early Important Works in the Development of Multicultural Literature.

Evaluation and Selection of Multicultural Literature

In addition to the standard requirement for high literary merit, *critical reading* with attention to whether characters are portrayed honestly and respectfully and to whether themes are worthwhile are of utmost importance in evaluating and selecting multicultural literature. The following criteria are

EARLY IMPORTANT WORKS *of* MULTICULTURAL LITERATURE		
Date	Literary Work/Event	Genre/Significance
1923	*The Voyages of Dr. Dolittle* by Hugh Lofting wins Newbery Medal	Modern fantasy. Crudely stereotyped microcultural characters accepted as the norm.
1932	*Waterless Mountain* by Laura Armer wins Newbery Medal	Realistic fiction. One of the few positive young adult books about people of color in the first half of the twentieth century.
1946	*The Moved-Outers* by Florence C. Means wins Newbery Honor	Realistic fiction. Signaled a departure from stereotyped depiction of people of color in books.
1949	*Story of the Negro* by Arna Bontemps wins Newbery Honor	Informational. First minority author to win a Newbery Honor.
1970–1974	*Sounder* by William Armstrong, *Julie of the Wolves* by Jean C. George, and *The Slave Dancer* by Paula Fox win Newbery Medals	Historical fiction. Books by Euro-Americans with multicultural protagonists or themes are accepted and honored.
1975	*M. C. Higgins, the Great* by Virginia Hamilton wins Newbery Medal	Realistic fiction. First book by a minority author to win the Newbery Medal.
1976	*Dragonwings* by Laurence Yep selected as Newbery Honor Book	Historical fiction. First Chinese American to win a Newbery Honor.
1977	*Roll of Thunder, Hear My Cry* by Mildred Taylor wins Newbery Medal	Historical fiction. Precedent established for members of a microculture to write most authoritatively about their own people and culture.

part of critical reading and should be considered when evaluating and selecting multicultural books for school and classroom libraries:

- Authentic depiction of the cultural experience *from the perspective of that group.* Either the story is told by someone of the culture or by someone not of the culture who has carefully researched the culture.
- Accuracy of cultural details in text and illustrations. This extends to accuracy when describing subgroups within a larger group—for example, a specific Native American tribe.
- Positive images of minority characters. Even in books about topics that have no positives, such as slavery, some pivotal characters should be shown as undaunted or hopeful for a better future. This can have a positive influence on readers' self-esteem.
- Balance between historic and contemporary views of groups. Native Americans of today, for example, do not always wear traditional dress and ride horses, and contemporary book images should depict them as they are.
- Adequate representation of any group. No one book can definitively describe a culture or a cultural experience. The more good books about a culture, the more complete the picture.

Book award programs have done much to promote excellence in multicultural literature for young people, especially the following:

- The Coretta Scott King Award (www.ala.org/ala/emiert/corettascottkingbookawards/corettascott .htm) is given to the African-American author whose book published in the preceding year is judged to be the most outstanding inspirational and educational literature for young readers.
- The Asian/Pacific American Award for Literature (www.apalaweb.org/awards/awards.htm) honors outstanding work of Asian-American authors and illustrators.
- The National Jewish Book Awards (www.jewishbookcouncil.org) and the Association of Jewish Libraries' Sydney Taylor Awards for Teen Readers (www.jewishlibraries.org/ajlweb/awards) promote Jewish literary creativity.
- The Américas Book Award for Children's and Young Adult Literature (www.uwm.edu/Dept/CLACS/ outreach/americas.html) annually recognizes the author of what is considered to be the best work written at the secondary level that authentically and engagingly portrays Latin America, the Caribbean, or Latinos in the United States.
- The Pura Belpré Award (www.ala.org; click on Awards & Scholarships; click on Book/ Media Awards; click on Belpré Medal) every other year honors the Latino author of what is considered to be the work that best portrays, affirms, and celebrates the Latino cultural experience.

In recent years, small presses have given teachers and librarians a source of books with a distinctly multicultural (versus Euro-American) point of view. For an extensive up-to-date list of small presses that publish multicultural books for children and young adults, go to www.education.wisc.edu/ ccbc/books/pclist.htm.

Evaluating, selecting, and then bringing multicultural literature to your classroom, though essential, are not enough to ensure that your students will actually read the books. Without guidance, young people tend to choose books about people like themselves (Rudman, 1984), so you must also purposefully expose young readers to multicultural books through reading aloud, booktalking, and selecting particular titles for literature circle reading.

Types of Multicultural Literature

Before discussing the literature of any ethnic group or culture, a general caution is in order. Each of these groups contains subgroups that differ remarkably from one another in characteristics such as country of origin, language, race, traditions, and present location. Teachers must be especially conscious of and sensitive to these differences and guard against presenting these groups as completely uniform or selecting literature that does so. Gross overgeneralization is not only inaccurate but also a form of stereotyping.

AFRICAN-AMERICAN LITERATURE   African Americans have produced the largest body of multicultural literature for young people in the United States. A genre particularly well represented in African-American literature is poetry. A good example is *Jazz* by Walter Dean Myers. African Americans have told the stories of their lives in the United States through both historical and realistic fiction. The stories often include painfully harsh but accurate accounts of racial oppression, as in Sharon Draper's historical fiction account of slavery in the eighteenth-century Carolinas, *Copper Sun,* or Mildred Taylor's historical fiction saga of the close-knit Logan family (*The Song of the Trees; Roll of Thunder, Hear My Cry; Let the Circle Be Unbroken; The Road to Memphis; The Land*) and in Jaime Adoff's contemporary realistic novel *The Death of Jayson Porter.* Such stories can be balanced with more positive, encouraging contemporary realistic stories, such as Angela Johnson's *Heaven* and *The First Part Last.*

ASIAN-AMERICAN LITERATURE   Asian-American literature for young people is mainly represented in the United States by stories about Chinese Americans and Japanese Americans, possibly because these groups have lived in the United States longer than others such as Vietnamese Americans. Recently, works by and about Korean Americans and Indian Americans have begun to appear with some regularity. A major theme in much of this literature is the oppression that drove the people out of their homelands and the prejudice that they face as newcomers in the United States. A more positive theme is that of learning to appreciate one's cultural heritage while adjusting to life in the United States. A good example is An Na's realistic story, *A Step from Heaven.*

The body of Asian-American young adult literature is small. Nonfiction, poetry, and fantasy are almost unrepresented, with the notable exception of Rhoda Blumberg's 1986 Newbery Honor book, a work of nonfiction, *Commodore Perry in the Land of the Shogun,* and her more recent biography *Shipwrecked! The True Adventures of a Japanese Boy.* The recently established Asian/Pacific American Award for Literature will help to improve this situation.

CROSS-CULTURAL LITERATURE   The term *cross-cultural* as it relates to literature can mean a work that addresses two or more different cultures, such as Yale Strom's *Quilted Landscape: Conversations with Young Immigrants.* It can also refer to a work in which the protagonist is of mixed heritage, such as *Rain Is Not My Indian Name* by Cynthia Leitich Smith. A common theme of many works of young adult cross-cultural literature is finding a way to fit into the cultures of which one is a part. Pearl F. Gaskins' collection of interviews, essays, and poetry by mixed-race young adults, *What Are You? Voices of Mixed-Race Young People,* and Claudine O'Hearn's collection of first person accounts of eighteen writers with

African-American

Christopher Paul Curtis, author whose characters cope with life in and around Flint, Michigan. *Bud, Not Buddy; Bucking the Sarge.* www.christopherpaulcurtis.com

Sharon Draper, author best known for contemporary African-American characters who confront real-life problems. *Forged by Fire; Battle of Jericho; Copper Sun* (historical fiction). www.sharondraper.com

Walter Dean Myers, author of gritty, contemporary realistic fiction with urban settings about African Americans growing up. *Scorpions; Somewhere in the Darkness; Monster.* www.walterdeanmyers.net

Jacqueline Woodson, author noted for introspective novels with strong characterization. *From the Notebooks of Melanin Sun; I Hadn't Meant to Tell You This; Miracle's Boys.* www.jacquelinewoodson.com

Asian-American

Cynthia Kadohata, author of historical fiction about Japanese Americans coping with prejudice and finding strength in family. *Kira-Kira; Weedflower.* www.kira-kira.us

Linda Sue Park, author of historical fiction novels set in Korea. *A Single Shard; When My Name Was Keoko; The Kite Fighters.* www.lindasuepark.com

Laurence Yep, author of historical and contemporary realistic fiction about growing up Chinese American. *Dragonwings; Child of the Owl.*

Cross-Cultural

Pearl Fuyo Gaskins, anthologist whose collections of interviews with young people focus on their mixed-heritage and varied religious beliefs. *What Are You? Voices of Mixed-Race Young People; I Believe In . . .: Christian, Jewish, and Muslim Young People Speak About Their Faith.* www.whatareyou.com/pearl.html

Naomi Shihab Nye, Palestinian-American poet and author whose works celebrate different cultures. *This Same Sky: A Collection of Poems from around the World; 19 Varieties of Gazelle: Poems of the Middle East; Habibi.*

Latino

Julia Alvarez, author who writes about life in the Dominican Republic and life in the United States as recent Dominican émigrés. *Before We Were Free; How the García Girls Lost Their Accents* (short stories). www.juliaalvarez.com

Francisco Jiménez, author of autobiographical stories of his childhood and young adulthood in California as an illegal immigrant from Mexico. *Breaking Through; Reaching Out.* www.scu.edu/fjimenez

Gary Soto, author of contemporary stories about the Mexican-American experience. *Trading Places; Baseball in April and Other Stories.* www.garysoto.com

Native American

Sherman Alexie, author of penetrating, often funny, novels and short story collections about Native Americans. *The Absolutely True Diary of a Part-Time Indian; The Toughest Indian in the World* (COL). www.fallsapart.com

Joseph Bruchac, author of fiction and nonfiction about the contributions of Native Americans. *Code Talker: A Novel about the Navajo Marines of World War Two; Pocahontas; Sacajawea.* www.josephbruchac.com

Louise Erdrich, author of historical fiction novels about Ojibwa life in northern Minnesota in the mid-nineteenth century. *The Birchbark House; The Game of Silence.*

Religious Cultures

Demi, author-illustrator of picture book biographies and story collections for older readers about important religious figures, with art inspired by traditional Chinese and Indian techniques. *Buddha; Buddha Stories; Muhammad.* http://authors.simonandschuster.com/Demi

Sonia Levitin, author of books about Jewish immigration to America. *Journey to America; Silver Days; Strange Relations.* www.sonialevitin.com

Types

biracial or bicultural backgrounds, *Half and Half: Writers Growing Up Biracial and Bicultural,* are worthy examples of books of this kind.

LATINO LITERATURE   Relatively few Latino books for young adults are published in the United States, despite the fact that Latinos represent the largest microcultural group—an estimated 14 percent of the population—and are the fastest-growing segment of the population (U.S. Census Bureau, 2004). In the books that are available, recurrent themes are life in barrios (e.g., *Baseball in April and Other Stories,* a collection of contemporary short stories by Gary Soto), identifying with one's native heritage and the culture of the United States (e.g., *Cubanita,* a work of contemporary realistic fiction by Gaby Triana), life under repressive Latin American political regimes (e.g., Julia Alvarez's work of historical fiction set in the Trujillo-era Dominican Republic, *Before We Were Free*), and immigration to the United States for economic or political reasons (e.g., Pam Muñoz Ryan's Depression-era historical fiction story, *Esperanza Rising,* and Ann Jaramillo's work of contemporary fiction, *La Línea*). In addition to the recommended books by and about Latinos at the end of this chapter, another source is the website of The Barahona Center for the Study of Books in Spanish for Children and Adolescents at the University of California San Marcos (www.csusm.edu/csb), which offers lists of books in English about Latinos and books in Spanish.

NATIVE AMERICAN LITERATURE   Native Americans have long suffered at the hands of Euro-Americans. Consequently, in books written from the Native American perspective, oppression by the white population is a pervasive theme. Appreciation, celebration, and protection of nature—central tenets of Native American cultures—are other recurrent themes in this body of literature.

Although much has been written *about* Native Americans, relatively little has been written *by* members of this microculture. Native Americans who are known for their young adult books include Louise Erdrich for her novels and Joseph Bruchac for his retellings of folklore, poems, and short stories. *The Absolutely True Diary of a Part-Time Indian,* a semiautobiographical work by Sherman Alexie, is another good example.

Non-Native writers have told the history of Native Americans in works of historical fiction and informational books. Scott O'Dell was particularly well known in the late twentieth century for his award-winning works of historical fiction featuring young Native American women, such as *Island of the Blue Dolphins.* A work of nonfiction, *Only the Names Remain: The Cherokees and the Trail of Tears,* by Alex W. Bealer, is another interesting work by a non-Native writer.

RELIGIOUS CULTURES LITERATURE   The United States is traditionally a Christian nation, but nonmainstream religious cultures are represented in young adult literature in the United States, including Buddhist, Hindu, Jewish, and Muslim themes. However, good contemporary young adult fiction set within the context of a religious culture and written from the perspective of a member of that religion is scarce. An example is Asma Mobin-Uddin's *My Name Is Bilal,* a picture book for older readers illustrated by Barbara Kiwak, which explores the topic of fitting into the U.S. mainstream while remaining true to one's Islamic culture and heritage. Nonfiction and folklore on the subject of religion are more plentiful. Author-illustrator Demi, for example, is known for her picture book biographies and story collections about Buddha and Buddhism and Muhammad and Islam.

The body of Jewish young adult literature is by far the largest produced from nonmainstream religious cultures in this country. The terrible experience of the Jewish Holocaust in Europe during the

1930s and 1940s has had a tremendous influence on Jewish literature for young people. The prejudice and cruelty that led to the Holocaust and the nightmare of the death camps themselves are recurring themes in both fiction and nonfiction. Since many Jewish people immigrated to the United States as the Nazi threat grew in Europe, much Holocaust literature has been written by eyewitnesses or by those whose relatives were victims. An outstanding early example is Aranka Siegal's work of historical fiction *Upon the Head of the Goat: A Childhood in Hungary 1939–1944.* A more recent example of holocaust literature is the biography *Fireflies in the Dark: The Story of Friedl Dicker-Brandeis and the Children of Terezin* by Susan Goldman Rubin.

Although the last several decades have seen positive changes in the status of multicultural literature in the United States, there is still a marked shortage of books of this kind. Multicultural authors and illustrators of books for young people are also in short supply. In 2006, only 215 (7%) of the approximately 3,000 books reviewed by the Cooperative Children's Book Center in Madison, Wisconsin, were written or illustrated by people of color (Horning, Lindgren, Rudiger, & Schliesman, 2007). A broader indication of this shortage is that in 2002 only 415 (8%) of the approximately 5,000 children's books published in the United States were by or about people of color, even though these groups represent approximately 30 percent of the country's population (U.S. Census Bureau, 2000).

NTERNATIONAL LITERATURE

Definition and Description

International literature in the United States is defined as literary selections that were originally published for young people in a country other than the United States in a language of that country and later published in the United States. The key elements of this definition are the book's country of origin and the primary audience for the book. If a book was written and published in the Netherlands for Dutch young adults and then translated and published for U.S. readers, it is considered an international book in the United States. Books that are classified as international literature by this definition include

1. English-language books that were originally written and published in English in another country, such as England, Canada, or Australia, and then published or distributed in the United States. Example: The Harry Potter books by J. K. Rowling (England). — ?
2. Translated books that were written and published in a foreign country and then translated into English and published in the United States. Example: *The Friends* by Kazumi Yumoto (Japan).
3. Foreign-language books that were written and published in a foreign language in another country for children of that country and later published or distributed in the United States in the foreign language. Example: *Le Petit Prince* by Antoine de Saint-Exupéry (France).

Some authors from the United States write books for young adults set in other countries. These books are written and published in the United States primarily for an audience of American young people and are a part of the body of U.S. literature. They include stories written by immigrants to this country about their lives and experiences in their countries of origin. Authors known for their books set in other countries include Nancy Farmer, who writes modern fantasies and works of magical realism such as *A Girl Named Disaster,* which is set in Mozambique and Zimbabwe; Suzanne Fisher Staples, who writes works of realistic fiction such as *Shabanu,* which is set in Pakistan; and Gloria Whelan, who writes works of realistic fiction such as *Homeless Bird,* which is set in India, and historical fiction such as *Angel on the Square,* which is set in early twentieth-century Russia. Books such as these are included in the recommended books lists in Chapters 3 through 7.

A book's publishing history page is the most reliable source of its country of origin. In most books the publishing history is placed after the title page, but in some cases it is placed at the end of the book. Look for a statement such as "First published in (year) by (name of foreign publisher), (country of origin) as (foreign title)." In the case of Mette Newth's work of historical fiction about leprosy in early-nineteenth-century Norway, *The Dark Light,* this statement reads, "First published in 1995 by H. Aschehoug & Co., Norway, as *Det mørke lyset*" (p. iv).

Much of the literature for young people that was available in the United States during the seventeenth, eighteenth, nineteenth, and early twentieth centuries came from Europe. These early books are an important part of our cultural heritage, but we seldom think of the fact that they were originally published in other countries and many in other languages. They are so familiar to us in the United States that we consider them *our* classics for young people, as they have indeed become. (See Early Important Works of International Literature.)

Evaluation and Selection of International Literature

International books should first be judged by the standards for all good literature as outlined in Chapter 2. In addition, the following criteria should be considered.

- Translated works should exhibit a good, fluent writing style. A flavor of the country of origin should remain, sometimes by leaving a few well-chosen words in the original language. A glossary of foreign words found in the text with their meanings and pronunciations is helpful.
- More introspection by the main character and less physical action than is usual for U.S. books should be expected and explored. Students can be alerted to this difference and asked to reflect on why the author may have chosen this manner of telling the story.
- In international picture books for older readers, expect a more abstract style and greater use of visual symbolism. See, for example, the works of modern fantasy *The Collector of Moments* by Quint Buchholz and *Fox* by Margaret Wild, illustrated by Ron Brooks.

The following selection sources will prove useful in locating good international book titles:

- Lists of the British, Australian, and Canadian awards for young adult books (see Appendix A)
- The United States Board on Books for Young People (USBBY) bibliography series—*Children's Books from Other Countries,* edited by Carl M. Tomlinson (1998); *The World through Children's Books,* edited by Susan Stan (2002); and *A Bridge of Children's Books: Children's Books from and about Other Countries,* edited by Doris Gebel (2006)—with extensive annotated lists of international books for children and young adults, strategies for sharing these books, and activities for promoting international understanding

EARLY IMPORTANT WORKS *of* INTERNATIONAL LITERATURE

Date	Literary Work	Genre/Country of Origin
1719	*Robinson Crusoe* by Daniel Defoe	Realistic fiction, adventure, survival/England
1726	*Gulliver's Travels* by Jonathan Swift	Modern fantasy, adventure/England
1813	*Pride and Prejudice* by Jane Austen	Realistic fiction/England
1846	*A Book of Nonsense* by Edward Lear	Poetry (limericks)/England
1847	*Jane Eyre* by Charlotte Brontë *Wuthering Heights* by Emily Brontë	Realistic fiction/England
1850, 1861	*David Copperfield* and *Great Expectations* by Charles Dickens	Realistic fiction/England
1864	*Journey to the Center of the Earth* by Jules Verne	Science fiction/France
1865	*Alice's Adventures in Wonderland* by Lewis Carroll	Modern fantasy/England
1869	*Twenty Thousand Leagues under the Sea* by Jules Verne	Science fiction/France
1883	*Treasure Island* by Robert Louis Stevenson	Realistic fiction, adventure/England (Scottish author)
1894	*The Jungle Book* by Rudyard Kipling	Modern fantasy/India (English author)
1908	*Anne of Green Gables* by Lucy M. Montgomery	Realistic fiction/Canada
1937	*The Hobbit* by J. R. R. Tolkien	Modern fantasy/England

International Books by World Regions

The international books that are most often available in the United States have been and continue to be books originally written in English from other English-speaking countries, mainly because they require no translation. The largest numbers of these books come from Great Britain, Canada, Australia, and the Republic of South Africa. These books are often edited for spelling, characters' names, place names, and, occasionally, titles and cover illustrations before being published in the United States. At best, these alterations make the story more understandable for American readers; at worst, they amount to censorship. Because of cultural similarities between the United States and these other English-speaking countries, teachers and librarians are often surprised to discover that one of their favorite authors is not American, but British, Canadian, or Australian. However, many English-language books do feature cultural attitudes and customs not typically found in the United States that warrant comparison and discussion by students.

NOTABLE   *Authors of International Literature*

Aidan Chambers, British author of sophisticated, multilayered stories of self-discovery for mature readers. *Postcards from No Man's Land; The Toll Bridge; Dance on My Grave.* www.aidanchambers.co.uk

Eoin (pronounced "Owen") **Colfer,** Irish author of the five-part fantasy crime Artemis Fowl series. *Artemis Fowl; Benny and Omar; Airman.* www.eoincolfer.com

Cornelia Funke, German author of magical realism novels. *The Thief Lord;* Inkworld triology. www.corneliafunkefans.com

Margo Lanagan, Australian author known for otherworldly short stories. *Black Juice* (COL); *White Time* (COL); *Tender Morsels.*

John Marsden, Australian author of edgy contemporary realism and the Tomorrow series about teenage adventure and survival during war. *So Much to Tell You; Letters from the Inside; Tomorrow, When the War Began.* www.johnmarsden.com.au/home.html

Geraldine McCaughrean (pronounced "Muh-cork-ran"), British author of historical fiction and fantasy novels. *A Pack of Lies; The Kite Rider; The White Darkness.* www.geraldinemccaughrrean.co.uk

Beverley Naidoo, South African-born author of novels dealing with the effects of political injustice on children. *No Turning Back; The Other Side of Truth.* www.beverleynaidoo.com

Uri Orlev, Israeli author of holocaust novels set in Nazi-occupied Poland. *Run, Boy, Run; The Island on Bird Street.*

Philip Pullman, British author of the His Dark Materials fantasy trilogy and the Sally Lockhart mystery series. *The Ruby in the Smoke; The Golden Compass; The Subtle Knife.* www.philip-pullman.com

Shaun Tan, Australian author and illustrator noted for illustrated books on social, political, and historical subjects illustrated in a surrealist style. *The Arrival; Tales from Outer Suburbia.* www.shauntan.net

Markus Zusak, Australian author of novels with enigmatic, unusual, but ultimatley successful characters. *I Am the Messenger; The Book Thief.* www.randomhouse.com/features/markuszusak

Translated books come to the United States mainly from Europe, and particularly from Sweden, Germany, the Netherlands, Belgium, France, Norway, and Denmark. Of the Mideastern countries, Israel produces the most young adult literature that comes to the United States. Examples of translated literature from Europe and the Middle East are two works of historical fiction, *Daniel Half Human: And the Good Nazi* by David Chotjewitz, translated from the German by Doris Orgel, and *Run, Boy, Run* by Uri Orlev, translated from the Hebrew by Hillel Halkin.

Translated young adult literature coming to the United States from Asia originates mostly in Japan. One example is *The Friends,* a work of contemporary realistic fiction by Kazumi Yumoto, translated from the Japanese by Cathy Hirano. Recent immigrants to the United States from Asian countries have written about their experiences in their homelands, but in English and originally for an American audience. For example, a number of excellent young adult books, such as *Red Scarf Girl: A Memoir of the Cultural Revolution* by Ji-li Jiang, chronicle this horrific pogrom in China. Translated titles can be found in Chapters 3 and 5. Books by recent immigrants about their experiences in their homelands are listed with the recommended multicultural books at the end of this chapter.

African nations, with the exception of the Republic of South Africa, and the developing countries of Central and South America have produced few young adult books that have been exported to the

United States. The reason is primarily economic. Publishing books is expensive, and if books for young people are published at all, they tend to be textbooks, not trade books. The more developed countries of Brazil and Venezuela have robust publishing industries but still export few young adult books, possibly as a result of lack of interest on the part of U.S. publishers. Most young adult works of fiction about life in developing countries that come to the United States have been written by citizens of developed countries who have lived in these places, as did Henning Mankell, author of the docu-novel *Secrets in the Fire* (translated from the Swedish by Anne Connie Stuksrud), a story about young people and landmines set in the African nation of Mozambique.

Ethnic prejudice and bias are not natural behaviors; they are learned. One of the most intriguing challenges to those who work with young people is to combat the ignorance that is at the root of racial, cultural, and religious prejudice and intolerance. Young adult literature, particularly the multicultural and international selections that are currently available, is a powerful tool in this effort, for it shows that the similarities between all people are much more fundamental than the differences.

Good

REFERENCES

Carlisle, L. R., Jackson, B. W., & George, A. (2006). Principles of social justice education: The social justice education in schools project. *Equity & Excellence in Education, 39*(1), 55–64.

Ford, D. Y., & Moore, J. L. (2004). Creating culturally responsive gifted education classrooms: Understanding "culture" is the first step. *Gifted Child Today, 27*(4), 34–39.

Gebel, D. (Ed.). (2006). *A bridge of children's books: Children's books from and about other countries.* Lanham, MD: Scarecrow.

Horning, K. T., Lindgren, M. V., Rudiger, H., & Schliesman, M., with Elias, T. (2007). *CCBC Choices, 2007.* Madison: University Communications, University of Wisconsin-Madison.

Lepman, J. (2002). *A bridge of children's books.* Dublin, Ireland: The O'Brien Press in association with IBBY Ireland and USBBY. (Originally published in 1964 as *Die Kinderbuchbrüke* by S. Fischer Verlag, Frankfurt am Main, Germany)

Rochman, H. (1993). *Against borders.* Chicago: ALA Books.

Rudman, M. (1984). *Children's literature: An issues approach* (2nd ed.). New York: Longman.

Schmidt, P. R. (2005). Culturally responsive instruction: Promoting literacy in secondary content areas. Naperville, IL: Learning Point Associates.

Stan, S. (Ed.). (2002). *The world through children's books.* Lanham, MD: Scarecrow.

Tomlinson, C. M. (Ed.). (1998). *Children's books from other countries.* Lanham, MD: Scarecrow.

U.S. Census Bureau. (2000). www.census.gov.

———. (2004). www.census.gov.

U.S. Department of Education, National Center for Education Statistics. (2002a). *Dropout rates in the United States.* Washington, DC: NCES.

U.S. Department of Education, National Center for Education Statistics. (2002b). *Minority population growth.* Washington, DC: NCES.

U.S. Department of Education, National Center for Education Statistics. (2003–2004). *Schools and staffing survey: Percentage distribution of school teachers by race/ethnicity, percentage minority, school type, and selected school characteristics: 2003–04.* Washington, DC: NCES.

U.S. Department of Education, National Center for Education Statistics. (2005). *The nation's report card: Reading 2005.* Retrieved from http://nces .ed.gov/nationsreportcard/pdf/main2005.

RECOMMENDED MULTICULTURAL BOOKS

Ages refer to approximate ages for which the book is appropriate. Book formats other than novels are coded as follows:

(GR)   *Graphic novel*
(PI)   *Picture book*
(COL) *Short story collection*

AFRICAN-AMERICAN LITERATURE

Adoff, Jaime. *The Death of Jayson Porter.* Hyperion, 2008. Ages 15–18. Crushing poverty, neighborhood violence, and lack of family support push a 16-year-old to the edge.

Berry, James. *Ajeemah and His Son.* HarperCollins, 1992. Ages 11–14. Slavery in nineteenth-century Jamaica.

Booth, Coe. *Kendra.* Scholastic, 2008. Ages 14–18. Kendra, 14, must deal with her mother's rejection while growing up in the Bronx and Harlem.

———. *Tyrell.* Scholastic, 2006. Ages 14–18. A 15-year-old boy's struggle to survive poverty and temptations in New York City's South Bronx.

Crisler, Curtis L. *Tough Boy Sonatas.* Illustrated by Floyd Cooper. Boyds Mills/Wordsong, 2007. Ages 15–18. Thirty-eight gritty poems about growing up male, African-American, and poor in Gary, Indiana.

Curtis, Christopher Paul. *Bucking the Sarge.* Random, 2004. Ages 13–18. A 15-year-old boy seeks self-identity and independence from his overbearing mother.

Draper, Sharon M. *Copper Sun.* Atheneum, 2006. Ages 13–18. A 15-year-old African girl is forced into slavery in the eighteenth-century Carolinas.

Feelings, Tom. *The Middle Passage: White Ships/Black Cargo.* Dial, 1995. (PI) Ages 11–18. The horrific transatlantic crossing of slaves bound for America.

Hamilton, Virginia. *The People Could Fly: The Picture Book.* Illustrated by Leo and Diane Dillon. Knopf, 2004. (PI) Ages 11–15. Retelling of a slave escape fantasy.

Jenkins, George, Sampson Davis, and Rameck Hunt. *The Pact: Three Young Men Make a Promise and Fulfill a Dream.* Riverhead, 2002. Ages 14–18. True account of three friends' journey from poverty to professional success.

Johnson, Angela. *The First Part Last.* Simon & Schuster, 2003. Ages 12–16. A 16-year-old father struggles to raise his infant daughter. Prequel to *Heaven.*

———. *Heaven.* Simon & Schuster, 1998. Ages 12–14. A 14-year-old girl wrestles with the true meaning of family and home.

Lester, Julius. *Day of Tears: A Novel in Dialogue.* Hyperion, 2005. Ages 12–15. Fictionalized account of the biggest slave auction in American history (Savannah, Georgia, 1859).

———. *From Slave Ship to Freedom Road.* Illustrated by Rod Brown. Dial, 1998. (PI) Ages 11–15. Graphic depiction of 250 years of slavery in America.

———. *The Old African.* Illustrated by Jerry Pinkney. Dial, 2005. (PI) Ages 11–13. Legend of Ibo slaves in Georgia who walked into the ocean to regain their freedom and spirit.

Mosley, Walter. *47.* Little, Brown, 2005. Ages 12–16. In 1832 a mystical runaway slave inspires the narrator to lead his people to freedom.

Myers, Walter Dean. *Autobiography of My Dead Brother.* HarperCollins, 2005. Ages 14–18. Three young, urban black males follow different paths, one downhill.

———. *The Beast.* Scholastic, 2003. Ages 14–18. A boy discovers that his girlfriend is addicted to drugs.

———. *The Glory Field.* Scholastic, 1994. Ages 11–18. Saga of one black family's American experience, 1753–1990.

———. *Handbook for Boys: A Novel.* HarperCollins, 2002. Ages 14–18. Adult mentoring helps a 16-year-old boy see a better future for himself.

———. *Jazz.* Illustrated by Christopher Myers. Holiday, 2006. (PI) Ages 10–15. Poems and illustrations exploring the forms, moods, and styles of jazz.

———. *Street Love.* HarperCollins/Amistad, 2006. Ages 14–18. Will love overcome Damien and Junice's different social classes and career paths?

———. *Sunrise over Fallujah.* Scholastic, 2008. Ages 14–18. An 18-year-old soldier in the Iraq War tells about the everyday life and frustrations of a soldier.

————. *What They Found: Love on 145th Street.* Random, 2007. **(COL)** Ages 12–18. Finding love and community against all odds.

————. *145th Street: Short Stories.* Ages 13–18. Delacorte, 2000. **(COL)** Ten stories portray life on a block in Harlem.

Smith, Hope A. *Keeping the Night Watch.* Illustrated by E. B. Lewis. Holt, 2008. Ages 10–14. C. J.'s father's return after a long absence causes some resentment.

Suskind, Ron. *A Hope in the Unseen: An American Odyssey from the Inner City to the Ivy League.* Random, 1999. Ages 14–18. The true story of an inner-city African-American boy's effort to get into an Ivy League college.

Taylor, Mildred. *Roll of Thunder, Hear My* Cry. Dial, 1976. (See others in the Logan family saga: *The Song of the Trees,* 1975; *Let the Circle Be Unbroken,* 1981; *The Road to Memphis,* 1990; *The Land,* 2001.) Ages 11–16. Racial prejudice and injustice against generations of a landowning black family in Mississippi.

Tillage, Leon W. *Leon's Story.* Illustrated by Susan L. Roth. Farrar, 1997. Ages 11–13. Nonfiction; illustrated. The hard life of African-Americans in the mid-twentieth century.

Williams-Garcia, Rita. *Every Time a Rainbow Dies.* HarperCollins, 2001. Ages 14–18. Love story set in present-day Brooklyn, NY.

Woodson, Jacqueline. *Miracle's Boys.* Putnam, 2000. Ages 11–18. Inner-city struggles of three recently orphaned brothers.

ASIAN-AMERICAN LITERATURE

Alisa, Kaarin. *The Hmong.* Ages 12–14. Greenhaven, 2007. Part of the Coming to America series on immigration.

Blumberg, Rhoda. *Commodore Perry in the Land of the Shogun.* Lothrup, 1985. Ages 11–15. Matthew Perry's 1853 expedition to open feudal Japan to American trade.

————. *Shipwrecked! The True Adventures of a Japanese Boy.* HarperCollins, 2001. Ages 11–14. Manjiro Nakahama, first Japanese person to come to the United States.

Brown, Jackie. *Little Cricket.* Hyperion, 2004. Ages 11–14. A Hmong immigrant family adjusts to life in St. Paul, Minnesota, in the 1970s.

Budhos, Marina. *Ask Me No Questions.* Atheneum, 2006. Ages 15–18. Fourteen-year-old Nadia, a Muslim from Bangladesh living illegally in New York, struggles to hold her family together.

Carey, Mike. *Re-Gifters.* Illustrated by Sonny Liew and Marc Hempel. Minx, 2007. **(GR)** Ages 13–18. Korean-American girl friends learn about life and love during a martial arts tournament.

Kadohata, Cynthia. *Kira-Kira.* Atheneum, 2004. Ages 11–14. Devoted siblings growing up Japanese-American in Georgia in the 1950s.

————. *Weedflower.* Simon & Schuster, 2006. Ages 11–14. Japanese-American internment during World War II in Arizona.

Lasky, Kathryn. *Jahanara, Princess of Princesses.* Scholastic, 2002. Ages 12–14. Part of the Royal Diaries series. Daughter of the seventeenth-century Indian emperor who built the Taj Mahal.

McKay, Lawrence, Jr. *Journey Home.* Illustrated by Dom and Keunhee Lee. Lee & Low, 1998. **(PI)** Ages 11–12. A Vietnamese American searches for her birth parents in Saigon.

Na, An. *A Step from Heaven.* Front Street, 2001. Ages 13–16. A Korean émigré family's struggles to adjust to life in the United States.

Salisbury, Graham. *Lord of the Deep.* Delacorte, 2001. Ages 11–14. Maturing as a result of facing a moral dilemma. Set in present-day Hawaii.

Shea, Peggy Deitz. *Tangled Threads: A Hmong Girl's Story.* Ages 12–15. Clarion, 2003. A 13-year-old Laotian refugee's assimilation into American culture.

Sheth, Kashmira. *Blue Jasmine.* Hyperion, 2004. Ages 11–14. An immigrant from India adjusts to life in America.

————. *Keeping Corner.* Hyperion, 2007. Ages 12–18. Leela, widowed at 12, faces a bleak future, but the politics of India's fight for independence (1940s) gives her hope for a brighter future.

Staples, Suzanne Fisher. *Shiva's Fire.* Farrar, 2000. Ages 12–16. An Indian girl acknowledges her destiny to live the life of an artist.

Whelan, Gloria. *Chu Ju's House.* HarperCollins, 2004. Ages 12–14. Overcoming (female) gender restrictions in present-day rural China.

————. *Homeless Bird.* HarperCollins, 2000. Ages 12–14. Married, widowed, then abandoned at 13 in present-day India.

Yang, Gene Luen. *American Born Chinese.* Roaring Brook/First Second, 2006. **(GR)** Ages 12–18. Postmodernist coming-of-age story about self-acceptance.

Yang, Kao Kalia. *The Latehomecomer: A Hmong Family Memoir.* Coffee House, 2008. Ages 15–18. The story of a woman who immigrated from Laos to Minnesota in 1986 and later founded a support service for immigrants.

Yep, Laurence. *Dragon's Gate.* HarperCollins, 1993. Ages 12–16. Chinese-American experiences working on the transcontinental railroad in 1867.

————. *Dragonwings.* Harper, 1975. Ages 11–14. Assimilation of American culture by Chinese immigrants in 1903 San Francisco.

————. *Thief of Hearts.* HarperCollins, 1995. Ages 11–14. Dealing with mixed heritage and racial stereotyping in 1995 San Francisco. (Sequel to *Child of the Owl.*)

————. *Traitor: Golden Mountain Chronicles, 1885.* HarperCollins, 2003. Ages 12–14. Friendship versus race-related hatred in an 1885 Wyoming mining community.

CROSS-CULTURAL LITERATURE

Gaskins, Pearl F., editor. *I Believe In . . . : Christian, Jewish, and Muslim Young People Speak about Their Faith.* Cricket, 2004. Ages 14–18. A look at how religion affects the lives of young people through interviews with 15–24-year-olds.

————. *What Are You? Voices of Mixed-Race Young People.* Holt, 1999. Ages 14–18. Interviews, essays, and poetry by forty-five mixed-race young people.

Gillan, Maria M., and Jennifer Gillan, editors. *Growing Up Ethnic in America: Contemporary Fiction about Learning to Be American.* Penguin, 1999. **(COL)** Ages 15–18. Stories and memoirs about adapting to American ways while holding onto one's native culture.

Nye, Naomi Shihab (anthologist). *The Space between Our Footsteps: Poems and Paintings from the Middle East.* Simon and Schuster, 1998. Ages 12–18. Poems and paintings from over 100 poets and artists from 19 Middle Eastern countries give insights into the culture of the region.

————. *This Same Sky: A Collection of Poems from around the World.* Four Winds, 1992. Ages 11–12. One hundred twenty-nine poets from sixty-eight countries.

O'Hearn, Claudine C. *Half and Half: Writers Growing Up Biracial and Bicultural.* Pantheon, 1998. Ages 12–18. First-person accounts of eighteen writers with biracial or bicultural backgrounds.

Smith, Cynthia Leitich. *Rain Is Not My Indian Name.* HarperCollins, 2001. Ages 11–14. A present-day teen discovers the meaning of her Indian heritage.

Strom, Yale. *Quilted Landscape: Conversations with Young Immigrants.* Simon & Schuster, 1996. Ages 11–18. Thoughts of twenty-six recent young adult immigrants to the United States.

LATINO LITERATURE

Alvarez, Julia. *Before We Were Free.* Knopf, 2002. Ages 11–14. Life during the Trujillo dictatorship in the Dominican Republic, 1960–1961.

————. *How the García Girls Lost Their Accents.* Algonquin, 1991. Ages 14–18. Four sisters' adjustment to life in the United States after fleeing the Dominican Republic in the 1960s.

Atkin, S. Beth. *Voices from the Fields: Children of Migrant Farmworkers Tell Their Stories.* Little, Brown, 1993. Ages 10–14. The stories of nine migrant Mexican-American children are told through interviews, poems, and photographs.

Canales, Viola. *The Tequila Worm.* Random, 2005. Ages 12–15. A Mexican-American girl's experiences on her way to becoming a *comadre,* or family-maker, in the barrio.

Carlson, Lori M., editor. *Cool Salsa: Bilingual Poems on Growing Up Latino in the United States.* Holt, 1994. Ages 14–18. English/Spanish. Eclectic collection of several generations of U.S. writers of Latino heritage.

————. *Red Hot Salsa: Bilingual Poems on Being Young and Latino in the United States.* Holt,

2005. Ages 14–18. English/Spanish. Poems (some by teens) about the complex challenges of being bicultural.

Cisneros, Sandra. *The House on Mango Street.* Arte Público, 1984. Ages 14–18. Growing up Mexican American in the Latino section of Chicago.

————. *Woman Hollering Creek and Other Stories.* Random, 1991. (COL) Ages 14–18. Lives of Mexican-American women living on the border between Mexico and Texas.

Cofer, Judith O. *An Island Like You.* Orchard, 1995. (COL) Ages 12–16. Twelve stories about being a teenager in the Puerto Rican barrio.

Delacre, Lulu, reteller. *Salsa Stories.* (COL) Ages 11–14. Scholastic, 2000. Family stories triggered by memories of favorite foods from various Latin American countries. Recipes included.

Freedman, Russell. *In the Days of the Vaqueros: America's First True Cowboys.* Clarion, 2001. Ages 10–14. Nonfiction. Role of the Central American cowherders, 1500s–1700s.

Hernandez, Gilbert. *Sloth.* DC Comics/Vertigo, 2006. (GR) Ages 15–18. Disillusioned Miguel and friends seek meaning in their small-town lives.

Herrera, Juan Felipe. *Crashboomlove: A Novel in Verse.* University of New Mexico Press, 1999. Ages 14–18. 16-year-old Mexican teen growing up in an American high school.

Jaramillo, Ann. *La Línea.* Roaring Brook, 2006. Ages 12–14. A brother and sister's experience immigrating illegally from Mexico to the United States.

Jiménez, Francisco. *The Circuit: Stories from the Life of a Migrant Child.* Houghton, 1999. (COL) (Sequels: *Breaking Through,* 2001; *Reaching Out,* 2008) Ages 11–18. Autobiographical account of the dreary, frustrating, poverty-stricken lives of migrant workers.

Joseph, Lynn. *The Color of My Words.* HarperCollins, 2000. Ages 10–14. Life, dreams, and sorrows of a Dominican teenage girl.

Nye, Naomi Shihab, editor. *The Tree Is Older Than You Are: A Bilingual Gathering of Poems and Stories from Mexico with Paintings by Mexican Artists.* Simon & Schuster, 1995. (COL) Ages 11–18. English/Spanish. Nature and rural life.

Resau, Laura. *What the Moon Saw.* Delacorte, 2006. Ages 11–15. Mexican-American 14-year-old Clara spends the summer with her grandparents in Mexico and awakens to her Mexican heritage.

Rice, David. *Crazy Loco.* Dial, 2001. (COL) Ages 12–18. Nine short stories about growing up Latino in southern Texas; family and traditions.

Ryan, Pam Muñoz. *Esperanza Rising.* Scholastic, 2001. Ages 11–15. Emigration from Mexico and adjustment to life in the United States in the 1930s.

————. *Becoming Naomi León.* Scholastic, 2004. Ages 11–15. Finding one's family, Mexican heritage, and talent.

Sáenz, Benjamin A. *Sammy and Juliana in Hollywood.* Cinco Puntos, 2004. Ages 15–18. Dreams and losses while growing up in the Hollywood barrio of Las Cruces, New Mexico, during the late 1960s.

Soto, Gary. *Baseball in April and Other Stories.* Harcourt, 1990. (COL) Ages 11–14. Eleven stories about everyday problems of growing up Latino in central California.

Sullivan, Charles, editor. *Here Is My Kingdom: Hispanic-American Literature and Art for Young People.* Abrams, 1994. (COL) Ages 13–18. Anthology of stories, poems, paintings. The Hispanic-American experience through works by more than 100 painters, poets, writers, photographers, activists, scholars, and historical figures.

Triana, Gaby. *Cubanita.* HarperCollins, 2005. Ages 15–18. A 17-year-old girl learns to value her Cuban heritage.

Veciana-Suarez, Ana. *Flight to Freedom.* Orchard, 2002. Ages 12–14. Flight from the Castro regime in Cuba in 1967 to Miami and the difficulties of living in exile in the United States.

NATIVE AMERICAN LITERATURE

Alexie, Sherman. *The Absolutely True Diary of a Part-Time Indian.* Little, Brown, 2007. Ages 12–18. Junior, a 14-year-old Spokane Indian, learns much about himself when he transfers to an all-white high school. Semiautobiographical.

Ancona, George. *Mayeros: A Yucatec Maya Family.* Lothrop, 1997. Ages 11–12. Photoessay about the daily life of a rural family in the Yucatan Peninsula.

Bealer, Alex. *Only the Names Remain: The Cherokees and the Trail of Tears.* Little, Brown, 1972. Ages

11–18. Tribal history from 1500s through the forced removal from Georgia in 1837.

Bruchac, Joseph. *Pocahontas.* Silver Whistle, 2003. Ages 12–18. Historically accurate account of the Powhatan girl and her relationship with Captain John Smith.

———. *Sacajawea.* Silver Whistle, 2000. Ages 12–18. Fact-based story of Lewis and Clark's Shoshone interpreter.

———. *The Winter People.* Dial, 2002. Ages 12–16. A tale (based on fact) of kidnap and rescue in Quebec in 1759 during the French and Indian War.

Carlson, Lori Marie, editor. *Moccasin Thunder: American Indian Stories for Today.* HarperCollins, 2005. Ages 15–18. (COL) Ten contemporary short stories by Native American writers about Native American teens.

Carvell, Marlene. *Sweetgrass Basket.* Dutton, 2005. Ages 13–16. Two Mohawk sisters' terrible experiences at the turn of the twentieth century in a boarding school for Native Americans.

Erdrich, Louise. *The Birchbark House.* Hyperion, 1999. Ages 11–14. (Sequel: *The Game of Silence,* 2005.) Ojibwa daily life in 1847 in the Lake Superior area.

———. *The Porcupine Year.* HarperCollins, 2008. Ages 10–14. Ojibwe Indian Omakaya's twelfth year (1852) is turbulent, as her family is displaced by the United States government and her transition to womanhood begins.

George, Jean Craighead. *Julie.* HarperCollins, 1994. Ages 11–14. (Sequel to *Julie of the Wolves.*) Wildlife conservation in the modern world.

———. *Julie of the Wolves.* Harper, 1972. Ages 11–13. Survival in the Alaskan tundra using traditional Inuit lore.

Hobbs, Will. *Bearstone.* Atheneum, 1989. Ages 11–14. (Sequel: *Beardance,* 1993.) A coming-of-age story involving a Ute boy, grizzly bears, and gold.

Mikaelsen, Ben. *Touching Spirit Bear.* HarperCollins, 2001. Ages 11–14. Healing one's spirit and atoning for wrongdoing by living for a year in the Alaskan wilderness.

O'Dell, Scott. *Island of the Blue Dolphins.* Houghton, 1960. Ages 11–13. A Native American girl learns to survive alone and prosper in the wild without destroying nature. Based on fact.

———. *Sing Down the Moon.* Houghton, 1970. Ages 12–16. Rebellion of a young Navajo woman during the forced removal of her tribe from Arizona to New Mexico in 1864.

Rappaport, Doreen. *The Flight of Red Bird: The Life of Zilkala-Sa.* Dial, 1997. Ages 11–14. Biography detailing the frustration of living between two cultures—the Nakota Sioux and white.

Viola, Herman J. *It Is a Good Day to Die: Indian Eyewitnesses Tell the Story of the Battle of the Little Bighorn.* Crown, 1998. Ages 11–18. Informational. Custer's Last Stand (1876) left no white survivors.

RELIGIOUS CULTURES LITERATURE

Ehrenberg, Pamela. *Ethan, Suspended.* Eerdmans, 2007. Ages 12–16. Sent to live with his Jewish grandparents in inner-city Washington, DC, Ethan learns much about his own and other cultures in school and at home.

Geras, Adèle. *My Grandmother's Stories: A Collection of Jewish Folk Tales.* Illustrated by Anita Lobel. Knopf, 2003. (COL) Ages 11–14. Ten traditional Russian Jewish folktales.

Hautzig, Esther. *The Endless Steppe: A Girl in Exile.* Crowell, 1968. Ages 11–14. A Jewish family's five years of starvation and forced labor in Siberia in World War II.

Hesse, Karen. *The Stone Lamp: Eight Stories of Hanukkah through History.* Illustrated by Brian Pinkney. Hyperion, 2003. (COL) Ages 11–13. Poems and narrative. Explanation of eight crucial periods in Jewish history.

Kimmel, Eric. *Wonders and Miracles: A Passover Companion.* Scholastic, 2004. (COL) Ages 11–14. Stories, songs, recipes, artwork, prayers, and commentary related to the Jewish holiday.

Levitin, Sonia. *Journey to America.* Atheneum, 1970. Ages 12–18. (Sequel: *Silver Days,* 1989.) Frightening escape of a Jewish family from Nazi Germany and their trials en route to America.

———. *Strange Relations.* Knopf, 2007. Ages 13–17. A 15-year-old Jewish-American girl wrestles with her religious traditions and the issue of faith.

Mobin-Uddin, Asma. *My Name is Bilal.* Illustrated by Barbara Kiwak. Boyds Mills, 2005. (PI) Ages 9–14.

A middle school boy and his sister, the only Muslims in their school, confront prejudice.

Reiss, Johanna. *The Upstairs Room.* Crowell, 1972. Ages 11–14. Jewish sisters hide for years in a small room in Nazi-occupied Netherlands during World War II.

Rogasky, Barbara. *Smoke and Ashes: The Story of the Holocaust* (expanded edition). Holiday, 2002. Ages 12–18. Anti-Semitism and hate groups from World War II to present.

Rubin, Susan Goldman. *Fireflies in the Dark: The Story of Friedl Dicker-Brandeis and the Children of Terezin.* Holiday, 2000. Ages 11–14. Biography of the woman who taught art to children in Nazi concentration camp (illustrated with archival children's art).

Schmidt, Gary. *Mara's Stories: Glimmers in the Darkness.* Holt, 2001. (COL) Ages 11–14. Traditional and original stories told by a Nazi concentration camp inmate during her imprisonment.

Siegal, Aranka. *Upon the Head of the Goat: A Childhood in Hungary, 1939–1944.* Farrar, 1981. (Sequel: *Grace in the Wilderness: After the Liberation, 1945–1948,* 1985.) Ages 11–16. Step-by-step account of the Jewish Holocaust through the experiences of one Hungarian family.

Vos, Ida. *The Key Is Lost.* Translated by Terese Edelstein. HarperCollins, 2000. Ages 10–13. Changing one's identity to escape the Nazis in Holland.

Yolen, Jane. *The Devil's Arithmetic.* Penguin, 1988. Ages 11–14. Time-warp Jewish Holocaust experience.

RECOMMENDED INTERNATIONAL BOOKS

Country of original publication is noted.

ENGLISH-LANGUAGE BOOKS

Abdel-Fattah, Randa. *Does My Head Look Big in This?* Scholastic, 2007. Ages 12–18. Australia. A humorous look at a teenager coping with issues of faith (Muslim) and different cultures (Australian-Palestinian). Also Cross-Cultural and Religious Cultures.

Almond, David. *Clay.* Delacorte, 2006. Ages 11–15. England. Three boys create a huge clay monster that obeys their wishes.

———. *Heaven Eyes.* Delacorte, 2001. Ages 11–14. England. Dreams, memories, reality, and imagination fuse as children seek their freedom from a dismal orphanage.

———. *Kit's Wilderness.* Delacorte, 2000. Ages 12–18. England. The influence of the past and the dead on the present and the living.

———. *Skellig.* Delacorte, 1999. Ages 11–14. England. Connected life-and-death struggles, one ethereal and one worldly.

Baker, Jeannie. *Window.* Julia McRae, 1991. (PI; wordless) Ages 11–13. Australia. Human destruction of the wilderness.

Boyce, Frank C. *Millions.* HarperCollins, 2004. Ages 11–14. England. Humor. An enormous, unexpected windfall helps brothers deal with losing their mother.

Brooks, Martha. *Mistik Lake.* Farrar, 2007. Ages 14–18. Canada. Seventeen-year-old Odella comes of age while coping with her mother's death, family secrets, and first romance.

Burgess, Melvin. *Doing It.* Holt, 2004. Ages 14–18. England. Sexual urges and anxieties of three teenage boys.

———. *Smack.* England. Holt, 1998. Ages 15–18. Heroin addiction.

Clark, Judith. *Kalpana's Dream.* Front Street, 2005. Ages 12–15. Australia. A girl is helped by her Indian great-grandmother in her search for self-identity.

Colfer, Eoin. *Artemis Fowl.* Hyperion, 2001. Ages 11–12. Ireland. A twelve-year-old masterminds a gold heist . . . from fairies!

Cornish, D. M. *Foundling.* Putnam, 2006. Ages 12–16. Australia. First book in the Monster Blood Tattoo series, a survival adventure set in a monster-filled, medieval world. Sequel: *Lamplighter.* Putnam, 2008. Ages 12–16.

Craig, Colleen. *Afrika.* Tundra, 2008. Ages 14–18. Canada. Kim, a 13-year-old Canadian, visits Africa in the 1980s during the era of apartheid. Also Cross-Cultural.

Crossley-Holland, Kevin. *The Seeing Stone*. Scholastic, 2001. Ages 11–14. England. A teenage boy in twelfth-century England is strangely connected to King Arthur.

Dhami, Narinder. *Bindi Babes*. Delacorte, 2004. Ages 11–14. England. Humor. Three Indian sisters living in England miss their mother and plot against their aunt.

Doctorow, Cory. *Little Brother*. Tor, 2008. Ages 13–18. Canada. After a 17-year-old boy is erroneously detained and subjected to brutal interrogation by Homeland Security, he vows to fight back.

Doherty, Berlie. *Dear Nobody*. Hamish Hamilton, 1991. Ages 12–18. England. Harsh truths about teenage pregnancy and parenthood.

Dowd, Siobhan. *Bog Child*. Random, 2008. Ages 13–18. Ireland. Intrigue following the discovery of a body buried in a bog in Ireland.

———. *The London Eye Mystery*. Random, 2008. Ages 11–14. England. A boy (possibly with Asperger's syndrome) tries to solve the mysterious disappearance of his cousin.

Doyle, Brian. *Mary Ann Alice*. Douglas & McIntyre, 2002. Ages 11–13. Canada. Gains and losses associated with "progress."

Doyle, Malachy. *Who Is Jesse Flood?* Bloomsbury, 2002. Ages 11–14. Northern Ireland. Teenaged angst and self-inquiry in a Northern Ireland small-town setting.

French, Jackie. *Hitler's Daughter*. HarperCollins, 2003. Ages 11–12. Australia. Ethical questions involving the Jewish Holocaust and Australia's Aboriginal people.

Gavin, Jamila. *Coram Boy*. Farrar, 2001. Ages 11–14. England. Child slavery, mystery, adventure, and romance in eighteenth-century England.

Gilmore, Rachna. *A Group of One*. Holt, 2001. Ages 11–14. Canada. A fifteen-year-old girl seeks her identity and acknowledges her Native heritage.

Golding, Julia. *The Diamond of Drury Lane*. Roaring Brook, 2008. Ages 14–16. England. Mystery involving a hidden diamond set in early eighteenth-century London's theatre district.

Greenwood, Kerry. *A Different Kind of Real: The Diary of Charlotte McKenzie, Melbourne, 1918–1919.*

Scholastic, 2001. Ages 11–13. Australia. Influenza pandemic.

Hartnett, Sonya. *Thursday's Child*. Candlewick, 2002. Ages 13–16. Australia. Living in the crushing poverty of an outback mining community during the Depression.

Henegan, James. *Flood*. Farrar, 2002. Ages 11–14. Canada. Finding one's family and home with the help of the Little People.

Herrick, Steven. *The Wolf*. Front Street, 2007. Ages 14–18. Australia. Jake and Lucy search for a predator in the Australian mountains, but find something else.

Honey, Elizabeth. *Remote Man*. Knopf, 2002. Ages 11–16. Australia. Tackling apathy, mental illness, and international wildlife poachers with the help of e-mail buddies.

Ibbotson, Eva. *Journey to the River Sea*. Illustrated by Kevin Hawkes. Dutton, 2001. Ages 11–13. England. Adventure along the Amazon River in 1910 Brazil.

———. *The Secret of Platform 13*. Dutton, 1998. Ages 11–13. England. The daring between-worlds rescue of a kidnapped prince.

———. *The Star of Kazan*. Dutton, 2004. Ages 11–13. England. A brave heroine encounters sly villains while seeking her true family in early-nineteenth-century Vienna.

———. *Which Witch?* Dutton, 1999. Ages 11–14. England. A tall, dark, and handsome wizard seeks a wife.

Ihimaera, Witi. *Whale Rider*. Harcourt, 2003. Ages 12–16. New Zealand. Combination Maori-creation-myth and girl-power adventure.

Jennings, Paul. *Unreal: Eight Surprising Stories*. Viking, 1991. (COL) Ages 11–14. Australia. (See also *Uncanny*, 1991, and *Unmentionable*, 1995.) Humor. Wacky, sometimes gross, tales of the supernatural. (High appeal to males.)

Jinks, Catharine. *Evil Genius*. Harcourt, 2007. Ages 12–16. Australia. Thirteen-year-old Cadel is being trained by his crooked father to dominate the world.

Jocelyn, Marthe. *How It Happened in Peach Hill*. Random, 2007. Ages 13–18. Canada. Fifteen-year-old Annie rebels against her mother and their life as swindlers in 1920s New York State.

————. *Would You.* Random, 2008. Ages 14–18. Canada. Natalie must cope with the aftermath of her sister's being hit by a car.

Johnston, Julie. *In Spite of Killer Bees.* Tundra, 2001. Ages 12–16. Canada. Reconstructing a long-lost family.

Kostick, Conor. *Epic.* Viking, 2007. Ages 12–18. England. Erik seeks to overcome the despots who rule his future world by beating them at their own fantasy computer game.

Lanagan, Margo. *Red Spikes.* Knopf, 2007. **(COL)** Ages 15–18. Australia. Ten stories focusing on what it means to be human.

————. *Tender Morsels.* Knopf, 2008. Ages 15–18. Australia. A 15-year-old mother and her two daughters experience good and evil in alternate worlds.

————. *White Time.* HarperCollins, 2006. **(COL)** Ages 13–18. Australia. Ten stories in a variety of genres.

Leavitt, Martine. *Keturah and Lord Death.* Front Street, 2006. Ages 13–17. Canada. A retelling of Sheherazade.

Little, Jean. *Willow and Twig.* Viking, 2003. Ages 11–14. Canada. Abandoned children try to establish a new home and family.

Lowry, Brigid. *Follow the Blue.* Holiday, 2004. Ages 14–18. New Zealand. A 15-year-old New Zealander tries to find her way in life while living in Australia.

Lunn, Janet. *Laura Secord: A Story of Courage.* Illustrated by Maxwell Newhouse. Tundra, 2001. Ages 11–12. Canada. A girl's nineteen-mile trek in 1813 to warn her country's troops of impending disaster.

Marchetta, Melina. *Saving Francesca.* Knopf, 2004. Ages 14–18. Australia. Coping with mental depression of a parent.

Marsden, John. *Letters from the Inside.* Houghton, 1994. Ages 15–18. Australia. Correspondence between two teenage girls for one year hints at impending disaster.

————. *So Much to Tell You.* Joy Street, 1989. Ages 12–18. Australia. Elective mutism as the result of a tragic accident.

————. *Tomorrow, When the War Began.* Houghton, 1995. Ages 12–18. Australia. (First of six books in the series.) A band of teenage guerilla warriors combat the foreign military occupiers of their country.

Matas, Carol. *Sparks Fly Upward.* Clarion, 2002. Ages 11–13. Canada. Coping with anti-Semitism in early-twentieth-century Canada.

McCaughrean, Geraldine. *Cyrano.* Harcourt, 2006. Ages 12–16. England. Retelling of the classic French play. Good for readers' theatre or read-aloud.

————. *The Kite Rider.* HarperCollins, 2002. Ages 11–14. England. A 12-year-old boy seeks to avenge his father's death and protect his mother in thirteenth-century China.

————. *A Pack of Lies.* Oxford, 1988. Ages 14–18. England. A master storyteller spins his web of intrigue and mystery in a London antiques shop.

————. *The White Darkness.* HarperCollins, 2007. Ages 12–16. England. Fourteen-year-old Sym makes some horrifying discoveries about her uncle in Antarctica.

McKay, Hilary. *The Exiles.* Macmillan, 1992. Ages 11–13. England. Humor. Four "bookish" sisters are exposed to hard work and fresh air during a summer visit with their grandmother.

————. *Indigo's Star.* McElderry, 2004. Ages 11–13. England. Dealing with bullies and an absentee father.

————. *Saffy's Angel.* McElderry, 2002. Ages 11–13. England. Humor. Being adopted and appreciating one's adoptive family.

Moriarty, Jaclyn. *The Year of Secret Assignments.* Scholastic, 2004. Ages 14–18. Australia. Friendship of three girls documented in letters, diaries, lists, e-mail, notes.

Morpurgo, Michael. *Private Peaceful.* Scholastic, 2004. Ages 14–18. England. Brutal trench warfare of World War I.

————. *Sir Gawain and the Green Knight.* Illustrated by Michael Foreman. Candlewick, 2004. Ages 11–13. England. A medieval tale of adventure and honor.

Murray, Martine. *The Slightly True Story of Cedar B. Hartley (Who Planned to Live an Unusual Life).* Scholastic, 2003. Ages 11–13. Australia. A 12-year-old girl contemplates a missing brother, a mysterious father, acrobatics, and budding romance.

Naidoo, Beverley. *Burn My Heart.* HarperCollins, 2008. Ages 12–18. South Africa. The Mau Mau uprising in early 1950s Kenya as seen through the eyes of a young white boy and a young Kikuyu boy.

———. *Chain of Fire.* Lippincott, 1990. Ages 11–18. South Africa. (Sequel to *Journey to Jo'burg.*) Effects of apartheid on families and children.

———. *Journey to Jo'burg.* Lippincott, 1986. Ages 11–13. South Africa. Effects of apartheid on families and children.

———. *No Turning Back: A Novel of South Africa.* HarperCollins, 1997. Ages 11–14. South Africa. Perils of homelessness in Johannesburg.

———. *The Other Side of Truth.* HarperCollins, 2001. Ages 11–14. South Africa (set in Nigeria and London). Two young political refugees from Nigeria cope with abandonment, culture shock, and fear in London.

———. *Out of Bounds: Seven Stories of Conflict and Hope.* HarperCollins, 2003. Ages 11–14. South Africa. Living under apartheid, 1948–2000.

Nicholson, William. *The Wind Singer.* Hyperion, 2000. Ages 11–13. (Also in Wind on Fire trilogy: *Slaves of the Master,* 2001; *Firesong,* 2002.) England. Dystopian quest fantasy in which the heroes seek freedom of choice for their people.

Orr, Wendy. *Peeling the Onion.* Holiday, 1997. Ages 11–16. Australia. Self-discovery through recovery from a car wreck.

Peacock, Shane. *Eye of the Crow.* Tundra, 2007. Canada. Ages 12–15. Mystery solved by a young Sherlock Holmes.

Peet, Mal. *Tamar.* Candlewick, 2007. Ages 14–18. England. Fifteen-year-old Tamar solves the mystery surrounding her grandfather's role as a resistance fighter in 1945 Netherlands. Also Religious Cultures.

Pratchett, Terry. *The Amazing Maurice and His Educated Rodents.* HarperCollins, 2001. Ages 11–16. England. Humor. Mystery involving con artist rats who uncover a sinister conspiracy.

———. *Nation.* HarperCollins, 2008. Ages 12–16. England. Two teens from different cultures are brought together when a tidal wave inundates an island.

———. *The Wee Free Men.* HarperCollins, 2003. Ages 11–14. England. Humor. A feisty young detective-witch-heroine and a band of fierce little men combat an evil Fairy Queen kidnapper.

Pullman, Philip. *The Golden Compass.* Knopf, 1996. Ages 12–16. (Also in His Dark Materials trilogy:

The Subtle Knife, Knopf, 1997; *The Amber Spyglass,* Knopf, 1999.) England. Quest fantasy pitting a young heroine against ruthless soul-thieves.

Rees, Celia. *Pirates!* Bloomsbury, 2003. Ages 12–16. England. Adventures of two young women aboard a pirate ship in 1725.

———. *Witch Child.* Candlewick, 2001. Ages 11–14. (Sequel: *Sorceress,* 2002.) England. Granddaughter of an herbal healer is suspected of witchcraft in 1600s Massachusetts.

Reeve, Philip. *Here Lies Arthur.* Scholastic, 2008. Ages 12–16. England. A new perspective on the events and characters in the Arthurian legend.

Rowling, J. K. *Harry Potter and the Sorcerer's Stone.* Scholastic, 1998. (Also in the Harry Potter quest fantasy series: *Harry Potter and the Chamber of Secrets,* 1999; *Harry Potter and the Prisoner of Azkaban,* 1999; *Harry Potter and the Goblet of Fire,* 2000; *Harry Potter and the Order of the Phoenix,* 2003; *Harry Potter and the Half-Blood Prince,* 2005; *Harry Potter and the Deathly Hallows,* 2007.) Ages 11–13. England. A young wizard battling a local evil in the real world (his foster family) and a cosmic evil threatening to take over the world in the realm of magic.

Selvadurai, Shyam. *Swimming in the Monsoon Sea.* Tundra, 2005. Ages 14–17. Canada. When his Canadian cousin visits, a 13-year-old Sri Lankan boy learns much about his family and himself.

Slade, Arthur. *Dust.* Wendy Lamb, 2003. Ages 11–14. Canada. Drought, missing children, and a stranger in town are mysteriously related.

Southall, Ivan. *Josh.* Macmillan, 1988. Ages 12–14. (Reissued by Front Street, 2005.) Australia. Misunderstanding escalates rapidly toward violence during a boy's three-day visit to the outback.

Stratton, Allan. *Chanda's Secrets.* Annick, 2004. Ages 14–18. Canada. The effect of AIDS on the lives of children and young adults in South Africa.

Tan, Shaun. *The Arrival.* Scholastic, 2007. (**GR**, wordless) Ages 12–18. Australia. A pictorial view of the immigrant experience of arriving in a strange new country.

———. *Tales from Outer Suburbia.* Scholastic, 2009. (**COL**) Ages 12–18. Australia. Fifteen illustrated stories about strange situations in suburbia and how people react to them.

Thompson, Kate. *The New Policeman.* Greenwillow, 2007. Ages 12–16. England. A 15-year-old boy visits an alternate world to repair a cosmic time leak.

———. *Wild Blood.* Hyperion, 2000. Ages 11–14. (Also in the Switchers series: *Switchers,* 1998; *Midnight's Choice,* 1999.) Ireland. A shape-changer must decide on her permanent form.

Updale, Eleanor. *Montmorency.* Scholastic, 2004. Ages 12–16. Suspense-filled London-based Victorian spy drama. Part of a series.

Valentine, Jenny. *Me, the Missing, and the Dead.* HarperTeen, 2008. Ages 14–18. England. While learning about a deceased concert pianist, Lucas solves the mystery of his missing father.

Venkatraman, Padma. *Climbing the Stairs.* Putnam, 2008. Ages 12–16. An ambitious, progressive 15-year-old Indian girl comes of age in a conservative household in Madras during World War II.

Wild, Margaret. *Fox.* Illustrated by Ron Brooks. Kane/Miller, 2001. **(PI)** Ages 11–13. Australia. A modern fable about friendship and betrayal.

Wynne-Jones, Tim. *The Boy in the Burning House.* Farrar, 2001. Ages 12–14. Canada. Investigations into two suspected murders reveal many secrets.

Yee, Paul. *Dead Man's Gold and Other Stories.* Illustrated by Harvey Chan. Douglas & McIntyre, 2002. **(COL)** Ages 10–16. Canada. Ten ghost stories about Chinese-Canadian immigrants.

Zusak, Markus. *The Book Thief.* Knopf, 2007. Ages 14–18. Australia. Stolen books help a girl cope with life and death in Nazi-era Germany. Also Religious Cultures.

TRANSLATED BOOKS

Bondoux, Anne-Laure. *The Killer's Tears.* Translated from the French by Y. Maudet. Delacorte, 2006. Ages 14–18. France. Crime, punishment, and the awakening of conscience are the focus of this story set in Chile.

Buchholz, Quint. *The Collector of Moments.* Translated from the German by Peter F. Niemeyer. Farrar, 1999. **(PI)** Ages 11–13. Germany. The stories found in art and their power to affect the viewer's life.

Chotjewitz, David. *Daniel Half Human: And the Good Nazi.* Translated from the German by Doris Orgel.

Atheneum, 2004. Ages 14–18. Germany. Discovering and coming to terms with one's Jewish heritage during the Holocaust.

de Saint-Exupéry, Antoine. *Le Petit Prince.* Harcourt, 1943/2001. Ages 6 and up. Childlike but profound views on life and human nature. French language version.

Funke, Cornelia. *The Thief Lord.* Translated from the German by Oliver Latsch. Scholastic, 2002. Ages 11–14. Germany. Young runaways form a ring of thieves in Venice.

Gandolfi, Silvana. *Aldabra, or the Tortoise Who Loved Shakespeare.* Translated from the Italian by Lynne Sharon Schwartz. Scholastic, 2004. Ages 11–16. Italy. An eccentric grandmother devises a way to prolong her life, with the help of her loving granddaughter.

Jansen, Hanna. *Over a Thousand Hills I Walk with You.* Translated from the German by Elizabeth D. Crawford. Carolrhoda, 2006. Ages 12–16. Germany. Fictionalized biography about a survivor of the 1994 Rwanda genocide.

Jung, Reinhard. *Dreaming in Black and White.* Translated from the German by Anthea Bell. Phyllis Fogelman, 2003. Ages 11–14. Germany. Attitudes toward those living with disabilities.

Kerner, Charlotte. *Blueprint.* Translated from the German by Elizabeth D. Crawford. Lerner, 2000. Ages 14–18. Germany. Psychological, sociological, and physical ramifications of human cloning.

Mankell, Henning. *Secrets in the Fire.* Translated from the Swedish by Anne C. Stuksrud. Ages 11–18. Annick, 2003. Sweden. Tragic effects of war on child victims of minefields in early 1990s Mozambique.

Michaelis, Antonia. *Tiger Moon.* Translated from the German by Anthea Bell. Abrams, 2008. Ages 15–18. Germany. Storytelling helps a young Indian maiden cope with her forced betrothal.

Mourlevat, Jean-Claude. *The Pull of the Ocean.* Translated from the French by Y. Maudet. Delacorte, 2006. Ages 10–14. France. A modern "Tom Thumb" story.

Newth, Mette. *The Dark Light.* Translated from the Norwegian by Faith Ingwersen. Farrar, 1998. Norway. Leprosy in nineteenth-century Norway.

Orlev, Uri. *Run, Boy, Run.* Translated from the Hebrew by Hillel Halkin. Houghton, 2003. Ages 11–13.

Israel. Survival in the Polish countryside during the Jewish holocaust.

Place, François. *The Old Man Mad about Drawing: A Tale of Hokusai.* Translated from the French by William Rodarmor. Godine, 2003. Illustrated. France. Woodblock engraving in nineteenth-century Japan.

Pressler, Mirjam. *Malka.* Translated from the German by Brian Murdoch. Philomel, 2003. Ages 11–16. Germany. Surviving in Nazi-occupied Germany as an abandoned 7-year-old.

Rabinovici, Schoschana. *Thanks to My Mother.* Translated from the German by James Skofield. Dial, 1998. Ages 12–18. Autobiographical account of surviving in Jewish ghettos and Nazi concentration camps in World War II.

Skármeta, Antonio. *The Composition.* Illustrated by Alfonso Ruano. Translated from the Spanish by Elisa Amado. Groundwood, 2000. **(PI)** Ages 11–12.

Family loyalty or betrayal in a Latin American police state.

Steinhofel, Andreas. *The Center of the World.* Translated from the German by Alisa Jaffa. Delacorte, 2005. Ages 16–18. A gay teenager comes to terms with himself and his family.

Stolz, Joëlle. *The Shadows of Ghadames.* Translated from the French by Catherine Temerson. Delacorte, 2004. Ages 11–14. Coming of age as a woman in late-nineteenth-century Libya.

van Dijk, Lutz. *Damned Strong Love: The True Story of Willi G. and Stefan K.* Translated from the German by Elizabeth D. Crawford. Holt, 1995. Ages 14–18. Germany. Affair between a Polish teenaged Jew and a Nazi soldier during World War II.

Yumoto, Kazumi. *The Friends.* Translated from the Japanese by Cathy Hirano. Farrar, 1996. Ages 11–14. Japan. Twelve-year-old boys interested in the concept of dying find an unexpected friend.

RELATED FILMS, VIDEOS, AND DVDS

The Devil's Arithmetic (1999). Author: Jane Yolen (1988). 95 minutes. (Jewish)

The Golden Compass (2007). Author: Philip Pullman (1996). 113 minutes. (Originally published in England)

A Hero Ain't Nothin' But a Sandwich (1991). Author: Alice Childress (1973). 107 minutes. (African-American)

Inkheart (2008). Author: Cornelia Funke (2003). 106 minutes. (Originally published in Germany)

Millions (2005). Author: Frank C. Boyce (2004). 98 minutes. (Originally published in England)

Miracle's Boys (2005). Author: Jacqueline Woodson (2000). 6 episodes; 133 minutes. (African American)

The Thief Lord (2006). Author: Cornelia Funke (2002). 98 minutes. (Originally published in Germany)

SOURCES FOR FILMS, VIDEOS, AND DVDS

The Video Source Book, Syosset, NY. National Video Clearinghouse, 1979–. Published by Gale Research, Detroit, MI. An annual reference work that lists media and provides sources for purchase and rental.

Websites of large video distributors

www.libraryvideo.com
www.knowledgeunlimited.com

part THREE

LITERATURE *in* the SCHOOLS

Chapter 9 focuses on planning for and implementing teaching strategies in the classroom. Having students experience and respond to literature are two major components of a good literature program. The ways students may experience literature are treated extensively, including suggestions for teachers on ways to make these experiences positive. This section is followed by a discussion of ways to encourage students to respond to what they have read, again accompanied by thorough explanations.

Chapter 10 explores the needs and interests of resistant readers and the challenges of finding ways to get all students to read widely and intensively. First, we define the term "resistant reader" and identify five specific groups to which the term applies. We present an overview of the reading interests of adolescents, and especially of adolescent resistant readers, and follow this with a discussion of ways to approach such readers to address their particular needs. Ways to create classroom and school library environments conducive to reading are treated extensively. The final section of this chapter deals with ways to achieve a schoolwide emphasis on reading and literature through collaboration with fellow teachers, school and public librarians, and school administrators.

Chapter 11 deals with issues related to censorship of literature, the use of literary classics in the curriculum, and the impact of accountability on reading and literature. These determine, to varying degrees, the current character and future direction of young adult literature and are therefore worthy of attention. A discussion of the increasing use of technologies and their real and potential impacts on classroom instruction concludes the chapter.

TEACHING STRATEGIES

Having students experience and respond to literature are major responsibilities that a teacher must assume to ensure a good literature program. Careful reflection, planning, and implementation by the teacher are necessary to fulfill these responsibilities. This chapter begins with a discussion of curriculum planning and then focuses on teaching strategies for engaging young adults and for encouraging student response to the literature they experience.

PLANNING FOR A LITERATURE CURRICULUM

Planning for a yearlong strand of literature instruction begins with choosing the approach. In each approach, there should be goals for the course of study, specific young adult trade books to be read or listened to by each student, guidelines for selection of materials, a schedule, and criteria for evaluating the course of study.

Choosing the Approach

Most often, teachers organize a literature curriculum by genre, author, literary element or device, notable book, or an inquiry approach. An alternative is to create a hybrid literature curriculum by including aspects of several of these approaches in the plan.

GENRE By organizing a literature curriculum around literary genres, teachers give students an opportunity to learn about the various types of literature and the characteristics of each genre. In the beginning, the teacher will have to direct students' attention to similarities in books of like genre. For example, students will learn that works of historical fiction are always set in the past or that works of science fiction are often set in the future. Soon students will begin to read with more genre awareness and will enjoy finding common elements within and differences between genres.

One advantage of this plan is that over the school year students gain useful frameworks for understanding and appreciating works of different genres. A genre approach can work in all grade levels and is suited to the use of literature circles, given thoughtful selection of titles and delivery of literary concepts. Planning involves choosing the genres to be studied, selecting the representative young adult books for each, and determining the order in which the genres will be studied.

AUTHOR The goal of a curriculum in literature organized by author is to make students more familiar with the works and writing styles of selected young adult book authors. An additional goal may be knowledge of the authors' lives insofar as their life experiences influenced their works. The choice of authors will naturally be guided both by students' reading interests and the teacher's desire to introduce students to important authors and their works. The number of works chosen to represent an author will vary, but even when an author's books are lengthy, more than one work is recommended.

As a class experiences a sampling of the chosen author's work, attention will be focused on trademark stylistic elements such as unusual use of words or prevalent themes, character types, or settings. Later, information about the author's life can be introduced through reports, audio and video recordings of interviews with the author, and even guest appearances by the author. Author websites, biographies, autobiographies, and biographical reference volumes, such as *Something about the Author* (2006) and *Children's Literature Review* (2006), are good resources for information about young adult book authors. Students are evaluated informally through observation of their recognition of featured authors' works and their ability to compare literary styles of various authors.

Success of author studies is not necessarily defined by wholesale student approval of the featured authors. Students must be allowed to decide whether they like a person's work or not and should be encouraged to discover why they have these feelings. Wholesale *disapproval* by students of the works of a featured author, however, is an important critique that indicates a need for self-evaluation by the teacher. In such a case, the teacher's choice of author or books to be studied was inappropriate for the purpose and should not be repeated without careful consideration of necessary changes.

LITERARY ELEMENT OR DEVICE   When teachers say that their teaching of literature is organized by literary element, they are usually referring to the elements of fiction, nonfiction, and poetry as presented in Chapters 2, 6, and 7. An example might be a focus on character development in a work of fiction. A *literary device is* "any literary technique deliberately employed to achieve a special effect" (Baldick, 1990, p. 55). Symbolism, foreshadowing, and circular plot are examples of devices that add richness to stories. The goal of a literature curriculum organized by literary elements and devices is to give students a better understanding of the craft of writing so that they can read more perceptively and appreciatively and possibly apply this knowledge to their own writing.

Careful selection of young adult books to accompany the investigation of each literary element or device is crucial to the success of this approach. The featured element or device must be prominent and must have been used by the author with extraordinary skill. In addition, the story itself must captivate readers. Note that in this approach books of various genres can be grouped to demonstrate the same literary element, permitting teachers to select five or six books for literature circles. Note also that picture books sometimes provide teachers with clear examples of literary elements and devices in relatively simple contexts so that they can be understood more easily by young people. An excellent resource to help middle and high school teachers select picture books for this use is Hall's *Using Picture Story Books to Teach Literary Devices,* Volumes 1–4 (1990, 1994, 2001, 2007).

Students' acquaintance with literary elements and devices can go far beyond mere definition. Close reading of key passages reveals the author's craft at developing character, establishing mood, authenticating setting, or using such devices as shifting point of view. Re-creation of these elements and devices in their own art, drama, and writing not only gives students a personal and more complete understanding of these concepts, but also gives teachers a way to evaluate their students' grasp of these concepts.

NOTABLE BOOK   *Notable,* in this context, means an exemplary work for young adults. Notable books can be classic or contemporary and of any genre. They can be award winners or not. Teachers using this approach often select works from several different genres, and the books are read and analyzed for the features that contribute to their excellence. They can be compared and contrasted, discussed in light of their relevance to the readers, or discussed in terms of the strength of the writing. Discussion of notable books can be organized by whole class, small groups, or pairs, and students can respond to these books in oral discussion or writing. Novels are usually read independently, but shorter works, such as selected poems or short stories, can be read aloud in class by the teacher or students.

Teachers who organize their literature curriculum by notable books must be careful to remain flexible in book selections from year to year so that the list of notable books reflects students' current interests and reading preferences. A list of notable books that never varies can result in a lack of student interest and stale teaching.

INQUIRY   The *inquiry approach* to literature shares some features of problem-based and constructivist learning. Teachers who choose this approach want their students to become aware of the power of literature to explain the human condition. The inquiry approach is characterized by the following precepts:

- Students' inquiry is guided by their own questions related to a work of literature—questions they honestly care about. During the inquiry process, students refine or alter their questions as they learn more through research and discuss, debate, and share information with other students. Collaborative learning, team projects, and small-group discussions are emphasized.
- Emphasis is placed on the process of how one gets and makes sense of information about literature so that knowledge gained will have wide application.
- Teachers operate as facilitators rather than dispensers of knowledge. They ask leading questions rather than tell answers.

An inquiry approach to literature can be managed as a whole-class inquiry into the same question, a small-group inquiry into various questions, or independent inquiry into individual questions by each student. This approach begins with the teacher identifying the theme or topic to be explored and a relevant work or works of literature. Students read the selected literature and then identify a question or questions to be answered.

Possible themes or topics that a class might explore through a year include

- Alienation and acceptance by peers
- Community involvement and activism
- Effects of technology on our lives
- The future world
- Health issues for today's teens
- Heroes and quests
- Independence and responsibility
- Prejudice at home and abroad
- Survival: learning through adversity
- Teens now and in history

Outlining a Yearlong Literature Curriculum

Planning

Outlining a yearlong literature curriculum helps teachers determine a practical scope of content and logical sequence of presentation and gives them time to gather the necessary resources by the time they are needed. Recommended steps in outlining for a yearlong literature curriculum are reviewed in the following subsections.

ESTABLISH GOALS   *Goals* in a literature curriculum are those aims one expects to accomplish by the end of the course of study. Central to this part of the planning process is deciding on the literary concepts to be taught. Since goals largely determine the parameters of the curriculum, they must be established early in the planning process.

Goals for a literature curriculum are established by individual teachers and sometimes by schools or school districts. Goals for a teacher who has chosen a mixed genre/author organization to teaching literature would include the following, among others:

- Students will enjoy reading a variety of genres of literature.

- Students will be familiar with the characteristics of modern fantasy, historical fiction, contemporary realistic fiction, mystery, and science fiction and will be able to classify a book as belonging to one of the featured genres when reading it.
- Students will become familiar with several leading authors of each of the preceding genres and will be able to identify characteristics of the writing of each author.

DETERMINE LITERATURE UNITS   After goals have been identified and set, the next step in outlining a literature curriculum is to determine the units of study through which the literature content will be delivered. In this way, a tentative schedule can be set in order to foresee needs in terms of time and materials and to coordinate delivery of the units with the school calendar.

SELECT FOCUS BOOKS   Early selection of unit titles is important for several reasons. Balance in the overall book selection, for instance, is achieved much more easily in the planning stages. Balance in book selection, as presented in Chapter 2, means that the books selected present a diversity of characters (type, gender, age, ethnicity, place of origin) who have relevance to adolescents' lives, settings (urban, rural, familiar, foreign), and themes. Another advantage of early selection is being able to estimate the time necessary for each unit. Some units will take longer than others, depending on such variables as the extent of content to be covered, the length and difficulty of books to be read, the type and complexity of planned book extension activities, and the ability to locate and obtain the books and related resources such as films and guest speakers.

Developing the Literature Units

Planning

Thinking through, organizing, and writing down the details of daily lessons and activities in the various units are the final steps in planning for a literature curriculum. Two helpful tools in organizing the details of literature units are webs and lesson plans.

WEBS   A *web* is a graphic planning tool that reveals relationships between ideas. It is like a map in that it helps teachers and students find the way to their goals and objectives, but unlike a map, it can be changed easily to encompass new ideas or be adapted for different uses or to meet special needs and circumstances. Involving students in creating webs benefits everyone; students are motivated by being given a voice in planning the learning unit; and teachers benefit when students have original ideas and see new relationships that improve the overall plan.

The web in Figure 9.1 is organized around a topic of current interest that is explored through various literacy and art activities and could be one approach to planning a teaching unit in language arts or English. This web could just as well be organized around concepts relating to immigration, such as facing prejudice as an immigrant, assimilation into a new culture, retaining one's native culture, the history of immigration in the United States, or the pros and cons of immigration. As such, it could be used as a planning tool for a teaching unit in social studies or history as well as in English or language arts. The web in Figure 9.2 is organized around concepts related to making moral choices and would be appropriate for planning a teaching unit in English, literature, or life skills.

A disadvantage of a web is that it gives no indication of the chronology of events or time allotments. The set of daily or weekly lesson plans that can be developed from a web provides the more linear format preferred by most teachers.

Literature-circle reading

The immigrant experience

Facing prejudice
La Línea by Ann Jaramillo
Dragon's Gate by Laurence Yep

Assimilation of a new culture
Blue Jasmine by Sheth Kashmira
A Step from Heaven by An Na

Retaining one's native culture
Two Lands, One Heart: An American Boy's Journey to His Mother's Vietnam by Jeremy Schmidt
Child of the Owl by Laurence Yep

Read-aloud

Immigration today

Who Belongs Here? An American Story by Margy Knight

Quilted Landscape: Conversations with Young Immigrants by Yale Strom

Independent reading

Immigration, 1840s–present

Fiction
Ask Me No Questions by Marina Budhos
Journey of the Sparrows by Fran Buss and Daisy Cubias (El Salvador)
Esperanza Rising by Pam M. Ryan
Letters from Rifka by Karen Hesse (Russia)
Journey to America by Sonia Levitin (Germany)
Tonight, by Sea by Frances Temple (Haiti)

Nonfiction
Welcome to America? A Pro/Con Debate over Immigration by Tom Streissguth
The Circuit: Stories from the Life of a Migrant Child by Francisco Jiménez (Mexico)
If Your Name Was Changed at Ellis Island by Ellen Levine
Coming to America: The Story of Immigration by Betsy Maestro

Reading

Coming to America: Immigration

Discussion ◄

What are the causes of prejudice against recent immigrants?

How do experiences of recent immigrants compare to those of the past?

Debate: "Should the U.S. allow immigrants into the country today? Why or why not?"

Listening

Invite someone who immigrated to the U.S. (a parent, grandparent, friend, someone from your community) to speak to your class. How does this person's experience compare to the experiences of the protagonists in the books you read?

Reading–writing connections ◄

Read a newspaper or news magazine article about immigration. Summarize the article by answering the five questions journalists must answer in their writing: "who, what, when, where, why."

Then write a newspaper article based on the work of fiction you read, being sure to fulfill the same five requirements of journalistic writing.

Writing

Adapt a pivotal scene from a book you read for a dramatic presentation.

Interview a recent immigrant to the U.S. Describe this person's experience.

Find out as much as you can about where your ancestors came from and their immigration story. Tell this story.

From your reading, list all the reasons people might wish to immigrate to the U.S.

Art

In a small group, design and create a mural that explains why people immigrate to the U.S.

Create a poster that expresses your thoughts about immigration to the U.S.

Design a postage stamp commemorating immigration to this country.

FIGURE 9.1 Web Demonstrating Use of Literature across the Curriculum, Grades 6–8

Cheating

Suggested Titles:
• *Crunch Time* by Mariah Fredericks
• *Wait for Me* by An Na
• *Teens and Cheating* by Hal Marcovitz

Bullying

Suggested Titles:
• *Don't Call Me Ishmael* by Michael G. Bauer
• *Nineteen Minutes* by Jodi Picoult

Illegal Drug Use

Suggested Titles:
• *Drugs and Sports* by William Dudley
• *Hole In My Life* by Jack Gantos
• *Smack* by Melvin Burgess
• "Stranger" by Walter Dean Myers in D. Gallo's *No Easy Answers*

Going against Societal Norms

Suggested Titles:
• *The Killer's Tears* by Anne-Laure Bondoux*
• *One Night* by Margaret Wild

DECIDING BETWEEN RIGHT AND WRONG

Suggested Activities:
Read aloud excerpts from *Bullying and Hazing* by Jill Hamilton. Discuss (1) the nature of moral decisions, (2) why people make bad choices, (3) whether situations ever justify such acts as bullying or cheating.
After reading one of the suggested titles, write a personal response to the prompts "Why are moral choices difficult to make? What is a good moral choice?"

TAKING A STAND ON ISSUES

Suggested Activities:
Read one of the titles, clarify the issue, and debate the two sides of the issue.
Take a stand on the issue presented in the book you read. Write an opinion paper.

STANDING UP TO PEER PRESSURE

Suggested Activities:
Read aloud excerpts from *Friends, Cliques, and Peer Pressure: Be True to Yourself* by Christine Koubek. After reading one of the suggested titles, respond in journals on the topic of how peer pressure affects you and your decisions.

Suggested Titles:
• *The Boy Who Dared* by Susan C. Bartoletti
• *The Chocolate War* by Robert Cormier
• *Geography Club* by Brent Hartinger
• *Stargirl* by Jerry Spinelli
• "X15s" by Jack Gantos in D. Gallo's *No Easy Answers*

Making Moral Choices

Genetic Engineering

Suggested Titles:
• *Blueprint* by Charlotte Kerner
• *The Debate Over Human Cloning* by David Goodnough

STANDING UP FOR ONE'S CONVICTIONS

Suggested Activity:
Students read one of the suggested titles; discuss in small groups the question "What would you have done in (your book character's) situation?"

Suggested Titles:
• *Bucking the Sarge* by Christopher Paul Curtis
• *Staying Fat for Sarah Byrnes* by Chris Crutcher
• *Tangerine* by Edward Bloor*

TAKING RESPONSIBILITY FOR ONE'S ACTIONS

Suggested Activities:
Students read and discuss one of the suggested titles in literature circles. After reading, discuss "If you had been the protagonist, what would you have done differently?" or "How, if ever, can one atone for a bad moral choice?"

Suggested Titles:
• *Driver's Ed* by Caroline Cooney
• *Inexcusable* by Chris Lynch
• *Speak* by Laurie Halse Anderson
• *Touching Spirit Bear* by Ben Mikaelsen*
• "The Unnumbing of Cory Willhouse" by Virginia Euwer Wolff in D. Gallo's *No Easy Answers*

FIGURE 9.2 Conceptual Literature Planning Web, Grades 9–12

*Titles for less able or resistant readers

Planning

LESSON PLANS   Lesson plans are organized by day or week. Specificity will vary according to the needs and experience of the teacher, but each day's or week's lesson plan usually includes the following components:

- *Objectives,* which are short-range aims to be accomplished day by day or week by week. An objective for a teacher conducting a literature unit on the topic of immigration, as found in Figure 9.1, might be for students to realize that most Americans or their ancestors are immigrants and deserve respect regardless of how recently they have arrived in this country.

- *Procedures and methods,* which tell what the teacher does, in what order and with what materials, what tasks or assignments students will be given, and what the teacher expects of them. Procedures of the teacher conducting the immigration unit in Figure 9.1 in order to fulfill the preceding objective might be to read aloud Margy Knight's book, *Who Belongs Here: An American Story* (1993) and then ask students to share in small groups their own or their families' stories of how they came to this country.

- *Evaluation,* in which teachers must consider how they intend to assess their students and themselves in terms of how well the students met the objectives and how well their plans worked. Classroom assessment is usually divided into summative and formative assessment. The aims of *summative assessment* are to make judgments about student performance and produce grades. This form of assessment usually involves tests that take place *after instruction.* The aim of *formative assessment,* on the other hand, is to inform both students and teachers *during instruction* about what is being learned well or not so well. Hallmarks of formative assessment are self-evaluated practice quizzes for students, frequent student-to-student discussions of material to be learned, and immediate feedback for both teachers and students on the effectiveness of their teaching and learning. The purpose of formative assessment is to improve learning and teaching. To comply with district and state demands, most teachers will use a combination of summative and formative assessment. In our opinion, maintaining a balance between these two forms of assessment is imperative. Even more important is avoiding *assessment overkill,* as it diminishes student interest and motivation and wastes valuable classroom time.

Because literature units are several weeks long, they usually include a culminating activity that gives students an opportunity to reflect on what they have learned, review major points, and sometimes celebrate the focus of the unit in some way. An overall unit evaluation is valuable to teachers, particularly if they intend to use the unit with another group of students. The unit should indicate the method of evaluation. Revisions can make the unit even more successful in the following years.

EXPERIENCING LITERATURE

Reading Aloud by Teachers

Reading aloud to students is an important teaching strategy for English/language arts teachers and teachers of other content-area subjects to incorporate into their courses. Many of you will associate reading aloud to students with primary and elementary grades. You may wonder why those who know how to read should be read to. In fact, many of the same benefits of reading aloud that apply to younger children also apply to middle and high school students. Foremost among these is motivation for students to read by proving to them that reading can be entertaining and rewarding (Blessing, 2005). Unless this message is conveyed, the many other entertainment options open to young people today—computer games, television, video arcades—will prevail, and the trend toward cessation of reading for pleasure in the middle grades will continue (Campbell, Voelkl, & Donahue, 1998). Research studies such as those noted in Table 1.2 (pp. 14–15) have suggested that reading aloud to students is a reading motivation activity that works (Livaudais, 1985; Carlsen & Sherrill, 1988).

Other important reasons to read aloud to young adults include the following:

- To improve their reading skills by motivating them to read more. Studies such as the one conducted by Fielding, Wilson, and Anderson (1986) listed in Table 1.2 have shown that students who read more tend to read better.
- To give teachers an opportunity to model fluent, expressive reading. This reason presupposes that the teacher is a good oral reader. Those who are not should make an effort to hone their oral reading skills by recording their reading, listening to it, and making improvements. Other options are to enlist the services of students who are excellent oral readers or to use audio books recorded by professional readers.
- To introduce students to authors and genres they might like to read independently. This idea prompts us to suggest that you need not always read the entire work to your students. Sometimes you can read a carefully selected passage from a book, poem, or short story to give your students a taste of what is in store for them if they choose to read the work in its entirety.
- To present examples of good writing (e.g., description, characterization, dialogue, expository writing) and new vocabulary. Dressel (1990) found that students' writing is directly affected by the characteristics of the stories they hear and discuss.

BOOK SELECTION   It is essential that you preread the books, poems, or short stories that you are considering as read-aloud choices. When you preread a work of literature, you can determine whether you and your students will find it enjoyable and worth the students' time, appropriate in terms of theme, language, and conceptual difficulty, and accessible to various forms of student response. Prereading also allows you to improve your reading fluency and expression and check for vocabulary words and examples of good writing to call to students' attention.

Over a school year you will want to vary your read-aloud selections by genre, author, mood, and setting, as well as by gender and ethnicity of protagonist. Books, poems, and short stories of varying degrees of difficulty should be selected with the understanding that complex but worthy works may require some teacher guidance to be fully appreciated by students. Adding some new works to your read-aloud list each year and choosing works that students have not heard or read before helps to keep both your own and your students' interest in read-aloud selections strong. For suggested read-aloud titles see the Excellent Books to Read Aloud box.

PREPARATION   Once a promising read-aloud selection has been made, establishing and enforcing a protocol for read-aloud sessions will further insure its success. During read-aloud sessions, students must listen. This is not a time to do other things. Note the underlying message of this protocol: *we are*

Excellent Books to Read Aloud

REALISTIC FICTION

Anderson, Laurie Halse. *Prom.* Ages 15–18. An ordinary high school senior dealing with friendship, dating, and the hypocrisies of high school life.

Cameron, Ann. *Colibrí.* Ages 11–16. Kidnapping; coming of age in Guatemala.

Curtis, Christopher Paul. *Bucking the Sarge.* Ages 13–18. Mother–son relationship; welfare system fraud. Humor.

Doctorow, Cory. *Little Brother.* Ages 13–18. A 17-year-old is subjected to brutal interrogation by Homeland Security and decides to fight back.

Dowd, Sioban. *The London Eye Mystery.* Ages 11–14. A boy tries to solve the mystery of his missing cousin.

Frost, Helen. *Keesha's House.* Ages 11–18. Seven teens leaving home and looking for shelter when facing problems. Monologues in poetic verse forms.

Gallo, Don, editor. *Ultimate Sports: Short Stories by Outstanding Writers for Young Adults.* Ages 13–18. Sixteen short stories about teenage athletes.

Tolan, Stephanie S. *Surviving the Applewhites.* Ages 11–14. Finding a home with an eccentric family; home-schooling; juvenile delinquency. Humor.

Westerfeld, Scott. *So Yesterday.* Ages 15–18. Market-research-trends thriller set in New York City; finding the next "cool thing."

MODERN FANTASY

Almond, David. *Kit's Wilderness.* Ages 12–18. English coal-mining families; ancestral ghosts. Magical realism.

Anderson, M. T. *Feed.* Ages 15–18. Dystopian novel featuring a collapsing environment and technology overload.

Cart, Michael, editor. *Tomorrowland: Ten Stories about the Future.* Ages 11–16. Futuristic stories by well-known authors; many suitable as read-alouds.

Clements, Andrew. *Things Not Seen.* Ages 12–15. Mystery involving an invisible boy and his blind friend.

Hoffman, Alice. *Green Angel.* Ages 13–18. Survival in the face of the tragic loss of one's entire family. Magical realism.

Mourlevat, Jean-Claude. *The Pull of the Ocean.* Ages 10–14. A modern "Tom Thumb" story.

HISTORICAL FICTION

Curtis, Christopher Paul, *Elijah of Buxton.* Ages 12–15. An 11-year-old boy born in Buxton, Canada, a haven for former slaves, risks his freedom in 1849 by crossing the U.S. border to recover stolen money.

Hughes, Dean. *Soldier Boys.* Ages 13–18. An American and a German in World War II era. Chapters alternate point of view.

Lawrence, Iain. *The Wreckers.* Ages 10–14. Adventures on the high seas; pirates, treasure, mystery in the 1800s. The trilogy includes *The Smugglers* (1999) and *The Buccaneers* (2001).

Peck, Richard. *A Year Down Yonder.* Ages 10–13. Southern Illinois, Depression era, 1937. Humor.

Ryan, Pam Muñoz. *Esperanza Rising.* Ages 11–15. Mexico and United States, Depression era, 1930s.

Yee, Paul. *Dead Man's Gold and Other Stories.* Illustrated by Harvey Chan. Ages 10–16. Chinese experience, United States and Canada, 1800s and 1900s.

NONFICTION

Bartoletti, Susan Campbell. *Black Potatoes: The Story of the Great Irish Famine, 1845–1850.* Ages 11–18. The impact of the famine on Ireland and the United States.

Bial, Raymond. *Tenement: Immigrant Life on the Lower East Side.* Ages 11–18. Photoessay describing the gritty life in New York tenements from the early 1800s to 1930.

Excellent Books to Read Aloud *(continued)*

NONFICTION *(continued)*

Giblin, James Cross. *The Amazing Life of Benjamin Franklin.* Illustrated by Michael Dooling. Ages 10–13. Picture book biography of the eighteenth-century American statesman, scientist, inventor, and author.

Hoose, Phillip. *We Were There, Too! Young People in U.S. History.* Ages 11–14. Contributions of dozens of young people who helped shape the nation.

Jiménez, Francisco. *Reaching Out.* Ages 12–18. Autobiography of the Mexican-American author's college days in the 1960s.

Rogasky, Barbara. *Smoke and Ashes: The Story of the Holocaust* (expanded edition). Ages 12–18. Nonfiction about anti-Semitism and hate groups from World War II to present.

Zenatti, Valérie. *When I Was a Soldier.* Translated from the French by Adriana Hunter. Ages 14–18. Memoir of a French immigrant's coming of age and beginning to question the politics of war as a result of her required two-year military service in the Israeli army, 1988–1990.

MULTICULTURAL LITERATURE

Draper, Sharon. *Copper Sun.* Ages 13–18. A 15-year-old girl is forced into slavery in the eighteenth-century Carolinas.

Erdrich, Louise. *The Birchbark House.* Ages 11–14. Novel about Ojibwa daily life in 1847 in the Lake Superior area.

Kadohata, Cynthia. *Kira-Kira.* Ages 11–14. Novel about devoted siblings growing up Japanese-American in Georgia in the 1950s.

Mikaelsen, Ben. *Touching Spirit Bear.* Ages 11–14. A young Native American heals his spirit and atones for wrongdoing by living alone for a year in the Alaskan wilderness.

Rice, David. *Crazy Loco.* Ages 12–18. Nine short stories about growing up Latino in southern Texas; family and traditions.

Woodson, Jacqueline. *Miracle's Boys.* Ages 11–18. Novel about the inner-city struggles of three recently orphaned brothers; African-American.

INTERNATIONAL LITERATURE

Mankell, Henning. *Secrets in the Fire.* Translated from the Swedish by Anne C. Stuksrud. Ages 11–18. Tragic effects of war on child victims of minefields in early 1990s Mozambique. Sweden.

McCaughrean, Geraldine. *Cyrano.* Ages 12–16. A retelling of the classic French play.

Morpurgo, Michael. *Private Peaceful.* Ages 14–18. Brutal trench warfare of World War I. England.

Naidoo, Beverley. *The Other Side of Truth.* Ages 11–14. Two young political refugees from Nigeria cope with abandonment, culture shock, and fear in London. South Africa.

Stratton, Allan. *Chanda's Secrets.* Ages 14–18. The effect of AIDS on the lives of children and young adults in South Africa. Canada.

taking valuable class time for this activity because it is important and worthy of your attention. None of the benefits associated with reading aloud applies if students do not listen.

Once the class is ready to listen to a new selection, you should briefly introduce it. The introduction might entail giving a historical context, if the selection is a work of historical fiction, or showing the geographical setting of the book on a large map, or mentioning other works by the author that the students have read and enjoyed. Some teachers like to list and define a few new words on the chalkboard for students to listen for. These word lists should be pointed out at this time. When beginning a new work, the reader should announce its title and author's name and begin reading. In subsequent read-aloud sessions of the same story, a brief reminder of what was happening in the story when the previous session ended can precede the reading.

READING ALOUD EFFECTIVELY

- Think of reading as a type of dramatic performance. Use different voices for different characters, if you can. Try accents, when appropriate, if you are good at such things. Use your voice to emphasize various moods suggested in the story, and employ pauses to heighten suspense.
- Maintain eye contact with your students. Not only will this help to keep listeners' attention, but it also will inform you when a word of explanation is necessary.
- Use body language and facial expressions to enhance the drama of the reading. Leaning forward during a suspenseful part of a story or chuckling during a funny part can convey your involvement in the story to your audience.
- Read the chapter or selection from beginning to end without interruption except as needed. When a word occurs during read-aloud that you suspect your students do not know, simply pause and give a synonym that the students know and continue reading. If you have posted the word with its meaning beforehand, simply point to it as it is read. You might want to call attention to a passage because it is an excellent example of a type of writing or is pivotal to the story. In this case say something like "That was an excellent description [or argument or comparison]. I'll reread it." Do so, then continue reading. In general, keep interruptions to a minimum.
- Research studies on reading aloud have shown that a brief follow-up to each read-aloud session is beneficial. In two to three minutes, students can ask questions, clarify plot developments, tell what they liked or did not like about the story developments, or project future plot developments.

When reading a novel aloud over several weeks, the following practices may help keep students involved:

- Keep a chart of the characters and their relationships and roles in the story, especially if the story has a large number of characters. This chart should be posted during read-aloud time so that students can easily see it.
- Draw and display a map of the story setting to track plot events in sequence. Maps are particularly helpful in quest fantasies.
- Develop a time line on which dates are set at intervals above the line, story events are placed below the line at the appropriate date, and, if necessary, historic events are noted on a third tier. A time line can serve as a mnemonic device for the story line as well as for historic events of the era.

Booktalks

A *booktalk* is an oral presentation by a teacher, librarian, or student who tells about a book to stimulate students' interest and motivate them to read it. Booktalks are not analyses of the author's style or the old-fashioned book report that discusses characters, setting, theme, and plot (Bodart, 1980). Booktalks have been used effectively for years by librarians who have developed this strategy into an art for the purpose of encouraging students to check out books from the library. Teachers can give booktalks on five to ten books each week from their school library media center collection; in this way, they can entice students to read and experience good literature.

Some teachers advocate having students give booktalks to induce other students to read the suggested books. One high school teacher videotaped students giving booktalks and showed the tape to other classes to motivate them to read the suggested titles and to learn how to give good booktalks. The following tips for giving successful booktalks are also useful.

- Read the book before booktalking it.
- Choose books that you have liked, wholly or in part, or that you think your students will enjoy. Sincere enthusiasm for a book is stimulating and infectious.
- Show the book to the students as you give the booktalk. Format aspects such as cover illustrations, length, and size of the book influence book choices and can be weighed by students only if they can see the book.
- Keep the booktalk brief, generally no more than two or three minutes. Do not tell too much about the book or the students will see no reason to read it. For most books, four to six sentences will suffice.
- State the topic and something about the action in the story, but *do not relate the plot*. You can focus on a scene or character that the story revolves around, but do not discuss a scene that gives away the ending.
- Booktalk a group of books that share the same theme; in this case you will want to talk briefly about each book and how it fits with the others.

The following is an example of a booktalk on *The House of the Scorpion* (2002) by Nancy Farmer:

> If you ever wonder about what life will be like 100 years from now, you will enjoy reading *The House of the Scorpion* by Nancy Farmer. In this story, Matt has spent his life locked away in a hut because he is a clone, an identical genetic copy of another human being, hated and outcast by human society. As Matt comes of age he discovers that he is the clone of El Patrón, the cruel ruler of Opium, a drug kingdom farmed by "eejits," clones whose brains have been destroyed. The country of Opium is located between the United States and Aztlán, once called Mexico. When Matt realizes that his life is at risk, he makes a break for freedom and escapes to Aztlán only to face more hardships and adventures. Matt wonders who he is, why he exists, and whether, as a clone, he has free will.

After you have given the booktalk, make the book available to students to peruse and consider for reading. You should booktalk a variety of books at different levels of reading difficulty, on different topics, and with male and female protagonists from many cultures. In this way, you will appeal to the wide range of interests and abilities that exist among students in your classroom.

Independent Reading by Students

Another way for students to experience good literature is to read it independently. Indeed, the ultimate goal of a literature program is to turn students into readers who voluntarily select and read good literature with enjoyment, understanding, and appreciation. To assist students in becoming independent lifelong readers, middle and high school teachers need to set aside as much time as possible during the week for students to read silently. This practice is particularly important because the demands on students' time outside school today often leave them with little or no time for reading. We advocate regular independent reading periods several days a week. The length of each period may vary, but there must be enough time for students to get well into their books and to gain some level of satisfaction from the reading. Furthermore, we advocate this practice for *all* students regardless of reading skill level. Students unaccustomed to independent reading may need shorter sessions at first until they develop longer reading attention spans.

Some middle schools have instituted sustained silent reading (SSR) programs on a schoolwide basis in order to promote the reading habit in students. In these SSR programs a certain time each day is set aside for all students, teachers, librarians, coaches, principals, custodians, and office and kitchen staff to take a "reading break." The philosophy behind SSR programs is that students need to see adults who read and who place a high priority on reading. In SSR programs, students read materials of their own choosing and are not required to write book reports or give oral reports on these materials.

Many schools have purchased ***computerized reading incentive programs*** to motivate and encourage students to read more widely. Programs such as Accelerated Reader (AR) pretest students to determine their reading levels, then assign each student to a level of books with predetermined numbers of points according to difficulty. After students finish reading a book silently, they complete multiple-choice tests to assess literal comprehension of the book to earn points based on the score. Students can then earn prizes according to their performance. Reports on the success of such programs are mixed. Many teachers and schools report disappointment in the programs. Teachers need to be cautious about whether such programs are having a positive impact on their students' interest in reading; possible concerns are noted in the following list.

- Levels to which books are assigned seem arbitrary to students.
- Extrinsic rewards diminish the desire of students to read for the pleasure of reading.
- Testing students' literal comprehension emphasizes inconsequential information, thus demeaning both the story and the reading act.
- Students find ways to gain the rewards without reading the books by, for example, asking other students for the answers, skimming the books for facts, or seeing the movie.
- Personal enjoyment of literature is often deemphasized.

Teachers can design their own reading incentive programs that avoid these drawbacks and still motivate students to read independently. In these programs students usually keep a record of their own independent reading, have opportunities to respond to books in a variety of ways, and work to achieve individual silent reading goals set by the student and teacher together. Rewards, such as a special celebration party, are given to the whole class for reading, as a group, more total pages or books than were read during the last grading period. Such group rewards avoid the negative consequences of highly competitive programs.

Here are some tips for having successful independent reading periods:

- Conduct booktalks regularly so that students become aware of books they may wish to read. These booktalks can be given by teachers, librarians, or students. Remember that young people are motivated to read books endorsed by their friends and peers.
- Have on hand a stock of short story collections and magazines for the inevitability that some students will forget to bring their independent reading books to class or will finish them during class.
- Insist on attentiveness to books during independent reading time.
- Set yourself as an example of a reader by spending the independent reading period engrossed in a book.
- Be knowledgeable about and interested in the books the students are reading.

Assigned Reading

Experience

The most common way for students to experience literature in schools today is through assigned reading. Teachers assign works of literature in order to direct students' attention to an aspect of the literature curriculum (e.g., characteristics of a genre, a literary device, a theme), to investigate the writing style of a particular author, or to connect to other curricular areas (see the following "Literature across the Curriculum" section).

LITERATURE ANTHOLOGIES   Most often, assigned reading selections are found in a *literature anthology* of short stories, excerpts from novels, essays, plays, and poems. Typically, each student has a copy of the anthology, and each student reads the same selection at the same time, as determined by the teacher. Though some excellent literature can be found in these anthologies, we cannot endorse their use as the sole source of reading material for students. There are inherent problems with matching students' interests and reading levels when only one title is assigned. Also, young people need the experience of reading complete novels in order to fully appreciate them. Excerpts cannot give readers the same experience. Another problem with anthologies is the comprehension questions and activities that follow nearly every selection and the tendency of teachers to depend on their edition of the anthology to supply the "preferred" answers. Not only do these questions often demean the literature by asking low-level recall questions, but, as noted by Zaharias (1989), literature anthologies typically control students' responses to literature. We advocate using only the best selections in anthologies and supplementing with other complete works of literature selected by teachers *with their students' interests and abilities in mind.* Moreover, it is not mandatory that all students in a class always read the same selections in an anthology at the same time. Sometimes students can be given a choice among several selections.

PAIRING CLASSICS AND YOUNG ADULT LITERATURE   Many school districts require the reading and teaching of specific works of classic literature in middle and high school. In many cases, students benefit from a pairing of the classic work with one or more young adult works having similar themes, characters, or settings to gain a greater appreciation for, and understanding of, the classic. Please see the section on classics in Chapter 11 for a discussion of this strategy.

TEXT SETS   Many teachers create text sets that address both curricular demands and the range of student interests and reading abilities. Using the school or public librarian's expertise and sources such as the recommended books lists at the end of each genre chapter in Part II of this text, Appendix A of this text (Book Awards), bibliographies such as NCTE's *Your Reading: An Annotated Booklist for Middle School and Junior High* (Brown & Stephens, 2003), *Books for You: An Annotated Booklist for Senior High* (Beers & Lesesne, 2001), and the American Library Association's Quick Picks for Reluctant Young Adult Readers (www.ala.org under Awards and Scholarships, Book/Media Awards), teachers can compile **text sets** of five to eight books that share a common theme, topic, genre, or writing style but vary by such features as reading level, length, complexity, gender and ethnicity of protagonist, and year of publication. The school librarian then orders multiple paperback copies of the selected titles. Alternate funding sources are the school's allocated materials budget or small grants written for this purpose. Other teachers use points garnered through publisher-owned book clubs to purchase these books. The advantage of using text sets is the likelihood of matching books and individual students' interests and reading abilities, thus increasing the success of the assigned reading experience. See Table 9.1 for examples of text sets.

Literature across the Curriculum

Students may also experience good literature in content-area classes when teachers supplement or replace textbooks with trade books for instruction. *Literature across the curriculum* refers to using works of literature as the content reading in social studies, health, science, and mathematics courses. Both students and teachers benefit from this practice, as we will show.

Using several trade books on the same topic but written at varying levels of readability allows teachers to meet students' varying levels of reading skill. Textbooks, often written at as much as two or more years above the average grade level of those who use them (Chall & Conard, 1991; Budiansky, 2001), can be difficult for some students to read and comprehend.

The stories and narrative of trade books are often more understandable, real, and memorable to young people than the expository language of textbooks. Works of historical fiction present historical events from a young person's point of view and feature well-defined characters and settings. Later, they move from an interest in the narrative to an interest in the history itself.

Trade books often address subjects or take perspectives omitted from textbooks, which are written to please all viewpoints. Trade books can fill in these gaps and permit students to read multiple perspectives on topics. The roles of women and various microcultural groups in U.S. history, for example, are often given short shrift in history textbooks. A related advantage to using trade books in content-area courses is the opportunity it offers students to verify facts by comparing them in different sources.

Trade books present political and social events in terms of the moral events related to them. Reading these books, young people can see how historical events affected the lives of ordinary people and can better understand the morality underlying the choices made by political leaders.

Teachers benefit from using literature across the curriculum because their course materials are richer, more interesting, more complete, and, particularly in the area of science, more up-to-date. When courses become more interesting, students are likely to become more involved and perform better.

A strategy teachers use when selecting text sets around a topic is to purposely look for books that contradict one another, present different information, or present viewpoints of different groups of people. Students may start with the textbook and then research the facts from other books, or read a work of fiction and then seek to verify to what extent the facts within the story are accurate or complete.

TABLE 9.1 Sample Text Sets by Genre, Theme, or Topic

Genre, Theme, or Topic	Titles
Escape with fantasy	*The Amazing Maurice and His Educated Rodents* by Terry Pratchett *Kit's Wilderness* by David Almond *Savvy* by Ingrid Law *Things Not Seen* by Andrew Clements *Which Witch* by Eva Ibbotson
War	*The Book Thief* by Markus Zusak *A Long Way Gone: Memoirs of a Boy Soldier* by Ishmael Beah *Private Peaceful* by Michael Morpurgo *Soldier Boys* by Dean Hughes *Under the Blood-Red Sun* by Graham Salisbury *Yellow Star* by Jennifer Roy
Finding oneself	*Bucking the Sarge* by Christopher Paul Curtis *Colibrí* by Ann Cameron *Flipped* by Wendelin Van Draanen *Hope Was Here* by Joan Bauer *Miracle's Boys* by Jacqueline Woodson *Petey* by Ben Mikaelsen
Mystery	*Eye of the Crow* by Shane Peacock *Holes* by Louis Sachar *The London Eye Mystery* by Siobhan Dowd *Me, the Missing, and the Dead* by Jenny Valentine *Sonny's House of Spies* by George Ella Lyon
Future worlds/science fiction	*The House of the Scorpion* by Nancy Farmer *The Hunger Games* by Suzanne Collins *A Matter of Profit* by Hilari Bell *The Knife of Never Letting Go: Chaos Walking* by Patrick Ness *The New Policeman* by Kate Thompson
Nonfiction: biography and memoir	*Lincoln through the Lens: How Photography Revealed and Shaped an Extraordinary Life* by Martin Sandler *Thanks to My Mother* by Schoschana Rabinovici *The Wall: Growing Up behind the Iron Curtain* by Peter Sís **(PI)** *We Are on Our Own* by Miriam Katin **(GR)** *We Were There, Too! Young People in U.S. History* by Phillip Hoose

Teachers can also ask students to compare facts presented in their textbooks with those found in various trade books on the same topic. This practice is particularly helpful in keeping course material up-to-date, given the rapidity of progress and change in the scientific fields today. Textbook information on global warming, for example, can be compared to facts in Laurence Pringle's *Global Warming:*

The Threat of Earth's Changing Climate (2001) and Alvin Silverstein, Virginia Silverstein, and Laura Silverstein Nunn's *Global Warming* (2003), two fairly short, well-written informational books. The human ramifications of this phenomenon can be explored in Marcus Sedgwick's science fiction novel *Floodland* (2001), in which a girl searches for her parents after the seas flood coastal areas and turn cities into islands as a result of global warming. Likewise, Nancy Farmer's work of science fiction *The House of the Scorpion* (2002), Charlotte Kerner's *Blueprint* (2000), and Marilyn Kaye's Replica series beginning with *Amy Number Seven* (1998) can become the basis of lively discussion and debate about the ramifications of human cloning in general science and biology courses.

Social studies classes can also be enlivened by incorporating well-selected trade books. By incorporating recent real-life stories of the immigrant experience in the United States, such as An Na's *A Step from Heaven* (2001) and Yale Strom's *Quilted Landscape: Conversations with Young Immigrants* (1996), teachers help students relate to the topic of immigration by showing that it is happening today in their world. These stories not only help students empathize with recent immigrants by revealing the difficulties of assimilating to a new culture, they often throw light on the political problems in the characters' home countries that necessitated the immigration.

Informational trade books can also be used as models for students' own expository writing. Teachers can show examples of clear, lively writing taken from works of nonfiction and also call attention to the use of captions, graphs, tables, figures, and authentic photographs as ways to present information effectively.

For ideas on planning social studies units incorporating trade books, fiction and nonfiction, see the Recommended Books lists at the end of Chapter 5, "Historical Fiction," and Chapter 6, "Nonfiction," which are organized by historical era, the planning webs in Figures 9.1 and 9.2, and the Literature across the Curriculum: Sample Book Lists box.

Content-area reading is reading to acquire and understand new content in a particular discipline. In content-area classes students are usually assigned textbooks, a type of expository text, as their sole source of information. When students enter schools with departmentalized organizations, the teaching of reading is often neglected, even though the demands of reading increase with the specialized vocabulary, abstract ideas, more complex syntax, and the need for prior knowledge required by textbooks (Allington, 2002). Content-area teachers feel more responsibility to impart knowledge about the particular subject matter in which they specialize and may ignore the need to assist students in their literacy development. Helping students learn technical vocabulary in a subject is one example of content-area reading instruction. Specialized vocabulary needs to be explained, practiced, and developed over time before students "own" it.

Not surprisingly, by the time students in the United States enter middle school, their reading achievement levels, on average, begin to fall (National Center for Educational Statistics, 2001). Allington (2002) reasoned that textbooks written at many students' frustration levels are partially to blame. He found that exemplary teachers avoid this problem by using multiple instructional resources written at varying levels of difficulty and then offer their students some choice in their assigned content-area reading. Also, teachers can make the reading of textbooks easier if they teach their students how such texts are structured and explain other specialized features in them. In Chapter 6, "Nonfiction," the elements of nonfiction are explained with examples provided. Robb (2003) also provides practical ideas for teaching reading in social studies, science, and mathematics classes.

Literature across the Curriculum: Sample Book Lists

ART

Balliett, Blue. *Chasing Vermeer.* Illustrated by Brett Helquist. Ages 10–14. Detective mystery involving a missing Vermeer painting and lots of puzzles.

Greenberg, Jan, and Sandra Jordan. *Chuck Close, Up Close.* Ages 11–14. Picture book biography of the American artist who creates oversized portraits despite paralysis.

Greenberg, Jan, and Sandra Jordan. *Vincent Van Gogh: Portrait of an Artist.* Ages 11–18. Biography of the nineteenth-century Dutch painter.

Greenberg, Jan, editor. *Heart to Heart.* Ages 12–18. Forty-three poets write poetic responses to pieces of modern art.

Hill, Laban C. *Casa Azul: An Encounter with Frida Kahlo.* Ages 12–16. Fictional account of two teens' witnessing the surreal life of artist Kahlo in Mexico City in 1940.

Mühlberger, Richard. *What Makes a Monet a Monet?* Ages 11–14. The artist's concerns, techniques, and uses of color.

ENGLISH LANGUAGE ARTS

Myers, Walter Dean. *Bad Boy: A Memoir.* Ages 12–18. Growing up in Harlem in the 1940s and 1950s.

Myers, Walter Dean. *Blues Journey.* Illustrated by Christopher Myers. New York: Holiday. Ages 10–14. A collection of original poems connect with the blues. Picture book.

Myers, Walter Dean. *Monster.* Ages 12–18. Being on trial as a murder accomplice; narrated from jail cell and courtroom. TV script form.

Myers, Walter Dean. *Scorpions.* Ages 11–15. Effects of gangs on young people; street violence.

Myers, Walter Dean. *Slam!* Ages 13–18. Struggling with academics; coping with family problems; basketball.

Myers, Walter Dean. *145th Street: Short Stories.* Ages 13–18. Ten stories portray life on a block in Harlem.

Myers, Walter Dean. *What They Found: Love on 145th Street.* Finding love and community against all odds.

FOOD AND NUTRITION

Delacre, Lulu. *Salsa Stories.* Ages 11–14. Family stories triggered by memories of favorite foods from various Latin American countries. Recipes included.

Gillies, Judi, and Jennifer Glossop. *The Kids Can Press Jumbo Cookbook.* Illustrated by Louise Phillips. Ages 10–14. Sturdy, well-illustrated, step-by-step cookbook with more than 125 recipes for novice to expert cooks.

Horvath, Polly. *Everything on a Waffle.* Ages 10–14. Novel set in a small-town café in British Columbia; finding a family; foster home. Recipes included.

Robbins, Paul R. *Anorexia and Bulimia.* Ages 12–18. Includes true stories of young people who have experienced these disorders and binge eating.

Rocklin, Joanne. *Strudel Stories.* Ages 10–14. Stories of a Jewish family's history told while making apple strudel. Strudel recipes included.

Schlosser, Eric, and Charles Wilson. *Chew on This: Everything You Didn't Want to Know about Fast Food.* The dangers of eating too much fast food.

(continued)

Literature across the Curriculum: Sample Book Lists *(continued)*

HEALTH

Anderson, Laurie Halse. *Fever 1793.* Ages 14–18. Historical fiction account of the eighteenth-century yellow fever epidemic in Philadelphia.

Choldenko, Gennifer. *Al Capone Does My Shirts.* Ages 10–14. A 12-year-old girl has responsibility for her severely autistic older sister while living on Alcatraz Island in 1935.

Davidson, Sue, and Ben Morgan. *Human Body Revealed.* Ages 10–14. How various parts of the human body fit together; uses double-page illustrations, photos, and overlays.

Farrell, Jeanette. *Invisible Allies: Microbes That Shape Our Lives.* Ages 12–18. Human dependence on microbes. See also by Farrell *Invisible Enemies: Stories of Infectious Disease.* Seven dreaded human diseases and efforts made to avoid or cure them.

Gantos, Jack. *Joey Pigza Swallowed the Key.* Ages 10–14. Life with attention deficit disorder.

Trueman, Terry. *Stuck in Neutral.* Ages 12–18. A 14-year-old boy with cerebral palsy suspects that his father plans to "put him out of his misery."

Vizzini, Ned. *It's Kind of a Funny Story.* Ages 14–18. Academic pressure results in depression and thoughts of suicide for high school freshman Craig.

MATHEMATICS

Ball, Johnny. *Go Figure! A Totally Cool Book about Numbers.* Ages 10–14. Filled with facts, figures, and brainteasers including geometry, predictability, and logic.

Devlin, Keith. *The Math Instinct: Why You're a Mathematical Genius (along with Lobsters, Birds, Cats and Dogs).* Ages 14–18. Intuitive math solutions by animals to problems of counting, trajectory, motion, and patterns.

Doak, Robin S. *Galileo: Astronomer and Physicist.* Ages 11–15. Traces the life of the Italian astronomer who defended the Copernican theory and invented a telescope.

Peters, Craig. *Bill Gates: Software Genius of Microsoft.* Ages 14–18. A profile of Microsoft founder and computer technology visionary Bill Gates. One of the Internet Biographies series.

Wise, Bill. *Whodunit Math Puzzles.* Illustrated by Lucy Corvino. Ages 10–14. A 12-year-old junior detective uses math to solve a series of twenty-two short mysteries.

Wishinsky, Frieda. *What's the Matter with Albert? A Story of Albert Einstein.* Illustrated by Jacques Lamontagne. Ages 9–13. Vignettes in picture book format of Albert Einstein's childhood, told from the viewpoint of a young newspaper reporter interviewing Albert Einstein.

MUSIC

Anderson, M. T. *Handel, Who Knew What He Liked.* Illustrated by Kevin Hawkes. Ages 10–13. Picture book biography of the eighteenth-century German-born English composer Handel.

Espejo, Roman. *Should Music Lyrics Be Censored for Violence and Exploitation?* Twelve essays on the pros and cons of censoring popular music lyrics.

Freedman, Russell. *The Voice that Challenged a Nation: Marian Anderson and the Struggle for Equal Rights.* Ages 11–18. Biography of the African-American singer.

Going, K. L. *Fat Kid Rules the World.* Ages 14–18. Two high school misfits start a new band.

Krull, Kathleen. *Lives of the Musicians: Good Times, Bad Times (and What the Neighbors Thought).* Illustrated by Kathryn Hewitt. Ages 10–14. Snapshot biographies of sixteen musical greats from classical to ragtime.

Marsalis, Wynton. *Jazz ABZ: An A to Z Collection of Jazz Portraits.* Illustrated by Paul Rogers. Ages 12–18. The greats of jazz commemorated in poems and art.

PHYSICAL EDUCATION

Bloor, Edward. *Tangerine.* Ages 11–14. A legally blind soccer-playing seventh-grader confronts several issues, including his amoral football hero brother.

Blumenthal, Karen. *Let Me Play: The Story of Title IX: The Law That Changed the Future of Girls in America.* Ages 12–18. The legislation that gave girls and women equal access to physical education classes, gymnasiums, universities, and graduate schools.

Crutcher, Chris. *Athletic Shorts: Six Short Stories.* Ages 14–18. High school athletes cope with racism, homophobia, sexism, and parents.

Freedman, Russell. *Babe Didrikson Zaharias.* Ages 10–18. Biography of one of the twentieth century's premier female athletes.

Gallo, Donald, editor. *Ultimate Sports.* Ages 12–18. Sixteen stories with sports settings or themes by top young adult authors.

Knudson, R. R., and M. Swenson (compilers). *American Sports Poems.* Ages 11–18. One hundred fifty-eight poems arranged by sport.

Morrison, Lillian. *Way to Go! Sports Poems.* Illustrated by Susan Spellman. Ages 10–14. Forty-two poems.

Ritter, John. *The Boy Who Saved Baseball.* Ages 10–14. The town's future rides on the outcome of a game between the ragtag local team and an all-star neighboring team.

SCIENCE

Collard, Sneed. *The Prairie Builders: Reconstructing America's Lost Grasslands.* Ages 11–14. Present-day re-creation of the tallgrass prairie in Iowa.

Dash, Joan. *The Longitude Prize.* Illustrated by Dušan Petričić. Ages 12–18. Life and times of the eighteenth-century clockmaker who invented a way of measuring longitude at sea.

Hiaasen, Carl. *Hoot.* Ages 10–14. Ecological mystery involving a proposed development project and endangered miniature owls.

Hoose, Phillip. *The Race to Save the Lord God Bird.* Ages 11–18. History of the ivory-billed woodpecker.

Lasky, Kathryn. *The Man Who Made Time Travel.* Illustrated by Kevin Hawkes. Ages 10–13. Picture book biography of the eighteenth-century British clockmaker John Harrison, who solved the problem of tracking longitude in shipboard navigation.

Latham, Jean Lee. *Carry On, Mr. Bowditch.* Ages 11–18. Eighteenth-century sailor and mathematician who laid the foundations for nautical navigation.

SOCIAL STUDIES

Blumberg, Rhoda. *York's Adventures with Lewis and Clark: An African-American's Part in the Great Expedition.* Ages 11–15. The biography of Clark's slave York and his role and adventures journeying west with the Lewis and Clark expedition.

Bruchac, Joseph. *Sacajawea: The Story of Bird Woman and the Lewis and Clark Expedition.* Ages 13–18. William Clark and a Shoshoni Indian interpreter and guide alternate in describing their experiences on the Lewis and Clark expedition.

Myers, Laurie. *Lewis and Clark and Me: A Dog's Tale.* Illustrated by Michael Dooling. Ages 9–13. Seaman, Meriwether Lewis's Newfoundland dog, describes Lewis and Clark's expedition, which he accompanied from St. Louis to the Pacific Ocean.

Smith, Roland. *The Captain's Dog: My Journey with the Lewis and Clark Tribe.* Ages 12–18. First-person fictionalized account by Lewis's dog of the 1804–1806 expedition to explore the western wilderness.

Sneve, Virginia Driving Hawk. *Bad River Boys: A Meeting of the Lakota Sioux with Lewis and Clark.* Illustrated by Bill Farnsworth. Ages 9–12. Told from a Native American perspective by a group of young Dakota Indians. Picture book.

Wolf, Allan. *New Found Land.* Ages 15–18. A novel told through free verse in narratives by fourteen different voices capturing the adventures of the Lewis and Clark expedition.

Reading development is a continuum and must be addressed at all grade levels and in all classes. Older students need to be encouraged to read widely from a variety of material, including trade books, magazines, newspapers, and textbooks. Time spent reading is closely related to reading success (Fielding et al., 1986).

Experience

Films Based on Young Adult Books

If films are to be a regular feature of your literature class, you will want your students to be active viewers and know how film is similar to and different from text. Both have plots, characters, settings, themes, styles, and points of view. Both are edited, and both can have dialogue and narration. Film differs from text in that it has sound (spoken words, music, and sound effects) and photography (use of color or black and white and use of angles, close-ups, or panoramas). Additionally, films have actual people inhabiting the character roles and actual settings, whereas books ask readers to form their own images of characters and settings. With this rudimentary background in the elements of cinema, students should become better "readers" of film and better equipped to discuss or write their reactions to films based on literature.

Teachers will want to select films based on young adult books for viewing in school settings that meet the following considerations and criteria:

- Teacher familiarity with, and approval of, the book on which the film is based
- A preview of the film itself
- Films that either support or contradict the content of the book
- Films that are age- and content-appropriate for viewing in a school setting to a young adult audience, based on the teacher's professional judgment and the film's rating, if there is one

RESPONDING TO LITERATURE

For readers to get optimal good from their reading, they must think about what they have read. Just handing students good books and giving them time to read is often not enough. Readers think about what they have read when they share their reading experiences with others through discussion, recommend a book to others, translate their reading into another form such as drama or art or poetry, describe their reactions to the story in writing, or apply their reading and learning to a content-area subject such as science, health, or history. In sharing their responses with others or translating them to new forms or media, students profit by reliving and rethinking the experience; they develop better understandings of what they experienced by organizing and deepening their feelings and thoughts on the experience; they discover that other readers' experiences with the same book may not have been the same as theirs; and they bring closure to the book experience. Although it is important to give students opportunities to respond to books, not every book needs or merits a lengthy response. Rosenblatt (1978) reminds us that no two people have the same prior experiences and that it is the transaction that occurs between the text and the reader within the present context that provokes a particular response. Teachers may generate opportunities for students to share their individual insights to literary experiences in many different ways.

Book Discussions

Response

Whole-class discussion usually accompanies the reading aloud of a book to the class. In these discussions, comprehension is assumed and the discussion centers on the different ways students feel and think about the book and its characters, events, and outcome. Good class discussions are stimulated by encouraging students to share their individual responses to open-ended questions, not by seeking supposedly right answers in order to check comprehension or recall. In a class discussion, the teacher has the pivotal role as discussion leader. The discussion tends to be a teacher-to-students, students-to-teacher interchange.

In large classes, only some of the students will have an opportunity to express their viewpoints, and yet adolescents crave social interaction with their peers. Another format that allows more students to discuss their responses to literature is the *literature circle,* in which a group of five to seven students share their responses with one another about a book they have read as a group or a book read aloud by the teacher to the whole class. One of the goals of literature circles is to have all participants learn to work with one another and to value the opinions and views of others. Using text sets for assigned reading lends itself to literature circles in which students who chose the same book from the text set meet daily to discuss what they have read. Usually, each person in the group is assigned a task, such as discussion leader, recorder, devil's advocate, vocabulary expert, or listener, and these tasks rotate daily. Under this system teachers assume the roles of facilitator, listener, clarifier, guide, and consensus builder. Teachers who have used this system note that the keys to success are careful training in each of the literature circle tasks, such as how to ask thought-provoking questions, and joint planning by teacher and class before groups begin working to set rules, goals, and time lines. They also note that student-led discussions in literature circles are superior to teacher-led discussions because more students become involved and have a greater opportunity to develop their thinking and speaking skills. It is natural for teachers to worry that students on their own will not address all of the points that they themselves would have addressed. Experience has proven that this is not the case, however. Teachers have stated that students who are well versed in the various tasks of literature circles and proficient in their execution not only address what they themselves consider important, but often have completely original insights into the works discussed.

The purpose of discussions of fiction is to find out what the students think and feel about the story. A question that can be answered by "yes," "no," or a single word or phrase will not lead to an interactive discussion. The question "Did you like the story?" may result in a simple "Yes." "Which part of the story did you like best, and what did you like about it?" is likely to elicit a more detailed response. *Divergent* questions have no one right answer but a number of possible answers. They naturally provoke more discussion than *convergent* questions, for which only one answer is correct.

The purpose of reading informational books, though perhaps partially aesthetic, is usually efferent; that is, the reader's attention is centered on what should be retained after the actual reading event. Locating specific pieces of information to support an argument and comparing information from two or more sources are examples of reasons for efferent reading of literature. Convergent questions in this case would reflect that purpose.

The following divergent questions can be adapted to different books and may help you in formulating good questions:

- What important ideas did you find in this story?
- How do you think the story should have ended, and why do you think so?
- How would you have acted if you had been *(book character)*?
- What do you think the author's main message (theme) was in this story? Why do you think so?
- Which part of the story did you like best or least? Why?
- Which character did you like best or least? Why?
- Which character do you identify with? Tell why and how you identify with him or her.
- What has happened in your life that you are reminded of by this story (character, situation)?
- What would *(character)* have done if . . . *(make a change in plot events)*?

Critical Thinking

Response

Thinking about what one has read is a fundamental form of response. An important teaching goal is to instill students with *critical thinking skills.* Hynd (1999) asserts that critical thinkers

- question what they read instead of accepting everything in print as true.
- notice discrepancies across different sources of information.
- place issues in perspective by asking, "How important is this?" and "What are the ramifications of this issue?"
- examine assumptions before accepting them as true.
- look for general agreement across sources before buying into an argument.

When teachers use text sets chosen to present different perspectives, different information, and contradictory conclusions, they set the stage for exercising students' critical thinking skills. This can happen in literature courses when text sets are used as reading material or in content-area courses when text sets are used to supplement the textbook. Consider the following example.

In studying the history of the nineteenth-century westward expansion in the United States, a history teacher could select trade books that present the perspectives of Native Americans who were displaced by the European settlers, focus on the roles of women pioneers, tell the contributions of the Chinese Americans in building the transcontinental railway, and detail the more harrowing aspects of the pioneers' lives. Generally, history textbooks either downplay the roles of women and minority groups in U.S. history or omit them altogether and present overviews rather than detailed accounts.

The following trade book selections are appropriate for such a unit:

The Ballad of Lucy Whipple by Karen Cushman (1996) (women pioneers, pioneer life)
Boston Jane series by Jennifer Holm (2001) (women pioneers)
Dragon's Gate by Laurence Yep (1993) (Chinese Americans' contributions)
The Game of Silence by Louise Erdrich (2005) (Native American perspective)
Hattie Big Sky by Kirby Larson (2006) (women homesteaders)
He Will Go Fearless by Laurie Lawlor (2006) (perils of the 1860s western frontier)
The Porcupine Year by Louise Erdrich (2008) (displaced Ojibwe family, 1852)

Students could be asked to choose and read one of these titles as a supplement to the pertinent chapter in their history textbook. During discussions, students could be asked to compare what they learned in the trade books to what they learned in their textbooks and to point out any omissions or contradictions in the two sources. For example, the U.S. government's Manifest Destiny policy of the 1840s (the belief of Euro-Americans that it was their mission to extend the "boundaries of freedom" to others by appropriating more land), usually addressed in history textbooks, could be contrasted with the Native Americans' resulting disenfranchisement and loss as addressed in selected trade books. Debates, essays, and stance papers are particularly appropriate response forms for honing students' critical thinking skills. Each student's writing ability must be considered in selecting an appropriate writing activity.

Sometimes a single trade book, rather than a text set, can encourage students' critical thinking. Avi's *Nothing but the Truth* (1991), written from several viewpoints about the escalating problems resulting from a ninth-grade boy's attempt to get transferred from one homeroom to another, is an example of a book that could be assigned reading for an entire literature class. Relevant to young people's lives and relatively easy to read, it should appeal to a broad range of students. As readers, students may take the boy's side or his homeroom teacher's side, but in discussions after finishing the novel they will likely be surprised that some of their peers view events differently than they did. This book and others like it help us to realize the importance of questioning our sources of information, of looking at the whole picture before deciding on what is true, and of projecting the ramifications of our actions.

Written Response

Response

The simplest and most direct way for teachers to elicit written responses to stories is to ask students to write their ideas and feelings about a book listened to or read. Using divergent, open-ended questions as writing prompts will evoke students' feelings and ideas about a scene, a character, or the story as a whole, and will help students explore their personal involvement with the story. For example, during or after the reading of Schmidt's (2007) *The Wednesday Wars* ask, "What do you see in the character of Holling that reminds you of yourself, and why?" Likewise, during or after reading Pratchett's (2008) *Nation,* ask, "In your opinion, why do Mau and Daphne get along as well as they do even though they come from such different cultures?"

Some teachers have found a literature journal to be a motivating tool. In these journals students make frequent written responses to the books they read. When teachers read and write responses in students' journals, the interaction becomes a dialogue and gives teachers an opportunity to guide students' thinking and growth as readers, if necessary. Atwell's (1987) seminal work *In the Middle,* and her updated *In the Middle: New Understandings about Writing, Reading, and Learning* (1998) offer advice to teachers and real-life examples on leading young people to learn through writing about what they have read.

Written response to literature can take many forms. For example, students can respond to what they have read in essays, letters, diary or journal entries as if they were a book character, poems, descriptions (of characters or settings), comparisons (to other books, of a character in the present book and a character in another book, of two characters in the present book), newspaper articles, and scripts for skits or radio plays. Teachers are advised to become familiar with these and other forms, since variety precludes boredom, both for students and teachers. Another advantage of these forms is that they vary in difficulty and can therefore match students' varying writing abilities. The traditional book report is definitely not the only way a student can respond to literature.

In some cases, reactions to books by one student can be enjoyed by the rest of the class. If a teacher has a classroom library, one way to accomplish this purpose is to clip blank response sheets inside the front covers of books. After reading a book, a student writes his or her name and a reaction to the book on the response sheet. Other students may enjoy reading the book to see whether their reactions will be the same. Another idea is to ask students to write their reactions to books on 4 × 6 note cards kept on file in the classroom so that each new reader can add his or her impressions.

Literary Works as Writing Models

Well-written stories and poems can serve as models for students' own writing that can be used as a means of response to a literary work. Kaywell (1996) notes that students can emulate professional writers' good opening lines, use of details, use of similes and metaphors, and significant insights. In addition, young people accumulate vocabulary, sentence structures, stylistic devices (such as use of dialect), and story ideas and structures to use in their own writing when they read and listen to stories. Table 9.2 provides suggestions for books that can be used as writing models. Ways that students could model on the work of young adult authors include the following:

- Create a new episode using the same characters.
- Write a summary of what would have happened in the story if the protagonist had made a different decision or if some external force had been different.
- Take the perspective of a character in the story other than the protagonist, and write your reflections on the situation. An example of changing points of view can be found in Wendelin Van Draanen's *Flipped* (2001) in which readers are treated to the same story seen from the different perspectives of a girl and a boy who are next-door neighbors.
- Write the synopsis of a *prequel* (a story in which events precede those detailed in an earlier work) to a story.
- Take a story set in the past and recast it with a modern-day setting. Write a plot summary of this new work. Alternatively, take a character from a work of historical fiction and make him or her a visitor to modern times. Describe how this character would be likely to react.

Newspapers and Newsletters

A collaborative endeavor in which students write about the books they have been reading and tell about their book-related projects can result in class *newspapers* and *newsletters.* Each issue of the paper can focus on a different topic, such as favorite authors, illustrators, story characters, and poetic forms. A different literature response group accepts editing responsibilities for the newsletter each month, selecting the focus, soliciting manuscripts, designing pages, and making editorial decisions. Since computers are generally available in schools, individuals with word-processing skills can usually be found, often among the students, to produce interesting newspapers and newsletters, which are sent home to parents with suggestions of good books to read and new authors to check out.

TABLE 9.2   Using Literary Works as Writing Models

Literary Device or Element	Suggested Books
Characterization	*The Goose Girl* by Shannon Hale *The Seeing Stone* by Kevin Crossley-Holland *Daniel Half Human: And the Good Nazi* by David Chotjewitz
Dialogue	*Ruby Holler* by Sharon Creech *Indigo's Star* by Hilary McKay *Me and Rupert Goody* by Barbara O'Connor
Metaphor	*Dovey Coe* by Frances O'Roark Dowell *Green Angel* by Alice Hoffman *Kira-Kira* by Cynthia Kadohata
Mood	*The Killer's Tears* by Anne-Laure Bondoux *Voss* by David Ives *Strays Like Us* by Richard Peck *At the Sign of the Sugared Plum* by Mary Hooper
Journal writing	*The Diary of Pelly D.* by L. J. Adlington *Stowaway* by Karen Hesse *Witch Child* by Celia Rees *Maata's Journal* by Paul Sullivan
Point of view	*Nothing but the Truth* by Avi *Flipped* by Wendelin Van Draanen *Letters from the Inside* by John Marsden *Making Up Megaboy* by Virginia Walter
Flashbacks	*Who Is Jesse Flood?* by Malachy Doyle *Racing the Past* by Sis Deans *Hush* by Jacqueline Woodson *A Northern Light* by Jennifer Donnelly

Traditional Book Reports   *Not so good*   *response*

Requiring students to list author, title, date, genre, setting, main characters, and a summary of the plot—the ***traditional book report***—seldom causes students to delve deeply into literature. In fact, students often report that they never read the books they report on, but instead read the bookflap and a page or two at the beginning and end and then write the report. We have the same negative view of the so-called literature response forms or worksheets that have been published for teachers who adopt literature-based reading approaches. Some of them are little more than thinly disguised book report forms. Such comprehension assessment may be justified occasionally in the reading class, but if your goal is to promote your students' interest in reading and elicit their authentic responses to what they read, you should stay away from traditional book reports and worksheets, as suggested in the Alternatives to Traditional Book Reports box.

Alternatives to Traditional Book Reports

INDIVIDUAL

1. List ten facts learned from this work of nonfiction.
2. Draw a picture of the main character in a major scene from this book. Then write a sentence below the picture that describes the scene.
3. Write a newspaper article summarizing this book. Be sure to include a title and to answer "who, what, when, where, and why."
4. Collect at least eight interesting words or phrases from your book. Tell what each means and why you think it is interesting.
5. Choose one of the main characters from this story. Tell the class the name of the character and five things that happened to him or her in the order that they happened.
6. Design and keep a word book in which you record interesting words, phrases, and sentences in each book you read for use in your own writing.
7. Select a character from each of two different stories you have read. Write or tell a story that might result if these two characters met.
8. Select a character from this story. Write interview questions for this character, based on what happened in the story and on what might have happened to the character after the story ended. Then, with a friend, tape the interview, with your friend being the interviewer and you being the character.
9. Select new vocabulary words from this book. Write each word on one card and the meaning of each word on another card. The cards may be designed to look like a feature symbolizing the story. For example, after reading *Donuthead* (2003) by Sue Stauffacher, design each word card to look like a donut and each meaning card to look like a filled doughnut. Then have your classmates try to match them.
10. Find out as much as you can about the topics that the author of this book writes about. Make a poster about this author to get others interested in his or her books. Use the author's website, if he or she has one.
11. Describe the author or book character you would like to meet in person. Explain why you want to meet this person or character.
12. Make a book cover for this book. Include an illustration, the book title, and author's name on the front. Design the illustration so that it is faithful to the story and will interest others in reading the book. On the front inside flap, write a story blurb, making sure not to give the story away. On the back inside flap, put your name and a description of your favorite part of the book. Display the book cover in the classroom reading center.
13. Plan a booktalk for this book. Broadcast your booktalk on the school sound system, or make a video or audio recording of it for the library media center or class use.
14. Write a letter to another classmate to recommend this book. Tell why you liked the book, but don't tell the ending! Alternatively, write the letter to your classmates and post it on the bulletin board.
15. Select a favorite author and look up information about the author either online or in the library. Then write a brief biography of the person and list two or three of the author's best-known books. Tell why you believe this author's books will be remembered.
16. Write the story's problem or conflict on 4×6 index cards. Tell how the author might have handled the problem differently. Finally, tell how the author did handle the problem.
17. Find objects that were part of this story. Place these objects in a bag. Then booktalk your story, and take out each object to show when appropriate.
18. Write a comparison of the movie and book versions of this story. Tell the similarities and differences and which version you preferred and why.

Alternatives to Traditional Book Reports *(continued)*

19. Contribute a card to the class book review file in which you write the title of this book, author, and your review of the book. Tell what you liked and didn't like. Finally, give the book a 1–5-star rating.

20. Select a character from this work of historical fiction. Divide a page into two columns, and compare your life with the life of that character. Include as many similarities and differences as you can.

21. What was the main problem in this story? State the problem, how the main character dealt with it, and how you would have dealt with it differently.

22. After reading this biography, list the subject's good and not-so-good qualities.

23. Write a letter to the main character of this book giving him or her advice about dealing with future problems.

24. Pretend that you are the main character of this book. Think about how the events in the story changed you. In two paragraphs, describe yourself at the beginning and at the end of this story.

25. Look carefully at the cover illustration of this book. List the ways that you would change the illustration and why. If you wish, draw an improved cover illustration.

26. Go online or ask a librarian to help you find five other books for someone your age about the same topic as this book. Write the topic at the top of a page, and list these titles. Display the list for others who might be interested in reading about this topic.

LITERATURE CIRCLES

1. Have a panel discussion for the class by 4–6 students who have read this book. Likely topics are why others would enjoy the book, why others would relate to the characters or theme, or what readers would gain from the book.

2. Select a brief, but important, scene from this book. Rewrite the scene as a readers' theatre script, and audiotape the group reading. Place the tape in the classroom listening center as a way to encourage others to read the book.

WHOLE CLASS

1. As a class, write news stories, personal ads, want ads, for-sale ads, advice columns, editorials, comic strips, and sports stories based on the books you have read. Write the headline and a brief news article about the events leading up to the publication of this newspaper. Collate all contributions into a class newspaper.

2. (For near the end of a school year) Nominate your favorite books read this year. Booktalk any books that are not well known and then vote on the five class favorites. Advertise the winning books to other classes for summer reading.

Creative Drama

Creative drama is informal drama that lends itself readily to the reenactment of story experiences. In discussing the features of creative drama, McCaslin (1990) urges teachers and librarians to keep the following in mind:

- The drama is based on a piece of literature.
- Dialogue is created by the actors; lines are not written or memorized.

Creative Drama

- Improvisation is an essential element.
- Movement on "stage" by actors is an integral part of creative drama.
- Scenery and costumes are not used, although an occasional prop may assist the students' imaginations.
- Drama is a process rather than a product. It is performed not for an audience, but for the benefit of the participants. Several different dramas or different dramatic interpretations of the same piece of literature can occur simultaneously in the classroom.

Using creative drama, a single scene from a novel may be enacted, or a short story may be dramatized in its entirety. Suitable stories to start with are relatively simple, involving two to six characters and high action. Folktales, because of their brevity and simplicity, are good choices for beginners.

These are the steps to follow in guiding creative drama in the classroom:

- Once a story has been selected, the students listen to it being read to them, or they read it independently.
- Next, they decide whether they like the story enough to want to act it out. If so, they listen to it again or read it, paying particular attention to the characters and the story scenes in sequence.
- The students then list the characters and the scenes on the chalkboard or on chart paper.
- They assign parts to actors. If enough students are interested in dramatizing the same story, you may want to assign two or more casts of actors immediately. In this way, each cast of characters can observe the performances of the others and learn from them.
- Next, each cast uses the list of scenes to review the plot, ensuring that all actors recall the events. Discuss the characters at this time, too, having students describe the actions, talk, and appearance for each.
- Give the cast of characters a few minutes to decide how to handle the performance. Then run through it. The first attempt may be a bit bumpy, but by the second time, it usually goes quite smoothly.
- After completing the drama, the class or the group of students then evaluates its success. Mc-Caslin (1990) suggests these questions:
  1. Did they tell the story?
  2. What did you like about the opening scene?
  3. Did the characters show that they were excited (angry, unhappy, etc.)?
  4. When we play it again, can you think of anything that would improve it?
  5. Was anything important left out? (p. 174)

Because of its improvisational nature and simplicity of costumes and scenery, creative drama appropriately places importance on the learning and experiencing process, not on performance, and it permits drama to become a frequent means of responding to literature in the classroom.

Response

Readers' Theatre

Readers' theatre is the oral presentation of literature by two or more actors, and usually a narrator, reading from a script. Participants' literary response is made evident through expressive oral reading and group interpretation. This form of response is especially enjoyable for those who are able to read aloud fluently. Features typically associated with readers' theatre include the following:

- The readers and narrator typically remain on the "stage" throughout the production.
- Readers use little movement; instead, they suggest action with simple gestures and facial expressions.
- Chairs or stools are used for readers and narrator to sit on, and performers usually remain seated throughout the performance. Sometimes, certain readers sit with their backs to the audience to suggest that they are not in a particular scene.
- No costumes or stage settings are necessary and, at most, should be suggestive, rather than complete or literal, to permit the imaginations of the audience to have full rein. The use of sound effects may enhance the performance and give the impression of a radio play.

Scripts adapted from a work of literature enjoyed by the class can be developed for readers' theatre by students. Short stories readily lend themselves to adaptation, as do well-selected scenes from a favorite novel (Figure 9.3). The qualities to seek in a story or scene are natural-sounding dialogue, strong characterization, drama or humor, and a satisfactory ending. If the original work has extensive dialogue, script writing is easy. When dialogue is separated by extensive narration, editing out all but the necessary narrative keeps the script lively, and deciding how best to do this editing is the students' challenge. The script begins with the title of the book or story from which the play is adapted, the name of the author, a list of characters, and usually an opening statement by the narrator. Following the introduction, the dialogue is written into script form. If you want your students to develop readers' theatre scripts from literature, first give them a model, such as the one provided in Figure 9.3. Students take readily to script development once they have a model to imitate.

Literature to adapt for use as readers' theatre can include virtually any literary genre—picture books for older readers, novels, short stories, biographies, poems, letters, diaries, and journals. Examples of novels suitable for script development are found in the Novels Adaptable for Readers' Theatre Scripts box. Variations on readers' theatre include the use of carefully selected background music, choral poems, and brief scenes from different stories tied together by a common theme.

Readers' theatre presentations give students a good opportunity to strengthen their oral reading abilities and expressive skills. The group typically reads through the script once or twice and then works on refining the interpretive aspects of each performer. Decisions can be made on the

Novels Adaptable for Readers' Theatre Scripts

The Boy Who Saved Baseball by John H. Ritter
Bull Run by Paul Fleischman
Easy Avenue by Brian Doyle
Gilbert & Sullivan Set Me Free by Kathleen Karr
Holes by Louis Sachar
Remote Man by Elizabeth Honey
The Star of Kazan by Eva Ibbotson

Street Love by Walter Dean Myers
Surviving the Applewhites by Stephanie S. Tolan
Under the Same Sky by Cynthia DeFelice
When Zachary Beaver Came to Town by Kimberly Willis Holt

Scorpions (adapted from Chapter 3, pp. 15–16)
by Walter Dean Myers
Harper, 1988

CHARACTERS NEEDED: 7

Narrator
Mama
Jamal
Sassy
Mr. Davidson, principal
Mrs. Rich, teacher
Christine, a student

Mama: Jamal, wait for Sassy so you can walk to school with her.

Jamal: I'm going to be late waiting for her.

Mama: Sassy put some vaseline on your face before you leave.

Narrator: Sassy went into the bathroom. Jamal saw her standing at the sink and went to the bathroom door to watch her. She took some Vaseline from the jar, rubbed it between her palms, and then put it on her face. She made a tight face as she smoothed it on her cheeks and squinted as she put it on the top of her nose. Then she turned toward Jamal and smiled.

Jamal: You think you cute or something?

Sassy: All I know is what I see in the mirror.

Narrator: Sassy walked past her brother.

Jamal: Mama, she think she cute.

Mama: She is cute.

Jamal: No she ain't.

Sassy: Tito think I'm cute.

Jamal: Tito told me you were ugly.

Sassy: No, he didn't, 'cause he told Mary I was the cutest girl in third grade.

Jamal: They must got some ugly girls in the third grade, then.

Mama: Y'all get on to school. And don't fool around on the way.

Etc. . . .

FIGURE 9.3   Sample Opening of a Script for Readers' Theatre

arrangement of chairs and speakers for greatest visual effect. Following each presentation, an evaluation is made by the group with the goal of improving future performances.

McCaslin (1990) states that "the simplicity of production and effectiveness of result make it [readers' theatre] singularly desirable in schools with inadequate stage facilities and where rehearsal time is at a premium" (p. 263). For these same reasons, readers' theatre is extremely well suited to classroom reenactments of literary experiences. In readers' theatre, students have the opportunity to translate their experiences with a literary work to the medium of drama, thereby deepening their understanding of, and pleasure from, the work.

Published Plays

Response

Plays, as a literary genre, refer to written dramatic compositions of scripts intended to be acted. Plays are usually published as *playbooks* or *acting editions* in 4 × 8 paperback books by publishers who specialize in plays. Playbooks are inexpensive and can be purchased directly from publishers or ordered through bookstores. Plays are also published in books and magazines. They may be enjoyed in several ways:

- Read independently
- Read in small groups
- Performed as readers' theatre
- Performed as *recreational drama,* a formal theatrical presentation before an audience (such as other students in the classroom).

As with other forms of literature, plays must be interesting to the target audience to be successful. A relevant topic, an interesting character or two, a character to whom the reader can relate, a plot that thickens but is ultimately resolved, conflict, humor, and natural-sounding dialogue all contribute to the interest a play has for young people. Some readers may even find the play's stage directions interesting, even if they are not able to produce the play as suggested.

In selecting plays for classroom use, the distinction between adaptations and original plays is important. Many adaptations, particularly of traditional literature, are available. Far fewer adaptations of contemporary works are available, and *original plays,* stories originating in play form, are scarce, even though young adults indicate a preference for them (Sather, 1976).

The American Alliance for Theatre and Education (AATE) sponsors the Distinguished Play Award, which is useful in identifying notable plays for young people. Established in 1983, this annual award honors the playwrights and publishers of the works voted as the best original plays for young people published during the preceding year. Category A is for plays primarily for middle school and secondary age audiences. Category C is for the best adaptation of an existing work of literature. For a complete list of award winners, go to www.aate.com/awards_winners.asp#distinguishedplay. Two publishers have published most of the award-winning plays for young adults during the last two decades: Anchorage Press Plays, P.O. Box 2901, Louisville, KY 40201-2901, and Dramatic Publishing Company, 311 Washington Street, Woodstock, IL 60098.

Anthologies are a good source of plays for young adults' reading enjoyment. One publisher, Smith and Kraus, Inc., has several play anthologies available on a variety of topics. Some recent anthologies from this publisher include *"Now I Get It!": 12 Ten-Minute Classroom Drama Skits for Science, Math, Language, and Social Studies* by L. E. McCullough; *Multicultural Monologues for Young Actors* by C. Slaight and J. Sharrar; *Most Valuable Player: And Four Other All-Star Plays for Middle and High School Audiences* and *Short Scenes and Monologues for Middle School Actors,* both by M. H. Surface.

Time Lines and Maps

A *time line* is a type of visual figure that details a period of time covered in a story. The figure is made by drawing a line on a long strip of mural paper and then placing dates below the line at scaled intervals. The story events are logged in above the line. This graphic aid organizes the events of the story and can permit students to compare events from a novel of historical fiction or from a biography with actual dates from history.

Time lines can be excellent visual aids when used in conjunction with reading aloud a progressive-plot novel. The time line is set up with the dates, and story events are recorded on the time line after each day's reading. The time line can also serve as a reminder of what has happened thus far as a review before beginning the next chapter.

Time lines can also be useful when students are reading a variety of material on a single period of history: biographies, historical fiction novels, and photoessays on World War II, for instance. Historical events from different sources can be compared for authenticity by using parallel time lines or by adding more tiers to the same time line. Individual students may develop time lines to follow the events of an entire series of books, such as science fiction novels and quest adventure stories.

Maps are especially suitable for charting the settings in novels. They can be designed by individuals or groups of students and make interesting and helpful visual aids for telling others about books. Books in which maps are included can be used by students as models for drawing story maps on other books. Examples are *The Thief Lord* (2002) by Cornelia Funke, *Stowaway* (2000) by Karen Hesse, and *The Great Fire* by Jim Murphy (1995). Maps are also suitable for laying out the events in books with a circular journey motif in which the protagonist leaves home, encounters adversity, overcomes it, and returns home, as in *The Kite Rider* (2001) by Geraldine McCaughrean.

Jackdaws

Jackdaws are collections of artifacts or copies of objects from a particular historical period or event. Jackdaws are often available in museums for study of a period of history, and some museums lend them to teachers for use in schools. The term "jackdaw" refers to a common European bird that is related to the crow and known to collect colorful objects for its nest. Educators have borrowed the term to refer to a teaching tool that can be used to connect historical books with the real events of the times depicted through concrete objects (Devitt, 1970). For example, a teacher may put together a jackdaw based on homesteaders in Oklahoma in the 1800s and then use the jackdaw to build background knowledge as an introduction to studying the historical fiction novel *Stop the Train!* (2001) by Geraldine McCaughrean.

Jackdaws are made by collecting a wide array of related materials in their original forms or in reproductions. Materials often collected are regional maps; photographs or models of homes, farms, or machines; household furnishings; toys and dolls; kitchen tools; recipes for foods commonly eaten; newspapers and books of the era; clothing; modes of transportation; information about the government of the time (president, legislature, political parties, statehood); pictures or models of educational institutions; and cultural artifacts such as songs, paintings, and architectural landmarks. The objects are placed in a decorated box with labels and explanations attached, if desired. The jackdaw can be used as an extension activity for a book read in class as well as for building background. Many teachers enlist students in the development of jackdaws and share jackdaws with other teachers who are studying the same historical book or era.

This chapter has presented options for planning for a literature curriculum and strategies for having students experience literature and respond to those literary experiences. It is important to remember that even the most motivating activity repeated to the point of monotony becomes little more than busywork to students. It is also important to remember that a response activity is *not* an absolute necessity for every literary work read. In many cases, a worthy response to a book, poem, or short story would be finding another work by the same author and reading it next. When more active response seems warranted, however, it is important to plan worthwhile ways for students to express those responses. It is then the teacher's job to provide students with a variety of interesting response options, the materials needed to complete them, and assistance in planning the execution of the response.

REFERENCES

Adlington, L. J. (2005). *The diary of Pelly D.* New York: HarperCollins.

Allington, R. L. (2002). You can't learn much from books you can't read. *Educational Leadership, 60*(3), 16–19.

Almond, D. (2000). *Kit's wilderness.* New York: Delacorte.

Anderson, L. H. (2000). *Fever 1793.* New York: Simon & Schuster.

———. (2005). *Prom.* New York: Viking.

———. (1999). *Speak.* New York: Farrar.

Anderson, M. T. (2001). *Handel, who knew what he liked.* Illustrated by Kevin Hawkes. Cambridge, MA: Candlewick.

———. (2002). *Feed.* Cambridge, MA: Candlewick.

Atwell, N. (1987). *In the middle.* Portsmouth, NH: Heinemann.

———. (1998). *In the middle: New understandings about writing, reading, and learning.* Portsmouth, NH: Boynton/Cook.

Avi. (1991). *Nothing but the truth.* New York: Orchard.

Baldick, C. (1990). *The concise Oxford dictionary of literary terms.* New York: Oxford University Press.

Ball, J. (2005). *Go figure!: A totally cool book about numbers.* New York: DK Publishing.

Balliett, B. (2004). *Chasing Vermeer.* New York: Scholastic.

Bartoletti, S. C. (2001). *Black potatoes: The story of the great Irish famine, 1845–1850.* Boston: Houghton Mifflin.

———. (2008). *The boy who dared.* New York: Scholastic.

Bauer, J. (2000). *Hope was here.* New York: Putnam.

Bauer, M. G. (2007). *Don't call me Ishmael.* New York: HarperCollins.

Beah, I. (2007). *A long way gone: Memoirs of a boy soldier.* New York: Farrar.

Beers, K., & Lesesne, T. S. (Eds.). (2001). *Books for you: An annotated booklist for senior high* (14th ed.). Urbana, IL: National Council of Teachers of English.

Bell, H. (2001). *A matter of profit.* New York: HarperCollins.

Bial, R. (2002). *Tenement: Immigrant life on the Lower East Side.* Boston: Houghton Mifflin.

Blessing, C. (2005). Reading to kids who are old enough to shave. *School Library Journal, 51*(4), 44–45.

Bloor, E. (1997). *Tangerine.* San Diego: Harcourt.

Blumberg, R. (2004). *York's adventures with Lewis and Clark: An African-American's part in the great expedition.* New York: HarperCollins.

Blumenthal, K. (2005). *Let me play: The story of Title IX: The law that changed the future of girls in America.* New York: Atheneum.

Bodart, J. (1980). *Booktalk!* New York: H. W. Wilson.

Bondoux, A. (2006). *The killer's tears.* New York: Delacorte.

Brown, J. E., & Stephens, E. C. (Eds.). (2003). *Your reading: An annotated booklist for middle school and junior high* (11th ed.). Urbana, IL: National Council of Teachers of English.

Bruchac, J. (2000). *Sacajawea: The story of Bird Woman and the Lewis and Clark expedition.* San Diego: Silver Whistle.

Budhos, M. (2006). *Ask me no questions.* New York: Atheneum.

Budiansky, S. (2001). The trouble with textbooks. *Prism, 10*(6), 24–27.

Burgess, M. (1998). *Smack.* New York: Holt.

Buss, F. L., & Cubias, D. (1991). *Journey of the sparrows.* New York: Lodestar.

Cameron, A. (2003). *Colibrí.* New York: Farrar.

Campbell, J. R., Voelkl, K. E., & Donahue, P. L. (1998). *Report in brief: NAEP 1996 trends in academic progress* (Pub. No. 98-530). Washington, DC: National Center for Education Statistics.

Carlsen, G. R., & Sherrill, A. (1988). *Voices of readers: How we come to love books.* Urbana, IL: National Council of Teachers of English.

Cart, M. (Ed.). (1999). *Tomorrowland: Ten stories about the future.* New York: Scholastic.

Chall, J. S., & Conard, S. S. (1991). *Should textbooks challenge students?* New York: Teachers College Press.

Children's literature review: Excerpts from reviews, criticism, and commentary on books for children and young people (Vols. 1–115). (1976–2006). Detroit: Thomson Gale.

Choldenko, G. (2004). *Al Capone does my shirts.* New York: Putnam.

Chotjewitz, D. (2004). *Daniel half human: And the good Nazi.* Translated from the German by D. Orgel. New York: Atheneum.

Clements, A. (2002). *Things not seen.* New York: Putnam/Philomel.

Collard, S. B. (2005). *The prairie builders: Reconstructing America's lost grasslands.* New York: Houghton Mifflin.

Collins, S. (2008). *The hunger games.* New York: Scholastic.

Cooney, C. (1994). *Driver's ed.* New York: Delacorte.

Cormier, R. (1974). *The chocolate war.* New York: Knopf.

Creech, S. (2002). *Ruby Holler.* New York: HarperCollins.

Crossley-Holland, K. (2001). *The seeing stone.* New York: Scholastic.

Crutcher, C. (1991). *Athletic shorts: Six short stories.* New York: Greenwillow.

———. (1993). *Staying fat for Sarah Byrnes.* New York: Greenwillow.

Curtis, C. P. (2004). *Bucking the Sarge.* New York: Random House.

———. (2007). *Elijah of Buxton.* New York: Scholastic.

Cushman, K. (1996). *The ballad of Lucy Whipple.* New York: Clarion.

Dash, J. (2000). *The longitude prize.* Illustrated by Dušan Petričić. New York: Farrar.

Davidson, S., & Morgan, B. (2002). *Human body revealed.* New York: DK Publishing.

Deans, S. (2001). *Racing the past.* New York: Holt.

DeFelice, C. (2003). *Under the same sky.* New York: Farrar.

Delacre, L. (2000). *Salsa stories.* New York: Scholastic.

Devitt, M. (Ed.). (1970). *Learning with jackdaws.* London: St. Paul's Press.

Devlin, Keith. (2005). *The math instinct: Why you're a mathematical genius (along with lobsters, birds, cats and dogs).* New York: Thunder's Mouth Press.

Doak, R. S. (2005). *Galileo: Astronomer and physicist.* Minneapolis: Compass Point Books.

Doctorow, C. (2008). *Little brother.* New York: Tor.

Donnelly, J. C. (2003). *A northern light.* San Diego: Harcourt.

Dowd, S. (2008). *The London Eye mystery.* New York: Random House.

Dowell, F. O. (2000). *Dovey Coe.* New York: Atheneum.

Doyle, B. (1998). *Easy avenue.* Toronto: Groundwood.

Doyle, M. (2002). *Who is Jesse Flood?* New York: Bloomsbury.

Draper, S. (2006). *Copper sun.* New York: Atheneum.

Dressel, J. H. (1990). The effects of listening to and discussing different qualities of children's literature on the narrative writing of fifth graders. *Research in the Teaching of English, 24*(4), 397–414.

Dudley, W. (Ed.). (2001). *Drugs and sports.* Farmington Hills, MI: Greenhaven.

Erdrich, L. (1999). *The birchbark house.* New York: Hyperion.

———. (2005). *The game of silence.* New York: HarperCollins.

———. (2008). *The porcupine year.* New York: HarperCollins.

Espejo, R. (2008). *Should music lyrics be censored for violence and exploitation?* Farmington Hills, MI: Greenhaven.

Farmer, N. (2002). *The house of the scorpion.* New York: Atheneum.

Farrell, J. (2005). *Invisible allies: Microbes that shape our lives.* New York: Farrar.

———. *Invisible enemies: Stories of infectious disease.* (Revised edition). (2005). New York: Farrar.

Fielding, L. G., Wilson, P. T., & Anderson, R. C. (1986). A new focus on free reading: The role of trade books in reading instruction. In T. Raphael (Ed.), *The contexts of school-based literacy* (pp. 149–160). New York: Random House.

Fleischman, P. (1993). *Bull Run.* New York: HarperCollins.

Fredericks, M. (2005). *Crunch time.* New York: Simon & Schuster.

Freedman, R. (1999). *Babe Didrikson Zaharias.* New York: Clarion.

———. (2004). *The voice that challenged a nation: Marian Anderson and the struggle for equal rights.* New York: Clarion.

Frost, H. (2003). *Keesha's house.* New York: Farrar.

Funke, C. (2002). *The thief lord.* Translated by O. Latsch. New York: Scholastic.

Gallo, D. (Ed.). (1995). *Ultimate sports: Short stories by outstanding writers for young adults.* New York: Delacorte.

———. (Ed.). (1997). *No easy answers: Short stories about teenagers making tough choices.* New York: Random House.

Gantos, J. (1998). *Joey Pigza swallowed the key.* New York: Farrar.

———. (2002). *Hole in my life.* New York: Farrar.

Giblin, J. C. (2000). *The amazing life of Benjamin Franklin.* Illustrated by M. Dooling. New York: Scholastic.

Gillies, J., & Glossop, J. (2000). *The Kids Can Press jumbo cookbook.* Illustrated by L. Phillips. Toronto: Kids Can Press.

Going, K. L. (2003). *Fat kid rules the world.* New York: Grosset & Dunlap.

Goodnough, D. (2003). *The debate over human cloning: A pro-con issue.* Berkeley Heights, NJ: Enslow.

Greenberg, J. (Ed.). (2001). *Heart to heart.* New York: Abrams.

Greenberg, J., & Jordan, S. (1998). *Chuck Close, up close.* New York: DK Ink.

———. (2001). *Vincent Van Gogh: Portrait of an artist.* New York: Delacorte.

Hale, S. (2003). *The goose girl.* New York: Bloomsbury.

Hall, S. (1990). *Using picture storybooks to teach literary devices: Recommended books for children and young adults.* Phoenix, AZ: Oryx.

———. (1994). *Using picture storybooks to teach literary devices: Recommended books for children and young adults* (Vol. 2). Phoenix, AZ: Oryx.

———. (2001). *Using picture storybooks to teach literary devices: Recommended books for children and young adults* (Vol. 3). Phoenix, AZ: Oryx.

———. (2007). *Using picture storybooks to teach literary devices: Recommended books for children and young adults* (Vol. 4). Santa Barbara, CA: Libraries Unlimited.

Hamilton, J. (2008). *Bullying and hazing.* Farmington Hills, MI: Greenhaven.

Hartinger, B. (2003). *Geography club.* New York: HarperCollins.

Hesse, K. (1998/1992). *Letters from Rifka*. New York: Holt.

———. (2000). *Stowaway*. New York: McElderry.

Hiassen, C. (2002). *Hoot*. New York: Knopf.

Hill, L. C. (2005). *Casa azul: An encounter with Frida Kahlo*. New York: Watson-Guptill.

Hoffman, A. (2003). *Green angel*. New York: Scholastic.

Holm, J. (2001). *Boston Jane: An adventure*. New York: HarperCollins. (Others in the series: *Boston Jane: Wilderness days*, 2002; *Boston Jane: The claim*, 2004.)

Holt, K. W. (1999). *When Zachary Beaver came to town*. New York: Holt.

Honey, E. (2002). *Remote man*. New York: Knopf.

Hooper, M. (2003). *At the sign of the sugared plum*. New York: Bloomsbury.

Hoose, P. (2001). *We were there, too! Young people in U.S. history*. New York: Farrar.

———. (2004). *The race to save the lord god bird*. New York: Farrar.

Horvath, P. (2001). *Everything on a waffle*. New York: Farrar.

Hughes, D. (2001). *Soldier boys*. New York: Atheneum.

Hynd, C. R. (1999). Teaching students to think critically using multiple texts in history. *Journal of Adolescent and Adult Literacy, 42*(6), 428–436.

Ibbotson, E. (1999). *Which witch?* New York: Dutton.

———. (2004). *The star of Kazan*. New York: Pan Macmillan.

Ives, D. (2008). *Voss*. New York: Putnam.

Jaramillo, A. (2006). *La línea*. New York: Roaring Brook.

Jiménez, F. (1999). *The circuit: Stories from the life of a migrant child*. Boston: Houghton Mifflin.

———. (2008). *Reaching out*. Boston: Houghton Mifflin.

Kadohata, C. (2004). *Kira-kira*. New York: Atheneum.

Karr, K. (2003). *Gilbert & Sullivan set me free*. New York: Hyperion.

Kashmira, S. (2004). *Blue jasmine*. New York: Hyperion.

Katin, M. (2006). *We are on our own*. Montreal: Drawn & Quarterly.

Kaye, M. (1998). *Amy number seven*. (Replica series.) New York: Skylark.

Kaywell, J. F. (1996). Enhancing your writing through the masters or what makes a good work good. *English Journal, 85*(5), 104–107.

Kerner, C. (2000). *Blueprint*. Minneapolis: Lerner.

Knight, M. B. (1993). *Who belongs here? An American story*. New York: Tilbury.

Knudson, R. R., & Swenson, M. (Comp.). (1996). *American sports poems* (reissue edition). New York: Orchard.

Koubek, C. W. (2002). *Friends, cliques, and peer pressure: Be true to yourself*. Berkeley Heights, NJ: Enslow.

Krull, K. (1993). *Lives of the musicians: Good times, bad times (and what the neighbors thought)*. Illustrated by K. Hewitt. San Diego: Harcourt.

Larson, K. (2006). *Hattie Big Sky*. New York: Delacorte.

Lasky, K. (2003). *The man who made time travel*. Illustrated by K. Hawkes. New York: Farrar.

Latham, J. L. (1955/2003). *Carry on, Mr. Bowditch*. New York: Houghton.

Law, I. (2008). *Savvy*. New York: Dial.

Lawlor, L. (2006). *He will go fearless*. New York: Simon & Schuster.

Lawrence, I. (1998). *The wreckers*. New York: Delacorte.

Levine, E. (1993). *If your name was changed at Ellis Island*. Illustrated by W. Parmenter. New York: Scholastic.

Levitin, S. (1999/1970). *Journey to America*. New York: Atheneum.

Livaudais, M. (1985). A survey of secondary students' attitudes toward reading motivational activities. Doctoral dissertation, University of Houston, 1985. *Dissertation Abstracts International, 46*(8), 2217A.

Lynch, C. (2005). *Inexcusable*. New York: Atheneum.

Lyon, G. E. (2004). *Sonny's house of spies*. New York: Atheneum.

Maestro, B. (1996). *Coming to America: The story of immigration*. Illustrated by S. Ryan. New York: Scholastic.

Mankell, H. (2003). *Secrets in the fire*. Toronto: Annick.

Marcovitz, H. (2005). *Teens and cheating*. Broomall, PA: Mason Crest.

Marsalis, W. (2005). *Jazz ABZ: An A to Z collection of jazz portraits*. Illustrated by P. Rogers. Cambridge, MA: Candlewick.

Marsden, J. (1994). *Letters from the inside.* Boston: Houghton Mifflin.

McCaslin, N. (1990). *Creative drama in the classroom* (5th ed.). New York: Longmann.

McCaughrean, G. (2001). *The kite rider.* New York: HarperCollins.

———. (2001). *Stop the train!* New York: Harper-Collins.

———. (2006). *Cyrano.* New York: Harcourt.

McCullough, L. E. (2000). *"Now I get it!": 12 ten-minute classroom drama skits for science, math, language, and social studies.* Manchester, NH: Smith and Kraus.

McKay, H. (2004). *Indigo's star.* New York: McElderry.

Mikaelsen, B. (1998). *Petey.* New York: Hyperion.

———. (2001). *Touching spirit bear.* New York: HarperCollins.

Morpurgo, M. (2004). *Private Peaceful.* New York: Scholastic.

Morrison, L. (2001). *Way to go! Sports poems.* Illustrated by S. Spellman. Honesdale, PA: Wordsong/Boyds Mills.

Mourlevat, J.-C. (2006). *The pull of the ocean.* New York: Delacorte.

Mühlberger, R. (2002). *What makes a Monet a Monet?* New York: Metropolitan Museum of Art/Viking.

Murphy, J. (1995). *The great fire.* New York: Scholastic.

Myers, L. (2002). *Lewis and Clark and me: A dog's tale.* Illustrated by M. Dooling. New York: Holt.

Myers, W. D. (1988). *Scorpions.* New York: Harper.

———. (1996). *Slam!* New York: Scholastic.

———. (1999). *Monster.* New York: Scholastic.

———. (2000). *145th street: Short stories.* New York: Delacorte.

———. (2001). *Bad boy: A memoir.* New York: HarperTempest.

———. (2003). *Blues journey.* Illustrated by C. Myers. New York: Holiday.

———. (2006). *Street Love.* New York: Amistad/HarperCollins.

———. (2007). *What they found: Love on 145th Street.* New York: Random.

Na, A. (2001). *A step from heaven.* Asheville, NC: Front Street.

———. (2006). *Wait for me.* New York: Putnam.

Naidoo, B. (2001). *The other side of truth.* New York: HarperCollins.

National Center for Education Statistics. (2001). *Outcomes of learning: Results from the 2000 program for international student assessment of 15-year-olds in reading, math, and science.* Washington, DC: U.S. Department of Education.

Ness, P. (2008). *The knife of never letting go: Chaos walking.* New York: Candlewick.

O'Connor, B. (1999). *Me and Rupert Goody.* New York: Farrar.

Peacock, S. (2007). *Eye of the crow.* Toronto: Tundra.

Peck, R. (1998). *Strays like us.* New York: Dial.

———. (2000). *A year down yonder.* New York: Dial.

Peters, C. (2003). *Bill Gates: Software genius of Microsoft.* Berkeley Heights, NJ: Enslow.

Picoult, P. (2007). *Nineteen minutes.* New York: Atria.

Pratchett, T. (2001). *The amazing Maurice and his educated rodents.* New York: HarperCollins.

———. (2008). *Nation.* New York: HarperCollins.

Pringle, L. (2001). *Global warming: The threat of earth's changing climate.* New York: Chronicle/Seastar.

Rabinovici, S. (1998). *Thanks to my mother.* Translated from the German by J. Skofield. New York: Dial.

Rees, C. (2001). *Witch child.* Cambridge, MA: Candlewick.

Rice, D. (2001). *Crazy loco.* New York: Dial.

Ritter, J. H. (2003). *The boy who saved baseball.* New York: Philomel.

Robb, L. (2003). *Teaching reading in social studies, science, and math.* New York: Scholastic.

Robbins, P. R. (1998). *Anorexia and bulimia.* Berkeley Heights, NJ: Enslow.

Rocklin, J. (1999). *Strudel stories.* New York: Delacorte.

Rogasky, B. (2002). *Smoke and ashes: The story of the Holocaust* (expanded edition). New York: Holiday.

Rosenblatt, L. M. (1978). *The reader, the text, the poem: The transactional theory of the literary work.* Carbondale: Southern Illinois University Press.

Roy, J. (2006). *Yellow star.* Tarrytown, NY: Marshall Cavendish.

Ryan, P. M. (2000). *Esperanza rising.* New York: Scholastic.

Sachar, L. (1998). *Holes.* New York: Farrar.

Salisbury, G. (1994). *Under the blood-red sun.* New York: Delacorte.

Sandler, M. W. (2008). *Lincoln through the lens: How photography revealed and shaped an extraordinary life.* New York: Walker.

Sather, S. P. (1976). A critical assessment of children's plays. *Children's Theatre Review, 25*(1), 2–5.

Schlosser, E., & Wilson, C. (2006). *Chew on this: Everything you didn't want to know about fast food.* Boston: Houghton Mifflin.

Schmidt, G. D. (2007). *The Wednesday wars.* New York: Clarion.

Schmidt, J. (1995). *Two lands, one heart: An American boy's journey to his mother's Vietnam.* New York: Walker.

Sedgwick, M. (2001). *Floodland.* New York: Delacorte.

Silverstein, A., Silverstein, V., & Nunn, L. S. (2003). *Global warming.* Kirkland, WA: 21st Century.

Sís, P. (2007). *The wall: Growing up behind the iron curtain.* New York: Farrar.

Slaight, C., & Sharrar, J. (1995). *Multicultural monologues for young actors.* Manchester, NH: Smith and Kraus.

Smith, R. (1999). *The captain's dog: My journey with the Lewis and Clark tribe.* San Diego: Harcourt.

Sneve, V. D. H. (2005). *Bad river boys: A meeting of the Lakota Sioux with Lewis and Clark.* Illustrated by B. Farnsworth. New York: Holiday.

Something about the author: Facts and pictures about authors and illustrators of books for young people (Vols. 1–169). (1971–2006). Detroit: Thomson Gale.

Spinelli, J. (2000). *Stargirl.* New York: Knopf.

Stauffacher, S. (2003). *Donuthead.* New York: Knopf.

Stratton, A. (2004). *Chanda's secrets.* Toronto: Annick.

Streissguth, T. (2008). *Welcome to America? A pro/con debate over immigration.* Berkeley Heights, NJ: Enslow.

Strom, Y. (1996). *Quilted landscape: Conversations with young immigrants.* New York: Simon & Schuster.

Sullivan, P. (2003). *Maata's journal.* New York: Atheneum.

Surface, M. H. (1999). *Most valuable player: And four other all-star plays for middle and high school audiences.* Manchester, NH: Smith and Kraus.

———. (2000). *Short scenes and monologues for middle school actors.* Manchester, NH: Smith and Kraus.

Temple, F. (1995). *Tonight, by sea.* New York: Orchard.

Thompson, K. (2007). *The new policeman.* New York: Greenwillow.

Tolan, S. S. (2002). *Surviving the Applewhites.* New York: HarperCollins.

Trueman, T. (2000). *Stuck in neutral.* New York: HarperCollins.

Valentine, J. (2008). *Me, the missing, and the dead.* New York: HarperTeen.

Van Draanen, W. (2001). *Flipped.* New York: Knopf.

Vizzini, N. (2006). *It's kind of a funny story.* New York: Miramax.

Walter, V. (1998). *Making up Megaboy.* Illustrated by K. Roecklelein. New York: DK Publishing.

Westerfeld, S. (2004). *So yesterday.* New York: Penguin.

Wild, M. (2004). *One night.* New York: Knopf.

Wise, B. (2001). *Whodunit math puzzles.* Illustrated by L. Corvino. New York: Sterling.

Wishinsky, F. (2002). *What's the matter with Albert? A story of Albert Einstein.* Illustrated by J. Lamontagne. Toronto: Maple Tree Press.

Wolf, A. (2004). *New found land.* Cambridge, MA: Candlewick.

Woodson, J. (2002). *Hush.* New York: Putnam.

———. (2000). *Miracle's boys.* New York: Putnam.

Yee, P. (2002). *Dead man's gold and other stories.* Illustrated by H. Chan. Toronto: Douglas & McIntyre. Distributed in United States by Publishers Group West, Berkeley, CA.

Yep, L. (1990/1977). *Child of the owl.* New York: HarperCollins.

———. (1993). *Dragon's gate.* New York: HarperCollins.

Zaharias, J. A. (1989). Literature anthologies in the United States: Impediments to good teaching practice. *English Journal, 78*(6), 22–27.

Zenatti, V. (2005). *When I was a soldier.* Translated from the French by A. Hunter. New York: Bloomsbury.

Zusak, Markus. (2007). *The book thief.* New York: Knopf.

chapter TEN

RESISTANT READERS *and* YOUNG ADULT LITERATURE

Independent reading, that is, reading done voluntarily in and out of school, has been in decline among young adults in the United States for several decades (Cline & Kretke, 1980; Anderson, Tollefson, & Gilbert, 1985; Shapiro & White, 1991; McKenna, Ellsworth, & Kear, 1995; Bradshaw & Nichols, 2004). Some national studies say that more than half of today's young people do not engage in independent reading (Bradshaw & Nichols, 2004). This trend is cause for concern, since research findings show that time spent reading correlates with reading achievement (Fielding, Wilson, & Anderson, 1986; Anderson, Wilson, & Fielding, 1988; Krashen, 1988; Postlethwaite & Ross, 1992; Moore, Bean, Birdyshaw, & Rycik, 1999). Research findings also show that reading practice helps to strengthen the skills learned through reading instruction and that the reading skills of those who do not engage in recreational reading, including good readers, often erode over time (Stanovich, 1986; Anderson et al., 1988; Mullis, Campbell, & Farstrup, 1993).

The term we will use for young people who can read but choose not to read is *resistant readers. Reluctant reader* is also commonly used to identify these readers. Most often, these students cite irrelevance of teacher-selected reading materials to their lives, instructional practices, too little time, peer pressure, past failures, a preference for electronic media, and a perception of reading as hard work as reasons for not reading. Consequently, the greatest challenge for teachers and librarians in middle and high schools is to break through this resistance to reading and find ways to get students to read widely and intensively.

DENTIFYING RESISTANT READERS

Beers (1996a) defines those who can read but do not as *aliterates,* but in this chapter we are referring to those who not only do not read but actively resist reading. Young people resist or reject reading for many reasons. We have identified five main groups of resistant readers.

Good to Average Readers Who Choose Not to Read

On entering middle school, some students who choose not to read have good to excellent comprehension, few difficulties in decoding, and average reading rates. They include males and females of all ethnic, racial, and socioeconomic groups. However, either because they have too little time or because they perceive the books they must read in school to be irrelevant to their lives and therefore boring, they rarely read or do not like to read. With little or no reading practice, they eventually lose their former reading achievement levels.

Students Who Struggle with Reading

By middle and high school, some struggling readers can decode, but this skill remains a conscious cognitive act rather than an automatic process. The act of concentrating on decoding words slows these students' reading rate and fluency, hampers their ability to recall what they have read to make sense of the text, and tires them mentally. Others in this group are fluent readers but have difficulty comprehending what they read. Possible ridicule by their peers and embarrassment in class for their reading difficulties makes them avoid reading whenever possible. But these are the students for whom regular reading practice is especially important to maintain and improve reading levels. Reading skills for these readers need constant reinforcement, or they weaken and can even be lost.

Ethnic and Racial Minorities Who Resist Reading

School instructional practices, teacher perceptions, low socioeconomic status, and self-perceptions molded by a cultural disbelief in the importance of intellectual development are given as possible reasons why some members of ethnic and racial minorities resist reading (Gilbert & Gilbert, 1998; Maynard, 2002; Tatum, 2005). The National Assessment for Educational Progress, since its inception in 1992, has reported a continuing reading achievement gap between whites and Asians on the one hand and American Indians, Hispanics, and blacks on the other. In 2005 the average reading score for eighth-grade whites and Asians was 271, compared to 249 for American Indians, 246 for Hispanics, and 243 for blacks (National Center for Education Statistics, 2005).

English Language Learners Who Resist Reading

Many students who are learning English as a second language are also adjusting to a new culture. Because they lack strong vocabularies and well-developed sentence structures to draw on when encountering English language texts and because the texts they are asked to read often portray unfamiliar experiences and cultural norms, they have difficulty reading, so they avoid it whenever possible. This group is large and growing. In 2000 about three and a half million children between the ages of 5 and 17 in the United States spoke English less than "very well" (U.S. Census Bureau, 2000).

Boys Who Resist Reading

Boys who resist reading may do so in part because of the preponderance of female teachers in American schools (75% in grades K–12) and their tendency to select reading materials that do not necessarily appeal to boys (Brozo, 2005). It also may stem from the perception that reading, because it is quiet and passive, is a female activity, or at least not macho. On average, boys exhibit more difficulty in reading and other language areas than girls (National Center for Education Statistics, 2005).

Not all young people who dislike reading school-based materials are resistant readers. Some, in fact, are avid readers, but of materials that schools do not traditionally recognize, such as magazines, Internet websites, and informational books (Taylor, 2004). Boys, in particular, fit this profile. Two informative sources about boys and their reading are *Reading Don't Fix No Chevys: Literacy in the Lives of Young Men* (Smith & Wilhelm, 2002) and *Teaching Reading to Black Adolescent Males: Closing the Achievement Gap* (Tatum, 2005).

The trend away from reading among young people today is a serious problem and a daunting challenge to teachers and librarians; but there are solutions, many of which are grounded in common sense and have been known and practiced for years. The first of these, acknowledging the importance of a person's interests as a reading motivator, is the subject of the next section.

 # KNOWING STUDENTS' GENERAL READING INTERESTS

Reading interest, reading preference, and reading choice studies provide useful information to those who purchase books for young adults and those who encourage them to read the books. Although the terms to describe the various studies and the procedures used in conducting the studies may vary, the studies try to infer what students like to read. Generally, a reading interest suggests a feeling one has toward particular reading material; a reading preference implies making a choice from two or more options; a reading choice study investigates "print materials selected and read from a predetermined collection" (Chance, 1999, p. 65). These studies do not always provide an opportunity for students to express their interests. If, for example, the study does not include illustrated books, then students will not be able to select illustrated books. Although the findings from this body of research can be useful, it is important to realize that the results of these studies are based on group data or aggregated data and reflect the interests of groups of students, but not individuals.

Reading Interests of Adolescents

Our common sense tells us that students will apply themselves more vigorously to read something they are interested in than something they find uninteresting or boring. Interest generates motivation, so knowing the general reading interests of your students' age group is essential. According to various research studies on reading interests over the years (Squire, 1969; McBroom, 1981; Carter & Harris, 1982; Samuels, 1989; Wilder & Teasley, 1999; Worthy, Moorman, & Turner, 1999; Hale & Crowe, 2001; Smith & Wilhelm, 2002), students over age 10 have indicated differences in interests by gender. It is important to remember that individual students' reading interests may vary from the following research-based generalizations.

REGARDING *TOPICS AND GENRES OF INTEREST,* ADOLESCENT MALES LIKE

- nonfiction on various subjects
- adventures
- sports
- mysteries
- science fiction and fantasy
- scary stories/horror

ADOLESCENT FEMALES LIKE

- romances
- mysteries
- scary stories/horror
- realistic stories

According to other reports (Carter & Harris, 1982; Samuels, 1989; Langerman, 1990; Worthy et al., 1999; Smith & Wilhelm, 2002) and our own observations, adolescents differ by gender in their preferences for books with certain characteristics.

REGARDING *FORMAT AND PRESENTATION OF MATERIAL,*
ADOLESCENT MALES LIKE

- short texts or texts with shorter sections or chapters; also short stories
- visual texts including illustrated books, picture books, comic books, and graphic novels
- books with cover illustrations, mostly of teenagers (covers can be a turnoff if the young person portrayed appears much younger than the reader; covers need to reflect the content of the book)
- books based on movies and television
- newspapers and popular magazines

ADOLESCENT FEMALES LIKE

- fiction, especially novels they can connect to
- books that convey characters' feelings
- newspapers and popular magazines

BOTH MALES AND FEMALES LIKE

- illustrations in books
- adolescent protagonists of their own gender
- characters the age of the reader or slightly older
- fast-paced stories
- humorous stories
- familiar experiences about teen life

In reading interest studies, males report a greater diversity of reading interests, more definitive likes and dislikes, and a lack of interest in reading other material, whereas females are more likely to read more, to share books with friends, and to see reading as a social act.

Reading Interests of Resistant Adolescent Readers

Although many of the preceding findings on the reading preferences of adolescents have remained fairly constant in studies for decades, less research has been conducted on the specific characteristics of reading material preferred by *resistant adolescent readers.* From reports (Beers, 1996a,b; Jones, 1994; Worthy, Patterson, Salas, Prater, & Turner, 2002; Beers, 2003) and from our own experiences, resistant adolescent readers indicate an interest in

- short books
- longer books with short chapters or sections
- lots of white space in books; fewer words per page; easy-to-read type face and font size
- books with illustrations, photographs, or sketches
- books *after* seeing the movie
- comic book–style illustrations
- comic books and graphic novels
- series books, such as R. L. Stine's Fear Street chillers   ←——————— *Cory?*

IN WORKS OF FICTION

- a rapid introduction to main characters
- only a few (2–4) characters, each with one name used consistently and each character well delineated
- characters the same age as the reader or only a few years older
- characters of the same racial or ethnic group or whose experiences seem similar to their own
- a quick start to the story with action beginning on the first or second page to hook the reader
- a fast pace throughout; less introspection and rumination by characters
- gripping and memorable stories with emotional impact
- a single narrator or single point of view

- episodic plots
- progressive chronological plots that can be easily followed
- familiar settings (needing little description) or settings described briefly or shown through illustrations (lengthy descriptions of the setting are disliked)
- dialogue with realistic everyday teen talk
- topics about teenagers' concerns

IN WORKS OF NONFICTION

- heavily illustrated books such as Dorling Kindersley's Eyewitness books
- trivia books such as the *Guinness Book of World Records*, sports statistics books, and joke books
- biographies of celebrities, actors, pop musicians, and sports figures
- game system guides for video and computer games
- books and magazines about cars, sports, teen advice, and other current topics

Reading interest research studies report what groups of students like, but individual student interests can differ from these descriptions. The topics and traits of literature in the preceding lists are helpful to a teacher only as a starting point in collecting and presenting books to groups of students. By themselves they are insufficient to guide a teacher to books for individual students.

DISCOVERING READING INTERESTS OF INDIVIDUAL STUDENTS

Individual students are the experts on what they enjoy reading. A consistent and important research finding is that being able to choose their own independent reading material is vital to adolescents (Beers, 1996a,b; Carlsen & Sherrill, 1988; Ivey, 1999; Wilder & Teasley, 1999; Worthy et al., 1999, 2002; Smith & Wilhelm, 2002). We cannot be assured that because we like a book our students will like it. Many probably will not. Teachers need to look at books that they would not typically select for their personal reading in order to tell students about these books, too.

Resistant readers want to choose their own books for independent reading, but they sometimes have difficulty selecting a book from an entire library, preferring instead to choose from a smaller collection of books. Beers (1996b) reported success with placing "30 drop-dead-great books" into a box labeled GOOD BOOKS. In visits to the school library, students began to select the books from the box and eventually, due to its success, a second box labeled MORE GOOD BOOKS was set up (p. 113). This procedure narrowed the choice but still allowed students to feel independent in their selections.

General interest surveys have not proved to be as helpful to us in a classroom situation as more book-specific ways of gathering information about individual students' interests. For example, a student may indicate on a survey an interest in reading mysteries but may only like mysteries that are realistic without supernatural elements; the answer "mystery" is not clear or sufficiently helpful in this case. Format and presentation are also important to many students, especially resistant readers, so students who indicate an interest in a topic or genre may only be interested if the book is short or illustrated. So we suggest that the teacher begin the year by presenting *actual books* selected on a variety of topics and formats for free-choice reading and then observe students' responses to the books presented. This purpose can be achieved quite easily in various ways, as described in the following paragraphs:

1. Early in the school year, spend a class period in the library media center. Give the students the task of finding a book on their own for free-choice reading. After twenty to thirty minutes you may observe some students who could be called "walkers," those who walk around the library looking for a book and never finding one, because they dislike reading or do not know how to find books. You need to pay particular attention to these students and give them individual help. Note what they tell you when interviewed or when asked to peruse books. Talk to them individually and show that you understand that it is sometimes difficult to find a book to read. Ask them for a book title or type of book they can recall liking in the past, and ask if they would like to read a similar book. You may need to go beyond the school and classroom collections to find satisfactory materials for these students. If you are to break through their resistance to reading, you must persist in your efforts to find the right materials (Worthy et al., 2002). Resistant readers need to understand that you are determined to help them find materials to read and will keep trying until they find something they want to read.

2. Present thirty or forty books in class by showing each book, telling the title and author, and describing in one or two sentences what the book is about. Showing the books is essential, especially for boys and some resistant readers who care greatly about the visual elements of the book, its cover, and its length. As you introduce each book, open it and show some of the inside pages. Then ask students to note on individual ballots whether they think they would or would not like to read the book by circling yes or no next to the book number. They must be assured that they will not be required to read the books they say they would like to read. These books are made available for checkout, for those who wish to read one.

3. During class ask students to tell you what they like to read. As they respond, write the topics, titles, and such on chart paper. Through this process you will gain a better sense of the class as a whole and some topics to begin including in your weekly booktalks for them to consider for free-choice books. Note those who do not contribute, and ask these students later to talk with you about what they like to read or might like to read. An individual or small-group conference will permit you to become better acquainted with students who do not respond in whole-class settings and have difficulty in finding books to read. The individual attention will make them realize that you want to help them.

4. Bring two or three books at a time into class for booktalking a few times a week, choosing a variety of topics, levels of difficulty, formats, and so on. Expect that students may dislike some of your choices. Accept their right to like or dislike your choices. Respect their preferences and insist that they respect each other's preferences. Ask them to guide you in finding books that they will like. The school librarian can be very helpful in pulling books for these purposes and will probably know what is currently popular with students in that grade. Booktalking throughout the school year is important in order to introduce students to new books they might not discover on their own. See Chapter 9 for ideas on how to do booktalks.

5. Display books in the classroom on a bookshelf, standing up with covers forward, and encourage students to take a few minutes of free time to look through them. Students often pick books by the cover, so displaying the books in this way will help some students find books. Change these books each week and place the books you have booktalked on that shelf. Note which books are selected by students and begin to build a collection of your "Good Books." Students may wish to suggest books for this collection.

6. Display forty books on large tables in the classroom or in the school media center. Include a good balance of types, topics, levels, and formats. Number the books 1 through 40 with self-stick notes. Make a list of the books and their numbers for your later use. Design a simple response ballot for students in which the numbers are listed with a simple YES–NO beside each number. Ask students to peruse the books from 1 to 40 and complete their forms as follows: "Next to the appropriate number on the ballot circle YES if you would like to read the book; circle NO if you would not like to read the book." Assure students before they begin that circling YES does not mean that they will be required to read the book. It is important that you let students know that you want to get to know them and their reading interests better and want their help in gaining this information. Each ballot is turned in with the student's name on it. The teacher can then analyze favored books for individual students, the students who enjoy reading many books, and those who enjoy almost none of the books.

This procedure has a dual purpose: It helps the teacher get a quick look at students' potential interests in reading, and it often results in students wanting to check some of the books out to read. Students enjoy doing the activity because they can get up, move around, and look at books they may want to read. Adolescents' interests change over the course of a year, so it is important to keep current on your students' reading interests. Repeating this procedure every few weeks results in students looking at new and different books in a collection that does not overwhelm them and allows you to keep abreast of their current reading interests.

JUDGING THE DIFFICULTY OF READING MATERIALS

Students' reading levels vary greatly in most classrooms by middle school and high school years, making it important to provide materials of varying difficulty. Being able to assess the difficulty of reading materials can be helpful to teachers and librarians.

The longstanding system that has been used in education to assign reading levels to books has been readability formulas such as the Fry Readability Graph (http://school.discovery.com/schrockguide/fry/fry.html) and the Lexile Framework (www.lexile.com; Schnick, 2000). *Readability* is defined as "the ease of comprehension because of style of writing" (Harris & Hodges, 1995, p. 203). Syntactic length and vocabulary difficulty are usually measured by a variety of means that vary by readability formula. Generally texts with shorter, less complex sentences and a predominance of common high-frequency words, such as *because, little,* and *everyone,* are rated as easier to comprehend.

Readability is expressed as a grade level (6.4 = sixth grade fourth month) or as an age level (11.5 = eleven years and five months) and refers to the approximate grade or age at which an average individual will be able to read the text with comprehension. Publishers often place this information on book covers, some databases include reading levels, and various school reading management programs, such as Accelerated Reader, grade the books for student reading by such formulas.

A teacher who looks carefully at a book can assess difficulty without using a formula, and most teachers do so with practice. Select a page of uninterrupted text, read the first sentence, count the words in the sentence, then look to see if this length appears to be typical on the rest of the page. Are the sentences generally short or long? Then read the page for word difficulty, noting words your students will likely not know. Are there many or few such words? We know that readers can figure out unknown words through context if they are infrequent. You can estimate a book's difficulty in this way.

Readability formulas may be helpful to teachers, librarians, and parents in selecting books, but they are not without their drawbacks and shortcomings. Different readability formulas give different estimates for the same text, so at best they give only a broad estimate of difficulty. Although the two factors of syntactic complexity and word choices are important, other factors make an important difference. A student's background knowledge on a particular topic cannot be factored into any formula, nor can a student's interest in a topic be measured by formula. Yet we know that students' interest and background knowledge are central to their willingness and ability to comprehend a text.

Conceptual difficulty is another factor not included in a readability formula. Conceptual difficulty pertains to the complexity of the ideas treated in the work and to how these ideas are presented. Symbolism, abstraction, and figurative language contribute to the complexity of ideas, just as the use of nonlinear plots or shifting points of view contributes to the complexity of plot presentation. Consider the work of magical realism *Skellig* (Almond, 1999), in which two young persons become involved with an otherworldly being who has hidden in a garage. The text, having easy vocabulary and short sentences, has a readability of about grade 3.5. Yet the concepts of spirituality, faith, and prejudice cast the conceptual level of this novel at a much higher level, probably appropriate for students ages 11 to 15. Readability is an issue only when the text is at such a high level that the reader cannot comprehend it.

The challenge is to find engaging materials for those students whose reading levels are lower. Some materials and lists of materials are labeled as *high interest–low reading* level and are believed to appeal to readers who are struggling readers and cannot easily read the same texts as their peers. Generally the materials are shorter texts but on age-appropriate topics. However, struggling readers just as any other readers have unique individual interests that must be considered.

So once more we return to the experts, individual students, in determining what they can read. The teacher can help students decide whether books are too difficult for them by encouraging them to open a book they are considering reading to a middle page and reading through it while counting the number of words they do not understand or cannot read. If they count more than five or six words they cannot read or do not know out of every 100 words, they may want to choose a different book.

REACHING RESISTANT READERS

Resistant readers have the same instructional needs as all readers except they need more persistent, adaptable teachers who can implement instructional practices flexibly and creatively and find new ways to meet their students' particular needs. Teachers and librarians who want to reach resistant readers must be willing to question established practices, to be objective, and to make changes in their practices when needed. Often, as teachers, we recall activities that worked with us and assume that they will work with our students, including resistant readers. These practices may be successful in some circumstances, but resistant readers often need something different.

School administrators also must reexamine their customary practices if they are to foster the development of lifelong reading habits in all students. They need to reconsider the traditions, rules, and policies that may be discouraging students from reading regularly and interfering with the efforts of teachers and librarians to promote reading.

Create a Classroom Environment Conducive to Reading

The teacher is the key element of the classroom environment and has the potential to exert a powerful positive influence on students and their reading. Following are some of the most important ways teachers can create a positive classroom atmosphere conducive to reading for all students and particularly for resistant readers.

BE A SUPPORTIVE TEACHER   A supportive teacher creates an atmosphere in which a student feels "comfortable, safe, and able to share his or her reading interests, reactions, and insights with the teacher and other students" (Barmore & Morse, 1977, p. 57). A good teacher of resistant readers is intelligent, caring, and accepting, encouraging students to read, and is a reader who shares his or her own reading with the students. A caring teacher knows that students want to succeed and be good readers and therefore sets high expectations for all students and builds their trust so they can meet those expectations (Landsman, 2006). Persistence is needed to reach some students.

A good teacher needs to be sensitive to the "turnoff" to reading that many students have developed as a result of assessment overkill. The various state tests cannot be avoided but the teacher can be careful not to contribute to the negative attitudes that tests engender in some students. The teacher can make an effort to steer clear of excessive testing in class and of placing undue pressure on students about tests.

Good teachers of resistant readers establish a respectful classroom environment. Moore, Bean, Birdyshaw, and Rycik (1999) describe such a classroom as one that "encourages the exchange of ideas among students. Respectful classrooms are safe enough for students to take risks when expressing themselves publicly. No rudeness, no put-downs or ugly remarks are allowed. Learners address others courteously and expect courteous treatment in turn. They disagree without being disagreeable, contesting others' ideas without personal insults" (p. 8). In respectful classrooms teachers accept the students' free reading choices, showing acceptance both verbally and nonverbally, and do not force students to defend their tastes in free-choice material. They accept different reading habits, such as picking a book to read and then deciding not to finish it or skipping some pages (Crowe, 1999). Good teachers encourage independent reading by showing an interest in what students choose to read, reading some of what their students are reading, even works that they typically would not select to read, and finding something to like in them. Good teachers accept that some students read more slowly and read much less than others, but they are pleased to see all students reading. Effective teachers guide students to good young adult literature but do not force it on them.

Effective teachers of resistant readers appreciate the social nature of adolescents and understand that for adolescents "working with others provides intrinsic motivation" (Smith & Wilhelm, 2002, p. 199). Effective teachers accommodate the social nature of teenagers by using strategies such as literature circles, drama activities, book clubs, and reading buddies (Smith & Wilhelm, 2002). Caring teachers of resistant readers are willing to change their choices of material and teaching strategies to meet the needs of their students. They accept the challenge of encouraging the lifetime reading habit (Barmore & Morse, 1977).

PROVIDE APPROPRIATE READING MATERIALS   Good teachers provide a classroom reading collection of materials that students can borrow. A wide variety of reading materials included in this collection, as delineated in the preceding sections on interests and difficulty, will offer students the opportunity to select their own material and begin to develop the habit of reading for pleasure. In the Carnegie Report, *Reading Next: A Vision for Action and Research in Middle and High School Literacy* (Biancarosa & Snow, 2004), the authors recommend that one of the elements needed to improve middle and high school literacy achievement is the use of diverse texts at a variety of difficulty levels and on a variety of topics. In *Voices of Readers: How We Come to Love Books* (1988), Carlsen and Sherrill report that rarely was a book's appeal associated with its degree of literary merit. They found that people usually remembered "the emotional impact of the book, the insights it provided whether for self or others, and the growth that it stimulated in the reader" (p. 86). These findings emphasize the importance of respecting students' choices in order to foster their desire to read.

Most students like to read about people like themselves, so good teachers provide books with characters that their students can identify with on some basis, be it gender, ethnicity, lifestyle, or circumstance. It is also appropriate for teachers to provide books about people who are different from their students, since some may enjoy learning about people of other cultures.

Our recommendation for building a classroom collection of trade books in which there are typically twenty-five students in each class is to first analyze the books on hand. First the teacher sorts the books by fiction or nonfiction, then by male or female protagonists and minority protagonists, then by approximate reading difficulty, topics of nonfiction, and so on. This analysis and sorting indicate what is needed to round the collection out. We recommend a collection of at least 200 books.

Of the 200 books, we recommend that about 55 percent be fiction and 45 percent be nonfiction. About 45 percent of the fiction books should have male protagonists, and 55 percent should have female protagonists. Nonfiction books should include biographies of male and female figures and informational books on topics that appeal to both females and males.

Subsequent expansion of the classroom collection should include materials acceptable to students as part of their independent reading. In addition to novels, consider magazines, driver's education manuals, cookbooks, trivia books, graphic novels, picture books for older readers, poetry collections, plays, and short story collections, and insure that lower, average, and challenging level books are included. An excellent source of books for resistant readers is available through the Young Adult Library Services

Association (YALSA), a division of the American Library Association (www.ala.org). It provides a list of Quick Picks for Reluctant Young Adult Readers that teens, ages 12 to 18, will pick up on their own and read for pleasure; it is geared to the teenager who, for whatever reason, does not like to read. This list is selected and published annually with approximately 100 briefly annotated titles divided between fiction and nonfiction. In addition, a top ten list of Quick Picks is selected each year.

Publisher-owned book clubs give teachers access to affordable trade books for their classroom reading collections. These clubs send monthly catalogs to teachers who then distribute them to students, collect and process student book orders, and receive bonus points for each item ordered. Paperback books representing a full range of quality and type of trade books are offered at prices far below bookstore cost. Book ownership has been shown to promote reading (Carlsen & Sherrill, 1988), and this is one of the main benefits of publisher book clubs. Teachers who participate in these clubs can use the bonus points to build their classroom book collections.

Many good works of young adult literature are available as *audiobooks.* In the best versions, professional readers enhance the literary experience with their use of dramatic devices, authentic dialects, and multiple voices. Sound effects and music make the stories more dramatic and moving. An important selection criterion for audiobooks is whether they are abridged or unabridged. We believe that unabridged versions are better. A source for good recommendations of audiobooks is the Young Adult Library Services Association (YALSA) Selected Audiobooks for Young Adults Web site at www.ala.org under Awards and Scholarships, Book/Media Awards.

Keeping one's classroom collection of reading materials current, strong, and inviting is an ongoing effort. As teachers learn about their students' interests, they add materials on these topics to their collections, and as books become dated and worn, teachers weed them out of the collection. They encourage their students to bring their own books to school for reading and, when particularly interesting or enjoyable, for recommending to other students. The sixth-grade students in Ivey and Broaddus's study (2001) reported that their classrooms were not sources of good reading material. This should not be the case, given the proven long-term benefits to students of having good reading materials close at hand.

READ ALOUD TO STUDENTS REGULARLY   Good teachers read aloud to their students at least twenty-five minutes a week by reading daily for five or more minutes or by reading aloud for longer periods a few times a week for a specific purpose. Generally, struggling readers have higher listening comprehension than reading comprehension abilities. Reading aloud is an opportunity to scaffold students into higher-level reading materials through the read-aloud program. Some teachers include audiobooks in place of normal daily read-aloud time on occasion to encourage the use of audiobooks and to justify their use as a valid learning activity. Ivey (2003) states, "The bottom line is that when teachers read to students they enhance students' understandings and their inclination to read independently" (p. 812). Furthermore, Ivey suggests that reading aloud is a means of exposing students to a variety of genres, formats, and topics, giving students access to texts they cannot yet make sense of on their own, and showing students thinking processes to use to make sense of text during reading. Wilder and Teasley (1998), in discussing the values of reading aloud to high school students, point out that students are more sophisticated listeners than expected and that they, as teachers, made adjustments in books selected for reading aloud accordingly.

Fisher, Frey, and Williams (2002) instituted a new literacy program in a low-scoring high school with predominantly minority students on free or reduced lunch and with 46 percent English language learners. This schoolwide effort set forth seven instructional strategies to permeate the school at every level. Reading aloud by teachers every day in all subjects for at least five minutes was one of these strategies. Usually the selections read aloud were not from textbooks but from materials to build students' background knowledge and for other purposes. This program has met with positive outcomes including improved student achievement. Reading aloud is one of the most effective ways for young adults to hear fluent reading.

PROVIDE STUDENTS TIME TO READ INDEPENDENTLY   Providing students time in class to read from free-choice materials every week informs them that independent reading is a worthwhile activity. Ivey and Broaddus (2001) found that, when 1,700 sixth-graders were asked which activities they most preferred in their reading and language arts classes, 63 percent selected independent reading, more than any other classroom practice. Students explained that uninterrupted reading allowed them to get into the content of the book and better comprehend what they had read.

Resistant readers will probably fare better during independent reading periods with shorter works that will not discourage them. Magazines, graphic novels, picture books for older readers, poetry, and short story collections are good for this purpose. As these students gain confidence and skill, the teacher can introduce them to short novels through booktalks as a way to expand their reading preferences.

Motivation is especially important for resistant readers, and there are no more powerful reading motivators than interest in and self-selection of reading materials. Hidi (1990) found that students' learning and motivation improve when instruction and materials are interesting to them. Ivey (1999) asserts, "The strong influence of self-selection on motivation to read makes a good case for free-choice reading, especially for struggling middle school readers" (p. 378).

Sustained silent reading (SSR) is a longstanding school practice that has been very successful in some schools. Clarke (2006), in considering the resistance that SSR programs face, states that "the teachers who motivate students to read independently are those who read themselves and who proactively talk with students about the need to read. If a teacher who has a solid relationship with a student models a love of reading, then the student is likely to read" (p. 67). Sustained silent reading programs have sometimes been unsuccessful because the reading materials available were uninteresting to students and the importance placed on the program was lacking. Bean (2002) states that "sustained silent reading is widely recommended but depends on books that capture students' interests" (p. 35). Students must be convinced that teachers believe that independent reading is time well spent. Teachers accomplish this purpose by reading themselves during SSR time, by introducing new material to students by booktalks and displays, by establishing and sticking with a regular time for independent reading, and by assuring that students are reading during this time and not doing other work.

PROVIDE MEANS FOR STUDENT RESPONSE TO LITERATURE   Resistant readers are often uncomfortable with verbal and written book reports, preferring instead graphic and artistic book response projects. To gain the cooperation of all students, teachers can provide alternatives to book reports as described in Chapter 9. To encourage varied ways of reporting on independent reading, teachers can select three or four response ideas to demonstrate each four to six weeks. This approach requires that the teacher make models of the art or graphic design projects for students to examine, such as those listed in the Graphic and Artistic Book Response Projects box. In this way students will gradually accumulate a variety of response methods to model on or innovate from. These book response projects are enjoyable and are only as difficult as a student chooses to make them. The artistic and graphic projects can be based on plots, scenes, characters, settings, or themes found in the books read (Hughes & Lynch-Brown, 2001). For example, a comic strip based on a work of fiction could depict the pivot points of the plot.

On some occasions it may be sufficient to have each student list on notebook paper the book, author, title, and what they liked best or least about the book, for sharing with a small group of class-mates. Providing opportunities for social interactions related to their reading is a good means for helping students find other books they may want to read.

ASSIGN READING FOR HOMEWORK   Independent reading should be part of homework requirements. Reading at home for a prescribed number of minutes from free-choice materials can be handled in various ways. We recommend assigning at least eighty minutes a week of independent reading time to be done at home. Students may read for twenty minutes each school evening or may read more on the weekend or on nights when other homework demands are less. Rewards or extra credit can be given for reading more minutes than requested. Continual encouragement may be needed for students who do not fulfill the reading assignment. It may help to ask students why they did not complete the reading and what you might be able to do to help. Do they need materials? Would it be helpful to come in before or after school to read? Can they offer you ideas for a solution? (Darling-Hammond & Ifill-Lynch, 2006)

Some teachers accept listening to audiobooks in place of reading for independent reading assignments at home. Listening to an audiobook does not help students' reading skills as much as independent reading does, but audiobooks may motivate students to reread the story or other stories by the same author. Students can gain vocabulary knowledge, conceptual understandings, and general information by listening as well as by reading. Stallworth (1998) suggests that audiobooks are wonderful options for experiencing books in a way that fits hectic schedules.

Content-area teachers can support independent reading by assigning some homework time as reading time. Lists of books that relate to the current focus of study in class can be made available to students to select from, or the books can be made available to check out and read as background

Graphic and Artistic Book Response Projects

Collage	Family tree	Project cube
Comic strip	Graph	Puppet
Computer graphic	Hidden picture	Sculpture
Costume	Map with legend	TV ad
Diorama	Mobile	Time line
Display	Painting	Travel brochure
Etching/crayon resist	Pop-up book	

knowledge and for other viewpoints on a topic. The students report on the book read near the end of the term.

Middle and high school teachers usually assign written homework because written products serve as evidence for teachers that assignments were completed. For the same reason, written products serve as motivators for students to do the work. Independent reading at home produces no physical evidence, and so it is rarely assigned as homework. If it is, students, and especially resistant readers, find it easy to ignore because there is nothing to hand in to their teachers. Parents who ask their children if they have any homework may very likely be told they do not, unless the assignment has an accountability component.

Darling-Hammond and Ifill-Lynch (2006) state that struggling students in particular must see their homework as worthy of their effort before they will do it. This finding suggests that teachers would receive more cooperation from their students if they explained why it is important for them to read independently at home—to become better readers, to learn more about the world, to gain a lifetime of enjoyment. But many students will require some form of accountability, such as a parent's signature, before they will comply with an independent reading homework assignment.

Judy Hughes, a middle school teacher in Panama City, Florida, has successfully used the program she describes in the Reading at Home box to encourage at-home reading by her students.

Provide a Library Media Center Environment Conducive to Reading

For all students the library media center should offer excellent resources for content-area studies and free voluntary reading. For some, the school library media center can also be a haven where reading and homework can be done in comfortable, quiet surroundings that they can find nowhere else.

Making teens feel welcome in the library media center is an important first step for the school librarian who wants to create an environment conducive to reading. Greeting students with a smile and calling them by name as they enter the library are natural ways to establish a welcoming atmosphere (Stevenson, 2005). The physical setup of the library media center plays a role in promoting reading as well. The latest popular titles should be prominently displayed cover side out where students will be most likely to see them, browse through them, and check them out. Comfortable armchairs, couches, and beanbag chairs placed in well-lit areas will invite students to sit and read.

Offering greater access to the library media center is another way to make it more conducive to reading. Flexible library media center hours that include before-school and after-school hours and access during all school hours correlate with successful schools (Lance, 2001; Baumbach, 2003). If extending library hours every day of the week is impossible, extending access at least some days of the week may still be greatly appreciated by students and their parents.

Promoting special reading programs enlivens a library's atmosphere and gives students the impression that the library is a place where interesting things happen. Book clubs focusing on popular special interests such as mystery, horror, fantasy, science fiction, graphic novels, or picture books for older readers attract young adults. These clubs are usually hosted by the school librarian or a teacher, but they could well be hosted by the school principal, a parent, or a qualified community volunteer. Parent–student book discussion clubs established for comparing reactions to books could generate much interest. A roster of these and other library programs prominently displayed in the hall outside the library promotes interest and advertises the programs.

Would love to try this!

The reading program RAH! (Reading at Home) is based on the theory that students need daily reading to improve their fluency, comprehension, and vocabulary as well as to practice reading strategies that they are learning in the classroom. The weekly requirement is 100 minutes (reading 20 minutes each night for 5 nights), but the students are allowed to meet the required number of minutes in any way that works for them to accommodate their after-school activities and family plans. They can read nightly as suggested or, for example, read all 100 minutes during the weekend. The selections are always personal choice and can include some—but not only—reading of magazines, Internet information, hobby instructions, and parent read-alouds. It is really important that RAH! not be used for unfinished class assignments unless approved ahead of time.

Each student has a RAH! folder in which to record at-home reading information for the week: book title, number of minutes read, number of pages, and parent or caregiver signature. I send a letter home at the beginning of the school year to all parents and to the parents of new student arrivals that explains the program and the importance of recording the student's reading information and turning in the signed report once a week. I have found that parents sometimes are unable to sign the folder, so I accept it without the signature if necessary.

The project that goes with the assignment is just as important as the reading. A one-page handout, sent home at the beginning of the year and posted in the classroom, lists project choices for RAH! presentations. Each student does two RAH! projects each nine-week grading period. RAH! projects not only cause students to reflect on the book, but they also add continuous book conversation to the classroom. The projects are homework assignments, but students are allowed to work on them in class when they have completed all their other work. The projects are presented as they are completed, not on a specific date. Although these presentations take only a few minutes throughout the week, their cumulative effect is fantastic. So often students just don't know what to read, and their peers' presentations give them book ideas on a regular basis. Books, and better yet, what books to read regularly, become the topics of conversation in the classroom.

A letter to the parents accompanies the report card each grading period and shows the RAH! reading results. Each grading period letter includes a comparison to the previously reported class totals of minutes read. The percentage of students reading above, on, and under the required minutes for the grading period is listed. Each student's individual minutes read are noted at the bottom of that student's letter so that this information is private. I include the names of the students with the top number of minutes read for the grading period to recognize incredible reading records. Parents often ask me how their son or daughter is doing, and what they often want to know is how their son or daughter is doing in comparison to the other students. This letter allows me to convey that information in an effective way that does not offend anyone.

I have watched students who entered my classroom saying that they hated reading grow to love reading. I have observed students helping other students find books they just know are wonderful—or find short books because they are behind on RAH! and need a quick read. I have recorded ever-increasing totals of minutes read each week as students become more proficient and more enthusiastic readers. Most recently, I have added to the program an end-of-year recommendation from each student of the one book that was his or her favorite for the year. Using this list, I add new books to the classroom library with a sticker giving the name of the student who recommended the book. This has turned out to be another layer of book selection available to my students and one they often use. Some books have many stickers, and that is good, too!

Students are often frustrated by having to return books to the library before they finish them or forgetting to return books and being fined. The traditional book loan period of two to three weeks is simply not enough time for many students, with their coursework and out-of-school activities, to finish a book, and fines may result in parents' disallowing their children to check books out, even though these students' need for reading materials is critical. Many librarians, in response, are extending their loan periods from the traditional two or three weeks to three or four weeks and are seeking ways to avoid fines or to adopt no-fine policies.

As noted in the first section of this chapter, some students resist reading in school because they find the reading materials sanctioned by schools and assigned by teachers irrelevant or boring and reject them (Baines, 1994; Worthy, 1996; Worthy, Turner, & Moorman, 1998). To make school media centers more conducive to reading, librarians must build up their collection of reading materials that are currently popular with young people. In 2001 these included popular magazines (see Appendix B), scary series stories, adventure stories, and nonfiction (Ivey & Broaddus, 2001).

Establish a School Environment Conducive to Reading

Although it is true that the teacher is the key element in creating a successful classroom literature program, it is also true that teachers' tasks are made easier, their teaching effectiveness is strengthened, and their pool of resources is richer when they have the support and collaboration of their administrators, school librarians, and fellow teachers.

COLLABORATE WITH SCHOOL ADMINISTRATORS   Principals who believe in the power of literature to help students become better readers and better students are godsends to teachers. Working with school librarians, they can allocate resources to purchase the reading materials requested by teachers. They can make schedule changes to accommodate before-school, during-school, or after-school reading clubs; and they can create policies that allow struggling students to take additional time to complete their assignments. Examples of teacher–administrator collaboration range from sharing with one another research findings about what works with resistant readers to setting up a place and time for students to come to do their homework and to receive help with it, if necessary, as described by Darling-Hammond and Ifill-Lynch (2006).

COLLABORATE WITH FELLOW TEACHERS   There is strength in teamwork. The following ideas for achieving a schoolwide emphasis on literature require a team effort, and the team will variously include teachers, the school librarian, and the school principal.

Summer Reading Programs   For decades middle and high school English teachers have developed lists of book titles for students to select from for summer reading. We believe that it is important to allow students the option of suggesting alternate titles, subject to their teacher's approval, for their summer reading so as to take advantage of their interests in particular topics or authors. The main purpose of these programs is to keep students reading during the months away from school to prevent loss of reading skills or regular reading habits. Another good reason to require summer reading is to create a shared experience among students, giving them something other than television shows, movies, or video games to discuss. We recommend that the book lists include twenty to thirty titles selected to cover a range of interests and levels of difficulty. To increase the likelihood that students will actually read some of the books listed, teachers could include with each title a brief booktalk with a hook to pique potential readers' interest. Coordinating selections within and across grade levels helps avoid duplication and makes the job of generating good lists easier, particularly if the school librarian is involved. Depending on students' reading abilities, summer reading requirements vary widely. Our advice is to require less reading, one or two full-length novels or their equivalent, for example, in order to achieve greater compliance on the students' part, and to avoid ponderous, gloomy, or problem-heavy selections.

Book Fairs   A book fair is a book sale that is organized by a book vendor, such as a local bookstore owner, large publisher, or book fair company. The latter two can be accessed by searching for "school book fairs" on a computer search engine. A book fair is usually held in the school building for a week. The purpose of a book fair is to promote reading, not to generate the greatest possible profit. Books are displayed so that students can browse and select items for purchase. Book fairs, like publisher-owned book clubs, promote book ownership and should be considered a reading motivator.

Book fairs send strong messages to young people about a school's stance on reading and about what sorts of reading materials teachers and librarians in the school endorse. Book fairs in which stickers, posters, and book spin-offs such as key chains, pins, and toys are prominent send the wrong message to students about reading. Book fairs in which a wide variety of good literature is prominent send an entirely different (and more defensible) message about reading. Excellent book fairs are the result of careful planning and active involvement in selection of books by teachers and school librarians. Book selection should be a collaborative effort between the independent, local book vendor and teachers. As for book fairs provided by large publishers, teachers have every right to set aside what they consider to be inappropriate materials.

Author Visits   Professional authors often visit schools to speak to young people about their careers and their books. Teachers and school librarians are usually instrumental in organizing these visits. A search for "school author visits" on the Internet produces a wealth of information on this subject, including step-by-step planning advice and contact information for many authors. Authors may be chosen on the basis of availability, but more often they are chosen because of the students' interest in their books or the relevance of their work to a topic that students are studying. Author visits are powerful reading motivators.

The standard procedure for an author visit is to contact the marketing director of the author's publishing house to determine availability and terms. Since most established authors of young adult literature charge an honorarium and travel expenses, schools within a system often share the author and the costs. Many state reading associations have developed lists of young adult authors who live in the same state. These lists can usually be found in public libraries.

COLLABORATE WITH STUDENTS' FAMILIES   Parents, grandparents, and other members of a young person's extended family can be helpful in supporting teen readers and encouraging them to read. Teachers can communicate with students' families and establish positive relations by maintaining contact in the following ways:

- Send home lists of books that will be read in class and encourage adult family members to read and discuss the books with their child.
- Explain reading-related class projects in letters to adult family members and suggest ways they can provide help and guidance.
- E-mail, call, or conference with family caregivers to ask about their students' reading interests and preferred materials. Family members often know what their teenager enjoys reading.
- Inform families about their public library, its location, and how they and their student can obtain library cards.
- Tell adult family members about the availability at the public or school library of audiobooks that would be appropriate for and appealing to resistant readers.
- Apprise families of special programs for teenagers available at the local library that would encourage the development of good reading habits, such as family literacy programs, upcoming author visits of interest to teens, volunteer opportunities, and employment available to teenagers.

MAKE GOOD USE OF THE LOCAL PUBLIC LIBRARY   The community has no more valuable resource than its public library. Each time students and teachers seek the educational resources they need in their public libraries, the natural link between schools and public libraries is reaffirmed. Public libraries provide many services in addition to loaning books, as indicated by the following examples:

- Provide a local public librarian to visit middle and high schools near the end of the school year to booktalk some of the library's best new young adult books and present their summer reading program.
- Support summer reading programs of nearby schools by purchasing multiple copies of books on the lists.
- Hold special programs such as teen poetry slams in which students read their own original poems and are judged on content and performance.
- Hold after-school programs in which booktalks and book discussion by students are combined with opportunities for social interaction.
- Sponsor author visits by young adult authors.
- Provide audiobook, DVD, and videotape versions of many young adult novels.
- Provide computers to use for Internet access to such sites as the international E-readers On-Line Book Discussion Club (www.e-readers.org).
- Provide the interlibrary loan system, which gives patrons access to library holdings throughout the state, region, or nation.

The ideas suggested in this chapter for reaching resistant readers apply to all readers and, in our opinion, are no more than all young people deserve. We trust that you, as teachers and librarians, will discover many additional ways to effectively motivate your students to read. We encourage you to take advantage of the national network of teachers and librarians created through professional journals and organizations and the Internet to find what works with others and to share what works with you.

REFERENCES

Almond, D. (1999). *Skellig.* New York: Delacorte.

Anderson, M. A., Tollefson, N. A., & Gilbert, E. C. (1985). Giftedness and reading: A cross-sectional view of differences in reading attitudes and behaviors. *Gifted Child Quarterly, 29*(4), 186–189.

Anderson, R., Wilson, P., & Fielding, L. (1988). Growth in reading and how children spend their time outside of school. *Reading Research Quarterly, 23*(3), 285–303.

Baines, L. (1994). Cool books for tough guys: 50 books out of the mainstream of adolescent literature that will appeal to males who do not enjoy reading. *ALAN Review, 22,* 43–46.

Barmore, J. M., & Morse, P. S. (1977). Developing lifelong readers in the middle schools: Teaching ideas. *English Journal, 66*(4), 57–61.

Baumbach, D. (2003). *Making the grade.* Retrieved from www.sunlink.ucf.edu/makingthegrade.

Bean, T. W. (2002). Making reading relevant for adolescents. *Educational Leadership, 60*(3), 34–37.

Beers, G. K. (1996a). No time, no interest, no way! The three voices of aliteracy, Part I. *School Library Journal, 42*(2), 30–33.

———. (1996b). No time, no interest, no way! The three voices of aliteracy, Part II. *School Library Journal, 42*(3), 110–113.

———. (2003). *When kids can't read: What teachers can do.* Portsmouth, NH: Heinemann.

Biancarosa, G., & Snow, C. E. (2004). *Reading next: A vision for action and research in middle and high school literacy, a report to Carnegie Corporation of New York.* Washington, DC: Alliance for Excellent Education.

Bradshaw, T., & Nichols, B. (2004). *Reading at risk: A survey of literary reading in America.* Research Division Report 46. Washington, DC: National Endowment for the Arts.

Brozo, W. G. (2005). Gender and reading literacy. *Reading Today, 22*(4), 18.

Carlsen, G. R., & Sherrill, A. (1988). *Voices of readers: How we come to love books.* Urbana, IL: National Council of Teachers of English.

Carter, B., & Harris, K. (1982). What junior high students like in books. *Journal of Reading, 26*(1), 42–46.

Chance, R. (1999). A portrait of popularity: An analysis of characteristics of novels from Young Adults' Choices for 1997. *ALAN Review, 27*(1), 65–68.

Clarke, B. (2006). Breaking through to reluctant readers. *Educational Leadership, 63*(5), 66–69.

Cline, R. K. L., & Kretke, G. L. (1980). An evaluation of long-term SSR in the junior high school. *Journal of Reading, 23*(6), 502–506.

Crowe, C. (1999). Dear teachers: Please help my kids become readers. *English Journal, 89*(1), 130–142.

Darling-Hammond, L., & Ifill-Lynch, O. (2006). If only they'd do their work! *Educational Leadership, 63*(5), 8–13.

Fielding, L. G., Wilson, P. T., & Anderson, R. C. (1986). A new focus on free reading: The role of trade books in reading instruction. In T. Raphael (Ed.), *The contexts of school-based literacy* (pp. 149–160). New York: Random House.

Fisher, D., Frey, N., & Williams, D. (2002). Seven literacy strategies that work. *Educational Leadership, 60*(3), 70–73.

Gilbert, R., & Gilbert, P. (1998). *Masculinity goes to school.* New York: Routledge.

Hale, L. A., & Crowe, C. (2001). "I hate reading if I don't have to": Results from a longitudinal study of high school students' reading interests. *ALAN Review, 28*(3), 49–57.

Harris, T. L., & Hodges, R. E. (1995). *The literacy dictionary: The vocabulary of reading and writing.* Newark, DE: International Reading Association.

Hidi, S. (1990). Interest and its contribution as a mental resource for learning. *Review of Educational Research, 60*(4), 549–571.

Hughes, J. E., & Lynch-Brown, C. (2001, July). *Motivating intermediate grade students to read.* Paper presented at the meeting of the European Conference on Reading, Dublin, Ireland.

Ivey, G. (1999). Reflections on teaching struggling middle school readers. *Journal of Adolescent and Adult Literacy, 42*(5), 372–381.

———. (2003). "The teacher makes it more explainable" and other reasons to read aloud in the intermediate grades. *The Reading Teacher, 56*(8), 812–814.

Ivey, G., & Broaddus, K. (2001). "Just plain reading": A survey of what makes students want to read in middle school classrooms. *Reading Research Quarterly, 36*(4), 350–377.

Jones, P. (1994). Thin books, big problems: Realism and the reluctant teen reader. *ALAN Review, 21*(2), 18–28.

Krashen, S. (1988). Do we learn to read by reading? The relationship between free reading and reading ability. In D. Tannen (Ed.), *Linguistics in context: Connecting observation and understanding* (pp. 269–298). Norwood, NJ: Ablex.

Lance, K. C. (2001). Proof of the power: Quality library media programs affect academic achievement. *Multimedia Schools, 8*(4), 14–16, 18, 20.

Landsman, J. (2006). Bearers of hope. *Educational Leadership, 63*(5), 26–32.

Langerman, D. (1990). Books and boys: Gender preferences and book selection. *School Library Journal, 36*(3), 132–136.

Maynard, T. (2002). *Boys and literacy: Exploring the issues.* New York: Routledge.

McBroom, G. (1981). Research: Our defense begins here. *English Journal, 70*(6), 75–78.

McKenna, M., Ellsworth, R., & Kear, D. (1995). Children's attitudes toward reading: A national survey. *Reading Research Quarterly, 30*(4), 934–957.

Moore, D. W., Bean, T. W., Birdyshaw, D., & Rycik, J. A. (1999). *Adolescent literacy: A position statement.* Newark, DE: International Reading Association.

Mullis, I., Campbell, J., & Farstrup, A. (1993). *NAEP 1992: Reading report card for the nation and states.* Washington, DC: U.S. Department of Education.

National Center for Education Statistics. (2005). *The nation's report card: Reading 2005.* Retrieved from http://nces.ed.gov/nationsreportcard/pdf/main2005.

Postlethwaite, T., & Ross, K. N. (1992). *Effective schools in reading: Implications for educational planners: An exploratory study.* The Hague: International Association for the Evaluation of Educational Achievement.

Samuels, B. G. (1989). Young adults' choices: Why do students "really like" particular books? *Journal of Reading, 32*(8), 714–719.

Schnick, T. (2000). *The Lexile framework: An introduction for educators.* Durham, NC: MetaMetrics.

Shapiro, J., & White, W. (1991). Reading attitudes and perceptions in traditional and nontraditional reading programs. *Reading Research and Instruction, 30*(4), 52–66.

Smith, M. W., & Wilhelm, J. D. (2002). *Reading don't fix no Chevys: Literacy in the lives of young men.* Portsmouth, NH: Heinemann.

Squire, J. R. (1969). What does research in reading reveal—about attitudes toward reading? *English Journal, 58*(4), 523–533.

Stallworth, B. J. (1998). The young adult literature course: Facilitating the integration of young adult literature into the high school English classroom. *ALAN Review, 26*(1), 25–30.

Stanovich, K. E. (1986). Matthew effects in reading: Some consequences of individual differences in the acquisition of literacy. *Reading Research Quarterly, 21*(4), 360–407.

Stevenson, S. (2005). When bad libraries go good. *School Library Journal, 51*(5), 46–48.

Tatum, A. (2005). *Teaching reading to black adolescent males: Closing the achievement gap.* Portland, ME: Stenhouse.

Taylor, D. L. (2004). "Not just boring stories": Reconsidering the gender gap for boys. *Journal of Adolescent and Adult Literacy, 48*(4), 290–298.

U.S. Census Bureau. (2000). Retrieved from www.census.gov.

Wilder, A., & Teasley, A. B. (1998). Young adult literature in the high school. *ALAN Review, 26*(1), 42–45.

———. (1999). Making the transition to lifelong reading: Books older teens choose. *ALAN Review, 27*(1), 42–46.

Worthy, J. (1996). Removing barriers to voluntary reading: The role of school and classroom libraries. *Language Arts, 73,* 483–492.

Worthy, J., Moorman, M., & Turner, M. (1999). What Johnny likes to read is hard to find in school. *Reading Research Quarterly, 34*(1), 12–27.

Worthy, J., Patterson, E., Salas, R., Prater, S., & Turner, M. (2002). "More than just reading": The human factor in reaching resistant readers. *Reading Research and Instruction, 41*(2), 177–202.

Worthy, J., Turner, M., & Moorman, M. (1998). The precarious place of free-choice reading. *Language Arts, 75,* 296–304.

chapter ELEVEN

CENSORSHIP, CLASSICS, ACCOUNTABILITY, TECHNOLOGY: ISSUES *and* TRENDS

Being aware of the trends and issues pertinent to young adult literature is basic to understanding how they affect you, your work, and the young adults you serve. The purpose of this chapter is to make you aware of the major issues and current trends that surround young adult literature.

CENSORSHIP

Censorship is "the actual removal, suppression, or restricted circulation of literary, artistic, or educational materials . . . on the grounds that they are morally or otherwise objectionable" (Reichman, 2001). When a person or persons attempt to remove material from the curriculum or library, thereby restricting the access of others, it is called a *challenge.* Most book challenges occur locally, and most fail. When a challenge is successful and materials are removed from the curriculum or library, it is called a *banning* (www.ala.org/ala/issuesadvocacy/banned/index.cfm). The issue is whether anyone has the right to deny others access to literary, artistic, or educational materials.

From its beginnings in the 1960s and 1970s, young adult literature has faced many challenges, partly because many contemporary novels for adolescents have focused on the real world of young people—drugs, premarital sex, alcoholism, divorce, gangs, school dropouts, racism, violence, and sensuality. Some people believe that these topics are unsuitable as subjects of books for adolescents. Others object to the use of profanity, mention of homosexuality, questioning authority figures, or criticism of the nation or government. The majority of censorship attempts of this kind come from individuals and groups adhering to ultraconservative political or religious beliefs. Censorship attempts also may come from the political left when there are concerns about stereotypes, bias, or misrepresentation found in books about minority cultures and females. The anonymity and facelessness of Africans taken as slaves in the Newbery Award–winning book *The Slave Dancer* (Fox, 1973), for example, have been offensive to many African Americans.

According to the censorship database of the American Library Association's Office of Intellectual Freedom (OIF), in the years from 2001 to 2008 the three groups from which most censorship attempts came were parents (51%), other library patrons (11%), and school administrators (6%) (www.ala.org/ala/issuesadvocacy/banned/frequentlychallenged/21stcenturychallenged/index.cfm). Of the 3,736 challenges reported to the OIF in these eight years, 32 percent were based on material perceived to be "sexually explicit," 27 percent were based on material perceived to have "offensive language," and 19 percent were based on material perceived to be "unsuited to the age group." It should be noted that the OIF estimates that 75 to 80 percent of censorship attempts are not reported, so these figures are approximate.

Another significant source of censorship that is unlikely to be included in the OIF's database is teachers themselves. A study by Wollman-Bonilla (1998) of pre- and in-service teachers' ideas about books acceptable and unacceptable for young people reveals a tendency toward teacher bias in book selection for the young people they serve. The researcher found that teachers "commonly objected to texts that reflect gender, ethnic, race, or class experiences that differed from their own" (p. 289). This subtle form of censorship is made worse by the fact that most teachers are unaware of their own biases in text selection (Luke, Cooke, & Luke, 1986; Jipson & Paley, 1991).

The long-term effects of continued censorship attempts, whether successful or not, can be subtle yet troubling. As reported by NCTE's Committee on the Right to Read, "Schools have removed from libraries and classrooms and English teachers have avoided using or recommending works which *might* [emphasis added] make members of the community angry. Many students are consequently 'educated' in a school atmosphere hostile to free inquiry. And many teachers learn to emphasize their own safety rather than their students' needs" (*The Students' Right to Read,* www.ncte.org/positions/statements/righttoreadguideline).

Our position as regards censorship is as follows:

Teachers and schools have the right and the obligation to select reading materials suitable for the education of their students. With this right comes the professional responsibility to select good-quality literature that furthers stated educational goals while remaining appropriate for the age and maturity level of the respective students.

Parents are within their rights to protect their children from materials or influences they see as potentially damaging. In the instance that a parent believes that material selected by a school or teacher is potentially harmful to his or her child, that parent has the right to bring this concern to the attention of the school and request that his or her child not be subjected to this material. Parents must indicate the reason for their concern.

The school must take the parent's objection seriously and provide a reasonable substitute for the material of concern. If an alternative procedure is necessary in order to effect the substitution (for example, the student will listen to a different book in the library while the teacher is reading aloud), the alternative provided should respect the student and be sensitive to his or her feelings.

The parent does not have the right to demand that the material in question be withheld from other students. Doing so would interfere with the right and professional duty of the teacher and school to educate students. Once a student is given a reasonable alternative, the school has fulfilled its obligation and should not interfere with the First Amendment rights of other students.

The First Amendment to the Constitution of the United States guarantees to its citizens the freedoms of religion, of speech, and of the press—collectively called "intellectual freedom." As adults, we cherish our right to choose our reading material and use it nearly every day of our lives. Middle and high school social studies and civics textbooks proudly proclaim the freedom of choice that citizens of the United States have in their daily lives. But do we, as parents, teachers, and librarians, actually extend these rights to our children and students? A positive response to the growth of censorship attempts is to teach young people about their First Amendment rights and what is at stake. *Censorship,* essays for teens edited by Tamara Roleff (2005), and Kathleen Krull's (1999) middle-school-level *A Kid's Guide to America's Bill of Rights* are examples of nonfiction that might be used in this regard. Good examples of young adult fiction about censorship to use in high schools are *The Sledding Hill* by Chris Crutcher (2005), *The Last Safe Place on Earth* by Richard Peck (1995), and *Save Halloween!* by Stephanie Tolan (1993). *The Landry News* by Andrew Clements (1999) would be appropriate for middle graders, and *Places I Never Meant to Be: Original Stories by Censored Writers,* edited by Judy Blume (1999), offers short story selections for both groups. As teachers and librarians, we should do everything possible to promote the kinds of books that encourage critical thinking, inquiry, and self-expression, while maintaining respect for the views of others.

The American Library Association's Office of Intellectual Freedom monitors the challenges made against books for children and young adults in the United States. Most adults and young adults who have read the highly regarded books that often appear on these "most challenged books" lists find the reasons given for the challenges perplexing, if not incredible. For example, the following young adult and crossover titles appeared on the ALA list of the Most Challenged Books of 2007 (www .ala.org/ala/aboutala/offices/oif/bannedbooksweek/challengedbanned/frequentlychallengedbooks .cfm#tmfcbo2007):

- *The Chocolate War* by Robert Cormier (1974), for sexually explicit content, offensive language, violence
- *Olive's Ocean* by Kevin Henkes (2003), for sexually explicit content, offensive language
- *The Golden Compass* by Philip Pullman (1996), for religious viewpoint
- *The Adventures of Huckleberry Finn* by Mark Twain (1884), for racism
- *The Color Purple* by Alice Walker (1982), for homosexuality, sexually explicit content, offensive language
- *I Know Why the Caged Bird Sings* by Maya Angelou (1970), for sexually explicit content
- *It's Perfectly Normal* by Robie Harris (1994), for sex education, sexually explicit content

Included in the OIF's *Most Frequently Challenged Books of the 21st Century (2000–2005)* (www.ala .org/ala/aboutala/offices/oif/bannedbooksweek/bbwlinks/topten2000to2005.cfm) are the Harry Potter series by J. K. Rowling, *The Chocolate War* by Robert Cormier (1974), the Alice series by Phyllis Reynolds Naylor, *Of Mice and Men* by John Steinbeck (1937), *I Know Why the Caged Bird Sings* by Maya Angelou (1970), and *Fallen Angels* by Walter Dean Myers (1988).

Often, individuals challenge books on the basis of a single word or phrase, or on hearsay, and have not read the book at all. Teachers and school librarians have found that being prepared for the would-be censor helps avoid problems. For example, a written procedure brings order and reason into discussions with those who want to censor school materials. Most procedures call for teachers and librarians to give would-be censors a complaint form and ask them to specify their concerns in writing. There are advantages to such a system: Both teachers and would-be censors are given time to reflect on the issue and to control their emotions; and would-be censors are given time to read the book in its entirety, if they have not done so already. Such a system for dealing with censorship attempts works best when the school or school system administration knows the process and pertinent laws, and is supportive and involved. Developing written procedures and complaint forms for dealing with a would-be censor are important tasks for a school's literature curriculum committee and administration. Figure 11.1 presents a model form produced by the National Council of Teachers of English (NCTE) for reconsideration of a work of literature. Another strategy that might prevent censorship attempts by parents is for teachers to send a permission slip home with students. This form would state the titles and nature of titles to be assigned for reading in school and at home, and parents would indicate their consent to let their child read these books by signing. Information about assigned reading also could be placed on a website for parents to read several weeks in advance of the actual assignment. Parents objecting to any title could work with the teacher to find an acceptable alternative.

An important part of teacher and librarian training is learning how to select books that are of good quality and appropriate for young people. Teachers must make book selections, and it is their obligation to make responsible choices on the bases of literary quality and knowledge of child and adolescent development and psychology. The NCTE guidelines, while stating that teachers are best qualified to

Author _____ Paperback _____ Hardcover _____
Title _____
Publisher (if known) _____
Request initiated by _____
Telephone _____
Address _____ City _____ Zip Code _____
Complainant represents
_____ Himself/Herself
_____ (Name organization) _____
_____ (Identify other group) _____
Have you been able to discuss this work with the teacher or librarian who ordered it or who used it?
_____ Yes _____ No
What do you understand to be the general purpose for using this work?
   a. Provide support for a unit in the curriculum? _____ Yes _____ No
   b. Provide a learning experience for the reader in one kind of literature? _____ Yes _____ No
   c. Other _____
 3. Did the general purpose for the use of the work, as described by the teacher or librarian, seem a
     suitable one to you? _____ Yes _____ No
     If not, please explain. _____
     _____
 4. What do you think is the general purpose of the author in this book? _____
     _____
 5. In what ways do you think a work of this nature is not suitable for the use the teacher or librarian
     wishes to carry out? _____
     _____
 6. Have you been able to learn the students' response to this work? _____ Yes _____ No
 7. What response did the students make? _____
     _____
 8. Have you been able to learn from your school library what book reviewers or other students of
     literature have written about this work? _____ Yes _____ No
 9. Would you like the teacher or librarian to give you a written summary of what book reviewers and
     other students have written about this book or film? _____ Yes _____ No
10. Do you have negative reviews of the book? _____ Yes _____ No
11. Where were they published? _____
12. Would you be willing to provide summaries of the reviews you have collected? _____ Yes _____ No
13. What would you like your library/school to do about this work?
     _____ Do not assign/lend it to my child.
     _____ Return it to the staff selection committee/department for reevaluation.
     _____ Other: Please explain _____
     _____
14. In its place, what work would you recommend that would convey as valuable a picture and perspective
     of the subject treated? _____
     _____

Signature _____ Date _____

FIGURE 11.1   Citizen's Request for Reconsideration of a Work

Source: Committee on the Right to Read. *The students' right to read.* Urbana, IL: National Council of Teachers of English.

make decisions about books, suggest that parents and community members be included on review committees, and, in addition, that schools develop written rationales for book selections to respond to challenges. We believe that such a practice may be necessary in some schools and can prevent attacks on books because parents were involved in the process. If your school does not have such a policy, we suggest that you make a practice of noting the reason for your choice of a book and how it supports your curricular goals, and keep these notes in a file in the event of an objection.

CLASSICS AND YOUNG ADULT LITERATURE

In Chapter 1 we stated that the study of adult classic works of literature was the tradition in American high schools throughout the twentieth century. In the last quarter of that century this tradition began to be challenged as young adult literature emerged as a distinct body of literature and was thought by some to be worthy of study on an equal basis with the classics. Conflicting opinions about this are at the heart of the issue. As the field of young adult literature matured, improved, and grew, the trend was to include more and more of these contemporary works in high school required reading lists.

We support the notion that some knowledge of our cultural heritage as found in the classics is important for our citizens to have and share. But a book list confined to the classics ignores the fact that we live in a rapidly changing culture and that literature should reflect the ongoing culture as well as that of the past. Culture is not static, nor is the body of literature referred to as "the classics" (Applebee, 1992). For titles often included on high school required reading lists, see Table 11.1. Change is inevitable; the literary works once considered essential will not be the same twenty years from now.

The classic works most often found on required reading lists have several serious shortcomings when examined by today's standards and as works suitable for young adults. They are gender and ethnically biased against women and people of color. The authors of most of these works are male and white. In some cases their language and writing styles are difficult for today's young readers to understand because of arcane expressions and convoluted syntax rarely used today. They are set in the world of the past. Few, if any, classics have teens as main characters. Even if the protagonist is a younger person who is still going through developmental changes in life, the author's (and, by extension, the

TABLE 11.1   Most Frequently Required Titles in Public Schools, Grades 9–12

Title	Percent	Title	Percent
Romeo and Juliet	84	*The Scarlet Letter*	62
Macbeth	81	*Of Mice and Men*	56
Huckleberry Finn	70	*Hamlet*	55
Julius Caesar	70	*The Great Gatsby*	54
To Kill a Mockingbird	69	*Lord of the Flies*	54

Source: Applebee (1992).

protagonist's) point of view, which is decidedly adult, should be carefully assessed as to whether an adolescent reader would comprehend the protagonist's interpretation of events and people. These characteristics make most classic works irrelevant or less relevant to most young people today, and especially so for females and minorities. We acknowledge that some classics still hold appeal and, if taught in an interesting way, can be enjoyed by young adults.

If our students are to become lifelong readers, they must be convinced that reading is worthwhile and enjoyable and that reading materials exist that are interesting and relevant to their lives. We urge those who develop required reading lists for middle and high school students to select only those classic works that hold interest for young people and to balance these works with excellent contemporary works that represent all sectors of society. Joan Kaywell in her multivolume *Adolescent Literature as a Complement to the Classics* (1993–2000) pairs classics with more accessible young adult novels with similar themes to improve students' understanding of the classic works and to encourage broader reading generally. Herz and Gallo's (2005) *From Hinton to Hamlet: Building Bridges between Young Adult Literature and the Classics* is a similar resource. Regular reevaluation of both classic and contemporary works and consequent updating of reading lists is essential. Teachers who stick rigidly to the same set of books year after year are, in effect, proclaiming that establishing their own personal literary canon is more important than addressing the needs and interests of the young people they teach.

Teachers who teach classic works such as those mentioned in Table 11.1 sometimes pair them with appropriate works of young adult literature for several reasons:

- *To serve as a bridge to understanding and appreciating the classic work.* In this case the two works will be the same genre or have similar themes. The young adult novel is read first and, because it is more accessible, helps readers create a schema for understanding the classic work and seeing its relevance to their lives.

- *To learn the vocabulary of literary criticism and to practice thinking about books critically.* In this case the paired works will have similar plots, characters, settings, themes, or writing styles. The young adult novel is read first and provides easily understandable examples of plot structure, character development, description and use of setting, development of theme, or writing style, thus preparing readers to find and understand how these elements work in the classic text.

- *To bring more diverse literature into the English curriculum.* Most classic works taught in schools in the United States are written by white males of British or Euro-American heritage. Paired works will feature similar plots or themes, but the young adult work will be written by or from the point of view of a protagonist from a culture other than European, Euro-American, or male.

In planning for young adult-classic literature pairings, teachers may elect to pair a classic work with one young adult novel or *several,* providing all have the required similarities. Pairing a classic work with several young adult selections allows a teacher to match students' reading abilities and interests more closely and to investigate several different themes (versus one major theme) or several different elements of fiction.

To get an idea of contemporary titles that might be paired with classics, consider the following examples, noting that the contemporary works cited are not the only ones possible to use in these pairings:

- William Shakespeare's (1597) *Romeo and Juliet,* widely taught in today's high schools, explores the themes of star-crossed love and prejudice. Contemporary works with a similar theme include Sharon Draper's (1999) *Romiette and Julio* (young love threatened by family prejudices and gangs), Walter Dean Myers' (2006) *Street Love* (love crossing social-class lines in Harlem), and Ellen Wittlinger's (1999) *Hard Love* (unrequited love).

- Aldous Huxley's (1932) classic, *Brave New World,* investigates the themes of utopias and dystopias, bioethical issues of genetic engineering, and the importance of individuality and self-determination. It could be paired with M. T. Anderson's (2002) *Feed* (consumer-driven dystopian world in which computer feeds are implanted in babies' brains), Suzanne Collins' (2008) *The Hunger Games* (dystopian near-future United States in which teens are pitted in gladiator-like combat), and Nancy Werlin's (2004) *Double Helix* (the perils of cloning).

- Nathaniel Hawthorne's often-assigned classic, *The Scarlet Letter* (1850), investigates the themes of alienation, acting on one's convictions, and the price of nonconformity. One finds the same themes in M. T. Anderson's (1999) *Speak* (alienation and acting on one's convictions), Jerry Spinelli's (2000) *Stargirl* (the price of nonconformity and alienation), and Margaret Wild's (2004) *One Night* (child out of wedlock, alienation, rejection).

Many classic works are available as audiobooks and can be downloaded free of charge at such sites as www.LibriVox.org and www.gutenberg.org.

ACCOUNTABILITY AND READING

Accountability is a demand by public and government agencies for school systems and teachers to improve students' school achievement as demonstrated by test scores, in the areas of reading, writing, mathematics, and science. In the United States, this trend began in the 1980s at the local school district level, then expanded to the state level in many states, and, with the enactment of the No Child Left Behind Act (NCLB) in 2002, became an important part of federal policy in education. NCLB expanded the original notion of accountability in two important ways: Annual testing of reading and mathematics achievement for all students in grades 3 to 8 became mandatory; and performance data had to be disaggregated according to race, gender, and other criteria to demonstrate progress in closing the achievement gap between disadvantaged students and other groups of students.

Under NCLB, each school is graded A, B, C, D, F, depending on student achievement by averages for the grade and by subgroups. Schools that receive failing grades are given a period of time to improve student achievement. Failure of a school to do so can result in reduced federal and state funding for the school, vouchers for students to attend another public school or charter school in the case of repeated failures by the school, or replacement of administrators and teachers, depending on state and local policies. States develop the actual tests used, the procedures for implementation of the policy, and timetables for implementation.

From its inception, NCLB has garnered widespread criticism. In Darling-Hammond's words, "Critics claim that the law's focus on complicated tallies of multiple-choice-test scores has dumbed down the curriculum, fostered a 'drill and kill' approach to teaching, mistakenly labeled successful schools as failing, driven teachers and middle-class students out of public schools and harmed special education students and English-language learners through inappropriate assessments and efforts to push out low-scoring students in order to boost scores. Indeed, recent analyses have found that rapid gains in education outcomes stimulated by reforms in the 1990s have stalled under NCLB, with math increases slowing and reading on the decline" (Darling-Hammond, 2007, p. 11). In light of such criticism, reauthorization of NCLB has been postponed until lawmakers can agree on how to revise it.

Although we, too, question the reliability of a score on a single test as the predominant measure of a student's progress or of a teacher's success over the course of a school year, this is the reality we face and must operate within. Because it directly affects students, teachers, schools, and school systems, accountability is a high-priority issue in education.

The curricular area that is of most concern to parents, teachers, and school administrators is reading, since reading scores have been in general decline across the nation for the last twenty-five years, especially at the middle school and high school levels. The National Association of Educational Progress tracks these trends in reading achievement and reports them in *The Nation's Report Card.* Data showing this trend can be seen at http://nationsreportcard.gov/reading_math_grade12_2005/s0203.asp.

We believe that a major reason for the decline in reading scores is a decrease in voluntary reading among our students. Young people have lost the reading habit. Voluntary reading of literature in the United States has been monitored by the Research Division of the United States Bureau of the Census and the National Endowment for the Arts (NEA) since 1982. From then until 2002 NEA reports showed a steady decline in voluntary reading across all age groups in the United States, but particularly among the youngest group surveyed, 18- to 24-year-olds. Although the NEA's 2008 report, *Reading on the Rise: A New Chapter in American Literacy,* showed growth in voluntary reading across all age groups since 2002 based on absolute numbers, it is important to note that when the nation's population growth from 2002 to 2008 is factored in, the percentage of 18- to 24-year-old Americans who read declined from 52 percent in 2002 to 50.7 percent in 2008. Moreover, our students do not compare favorably with those in other developed nations, as the Programme for International Student Assessment (PISA; http://nces.ed.gov/surveys/pisa) 2000, 2003, and 2006 reports on the reading, mathematics, and science literacy of 15-year-olds have demonstrated.

The NEA's 2004 report found a correlation between the decline in reading and increased participation in a variety of electronic media, including the Internet, video games, and portable digital devices (Bradshaw & Nichols, 2004, pp. xi–xii). Despite the 9 percent growth in reading from 2002 to 2008 among 18- to 24-year-olds (based on absolute numbers), reported by the NEA in 2008 (www.arts.gov/research/Research_brochures.php), we believe that it is too early to detect or claim a lasting trend toward more voluntary reading, and we doubt that the use or appeal of electronic media will diminish. It is, nonetheless, important to try to understand the reasons behind the growth in voluntary reading as reported by the NEA in 2008. Dana Gioia, chairman of the NEA, offers the following explanation: "Faced by a clear and undeniable problem, millions of parents, teachers, librarians, and civic leaders took action (inspired by thousands of journalists and scholars who publicized the issues at stake). Reading became a higher priority in families, schools, and communities. Thousands of programs, large and small, were created or significantly enhanced to address the challenge" (NEA, 2008, p. 2).

The 2008 NEA report also includes the following findings of interest to middle and high school teachers and librarians:

- Young adults read books at a slightly lower rate than older adults, but they also did more reading online than older Americans.
- Greater reading of fiction was responsible for the new growth in adult literary readers.

Much more than falling reading scores and a loss of accountability is at stake when people stop reading voluntarily. Commenting on the effects of a decline in literacy, Dana Gioia, NEA Chairman, states that "print culture affords irreplaceable forms of focused attention and contemplation that makes complex communications and insights possible. To lose such intellectual capacity—and the many sorts of human continuity it allows—would constitute a vast cultural impoverishment." He goes on to state that "readers play a more active and involved role in their communities. [A] decline in reading, therefore, parallels a larger retreat from participation in civic and cultural life. The long-term implications of [a decline in literacy] not only affect literature but all of the arts—as well as social activities such as volunteerism, philanthropy, and even political engagement." He concludes by saying, "Advanced literacy is a specific intellectual skill and social habit that depends on a great many educational, cultural, and economic factors. As more Americans lose this capability, our nation becomes less informed, active, and independent-minded. These are not qualities that a free, innovative, or productive society can afford to lose" (Bradshaw and Nichols, 2004, p. vii).

It is little wonder that teachers feel pressured by the demands of accountability to improve their students' reading ability when the population in general is moving away from reading. How do we inspire young people to love reading and to become aware of its power to inform, entertain, educate, and change? How do we instill in them the reading habit?

Accountability and falling reading scores make it mandatory that the efforts to improve test scores of all students at all achievement levels involve the entire school. Many middle schools and high schools have added reading courses and have required English teachers to place greater emphasis on teaching reading skills in their classes. Content-area teachers have been required to integrate the teaching of reading into their courses. These additional and revised courses give teachers opportunities to explicitly teach reading skills and to motivate students to read more. Some teachers provide students time in school to read, since it has been shown that students' reading ability improves when they read more. On a broader scale, programs such as the NEA's Big Read (www.arts.gov/national/bigread/index.html) offers support for people to read and discuss books—many of which are appropriate for young adults—within their communities.

Publishers, aware of falling test scores in reading and the demands of the public and the policymakers for schools to reverse this trend, have produced books written specifically for low-level readers. The aim of publishers, teachers, and librarians is to bring these students back to the reading habit by placing in their hands reading materials that will interest and not intimidate them. These include books, short stories, and magazines with high-interest topics relevant to young adults but written at third- to fifth-grade reading levels, short novels of about one hundred pages, and, in the case of nonfiction, well-illustrated books written in a lively style.

Regardless of students' reading ability, promoting reading is, in many cases, mainly a matter of helping students select appropriate reading materials. Note the success of various television programs, from "Reading Rainbow" to "Oprah Winfrey," in convincing people to read recommended books. These people are saying, "I read this book and loved it. I recommend it to you." To be a successful promoter of reading, you yourself must be a reader. Recommending a book that you have enjoyed is an effective reading motivator. In light of the NEA's *Reading on the Rise* report, there is hope that the curricular changes, programs, and strategies as outlined here may have positive results and that students may regain the reading habit.

ECHNOLOGY

The phenomenal growth in the availability, capability, and use of electronic devices that enable users to read, write, communicate, and gather and share information makes technological development a topic and trend worthy of attention by teachers. In this section, we will address technologies that have in-school applications and are currently affecting instruction and learning in schools.

The computer and its hand-held wireless versions, along with cellphones with Internet browsing, e-mail, and text messaging capabilities are currently the most-used technological devices. These technologies have already shown their potential for assisting in effective language and literature instruction and learning consistent with curricular goals. Guidelines for the appropriate use of these instructional devices in the classroom will need to be set by teachers to prevent their being used for socializing or game playing.

The Internet is very useful to teachers for research and lesson planning. For instance, teachers can use information they find on the Internet to corroborate information from other sources, to develop overviews of content being studied, and to update information found in textbooks. Online professional sources can assist in lesson planning. See, for example, www.readwritethink.org and www. webenglishteacher.com for lessons developed by teachers. Such lessons, if they meet teachers' curricular goals, can provide new ideas and sources for those ideas.

Teachers can use closed networks within their schools—*Intranets*—to conduct lessons in which students share their responses to literature being studied in class, to enable students to share drafts of writing in partner writing, and to require or encourage journaling by students. In our experience, adolescents are more willing to share their responses to literature on a computer, through the Internet, or by text messaging. In-school use of the Internet, interactive websites, weblogs, and class-created chat rooms must, of course, be operated within the safety guidelines of the school system.

Students can use the Internet to research topics for literature-related units of study, to locate websites for author studies, or to identify sources for further research on a theme. Students often enjoy finding titles of young adult books on topics of interest and reading others' comments about them. See, for example, www.teenreads.com. Students can also access free audios of many books through the websites www.librivox.com and www.gutenberg.org. Auditory learners especially appreciate audiobooks.

Promising Newer Technologies

E-BOOK READERS   A device growing in popularity is the *electronic book (e-book) reader,* an electronic device used to read *e-books* (the digital equivalent of a conventional printed book). Although e-books are not yet widely used in schools, they are growing in popularity among the general public and appear to have potential for use in classrooms as the technology develops and becomes more affordable. E-books are generally cheaper than paper books, take up less space, are environmentally less wasteful to produce, and are more easily distributed. They have the potential to make the concept of a book's being out of print obsolete and to make virtually any book available to readers who have access to the Internet. Furthermore, e-book readers provide access not only to books, but also to newspapers, magazines, and blogs. As a result, teachers may have access to greatly expanded choices of reading material for their students and of literature for text sets and books for in-class reading. An important disadvantage of e-book readers currently available is the lack of color graphic capability that makes picture books, illustrated informational books, and graphic novels using color ineffective as e-books. Access to full-text books is becoming possible on smartphones such as the iPhone and the Blackberry.

Capabilities of e-book readers such as Amazon's Kindle2 and the Sony Reader that may facilitate reading include

- a built-in dictionary so that readers can get a definition of a word simply by clicking on it
- automatic searching and cross-referencing of text (useful, for example, for finding earlier references to characters or events)
- nonpermanent highlighting
- text-to-speech software that can convert e-books to audiobooks automatically

Our interest is in how e-books and e-book readers will affect the teaching of literature in schools. Will they permit teachers to make available more choices for text sets? Will the cost of books decrease but availability increase as more e-books become available? Also, will these technologies *change* the way people read and think? Will they enable readers to *improve their reading ability,* or *motivate* them to read more? Supporters of reading on the Internet say that it is a new kind of reading and that ease of access to books on the Internet may increase the time young people spend reading and therefore help them to become better readers. Critics say that Internet reading is reducing readers' attention spans and diminishing literacy. Teacher observation and research into these questions will, in time, provide some answers.

INTERACTIVE ELECTRONIC WHITEBOARDS

This instructional tool, currently in use in some schools, is, in essence, a computer with a screen large enough to be seen by everyone in a normal-sized classroom. Software enables teachers to download and present interactive lessons on any subject. One software source, for example, offers recent news articles from the AP wire service accompanied by guides to interpretation, vocabulary, and comprehension. Various interactive programs assist students in brainstorming, mapping, writing, and editing their written responses to literature. Interactive electronic whiteboards, such as Smartboard, allow instructors to add interest and depth to their lessons by accessing photographs, drawings, maps, video and audio clips, and related sources of information.

With the field of technology changing rapidly, it is important for teachers to stay informed about newer technologies that have potential for teaching. Information sources include school technology managers who offer assistance and workshops for teachers on promising new instructional technologies available for use in their school system, educational technology conferences, and professional

subscribe to this →

organizations such as NCTE and IRA. These organizations provide conference workshops, Internet newsletters such as the NCTE Inbox, and publications that include information on emerging technologies.

REFERENCES

American Library Association. (1986). Banned and challenged books. Retrieved from www.ala/issues advocacy/banned/index.cfm.

————. (2009). *Frequently challenged books of the 21st century.* Retrieved from www.ala.org/issues advocacy/banned/frequentlychallenged/21st-centurychallenged/index.cfm.

Anderson, M. T. (2002). *Feed.* New York: Candlewick.

————. (1999). *Speak.* New York: Farrar.

Angelou, M. (1970). *I know why the caged bird sings.* New York: Random House.

Applebee, A. N. (1992). Stability and change in the high-school canon. *English Journal, 81*(5), 27–32.

Blume, J. (Ed.). (1999). *Places I never meant to be: Original stories by censored writers.* New York: Simon & Schuster.

Bradshaw, T., & Nichols, B. (2004). *Reading at risk: A survey of literary reading in America.* Research Division Report 46. Washington, DC: National Endowment for the Arts.

Clements, A. (1999). *The Landry news.* New York: Simon & Schuster.

Collins, S. (2008). *The hunger games.* New York: Scholastic.

Cormier, R. (1974). *The chocolate war.* New York: Pantheon.

Crutcher, C. (2005). *The sledding hill.* New York: HarperCollins.

Darling-Hammond, L. (2007). Evaluating "No Child Left Behind." *The Nation, 284*(20), 11–21.

Draper, S. (1999). *Romiette and Julio.* New York: Atheneum.

Fox, P. (1973). *The slave dancer.* New York: Bradbury.

Harris, R. H. (1994). *It's perfectly normal: A book about changing bodies, growing up, sex, and sexual health.* New York: Candlewick.

Hawthorne, N. (1850/2000). *The scarlet letter.* New York: Modern Library.

Henkes, K. (2003). *Olive's ocean.* New York: Greenwillow.

Herz, S. K., & Gallo, D. R. (2005). *From Hinton to Hamlet: Building bridges between young adult literature and the classics* (2nd ed.). Westport, CT: Greenwood.

Huxley, A. (1932/2006). *Brave new world.* New York: HarperCollins.

Jipson, J., & Paley, N. (1991). The selective tradition in children's literature: Does it exist in the elementary classroom? *English Education, 23,* 148–159.

Kaywell, J. F. (Ed.). (1993–2000). *Adolescent literature as a complement to the classics* (Vols. 1–4). Norwood, MA: Christopher-Gordon.

Krull, K. (1999). *A kid's guide to America's bill of rights: Curfews, censorship, and the 100-pound giant.* New York: HarperCollins.

Luke, A., Cooke, J., & Luke, C. (1986). The selective tradition in action: Gender bias in student teachers' selections of children's literature. *English Education, 18,* 209–218.

Myers, W. D. (1988). *Fallen angels.* New York: Scholastic.

————. (2006). *Street love.* New York: Amistad.

National Assessment of Educational Progress. (2005). *The nation's report card.* Retrieved from http://nationsreportcard.gov/reading_math_grade12_2005/s0203.asp.

National Council of Teachers of English. (1981/2009). *Guidleines on the students' right to read.* Retrieved from www.ncte.org/positions/statements/righttoreadguideline.

National Endowment for the Arts. (2008). *Reading on the rise: A new chapter in American literacy.* Retrieved from http://www.arts.gov/research/Research_brochures.php.

Peck, R. (1995). *The last safe place on earth.* New York: Delacorte.

Pullman, P. (1996). *The golden compass.* New York: Knopf.

Reichman, H. (2001). *Censorship and selection: Issues and answers for schools.* Chicago: American Library Association Editions.

Roleff, T. (2005). *Censorship.* Chicago: Greenhaven.

Shakespeare, W. (1597–1609?/1993). *Romeo and Juliet.* Mineola, NY: Dover.

Spinelli, J. (2000). *Stargirl.* New York: Knopf.

Steinbeck, J. (1937). *Of mice and men.* New York: Viking.

Tolan, S. (1993). *Save Halloween!* New York: HarperCollins.

Twain, M. (2002/1884). *The adventures of Huckleberry Finn.* Berkeley: University of California Press.

Walker, A. (1982). *The color purple.* New York: Harcourt.

Werlin, N. (2004). *Double helix.* New York: Dial.

Wild, M. (2004). *One night.* New York: Knopf.

Wittlinger, E. (1999). *Hard love.* New York: Simon & Schuster.

Wollman-Bonilla, J. E. (1998). Outrageous viewpoints: Teachers' criteria for rejecting works of children's literature. *Language Arts, 75*(4), 287–295.

Book Awards

Some of the awards listed in this appendix were established prior to the late 1960s, the approximate time that young adult literature emerged as a distinct body of literature. When this is the case, we omit those entries dated prior to 1970 and give a website for those who wish to access the complete list online. Some programs, such as the Boston Globe–Horn Book Awards and the Coretta Scott King Awards, confer separate awards for text and picture books. In these cases we omit the picture book awards but again give a website for those who wish to access the complete list.

Michael L. Printz Award for Excellence in Young Adult Literature

The Michael L. Printz Award is an award for a book that exemplifies literary excellence in young adult literature. It was established under the auspices of the Young Adult Library Services Association of the American Library Association in 2000. It is named for a Topeka, Kansas, school librarian who was a long-time active member of the Young Adult Library Services Association. The award is sponsored by Booklist, a publication of the American Library Association.

2009 *Jellicoe Road* by Melina Marchetta. HarperCollins. (Realism, ages 14–18.)

HONOR BOOKS

The Astonishing Life of Octavian Nothing, Traitor to the Nation, Volume II: *The Kingdom on the Waves* by M. T. Anderson. Candlewick. (Historical fiction [Colonial America, Revolutionary War era], ages 15–18.)

The Disreputable History of Frankie Landau-Banks by E. Lockhart. Hyperion. (Realism, ages 14–18.)

Nation by Terry Pratchett. HarperCollins. (Modern fantasy/survival, ages 14–18.)

Tender Morsels by Margo Lanagan. Knopf. (Modern fantasy, ages 15–18.)

2008 *The White Darkness* by Geraldine McCaughrean. HarperCollins. (Realism/survival, ages 12–16.)

HONOR BOOKS

Dreamquake: Book Two of the Dreamhunter Duet by Elizabeth Knox. Farrar. (Modern fantasy, ages 15–18.)

One Whole and Perfect Day by Judith Clarke. Front Street. (Realism, ages 14–16.)

Repossessed by A. M. Jenkins. HarperCollins. (Modern fantasy, ages 14–18.)

Your Own, Sylvia: A Verse Portrait of Sylvia Plath by Stephanie Hemphill. Knopf. (Biography/poetry, ages 14–18.)

2007 *American Born Chinese* by Gene Luen Yang. First Second. (Mixed genre graphic novel, ages 12–18.)

HONOR BOOKS

The Astonishing Life of Octavian Nothing, Traitor to the Nation, Volume I: *The Pox Party* by M. T. Anderson. Candlewick. (Historical fiction [Colonial America, Revolutionary War era], ages 15–18.)

An Abundance of Katherines by John Green. Dutton. (Realism, ages 15–18.)

Surrender by Sonya Hartnett. Candlewick. (Realism/psychological thriller, ages 15–18.)

The Book Thief by Markus Zusak. Knopf. (Historical fiction [Nazi-era Germany], ages 14–18.)

2006 *Looking for Alaska* by John Green. Dutton. (Realism, ages 15–18.)

HONOR BOOKS

Black Juice by Margo Lanagan. EOS/HarperCollins. (Modern fantasy/short stories, ages 15–18.)

I Am the Messenger by Marcus Zusak. Knopf. (Realism/mystery, ages 15–18.)

John Lennon: All I Want Is the Truth by Elizabeth Partridge. Viking. (Biography, ages 15–18.)

A Wreath for Emmett Till by Marilyn Nelson. Illustrated by Philippe Lardy. Houghton. (Nonfiction/poetry, ages 15–18.)

2005 *How I Live Now* by Meg Rosoff. Random House. (Realism, ages 14–18.)

HONOR BOOKS

Airborn by Kenneth Oppel. HarperCollins. (Modern fantasy, ages 12–16.)

Chanda's Secrets by Allan Stratton. Annick. (Realism, ages 14–18.)

Lizzie Bright and the Buckminster Boy by Gary D. Schmidt. Clarion. (Historical fiction [Maine, 1912]/multicultural [African-American], ages 13–16.)

2004 *The First Part Last* by Angela Johnson. Simon & Schuster. (Realism/multicultural [African-American], ages 14–18.)

HONOR BOOKS

A Northern Light by Jennifer Donnelly. Harcourt. (Historical fiction [USA, 1906], ages 14–18.)

Keesha's House by Helen Frost. Farrar. (Realism/poetry, ages 14–18.)

Fat Kid Rules the World by K. L. Going. Putnam. (Realism, ages 14–18.)

The Earth, My Butt, and Other Big Round Things by Carolyn Mackler. Candlewick. (Realism, ages 13–16.)

2003 *Postcards from No Man's Land* by Aidan Chambers. Dutton. (Realism, ages 15–18.)

HONOR BOOKS

The House of the Scorpion by Nancy Farmer. Simon & Schuster. (Science fiction, ages 11–15.)

My Heartbeat by Garret Freymann-Weyr. Houghton. (Realism, ages 14–18.)

Hole in My Life by Jack Gantos. Farrar. (Autobiography, ages 13–18.)

2002 *A Step from Heaven* by An Na. Front Street. (Realism/multicultural [Korean-American], ages 14–18.)

HONOR BOOKS

The Ropemaker by Peter Dickinson. Delacorte. (Modern fantasy, ages 13–16.)

Heart to Heart: New Poems Inspired by Twentieth-Century American Art by Jan Greenberg. Abrams. (Poetry/picture book, ages 11–18.)

Freewill by Chris Lynch. HarperCollins. (Realism/mystery, ages 14–18.)

True Believer by Virginia Euwer Wolff. Atheneum. (Realism, ages 14–18.)

2001   *Kit's Wilderness* by David Almond. Delacorte. (Magical realism, ages 12–16.)
HONOR BOOKS
Many Stones by Carolyn Coman. Front Street. (Realism, ages 14–18.)

The Body of Christopher Creed by Carol Plum-Ucci. Harcourt. (Realism/mystery, ages 13–18.)

Angus, Thongs, and Full Frontal Snogging: Confessions of Georgia Nicolson by Louise Rennison. HarperCollins. (Realism, ages 12–16.)

Stuck in Neutral by Terry Trueman. HarperCollins. (Realism, ages 11–16.)

2000   *Monster* by Walter Dean Myers. HarperCollins. (Realism; play script, ages 15–18.)
HONOR BOOKS
Skellig by David Almond. Delacorte. (Magical realism, ages 11–13.)

Speak by Laurie Halse Anderson. Farrar. (Realism, ages 14–18.)

Hard Love by Ellen Wittlinger. Simon & Schuster. (Realism, ages 14–18.)

National Book Award for Young People's Literature

The National Book Award for Young People's Literature, sponsored by the National Book Foundation, is presented annually to recognize what is judged to be the outstanding contribution to children's literature in terms of literary merit, published during the previous year. The award committee considers books of all genres written for children and young adults by U.S. writers. The award, which was added to the U.S. National Book Awards in 1996, carries a $10,000 cash prize.

2008   *What I Saw and How I Lied* by Judy Blundell. Scholastic. (Realism/mystery, ages 14–18.)

2007   *The Absolutely True Diary of a Part-Time Indian* by Sherman Alexie. Little, Brown. (Fictionalized autobiography, ages 14–18.)

2006   *The Astonishing Life of Octavian Nothing, Traitor to the Nation,* Volume I: *The Pox Party* by M. T. Anderson. Candlewick. (Historical fiction [Colonial America, Revolutionary War era], ages 15–18.)

2005   *The Penderwicks: A Summer Tale of Four Sisters, Two Rabbits, and a Very Interesting Boy* by Jeanne Birdsall. Knopf. (Realism, ages 9–13.)

2004   *Godless* by Pete Hautman. Simon & Schuster. (Realism, ages 13–18.)

2003   *The Canning Season* by Polly Horvath. Farrar. (Realism, ages 12–15.)

2002   *The House of the Scorpion* by Nancy Farmer. Atheneum. (Science fiction, ages 11–15.)

2001   *True Believer* by Virginia Euwer Wolff. Atheneum. (Realism, ages 14–18.)

2000   *Homeless Bird* by Gloria Whelan. HarperCollins. (Realism [set in India], ages 12–15.)

1999   *When Zachary Beaver Came to Town* by Kimberley Willis Holt. Holt. (Realism, ages 11–15.)

1998   *Holes* by Louis Sachar. Farrar. (Magical realism/mystery, ages 11–15.)

1997   *Dancing on the Edge* by Han Nolan. Harcourt. (Realism, ages 12–16.)

1996   *Parrot in the Oven: Mi Vida* by Victor Martinez. HarperCollins. (Realism/multicultural [Mexican-American], ages 13–16.)

Newbery Medal

The Newbery Medal, sponsored by the Association for Library Service to Children division of the American Library Association, is given to the author of the most distinguished contribution to children's literature published during the previous year. It was established in 1922. Only U.S. citizens are eligible for this award. Books appropriate for both children and young adults are included in this award. For access to the entire list, go to www.ala.org, click on Awards & Grants, then Book, Print & Media Awards, then Children and Young Adults, then Newbery Medal.

2009 *Graveyard Book* by Neil Gaiman. Illustrated by Dave McKean. HarperCollins. (Modern fantasy, ages 10–15.)

HONOR BOOKS

The Underneath by Kathi Appelt. Illustrated by David Small. Atheneum. Modern fantasy/magical realism, ages 10–14.)

The Surrender Tree: Poems of Cuba's Struggle for Freedom by Margarita Engle Holt. (Poetry, ages 11–18.)

Savvy by Ingrid Law. Dial. (Modern fantasy, ages 12–15.)

After Tupac & D Foster by Jacqueline Woodson. Putnam. (Realism/multicultural [African-American], ages 12–16.)

2008 *Good Masters! Sweet Ladies! Voices from a Medieval Village* by Laura Amy Schlitz. Illustrated by Robert Byrd. Candlewick. (Monologues/dialogues, ages 10–15.)

HONOR BOOKS

Elijah of Buxton by Christopher Paul Curtis. Scholastic. (Historical fiction/multicultural [African-American, 1840s], ages 10–14.)

The Wednesday Wars by Gary D. Schmidt. Clarion. (Realism, ages 11–14.)

Feathers by Jacqueline Woodson. Putnam. (Realism/multicultural [African-American], ages 10–14.)

2007 *The Higher Power of Lucky* by Susan Patron. Illustrated by Matt Phelan. Simon & Schuster. (Realism, ages 10–13.)

HONOR BOOKS

Penny from Heaven by Jennifer L. Holm. Random. (Historical fiction [1950s America], ages 11–14.)

Hattie Big Sky by Kirby Larson. Delacorte. (Historical fiction [1918 Montana], ages 14–18.)

Rules by Cynthia Lord. Scholastic. (Realistic, ages 10–13.)

2006 *Criss Cross* by Lynne Rae Perkins. Greenwillow. (Realism, ages 11–15.)

HONOR BOOKS

Whittington by Alan Armstrong. Illustrated by S. D. Schindler. Random. (Animal fantasy, ages 10–14.)

Hitler Youth: Growing Up in Hitler's Shadow by Susan Campbell Bartoletti. Scholastic. (Nonfiction, ages 11–15.)

Princess Academy by Shannon Hale. Bloomsbury. (Fantasy, ages 11–15.)

Show Way by Jacqueline Woodson. Illustrated by Hudson Talbott. Putnam. (Multicultural [African-American]/poetry, ages 8–11.)

2005 *Kira-Kira* by Cynthia Kadohata. Atheneum. (Realism/multicultural [Japanese-American], ages 11–14.)

HONOR BOOKS

Al Capone Does My Shirts by Gennifer Choldenko. Putnam. (Realism, ages 11–14.)

The Voice That Challenged a Nation: Marian Anderson and the Struggle for Equal Rights by Russell Freedman. Clarion. (Biography, ages 11–14.)

Lizzie Bright and the Buckminster Boy by Gary D. Schmidt. Clarion. (Historical fiction [Maine, 1912]/multicultural [African-American], ages 13–16.)

2004 *The Tale of Despereaux: Being the Story of a Mouse, a Princess, Some Soup, and a Spool of Thread* by Kate DiCamillo. Illustrated by Timothy Basil Ering. Candlewick. (Modern fantasy [animal], ages 5–8.)

HONOR BOOKS

Olive's Ocean by Kevin Henkes. Greenwillow. (Realism, ages 11–14.)

An American Plague: The True and Terrifying Story of the Yellow Fever Epidemic of 1793 by Jim Murphy. Clarion. (Informational, ages 12–18.)

2003 *Crispin: The Cross of Lead* by Avi. Hyperion. (Fantasy, ages 11–15.)

HONOR BOOKS

The House of the Scorpion by Nancy Farmer. Atheneum. (Fantasy, ages 11–15.)

Pictures of Hollis Woods by Patricia Reilly Giff. Random House. (Realism, ages 10–13.)

Hoot by Carl Hiaasen. Knopf. (Realism, ages 9–12.)

A Corner of the Universe by Ann M. Martin. Scholastic. (Realism, ages 11–14.)

Surviving the Applewhites by Stephanie S. Tolan. HarperCollins. (Realism, ages 12–16.)

2002 *A Single Shard* by Linda Sue Park. Clarion/ Houghton. (Realism, ages 10–14.)
HONOR BOOKS
Everything on a Waffle by Polly Horvath. Farrar. (Realism, ages 12–14.)
Carver: A Life In Poems by Marilyn Nelson. Front Street. (Poetry/biography, ages 12–14.)

2001 *A Year Down Yonder* by Richard Peck. Dial. (Realism, ages 10–15.)
HONOR BOOKS
Because of Winn-Dixie by Kate DiCamillo. Candlewick. (Realism [animal], ages 8–12.)
Hope Was Here by Joan Bauer. Putnam. (Realism, ages 12–14.)
Joey Pigza Loses Control by Jack Gantos. Farrar. (Realism, ages 9–12.)
The Wanderer by Sharon Creech. HarperCollins. (Realism, ages 12–14.)

2000 *Bud, Not Buddy* by Christopher Paul Curtis. Delacorte. (Multicultural [African-American], ages 9–12.)
HONOR BOOKS
Getting Near to Baby by Audrey Couloumbis. Putnam. (Realism, ages 10–13.)
26 Fairmount Avenue by Tomie dePaola. Putnam. (Biography, ages 7–9.)
Our Only May Amelia by Jennifer L. Holm. HarperCollins. (Historical fiction [U.S., 1899], ages 10–14.)

1999 *Holes* by Louis Sachar. Farrar. (Magical realism/ mystery, ages 11–15.)
HONOR BOOK
A Long Way from Chicago by Richard Peck. Dial. (Realism, ages 10–15.)

1998 *Out of the Dust* by Karen Hesse. Scholastic. (Historical fiction [U.S., 1920–1934], ages 13–16.)
HONOR BOOKS
Lily's Crossing by Patricia Reilly Giff. Delacorte. (Historical fiction [U.S., 1944], ages 9–12.)
Ella Enchanted by Gail Carson Levine. HarperCollins. (Modern fantasy, ages 9–12.)
Wringer by Jerry Spinelli. HarperCollins. (Realism, ages 9–12.)

1997 *The View from Saturday* by E. L. Konigsburg. Atheneum. (Realistic, ages 9–12.)
HONOR BOOKS
A Girl Named Disaster by Nancy Farmer. Orchard. (Realistic/multicultural [Black African], ages 12–14.)
The Moorchild by Eloise McGraw. McElderry/ Simon & Schuster. (Modern fantasy, ages 9–12.)
The Thief by Megan Whalen Turner. Greenwillow. (Modern fantasy, ages 12–16.)
Belle Prater's Boy by Ruth White. Farrar. (Realistic, ages 10–13.)

1996 *The Midwife's Apprentice* by Karen Cushman. Clarion. (Historical fiction [England, 1200s], ages 10–14.)
HONOR BOOKS
The Great Fire by Jim Murphy. Scholastic. (Informational, ages 11–15.)
The Watsons Go to Birmingham, 1963 by Christopher Paul Curtis. Delacorte. (Historical fiction [southern U.S., 1960s; African-American], ages 10–14.)
What Jamie Saw by Carolyn Coman. Front Street. (Realistic, ages 10–14.)
Yolanda's Genius by Carol Fenner. McElderry. (Realistic/multicultural [African-American], ages 10–14.)

1995 *Walk Two Moons* by Sharon Creech. HarperCollins. (Realism [Native American], ages 11–14.)
HONOR BOOKS
Catherine, Called Birdy by Karen Cushman. Clarion. (Historical fiction [England, 1200s] ages 10–14.)
The Ear, the Eye and the Arm by Nancy Farmer. Orchard. (Modern fantasy, ages 10–14.)

1994 *The Giver* by Lois Lowry. Houghton. (Modern fantasy, ages 10–14.)
HONOR BOOKS
Crazy Lady! by Jane Leslie Conly. HarperCollins. (Realism, ages 11–14.)
Dragon's Gate by Laurence Yep. HarperCollins. (Historical fiction [China, U.S. West, 1860s], ages 12–14.)
Eleanor Roosevelt: A Life of Discovery by Russell Freedman. Clarion. (Biography, ages 10–14.)

1993 *Missing May* by Cynthia Rylant. Orchard. (Realism, ages 10–13.)
HONOR BOOKS
The Dark-Thirty: Southern Tales of the Supernatural by Patricia McKissack. Knopf. (Modern fantasy/ghost stories [African-American], ages 8–12.)
Somewhere in the Darkness by Walter Dean Myers. Scholastic. (Realism [African-American], ages 11–14.)
What Hearts by Bruce Brooks. HarperCollins. (Realism, ages 11–14.)

1992 *Shiloh* by Phyllis Reynolds Naylor. Atheneum. (Realism [animal], ages 8–10.)
HONOR BOOKS
Nothing but the Truth by Avi. Orchard. (Realism, ages 10–14.)
The Wright Brothers: How They Invented the Airplane by Russell Freedman. Holiday. (Informational/biography, ages 9–14.)

1991 *Maniac Magee* by Jerry Spinelli. Little, Brown. (Magical realism, ages 10–13.)
HONOR BOOK
The True Confessions of Charlotte Doyle by Avi. Orchard. (Historical fiction [England–U.S., 1830], ages 10–13.)

1990 *Number the Stars* by Lois Lowry. Houghton. (Historical fiction [Denmark, 1940s], ages 10–14.)
HONOR BOOKS
Afternoon of the Elves by Janet Taylor Lisle. Orchard. (Realism, ages 10–13.)
Shabanu, Daughter of the Wind by Suzanne Fisher Staples. Knopf. (Realism, ages 12–16.)
The Winter Room by Gary Paulsen. Orchard. (Realism, ages 10–13.)

1989 *Joyful Noise: Poems for Two Voices* by Paul Fleischman. Harper. (Poetry, ages 9–14.)
HONOR BOOKS
In the Beginning: Creation Stories from Around the World by Virginia Hamilton. Harcourt. (Traditional fantasy, ages 9–14.)
Scorpions by Walter Dean Myers. Harper. (Realism/multicultural [African-American, Hispanic-American], ages 10–13.)

1988 *Lincoln: A Photobiography* by Russell Freedman. Clarion/Houghton. (Biography, ages 8–14.)
HONOR BOOKS
After the Rain by Norma Fox Mazer. Morrow. (Realism, ages 12–16.)
Hatchet by Gary Paulsen. Bradbury. (Realism, ages 9–13.)

1987 *The Whipping Boy* by Sid Fleischman. Greenwillow. (Historical fiction [medieval England], ages 9–12.)
HONOR BOOKS
On My Honor by Marion Dane Bauer. Clarion. (Realism, ages 8–12.)
Volcano: The Eruption and Healing of Mount St. Helens by Patricia Lauber. Simon & Schuster. (Informational, ages 8–13.)
A Fine White Dust by Cynthia Rylant. Bradbury. (Realism, ages 10–13.)

1986 *Sarah, Plain and Tall* by Patricia MacLachlan. Harper. (Historical fiction [U.S. western frontier, 1800s], ages 8–10.)
HONOR BOOKS
Commodore Perry in the Land of the Shogun by Rhoda Blumberg. Lothrop. (Informational, ages 10–14.)
Dogsong by Gary Paulsen. Bradbury. (Realism/multicultural [Native American], ages 10–13.)

1985 *The Hero and the Crown* by Robin McKinley. Greenwillow. (Modern fantasy [quest], ages 12–15.)
HONOR BOOKS
Like Jake and Me by Mavis Jukes. Illustrated by Lloyd Bloom. Knopf. (Picture book. Realism, ages 7–9.)
The Moves Make the Man by Bruce Brooks. Harper. (Realism/multicultural [African-American], ages 11–15.)
One-Eyed Cat by Paula Fox. Bradbury. (Realism, ages 10–12.)

1984 *Dear Mr. Henshaw* by Beverly Cleary. Morrow. (Realism, ages 8–10.)
HONOR BOOKS
The Sign of the Beaver by Elizabeth George Speare. Houghton. (Historical fiction [Colonial America], ages 9–12.)

A Solitary Blue by Cynthia Voigt. Atheneum. (Realism, ages 11–14.)

Sugaring Time by Kathryn Lasky. Photographs by Christopher Knight. Macmillan. (Informational, ages 9–13.)

The Wish Giver by Bill Brittain. Harper. (Modern fantasy, ages 9–12.)

1983   *Dicey's Song* by Cynthia Voigt. Atheneum. (Realism, ages 11–14.)
HONOR BOOKS
The Blue Sword by Robin McKinley. Greenwillow. (Modern fantasy [quest], ages 12–15.)

Dr. DeSoto by William Steig. Farrar. (Picture book. Modern fantasy [animal], ages 5–8.)

Graven Images by Paul Fleischman. Harper. (Modern fantasy, ages 10–12.)

Homesick: My Own Story by Jean Fritz. Putman. (Biography, ages 9–11.)

Sweet Whispers, Brother Rush by Virginia Hamilton. Philomel. (Fantasy/multicultural [African-American], ages 12–16.)

1982   *A Visit to William Blake's Inn: Poems for Innocent and Experienced Travelers* by Nancy Willard. Illustrated by Alice and Martin Provensen. Harcourt. (Picture book. Poetry, ages 9–11.)
HONOR BOOKS
Ramona Quimby, Age 8 by Beverly Cleary. Morrow. (Realism, ages 7–9.)

Upon the Head of the Goat: A Childhood in Hungary, 1939–1944 by Aranka Siegal. Farrar. (Historical fiction, ages 10–13.)

1981   *Jacob Have I Loved* by Katherine Paterson. Crowell. (Historical fiction [U.S., 1940s], ages 12–16.)
HONOR BOOKS
The Fledgling by Jane Langton. Harper. (Modern fantasy, ages 9–11.)

A Ring of Endless Light by Madeleine L'Engle. Farrar. (Science fiction, ages 13–16.)

1980   *A Gathering of Days: A New England Girl's Journal, 1830–32* by Joan Blos. Scribner's. (Historical fiction [New England, 1830s], ages 11–14.)

HONOR BOOK
The Road from Home: The Story of an Armenian Girl by David Kherdian. Greenwillow. (Historical fiction [Turkey, Greece, 1907–1924], ages 11–15.)

1979   *The Westing Game* by Ellen Raskin. Dutton. (Realism/mystery, ages 10–12.)
HONOR BOOK
The Great Gilly Hopkins by Katherine Paterson. Crowell. (Realism, ages 9–12.)

1978   *The Bridge To Terabithia* by Katherine Paterson. Crowell. (Realism, ages 9–11.)
HONOR BOOKS
Anpao: An American Indian Odyssey by Jamake Highwater. Lippincott. (Traditional fantasy/multicultural [Native American], ages 10–12.)

Ramona and Her Father by Beverly Cleary. Morrow. (Realism, ages 7–9.)

1977   *Roll of Thunder, Hear My Cry* by Mildred D. Taylor. Dial. (Historical fiction [Mississippi, 1934]/multicultural [African-American], ages 9–13.)
HONOR BOOKS
Abel's Island by William Steig. Farrar. (Fantasy [animal], ages 8–10.)

A String in the Harp by Nancy Bond. Atheneum/McElderry. (Modern fantasy, ages 11–13.)

1976   *The Grey King* by Susan Cooper. Atheneum/McElderry. (Modern fantasy [quest], ages 11–14.)
HONOR BOOKS
The Hundred Penny Box by Sharon Bell Mathis. Viking. (Realism/multicultural [African-American], ages 8–11.)

Dragonwings by Laurence Yep. Harper. (Historical fiction [San Francisco, 1903–1909]/multicultural [Chinese-American], ages 10–13.)

1975   *M. C. Higgins, the Great* by Virginia Hamilton. Macmillan. (Realism/multicultural [African-American], ages 10–13.)
HONOR BOOKS
Figgs & Phantoms by Ellen Raskin. Dutton. (Realism, ages 10–13.)

My Brother Sam Is Dead by James Lincoln Collier and Christopher Collier. Four Winds. (Historical fiction [Colonial America, 1700s], ages 10–14.)

The Perilous Gard by Elizabeth Marie Pope. Houghton. (Historical fiction [England, 1558], ages 12–15.)

Philip Hall Likes Me, I Reckon Maybe by Bette Greene. Dial. (Realism/multicultural [African-American], ages 9–11.)

1974 *The Slave Dancer* by Paula Fox. Bradbury. (Historical fiction [U.S., Africa, 1840s], ages 10–13.)

HONOR BOOK

The Dark Is Rising by Susan Cooper. Atheneum/McElderry. (Modern fantasy [quest], ages 11–14.)

1973 *Julie of the Wolves* by Jean Craighead George. Harper. (Realism/multicultural [Native American], ages 10–13.)

HONOR BOOKS

Frog and Toad Together by Arnold Lobel. Harper. (Picture book. Modern fantasy, ages 3–7.)

The Upstairs Room by Johanna Reiss. Crowell. (Historical fiction [Holland, 1940s], ages 9–13.)

The Witches of Worm by Zilpha Keatley Snyder. Atheneum. (Realism, ages 10–12.)

1972 *Mrs. Frisby and the Rats of NIMH* by Robert C. O'Brien. Atheneum. (Fantasy [animal], ages 10–12.)

HONOR BOOKS

Incident at Hawk's Hill by Allan W. Eckert. Little, Brown. (Historical fiction [Canada, 1870]/realism [animal], ages 10–12.)

The Planet of Junior Brown by Virginia Hamilton. Macmillan. (Realism/multicultural [African-American], ages 12–16.)

The Tombs of Atuan by Ursula K. Le Guin. Atheneum. (Modern fantasy [quest], ages 10–16.)

Annie and the Old One by Miska Miles. Little, Brown. (Picture book. Realism/multicultural [Native American], ages 8–10.)

The Headless Cupid by Zilpha Keatley Snyder. Atheneum. (Realism/mystery, ages 10–12.)

1971 *Summer of the Swans* by Betsy Byars. Viking. (Realism, ages 10–13.)

HONOR BOOKS

Kneeknock Rise by Natalie Babbitt. Farrar. (Modern fantasy, ages 9–13.)

Enchantress from the Stars by Sylvia Louise Engdahl. Atheneum. (Science fiction, ages 11–16.)

Sing Down the Moon by Scott O'Dell. Houghton. (Historical fiction [USA, 1860s], ages 12–18.)

1970 *Sounder* by William H. Armstrong. Harper. (Historical fiction [southern U.S., early 20th century], ages 10–13.)

HONOR BOOKS

Our Eddie by Sulamith Ish-Kishor. Pantheon. (Realism, ages 11–15.)

The Many Ways of Seeing: An Introduction to the Pleasure of Art by Janet Gaylord Moore. World. (Informational, ages 10–18.)

Journey Outside by Mary Q. Steele. Viking. (Modern fantasy, ages 10–13.)

Carnegie Medal: Great Britain

The Carnegie Medal, sponsored by the Chartered Institute of Library and Information Professionals, is given to the author of the most outstanding children's book first published in English in the United Kingdom during the preceding year. It was established in 1936. Books appropriate for both children and young adults are included in this award. For the entire list, go to www.carnegiegreenaway.org.uk/carnegie and click on Full List of Winners.

2008 *Here Lies Arthur* by Philip Reeve. Scholastic. (Modern fantasy, ages 12–16.)

2007 *Just in Case* by Meg Rosoff. Penguin. (Magical realism, ages 15–18.)

2006 *Tamar* by Mal Peet. Walker. (Realism/mystery, ages 14–18.)

2005 *Millions* by Frank Cottrell Boyce. Macmillan. (Realism, ages 11–14.)

2004 *A Gathering Light* (U.S. edition entitled *A Northern Light*) by Jennifer Donnelly. Bloomsbury. (Historical fiction [U.S., 1906], ages 14–18.)

2003 *Ruby Holler* by Sharon Creech. Bloomsbury/HarperCollins. (Realism, ages 9–13.)

2002 *The Amazing Maurice and His Educated Rodents* by Terry Pratchett. Doubleday/HarperCollins. (Modern fantasy [animal], ages 12–16.)

2001 *The Other Side of Truth* by Beverly Naidoo. Puffin/HarperCollins. (Realism, ages 12–15.)

2000 *Postcards from No Man's Land* by Aidan Chambers. Bodley Head. (Realism, ages 14–18.)

1999 *Skellig* by David Almond. Delacorte. (Magical realism, ages 11–14.)

1998 *River Boy* by Tim Bowler. Oxford. (Realism, ages 11–16.)

1997 *Junk* (U.S. edition entitled *Smack*) by Melvin Burgess. Andersen. (Realism, ages 13–18.)

1996 *Dark Materials,* book 1: *Northern Lights* by Philip Pullman. Scholastic. (Modern fantasy, ages 12–18.)

1995 *Whispers in the Graveyard* by Theresa Breslin. Methuen. (Modern fantasy, ages 11–14.)

1994 *Stone Cold* by Robert Swindells. Hamish Hamilton. (Realism, ages 13–16.)

1993 *Flour Babies* by Anne Fine. Hamish Hamilton. (Realism, ages 14–18.)

1992 *Dear Nobody* by Berlie Doherty. Hamish Hamilton. (Realism, ages 13–18.)

1991 *Wolf* by Gillian Cross. Oxford. (Realism/mystery, ages 12–14.)

1990 *My War with Goggle-Eyes* by Anne Fine. Joy Street. (Realism, ages 11–14.)

1989 *A Pack of Lies* by Geraldine McCaughrean. Oxford. (Modern fantasy, ages 13–18.)

1988 *The Ghost Drum: A Cat's Tale* by Susan Price. Faber. (Modern fantasy, ages 9–14.)

1987 *Granny Was a Buffer Girl* by Berlie Doherty. Methuen. (Realism, ages 13–16.)

1986 *Storm* by Kevin Crossley-Holland. Heinemann. Illustrated by Alan Marks. (Modern fantasy, ages 9–13.)

1985 *The Changeover* by Margaret Mahy. Dent. (Modern fantasy, ages 14–18.)

1984 *Handles* by Jan Mark. Kestrel. (Realism, ages 10–14.)

1983 *The Haunting* by Margaret Mahy. Dent. (Magical realism, ages 9–12.)

1982 *The Scarecrows* by Robert Westall. Chatto and Windus. (Modern fantasy, ages 12–15.)

1981 *City of Gold* by Peter Dickinson. Gollancz. (Traditional fantasy [Old Testament], ages 10–14.)

1980 *Tulku* by Peter Dickinson. Dutton. (Historical fiction [China, 1900], ages 12–15.)

1979 *The Exeter Blitz* by David Rees. Hamish Hamilton. (Historical fiction [England, World War II], ages 12–15.)

1978 *The Turbulent Term of Tyke Tiler* by Gene Kemp. Faber. (Realism, ages 8–11.)

1977 *Thunder and Lightnings* by Jan Mark. Kestrel. (Realism, ages 11–14.)

1976 *The Machine-Gunners* by Robert Westall. Macmillan. (Historical fiction [England, World War II], ages 12–14.)

1975 *The Stronghold* by Mollie Hunter. Hamilton. (Historical fiction [England, 1st century A.D.], ages 14–16.)

1974 *The Ghost of Thomas Kempe* by Penelope Lively. Heinemann. (Modern fantasy, ages 12–14.)

1973 *Watership Down* by Richard Adams. Rex Collings. (Modern fantasy [animal], ages 11–18.)

1972 *Josh* by Ivan Southall. Angus and Robertson. (Realism, ages 12–16.)

1971 *The God beneath the Sea* by Leon Garfield and Edward Blishen. Kestrel. (Mythology, ages 11–14.)

1970 *The Edge of the Cloud* by K. M. Peyton. Oxford. (Historical fiction [England, 1910s], ages 13–18.)

Boston Globe–Horn Book Awards

The Boston Globe–Horn Book Awards, sponsored by the Boston Globe and the Horn Book, are given to an author for outstanding fiction or poetry for children, to an illustrator for outstanding illus-

tration in a children's book, and, since 1976, to an author for outstanding nonfiction for children. This program was established in 1967. Only the awards for fiction are listed here. For the entire list go to www.hbook.com and click on Magazine, then Awards.

2008 Fiction: *The Absolutely True Diary of a Part-Time Indian* by Sherman Alexie. Little, Brown. (Fictionalized autobiography, ages 14–18.)

2007 Fiction: *The Astonishing Life of Octavian Nothing, Traitor to the Nation,* Volume I: *The Pox Party* by M. T. Anderson. Candlewick. (Historical fiction [Colonial America, Revolutionary War era], ages 15–18.)

2006 Fiction: *The Miraculous Journey of Edward Tulane* by Kate DiCamillo. Illustrated by Bagram Ibatoulline Candlewick. (Modern fantasy, ages 8–11.)

2005 Fiction: *The Schwa Was Here* by Neal Shusterman. Dutton. (Realism, ages 12–16.)

2004 Fiction: *The Fire-Eaters* by David Almond. Delacorte. (Historical fiction [England, 1962/Cuban missile crisis], ages 12–16.)

2003 Fiction: *The Jamie and Angus Stories* by Anne Fine. Illustrated by Penny Dale. Candlewick. (Modern fantasy, ages 5–7.)

2002 Fiction: *Lord of the Deep* by Graham Salisbury. Delacorte. (Realism, ages 11–15.)

2001 Fiction: *Carver: A Life In Poems* by Marilyn Nelson. Front Street. (Biography in poems, ages 12–14.)

2000 Fiction: *The Folk Keeper* by Franny Billingsley. Atheneum. (Modern fantasy, ages 11–15.)

1999 Fiction: *Holes* by Louis Sachar. Farrar. (Magical realism/mystery, ages 11–15.)

1998 Fiction: *The Circuit: Stories from the Life of a Migrant Child* by Francisco Jiménez. University of New Mexico Press. (Autobiography, ages 11–14.)

1997 Fiction: *The Friends* by Kazumi Yumoto. Farrar. (Realism [set in Japan], ages 11–14.)

1996 Fiction: *Poppy* by Avi. Illustrated by Brian Floca. Orchard. (Modern fantasy [animal], ages 8–11.)

1995 Fiction: *Some of the Kinder Planets* by Tim Wynne-Jones. Orchard. (Short stories of various genres, ages 10–14.)

1994 Fiction: *Scooter* by Vera B. Williams, Greenwillow. (Realism/picture book, ages 8–12.)

1993 Fiction: *Ajeemah and His Son* by James Berry. Harper. (Historical fiction [Africa–Jamaica, 1807]/multicultural [African–Caribbean], ages 12–15.)

1992 Fiction: *Missing May* by Cynthia Rylant. Orchard. (Realism, ages 10–13.)

1991 Fiction: *The True Confessions of Charlotte Doyle* by Avi. Orchard. (Historical fiction [England–U.S., 1830], ages 10–13.)

1990 Fiction: *Maniac Magee* by Jerry Spinelli. Little, Brown. (Magical realism, ages 10–13.)

1989 Fiction: *The Village by the Sea* by Paula Fox. Orchard. (Realism, ages 11–13.)

1988 Fiction: *The Friendship* by Mildred Taylor. Dial. (Historical fiction [Mississippi, 1933]/multicultural [African-American], ages 10–12.)

1987 Fiction: *Rabble Starkey* by Lois Lowry. Houghton. (Realism, ages 11–14.)

1986 Fiction: *In Summer Light* by Zibby Oneal. Viking Kestrel. (Realism, ages 13–18.)

1985 Fiction: *The Moves Make the Man* by Bruce Brooks. Harper. (Realism/multicultural [African-American], ages 11–16.)

1984 Fiction: *A Little Fear* by Patricia Wrightson. McElderry/Atheneum. (Modern fantasy, ages 12–14.)

1983 Fiction: *Sweet Whispers, Brother Rush* by Virginia Hamilton. Philomel. (Modern fantasy, ages 13–18.)

1982 Fiction: *Playing Beatie Bow* by Ruth Park. Atheneum. (Historical fantasy [Australia, 1880s], ages 13–18.)

1981   Fiction: *The Leaving* by Lynn Hall. Scribner's. (Realism, ages 15–18.)

1980   Fiction: *Conrad's War* by Andrew Davies. Crown. (Historical fantasy [England, World War II], ages 11–14.)

1979   Fiction: *Humbug Mountain* by Sid Fleischmann. Atlantic/Little, Brown. (Historical fiction [U.S. frontier, 1800s], ages 9–12.)

1978   Fiction: *The Westing Game* by Ellen Raskin. Dutton. (Realism/mystery, ages 10–12.)

1977   Fiction: *Child of the Owl* by Laurence Yep. Harper. (Realism/multicultural [Chinese-American], ages 11–13.)

1976   Fiction: *Unleaving* by Jill Paton Walsh. Farrar. (Realism, ages 10–13.)

1975   Text: *Transport 7-41-R* by T. Degens. Viking. (Historical fiction [Germany, 1946], ages 12–15.)

1974   Text: *M. C. Higgins, the Great* by Virginia Hamilton. Macmillan. (Realism/multicultural [African-American], ages 13–16.)

1973   Text: *The Dark Is Rising* by Susan Cooper. Atheneum/McElderry. (Modern fantasy, ages 11–14.)

1972   Text: *Tristan and Iseult* by Rosemary Sutcliff. Dutton. (Traditional fantasy [Legend], ages 10–13.)

1971   Text: *A Room Made of Windows* by Eleanor Cameron. Atlantic/Little, Brown. (Realism, ages 11–13.)

1970   Text: *The Intruder* by John Rowe Townsend. Lippincott. (Realistic, ages 12–14.)

1969   Text: *A Wizard of Earthsea* by Ursula K. Le Guin. Houghton. (Modern fantasy, ages 12–16.)

1968   Text: *The Spring Rider* by John Lawson. Crowell. (Modern fantasy, ages 9–12.)

1967   Text: *The Little Fishes* by Erik Christian Haugaard. Houghton. (Historical fiction [World War II], ages 11–13.)

Governor General's Literary Awards: Canada

The Governor General's Literary Awards were inaugurated in 1937, with separate prizes for children's literature (text and illustration) being added in 1987. Only the awards for text are listed here. For the entire list, go to www.canadacouncil.ca/prizes/ggla.

2008   *The Landing* by John Ibbitson. Kids Can.

2007   *Gemini Summer* by Iain Lawrence. Delacorte.

2006   *Ingrid and the Wolf* by André Alexis. Tundra.

2005   *The Crazy Man* by Pamela Porter. Groundwood.

2004   *Airborn* by Kenneth Oppel. HarperCollins.

2003   *Stitches* by Glen Huser. Groundwood.

2002   *True Confessions of a Heartless Girl* by Martha Brooks. Groundwood.

2001   *Dust* by Arthur Slade. HarperCollins Canada.

2000   *Looking for X* by Deborah Ellis. Groundwood.

1999   *A Screaming Kind of Day* by Rachna Gilmore. Fitzhenry & Whiteside.

1998   *The Hollow Tree* by Janet Lunn. Knopf Canada.

1997   *Awake and Dreaming* by Kit Pearson. Viking.

1996   *Ghost Train* by Paul Yee. Groundwood.

1995   *The Maestro* by Tim Wynne-Jones. Groundwood.

1994   *Adam and Eve and Pinch Me* by Julie Johnston. Lester.

1993   *Some of the Kinder Planets* by Tim Wynne-Jones. Groundwood.

1992   *Hero of Lesser Causes* by Julie Johnston. Lester.

1991   *Pick-Up Sticks* by Sarah Ellis. Groundwood.

1990   *Redwork* by Michael Bedard. Lester & Orpen Dennys.

1989   *Bad Boy* by Diana Wieler. Douglas & McIntyre.

1988   *The Third Magic* by Welwyn Wilton Katz. Douglas & McIntyre.

1987 *Galahad Schwartz and the Cockroach Army* by Morgan Nyberg. Douglas & McIntyre.

Book of the Year for Older Readers Award: Australia

The Children's Book Council of Australia sponsors five awards for excellence in children's books: The Picture Book of the Year Award; the Book of the Year for Early Childhood (since 2001); the Book of the Year for Younger Readers Award; the Book of the Year for Older Readers Award; and the Eve Pownall Award for Information Books. Only the Book of the Year for Older Readers Award is listed here. For the entire list, go to www.cbca.org.au/awards.htm.

2008 *The Ghost's Child* by Sonya Hartnett. Candlewick.

2007 *Red Spikes* by Margo Lanagan. Knopf.

2006 *The Story of Tom Brennan* by J. C. Burke.

2005 *The Running Man* by Michael Gerard Bauer. Omnibus.

2004 *Saving Francesca* by Melina Marchetta. Viking.

2003 *I Am the Messenger* by Markus Zusak. Pan Macmillan Australia.

2002 *Forest* by Sonya Hartnett. Viking.

2001 *Wolf on the Fold* by Judith Clarke. Allen & Unwin.

2000 *48 Shades of Brown* by Nick Earls. Penguin.

1999 *Deadly, Unna?* by Phillip Gwynne. Penguin.

1998 *Eye to Eye* by Catherine Jinks. Penguin.

1997 *A Bridge to Wiseman's Cove* by James Moloney. University of Queensland Press.

1996 *Pagan's Vows* by Catherine Jinks. Omnibus.

1995 *Foxspell* by Gillian Rubinstein. Hyland House.

1994 *The Gathering* by Isobelle Carmody. Penguin.

Angel's Gate by Gary Crew. Heinemann.

1993 *Looking for Alibrandi* by Melina Marchetta. Penguin.

1992 *The House Guest* by Eleanor Nilsson. Viking.

1991 *Strange Objects* by Gary Crew. Heinemann Australia.

1990 *Came Back to Show You I Could Fly* by Robin Klein. Viking/Kestrel.

1989 *Beyond the Labyrinth* by Gillian Rubinstein. Hyland House.

1988 *So Much to Tell You* by John Marsden. Walter McVitty Books.

1987 *All We Know* by Simon French. Angus & Robertson.

1986 *The Green Wind* by Thurley Fowler. Rigby.

1985 *The True Story of Lilli Stubeck* by James Aldridge. Hyland House.

1984 *A Little Fear* by Patricia Wrightson. Hutchinson.

1983 *Master of the Grove* by Victor Kelleher. Penguin.

1982 *The Valley Between* by Colin Thiele. Rigby.

1981 *Playing Beatie Bow* by Ruth Park. Nelson.

1980 *Displaced Person* by Lee Harding. Hyland House.

1979 *The Plum-Rain Scroll* by Ruth Manley. Hodder & Stoughton.

1978 *The Ice Is Coming* by Patricia Wrightson. Hutchinson.

1977 *The October Child* by Eleanor Spence. Oxford.

1976 *Fly West* by Ivan Southall. Angus & Robertson.

1975 No award

1974 *The Nargun and the Stars* by Patricia Wrightson. Hutchinson.

1973 *Family at the Lookout* by Noreen Shelly. Oxford.

1972 *Longtime Passing* by Hesba F. Brinsmead. Angus & Robertson.

1971 *Bread and Honey* by Ivan Southall. Angus & Robertson.

1970 *Uhu* by Annette Macarther-Onslow. Ure Smith.

Coretta Scott King Awards

The Coretta Scott King Awards, founded in 1970 to commemorate Dr. Martin Luther King Jr. and his wife, Coretta Scott King, for their work in promoting peace and world brotherhood, are given to an African-American author and, since 1974, an African-American illustrator whose children's books, published during the preceding year, made outstanding inspirational and educational contributions to literature for children and young people. The awards are presented annually by the Coretta Scott King Committee of the American Library Association's Ethnic Multicultural Information Exchange Round Table (EMIERT). Only the author awards are listed here. For the entire list, go to www.ala.org/ala/mgrps/rts/emiert/cskbookawards/recipients.cfm.

2009 *We Are the Ship: The Story of Negro League Baseball* by Kadir Nelson. Hyperion.

2008 *Elijah of Buxton* by Christopher Paul Curtis. Scholastic.

2007 *Copper Sun* by Sharon Draper. Atheneum.

2006 *Day of Tears: A Novel in Dialogue* by Julius Lester. Jump At the Sun.

2005 *Remember: The Journey to School Integration* by Toni Morrison. Harcourt.

2004 *The First Part Last* by Angela Johnson. Simon & Schuster.

2003 *Bronx Masquerade* by Nikki Grimes. Dial.

2002 *The Land* by Mildred D. Taylor. Fogelman/Penguin Putnam.

2001 *Miracle's Boys* by Jacqueline Woodson. Putnam.

2000 *Bud, Not Buddy* by Christopher Paul Curtis. Delacorte.

1999 *Heaven* by Angela Johnson. Simon & Schuster.

1998 *Forged by Fire* by Sharon M. Draper. Atheneum.

1997 *Slam!* by Walter Dean Myers. Scholastic.

1996 *Her Stories: African American Folktales, Fairy Tales, and True Tales* by Virginia Hamilton. Illustrated by Leo and Diane Dillon. Scholastic.

1995 *Christmas in the Big House, Christmas in the Quarters* by Patricia C. McKissack and Fredrick L. McKissack. Illustrated by John Thompson. Scholastic.

1994 *Toning the Sweep* by Angela Johnson. Orchard.

1993 *The Dark-Thirty: Southern Tales of the Supernatural* by Patricia McKissack. Knopf.

1992 *Now Is Your Time! The African-American Struggle for Freedom* by Walter Dean Myers. HarperCollins.

1991 *The Road to Memphis* by Mildred D. Taylor. Dial.

1990 *A Long Hard Journey* by Patricia and Fredrick McKissack. Walker.

1989 *Fallen Angels* by Walter Dean Myers. Scholastic.

1988 *The Friendship* by Mildred D. Taylor. Illustrated by Max Ginsburg. Dial.

1987 *Justin and the Best Biscuits in the World* by Mildred Pitts Walter. Lothrop.

1986 *The People Could Fly: American Black Folktales* by Virginia Hamilton. Knopf.

1985 *Motown and Didi* by Walter Dean Myers. Viking.

1984 *Everett Anderson's Good-Bye* by Lucille Clifton. Holt.

1983 *Sweet Whispers, Brother Rush* by Virginia Hamilton. Philomel.

1982 *Let the Circle Be Unbroken* by Mildred Taylor. Dial.

1981 *This Life* by Sidney Poitier. Knopf.

1980 *The Young Landlords* by Walter Dean Myers. Viking.

1979 *Escape to Freedom* by Ossie Davis. Viking.

1978 *Africa Dream* by Eloise Greenfield. Day/Crowell.

1977 *The Story of Stevie Wonder* by James Haskins. Lothrop.

1976 *Duey's Tale* by Pearl Bailey. Harcourt.

1975 *The Legend of Africana* by Dorothy Robinson. Johnson.

1974 *Ray Charles* by Sharon Bell Mathis. Crowell.

1973 *I Never Had It Made* by Jackie Robinson as told to Alfred Duckett. Putnam.

1972 *17 Black Artists* by Elton C. Fax. Dodd.

1971 *Black Troubador: Langston Hughes* by Charlemae Rollins. Rand.

1970 *Martin Luther King, Jr.: Man of Peace* by Lillie Patterson. Garrard.

Pura Belpré Awards

The Pura Belpré Award honors Latino writers and illustrators whose work best portrays, affirms, and celebrates the Latino cultural experience in a work of literature for youth. This biennial award is sponsored by the Association for Library Service to Children and the National Association to Promote Library Services to the Spanish Speaking. Only the author awards are listed here. For the entire list, go to www.ala.org, click on Awards & Grants, Book, Print & Media Awards, Children & Young Adults, Belpré Medal.

2008 *The Poet Slave of Cuba: A Biography of Juan Francisco Manzano* by Margarita Engle. Illustrated by Sean Qualls. Holt.

2006 *The Tequila Worm* by Viola Canales. Random.

2004 *Just a Minute: A Trickster Tale and Counting Book* by Yuyi Morales. Chronicle.

2002 *Esperanza Rising* by Pam Muñoz Ryan. Scholastic.

2000 *Under the Royal Palms: A Childhood in Cuba* by Alma Flor Ada. Atheneum.

1998 *Parrot in the Oven: Mi Vida* by Victor Martinez. HarperCollins.

1996 *An Island Like You: Stories of the Barrio* by Judith Ortiz Cofer. Orchard.

Margaret A. Edwards Award

The Margaret A. Edwards Award, established in 1988, honors an author's lifetime achievement for writing books that have been popular over a period of time. The annual award is administered by the Young Adult Library Services Association of the American Library Association and is sponsored by School Library Journal. It recognizes an author's work in helping adolescents become aware of themselves and addressing questions about the importance of and their role in relationships, society, and the world.

2009 Laurie Halse Anderson

2008 Orson Scott Card

2007 Lois Lowry

2006 Jacqueline Woodson

2005 Francesca Lia Block

2004 Ursula K. Le Guin

2003 Nancy Garden

2002 Paul Zindel

2001 Robert Lipsyte

2000 Chris Crutcher

1999 Anne McCaffrey

1998 Madeleine L'Engle

1997 Gary Paulsen

1996 Judy Blume

1995 Cynthia Voigt

1994 Walter Dean Myers

1993 M. E. Kerr

1992   Lois Duncan

1991   Robert Cormier

1990   Richard Peck

1988   S. E. Hinton

Phoenix Award

The Phoenix Award, sponsored by the Children's Literature Association, is given to the author of a book first published twenty years earlier. The book must have been originally published in English and cannot have been the recipient of a major children's book award.

2009   *Weetzie Bat* by Francesca Lia Block. Harper-Collins.

2008   *Eva* by Peter Dickinson. Delacorte.

2007   *Memory* by Margaret Mahy. McElderry.

2006   *Howl's Moving Castle* by Diana Wynne Jones. Greenwillow.

2005   *The Catalogue of the Universe* by Margaret Mahy. Atheneum.

2004   *White Peak Farm* by Berlie Doherty. Orchard.

2003   *The Long Night Watch* by Ivan Southall. Methuen.

2002   *A Formal Feeling* by Zibby Oneal. Orion.

2001   *Seventh Raven* by Peter Dickinson. Penguin.

2000   *The Keeper of the Isis Light* by Monica Hughes. Atheneum.

1999   *Throwing Shadows* by E. L. Konigsburg. Collier.

1998   *A Chance Child* by Jill Paton. Walsh.

1997   *I Am the Cheese* by Robert Cormier. Random.

1996   *The Stone Book* by Alan Garner. Collins. [Titles in the Stone Book Quartet: *The Stone Book* (1976); *Granny Reardun* (1978); *The Aimer Gate* (1979); *Tom Fobble's Day* (1979).]

1995   *Dragonwings* by Laurence Yep. Harper.

1994   *Of Nightingales That Weep* by Katherine Paterson. Harper.

1993   *Carrie's War* by Nina Bawden. Puffin.

1992   *A Sound of Chariots* by Mollie Hunter. Harper.

1991   *A Long Way from Verona* by Jane Gardam. Macmillan.

1990   *Enchantress from the Stars* by Sylvia Louise Engdahl. Macmillan.

1989   *The Night Watchman* by Helen Cresswell. Macmillan.

1988   *The Rider and His Horse* by Eric Christian Haugaard. Houghton.

1987   *Smith* by Leon Garfield. Constable.

1986   *Queenie Peavy* by Robert Burch. Viking.

1985   *Mark of the Horse Lord* by Rosemary Sutcliff. Walck.

MAGAZINES

The following list includes some of the most popular magazines available to young people today.

Art

Scholastic Art. Themed issues featuring lessons, reproductions, posters, and artist profiles to supplement the art curriculum. Ages 13–18. Six issues/year. Order at http://teacher.scholastic.com/products/classmags.

Drama

Plays, the Drama Magazine for Young People. Scripts for plays, skits, puppet shows, and round-the-table readings (a type of readers' theatre). Ages 6–17. Seven issues/year; 8–10 scripts per issue. Order at www.playsmag.com.

History

Calliope. Articles, stories, interviews, time lines, maps, and authentic photos to generate an interest in world history. Themed issues. Ages 9–14. Nine issues/year. Order at www.cricketmag.com.

Cobblestone. Articles about U.S. history. Themed issues. Ages 9–14. Nine issues/year. Order at www.cricketmag.com.

Languages

Each of the following magazines includes teen-interest articles and features interviews with pop culture personalities and sports figures as well as teen perspectives on other countries and cultures; extension lessons that build reading, grammar, and vocabulary skills; read-aloud plays for reading, writing, and listening skills; and free language CDs to help students develop pronunciation skills. Ages 12–18. Six issues/year. Order at http://teacher.scholastic.com/products/classmags.

French

Allons-Y (beginners); *Bonjour* (advanced beginners); *Ça-Va?* (intermediate); *Chez Nous* (advanced)

German

Das Rad (beginners); *Schuss* (advanced beginners)

Spanish

¿Qué Tal? (beginners); *Ahora* (advanced beginners); *El Sol* (intermediate and advanced)

Language Arts

Scholastic Action. High interest–low reading level (3rd to 5th grade). Readers' theatre plays, true teen nonfiction, celebrity profiles, debate prompts, language arts skill-builders for struggling and resistant readers. Ages 12–18. Fourteen issues/year. Order at http://teacher.scholastic.com/products/classmags.

Scholastic Scope. Readers' theatre plays, classic and contemporary literature, nonfiction, first person true teen stories, reading comprehension activities, vocabulary builders, writing prompts. Ages 12–18. Seventeen issues/year. Order at http://teacher.scholastic.com/products/classmags.

Stone Soup: The Magazine by Young Writers and Artists. Stories, poems, book reviews, and art by young people 8–13. Six issues/year. Order at www.stonesoup.com.

Teen Ink. A national teen magazine, book series, and website devoted entirely to teenage writing and art. Ages 12–18. Ten issues/year. Order at www.teenink.com.

Literature

Cicada. Stories and poems written by outstanding adult authors and teens. Ages 14–18. Six issues/year. Order at www.cricketmag.com.

Cricket. Fiction, nonfiction, book reviews, activities. Features international literature. Ages 9–14. Nine issues/year. Order at www.cricketmag.com.

Mathematics

Scholastic Math Magazine. Math problems, computation, statistics, consumer math, real-life applications, career math, critical reasoning. Ages 12–15. Twelve issues/year. Order at http://teacher.scholastic.com/products/classmags.

Recreation and Entertainment

Black Beat. Urban music news and trends, hip-hop culture, gossip. Ages 15–20. Six issues/year. Order at www.magazine-agent.com/black-beat/magazine.

BMX Plus! Reviews and tests of bikes and equipment, worldwide race coverage, interviews with top personalities. Ages 11–18. Twelve issues/year. Order at www.bmxplusmag.com.

Boys' Life. News, nature, sports, history, fiction, science, comics, Scouting, colorful graphics, and photos. Published by the Boy Scouts of America. Ages 8–18. Twelve issues/year. Order at www.boyslife.org.

GamePro. Video game magazine for serious gamers. Reviews and previews of video games plus tips and strategies. Ages 11–18. Twelve issues/year. Order at www.gamepro.com.

New Moon Girls. An international magazine by and about girls. Designed to build self-esteem and promote a positive body image. Ages 8–15. Six issues/year. Order at www.newmoon.com.

Right On! Entertainment news and celebrity profiles for black teens. Ages 11–18. Six issues/year. Order at www.rightonmag.com.

Seventeen. Fashion, health, beauty, celebrity interviews for female teens. Ages 14–18. Twelve issues/year. Order at www.seventeen.com.

Sports Illustrated. Sports news, analysis, and personality profiles. Ages 14–18. Fifty-six issues/year. Order at www.si.com/subscribe.

Teen Voices. A print (2 issues/year) and online (monthly) social justice magazine publishing essays and articles by teens on their lives, their world, and the issues affecting them. Provides an educational forum that challenges media images of women and serves as a vehicle of change. Order at www.teenvoices.com.

Science and Health

Choices. Articles and activities to teach and promote family and consumer sciences, prevention of drug abuse, personal responsibility, careers, and health. Ages 13–18. Six issues/year. Order at http://teacher.scholastic.com/products/classmags.

Current Health 2. Articles and news about nutrition, fitness, personal health, and the harmful effects of drugs and alcohol. *Optional:* **Human Sexuality Newsletter.** Ages 12–18. Eight issues/year. Order at www.weeklyreader.com.

Current Science. News in science, health, and technology; science activities. Ages 12–16. Sixteen issues/year. Order at www.weeklyreader.com.

Odyssey. Themed issues on the latest science news and discoveries. Ages 9–14. Nine issues/year. Order at www.cricketmag.com.

Science World. Articles, experiments, and news to supplement the science curriculum. Ages 12–16. Fourteen issues/year. Order at http://teacher.scholastic.com/products/classmags.

Social Studies

Career World. Practical advice and information on career awareness, college planning, and vocational/technical opportunities. Ages 12–18. Six issues/year. Order at www.weeklyreader.com.

Current Events. Important national and world news; debates on topics relevant to students' lives, maps, charts, diagrams. Ages 11–16. Twenty-five issues/year. Order at www.weeklyreader.com.

Faces. Articles and activities exploring world cultures. Ages 9–14. Nine issues/year. Order at www.cricketmag.com.

Junior Scholastic. Features U.S. and world current events, world cultures, map skills, geography, plays, and debates. Ages 11–14. Eighteen issues/year. Order at http://teacher.scholastic.com/products/classmags.

Muse. Nonfiction articles, photoessays, and jokes relating to history, science, and art. Ages 10–18. Nine issues/year. Order at www.cricketmag.com.

New York Times Upfront. Current national and international news, debates on issues, op-ed pieces, essays by teens, eight-page teacher edition. Ages 15–18. Fourteen issues/year. Order at http://teacher.scholastic.com/products/classmags.

Skipping Stones. An international, multicultural children's magazine. Articles by, about, and for children about world cultures and cooperation. Multilingual. Ages 7–17. Five issues/year. Order at www.skippingstones.org.

INDEX TO BOOKS AND AUTHORS

Page numbers followed by *f* or *t* indicate figures or tables, respectively.

SUBJECT INDEX

Page numbers followed by *f* or *t* indicate figures or tables, respectively.